"In this book, Kofoed has given us an investigation that is both exegetically precise and theologically and philosophically ambitious. In this way, he succeeds in documenting that the biblical texts are governed by a difference between nature and person that informs the givenness of one's biological sex as an unchangeable point of orientation. The analyses are carried by a depth that commands respect and invites further reflection."

—**KNUT ALFSVÅG**, professor in systematic theology,
Faculty of Theology and Social Sciences, VID
Specialized University, Stavanger, Norway

"This volume by Jens Bruun Kofoed offers the church and the academy the best treatment of currently discussed gender issues that I have read. With keen exegetical skill the author examines every relevant biblical text in the light of all Scripture as well as their place in ancient Near Eastern and classical Greek and Roman writings and practice. He interacts intensely with contemporary scientific, theological, and philosophical writings on the subject, but he grounds his appeal for a binary understanding of what it means for human beings to be male and female in divine creation theology as presented in the Bible. This book should be at the top of anyone's list of resources for answering questions related to gender and sexuality that Christ-followers confront today."

—**DANIEL I. BLOCK**, DPhil, Gunther H. Knoedler Professor Emeritus of Old Testament, Wheaton College, Wheaton, Illinois

"This is a very important book for those who take the Bible seriously in the modern controversy over sex and gender. The extensive background of the author in the Hebrew Old Testament and the Greek New Testament, as well as their background worlds, comes through in his detailed treatment of all the relevant biblical texts and biblical creation theology. He brings all this to bear on a very well defined and carefully articulated understanding of the cultural, sociological, and philosophical realities that permeate the discussion today. The author takes a definite position, holding that biblical creation theology offers a binary approach to sexuality, but shows full awareness of the issues involved and debates surrounding them. He is also sensitive to the pastoral concerns and need to show God's grace to those who suffer with gender dysphoria of one kind or another."

—**Richard E. Averbeck**, professor emeritus of Old Testament and Semitic Languages, Trinity Evangelical Divinity School

Majestic Mirror
or Mind-Bending Mirage

Majestic Mirror
or **Mind-Bending Mirage**

*Exploring Gender and Sexuality
in the Context of Biblical Creation Theology*

Jens Bruun Kofoed

WIPF & STOCK · Eugene, Oregon

MAJESTIC MIRROR OR MIND-BENDING MIRAGE
Exploring Gender and Sexuality in the Context of Biblical Creation Theology

Copyright © 2025 Jens Bruun Kofoed. All rights reserved. Except for brief quotations in critical publications or reviews, no part of this book may be reproduced in any manner without prior written permission from the publisher. Write: Permissions, Wipf and Stock Publishers, 199 W. 8th Ave., Suite 3, Eugene, OR 97401.

Wipf & Stock
An Imprint of Wipf and Stock Publishers
199 W. 8th Ave., Suite 3
Eugene, OR 97401

www.wipfandstock.com

PAPERBACK ISBN: 979-8-3852-3723-4
HARDCOVER ISBN: 979-8-3852-3724-1
EBOOK ISBN: 979-8-3852-3725-8

VERSION NUMBER 03/13/25

Scripture quotations are from the ESV® Bible (The Holy Bible, English Standard Version®), © 2001 by Crossway, a publishing ministry of Good News Publishers. Used by permission. All rights reserved. The ESV text may not be quoted in any publication made available to the public by a Creative Commons license. The ESV may not be translated in whole or in part into any other language.

Photos and illustrations (fig. 3–5) are used with permission from Yale University Art Gallery, Yitzhak Paz, Ianir Milevski, Nimrod Getzov, and Othmar Keel.

To our Children Line, Ditte, Nicolai, Mikkel,
and Emil—as different as they are.

Contents

List of Illustrations | ix
Abbreviations | xi
Online Resources | xv
Author's Foreword | xvii

Part One: Deconstructing Gender Studies | 1
    Basic Stuff | 1
    Falsification | 27
    Cards on the Table | 28

Part Two: Comparative Material on Gender Identity and Sexuality | 30
    Mesopotamia | 30
    A Methodological Afterword | 54

Part Three: Gender and Body in Biblical Creation Theology | 67
    Lord-of-the-Rings-Theology | 67
    Gender Hermeneutics | 75
    Created Matter Matters | 95
    Man, Male, and Mate | 126
    Solitude, Unity, Nakedness | 154
    Spousal Bookends | 159
    Eroticism and Reproduction | 168
    Separation and Oneness | 178
    Cross-Dressing | 188
    Cultic Prostitution | 190
    Neighboring Sexes | 203

CONTENTS

    Eunuchs, Intersex, and Transgender | 217
    Same-Sex Relations | 233
    Summary and Conclusion | 286

Part Four: Pastoral Implications | 303
    Epilogue | 317

Bibliography | 327

List of Illustrations

Fig. 1: The Genderbread Person Version 4. Created and uncopyrighted 2017 by Sam Killerman, https://www.itspronouncedmetrosexual.com/2018/10/the-genderbread-person-v4. | 17

Fig. 2: The Gender Unicorn. Trans Student Educational Resources, 2015. http://www.transstudent.org/gender. Used by permission. | 18

Fig. 3: Building attached to the temple for Atargatis at Dura-Europos. Used with permission from Yale University Art Gallery. | 45

Fig. 4: Reconstruction of sacred marriage scenes. Credit: N. Getzov. Used with permission from the authors. | 53

Fig. 5: MB IIB scarab depicting a *coitus a posteriori*. Used with permission from the author. | 54

Fig. 6: Old Babylonian Sign for Woman | 58

Fig. 7: Abstract Rendering of Sign for Woman rotated 45 degrees right. | 58

Fig. 8: Israel's King Jehu Submits to Shalmaneser III. Credit: Osama Shukir Muhammed Amin. Source: https://commons.wikimedia.org/wiki/File:The_Assyrian_king_Shalmaneser_III_receives_tribute_from_Sua,_king_of_Gilzanu,_The_Black_Obelisk.JPG. Licensed under the Creative Commons Attribution-Share 4.0 International License. | 200

Fig. 9: Hofstede Diagram. Created by the author. | 215

Fig. 10: Nicolai Winther-Nielsen's model. Created by the author. | 313

Abbreviations

ANE	Ancient Near East (sometimes including Egypt)
AOAT	Alter Orient und Altes Testament (Münster: Ugarit Verlag)
BDB	Brown-Driver-Briggs *Hebrew and English Lexicon of the Old Testament*
BHS	Biblia Hebraica Stuttgartensia
CAD	Chicago Assyrian Dictionary (Chicago: Oriental Institute)
CBS	University of Pennsylvania Museum's Catalogue of the Babylonian Section
CSB	Christian Standard Bible
CCEL	Christian Classics Ethereal Library
CCSD	Congenital Conditions of Sexual Development
CDLI	Cuneiform Digital Library Initiative
CHL	Catechesis of Human Love (John Paul II)
COS	William W. Hallo and K. Lawson Younger, eds. *The Context of Scripture: Canonical Compositions from the Biblical World*. Leiden: Brill, 1997.
COSD	Composite Substance Dualism
D	The Deuteronomist Source
DSD	Differences of Sexual Development
DO92	Danish Authorized Bible Translation of 1992
E	The Elohist Source

ABBREVIATIONS

EA	El Amarna Letter(s)
ETCBC	Eep Talstra Center for Bible and Computer
ESV	English Standard Version
GE	Gilgamesh Epic
HALOT	William L. Holladay. *Hebrew and Aramaic Lexicon of the Old Testament.* Leiden: Brill, 2000.
IM	Iraq Museum Catalogue
J	The Yahwist Source
JPS	The Jewish Publication Society Bible Translation
KAR	Kuyunjik (Nineveh) Archive or Kuyunjik Assyrian Records
KTU	Keilalphabetische Texte aus Ugarit
LAS	Lexical Akkadian Series
LGBTQ2IA/ LGBT+	Lesbian, Gay, Bisexual, Transgender/Transsexual, Questioning/Queer, Intersex, Two-Spirited, Allied/Asexual/Aromantic/Agender
LW	*Luther's Works*
LXX	The Greek Septuagint Version
MT	The Masoretic Hebrew Text
NASB	New American Standard Bible
NRSV	New Revised Standard Version
NDE	Near-Death Experience
NET	New English Translation
NIV	New International Version
NJB	New Jerusalem Bible
NJPS	New Jewish Publication Society Tanakh
NLT	New Living Translation
OBO	Orbis Biblicus et Orientalis (Fribourg: Academi Press Fribourg)
P	The Priestly Code/Source
REB	Revised English Bible

ABBREVIATIONS

Sib. Or.	Sibbylene Oracles
SMN	Sumerian Monolingual Lexical Texts
T. Benj.	Testament of Benjamin
T. Naph.	Testament of Naphtali
TEV	Today's English Version
TSER	Trans Student Educational Resources
TWOT	*Theological Wordbook of the Old Testament*
VAS	Vorderasiatische Sammlung (Near Eastern Collection), referring to the collection of ancient Near Eastern artifacts housed in the Museum of the Ancient Near East at the Berlin State Museums (Altes Museum) in Germany.
VSD	Variations of sexual development

Online Resources

Chavad
A digital library of classical Jewish texts (e.g., Mishnah, Talmud, Haggadah, Rambam) and Chassidic texts is located at https://www.chabad.org/library.

Christian Classics Ethereal Library
A digital library of hundreds of classic Christian books selected for edification and education at https://ccel.org.

Cuneiform Digital Library Initiative
A digital library that represents the efforts of an international group of Assyriologists, museum curators, and historians of science to make digitally available the form and content of cuneiform inscriptions dating from the beginning of writing, ca. 3350 BC. Several of these artifacts are currently kept in public and private collections to exceed 500,000 exemplars, of which now more than 360,000 have been cataloged in electronic form by the CDLI. Located at https://cdli.mpiwg-berlin.mpg.de.

New Advent
This website contains The Catholic Encyclopedia with information on the entire cycle of Catholic interests, action, and doctrine, as well as a digital library of the writings of the church fathers and the *Summa Theologica* of St. Thomas Aquinas. It is located at https://www.newadvent.org.

Perseus Digital Library
A digital library with a flagship collection of texts on the Greco-Roman world's history, literature, and culture, including a vast number of primary texts, is located at https://www.perseus.tufts.edu.

Sephora
Digital library with the original text and translations of Mishnah, Talmud, Midrash, Tosefta, Apocrypha, Philo, and Josephus. It is located at https://www.sefaria.org.

The Gnostic Library
A vast collection of primary documents relating to the Gnostic tradition, in-depth audio lectures, and brief archive notes designed to orient the study of the documents, their sources, and the religious tradition they represent are located at http://gnosis.org/library.html.

The Holy See
The Vatican's online library of apostolic letters, encyclicals, catechisms, etc., is located at https://www.vatican.va.

Zürich Open Repository and Archive
Open access to digital editions of all volumes in the Orbis Biblical et Orientalis Series. It is located at https://www.zora.uzh.ch/view/subjects/OBO.html.

Author's Foreword

THE BOOK THAT RESISTED its creation is one way to describe the present work. Firstly, because for the pragmatically inclined author, it has been far from evident to delve into such a controversial subject as gender identity and sexual orientation—especially when the result, as will become apparent from further reading, can be described as one of the most politically incorrect statements one could imagine in a Danish, Scandinavian, and indeed Western context. Secondly, gender identity and sexual orientation are, if not synonymous, at least closely connected to who we are, making it difficult to analyze them as "something" without also discussing "someone." Thirdly, transitioning from the interpretive analysis of individual biblical texts to the construction of a biblical-theological synthesis and subsequently deriving ethical principles for church and societal engagement is a nuanced process that has required a long career as a professional reader of the Bible to develop. The book demonstrates this aspect by constructing the biblical-theological synthesis not solely through the exegesis of isolated texts but by considering their placement within the overarching creation-theological framework that has shaped them all. Nevertheless, I decided to write it for several reasons.

Abigail Favale, in *The Genesis of Gender*, explains how her belief that the dignity of every human being and the dignity of the body are entwined and inseparable puts her in a double bind, a no-win scenario: "If I say that [biological] sex matters, I'm put on a one-way train to presumptive transphobia. If I say that sex doesn't matter, I'm betraying the truth of my embodiment and the truth of God's self-revelation. I need to make peace with being misunderstood because both prongs of the twofold truth need to be spoken—with compassion, to be sure, but spoken nonetheless."[1]

When I began my theological studies in the early 1980s, existentialism, social constructivism, and the third wave of feminism were gaining momentum, eroding the Christian unity culture that had characterized Danish society for centuries. The Association of 1948 (Forbundet af 1948), the precursor to LGBT+ Denmark, had begun to gain momentum in its political lobbying efforts, and the media increasingly reported on these new trends. This was particularly evident in the Danish Broadcasting Corporation's Children's and Youth Department (Danmark's Radio B&U), which became a standard-bearer for the era's norm-disruptive ideology. The liberalization of the state monopoly on radio and television also contributed to this pluralization. Since the 1990s, change has been rapid and profound. While advocating for a classical biblical ethic was still widely considered politically correct and legitimate when I began my professional career in 1992, it has increasingly become a minority viewpoint in the post-Constantinian society that Denmark has evolved into. Today, it is considered exotic—bordering on homophobic—to argue for ethical positions that exclude or illegitimatize other ethical choices, especially when referencing a normative sacred text. Classical Christianity has thus found itself in an intimidating situation where the most superficial human response would be to relinquish the normative and surrender to the "interlocking forces of oppression," which, according to Favale, is all about group membership: "We are not unique individuals; we are Frankensteinian composites, stitched-together hubs of group membership. These group affiliations are hierarchically ordered and awarded varying degrees of social capital in an attempt to reverse oppressive power dynamics, to recenter the marginalized, to privilege the underprivileged."[2] Rather than contributing to a self-pitying elegy, I resonate with Favale's invitation to view the current situation as *kairos*, a welcome and necessary opportunity to reevaluate and reformulate Biblical ethics on gender and identity positively, especially since the attempt in current gender identity theory to reverse power dynamics "does nothing to undo an underlying preoccupation with power and domination. Claiming an oppressed identity itself becomes a mode of power."[3] All of this will be revisited, but it must be mentioned here to emphasize the

1. Favale, *Genesis of Gender*, 205–6.
2. Favale, *Genesis of Gender*, 80.
3. Favale, *Genesis of Gender*, 81.

proactive and constructive approach guiding my work in this study. This does not mean that it's not also defensive or apologetic, as it defends in many ways a classical biblical ethic regarding gender and identity. However, it also engages with the latest gender identity theory, critically rejecting it and seeking to incorporate insights that align with biblical ontology and anthropology.

The inception of this book can be traced back to an invitation to present a conference paper on gender and sexuality at Fjellhaug International University College in Oslo on November 29, 2021. However, I would not have received this invitation without my extensive background in teaching biblical texts related to gender identity and my specialization in creation theology, which has defined my research focus for the past two decades. Additionally, my role as a pastor and counselor at Copenhagener Church (Københavnerkirken) has required me to contemplate the interplay between the biblical-theological synthesis and the formulation of concrete ethical guidance in the context of church leadership. In September 2023, the initial outcomes of my research were published in Danish by Kolon Publishers,[4] and the current volume naturally builds upon that foundation. However, comparative studies will reveal that significant new insights, perspectives, and emphases have emerged, and thus, the book must be read and evaluated on its own merits.

The parts of the book have been presented at various research seminars, and I am grateful for the constructive critique I have received in connection with presentations under the auspices of Fjellhaug International University College in Copenhagen. I would also like to extend my gratitude to my conversation partners in Københavnerkirken, including especially my cell group, our pastors Claus Sode Grønbæk and Peter Techow, and longtime friends Johannes Miðskarð and Mikkel Vigilius. Conversations with Margrethe Rye Bang Kofod and discussions in a study group organized by True Freedom Trust have been crucial for understanding challenged gender identities. I am also profoundly grateful for the help provided by Maha Golestaneh-Lubbers. This includes both inspiring discussions about the content and proofreading. While I take full responsibility for the result, I acknowledge that it would not have become what it is without the many constructive contributions I have received from the individuals, institutions, and organizations above.

---

4. Kofoed, *Fra begyndelsen*.

AUTHOR'S FOREWORD

The book comprehensively explores the Bible's perspective on gender and sexuality, focusing on the Old Testament. This emphasis is deliberate, as the New Testament builds upon the Old Testament's theology of creation. The book's structure is carefully designed to facilitate understanding of the topic, with a logical sequence of chapters and sections.

While there may be agreement on what the biblical texts say, diverse interpretations of their meaning are common. Even if consensus is reached on meaning, debate will likely persist regarding significance. When biblical texts are reinterpreted within a different hermeneutical framework, it is not because the texts have changed but because our understanding of them has shifted. This shift is often driven by fundamental changes in society's ontology and epistemology.

Eugene Rogers aptly notes that "there is no 'strategy' apart from better theology"[5] in applying biblical sexual ethics to contemporary issues. And better theology requires better exegesis, Christology, liturgy, and recovery of patristic and medieval resources. The book's first part examines the changes in ideological and methodological underpinnings that have influenced the approach to gender issues in the academy with trickle-down effects on church and society. The central part of the book shifts focus to exegesis and theology, proposing a thesis that articulates what the relevant biblical texts say, mean, and signify about gender identity and sexuality.

Karlslunde
November 15, 2024.

---

5. Rogers, "Doctrine and Sexuality," 53.

Part One

Deconstructing Gender Studies

BASIC STUFF

In *Gender as Love*, Felipe do Vale mentions two bifurcations in biblical gender studies, one *ontological* between gender as biologically essential or socially constructed, and one methodological between those who "anchor their views in some neighboring academic discipline, perceiving that discipline to provide whatever warrant is putatively missing from theological work," and those who "confine themselves to texts and questions of their traditions, and if gender is treated in their discussions at all, it's done with a sense of suspicion and reservation."[1] In the following, we will focus on the ontological divide and the methodological challenges of incorporating comparative material. But first, here are a few words on definitions.

The Gender Hydra

Definitions in studies of gender identity and sexuality show respect and create clarity. Therefore, it would be obvious to include—either here or as an appendix—a glossary for the many terms used. However, the challenge is that the taxonomy is like a terminological Hydra, where terms constantly disappear or fall out of use and new ones emerge or are added. LGBT has become LGBT+ or LGBTQI2A to explicitly state what the "+"

---

1. do Vale, *Gender as Love*, 6.

stands for: Lesbian, Gay, Bisexual, Transgender/Transsexual, Questioning/Queer, Intersex, Two-Spirited, Allied/Asexual/Aromantic/Agender. Providing a comprehensive list of terms would be nearly impossible. Therefore, readers are directed to such endeavors in other literature. Nonetheless, a few definitions and clarifications are pertinent. As we explore these topics, different terms will be introduced and explained along the way.

Sex refers to the biological or anatomical (physiological) traits used to identify humans as male, female, or intersex based on chromosomal, gonadal, or anatomical differences. As will become evident from the discussion below, it's essential to be attentive to the distinction between biological and anatomical sex, a differentiation characterizing the latest development within gender studies.

Sexual orientation is about whom you are sexually and romantically attracted to. A person may be monosexual (heterosexual, homosexual), bisexual, polysexual (attracted to multiple but not all genders), pansexual (attracted to all genders), asexual, or another orientation.

Gender refers to the social, cultural, and psychological aspects of being male, female, or another gender identity. It includes roles, behaviors, expressions, and expectations that societies assign to individuals based on their perceived sex. Gender is a complex and multifaceted concept that goes beyond biological characteristics.

Gender identity refers to the psychological identity that individuals construct based on or in opposition to their biological traits and the social gender role pattern introduced through upbringing.

Gender expression refers to the sociological part of gender and is the way an individual acts out gender through things like clothing, hair, voice, and mannerisms.

Gender role represents the societal manifestation of gender, relating to the expectations and stereotypes a specific culture has constructed around gender (i.e., stereotypes).

Gender essentialism is the belief that there are innate, unchangeable differences between men and women, that a man has a particular male essence that makes him who he is, and that his essence is the biological and spiritual opposite of the essence that a woman has that makes her who she is.

Gender dysphoria refers to the feelings of discomfort, anxiety, or distress that may arise from a mismatch between a person's gender identity and their assigned sex at birth. While gender dysphoria is common among transgender individuals, it's not a universal experience.

A *transgender* person is an individual whose gender identity, to a greater or lesser extent, does not correspond with the gender assigned to them at birth. In academic contexts, the term "trans*" is often used instead of "transgender" to acknowledge and encompass a broader spectrum of gender identities and expressions. This asterisk at the end of "trans*" is a wildcard, indicating numerous variations and nuances within the transgender umbrella. By using "trans*," scholars and activists aim to emphasize that gender identity is diverse and not limited to a binary understanding. It signals an openness to recognizing and validating all individuals who do not conform to traditional gender norms or expectations. This linguistic choice aligns with the evolving understanding within gender studies that gender is a complex, multifaceted aspect of identity. Recent estimates in a report from 2019 are that 0.5–1 percent of the Danish population identified as transgender.[2] According to a study from 2022, the numbers for the US are 0.52 percent for adults (ages 17 or older) and 1.4 percent for youth (ages 13–17).[3] These numbers correspond to recent European studies in which the percentage is between 0.6–1.1 percent.[4]

An *intersex* person is someone who is born with a variation in physical characteristics that do not fit typical binary notions of male or female bodies. This variation is congenital. It can involve aspects such as chromosomes, gonads, or genitals. Medical literature tends to use the terms "disorders of sexual development" or "differences of sexual development" (DSD), "variations of sexual development" (VSD), and "congenital conditions of sexual development" (CCSD) to describe these conditions as biologically based variation *within* maleness or femaleness. While the term "hermaphrodite" was previously used, it's now considered outdated and potentially offensive. The term "intersex" is the preferred terminology in both medical and sociocultural contexts. Intersex is about biological variations and not about gender identity or sexual orientation. It's estimated that individuals encompassing diverse identities under the intersexuality spectrum constitute approximately 0.05 percent to 1 percent of our societies, depending on the definition of "intersex."[5]

2. Frisch et al., "Sex in Denmark."
3. Herman et al., "How Many Adults."
4. Glintborg et al., "Socioeconomic Status," 1156.
5. Boyce et al., "Estimates," 1941–42.

Appareo, Ergo Sum

The evolution in understanding gender and sexuality can be described as a gradual detachment of the connection between a person's biological and psychosocial gender. Initially, the dominant perspective was that "I am embodied, therefore I am," where biological gender defined psychosocial gender. However, gender studies eventually flipped Descartes's famous phrase "I think, therefore I am" on its head, transforming it into "I appear, therefore I am." In essence, this shift suggests that it is our personal decision about how we want to present ourselves that defines who we are and that our biological gender and physical body must be subordinated and manipulated to fit this chosen appearance.

One of the most insightful reviews of the ontological changes in gender studies is provided by Abigail Favale, who has navigated a journey from birthright evangelicalism to postmodern feminism and ultimately to Roman Catholicism.[6] In her book *The Genesis of Gender*, Favale identifies four waves of feminism that have significantly impacted gender studies. The first wave, which emerged in the nineteenth and early twentieth centuries, focused on securing legal rights, such as voting. The second wave began in the 1960s and 1970s and expanded to address broader social and cultural issues, including reproductive rights and challenging traditional gender roles. A key aspect of this wave was the emphasis on reproductive freedom through contraception and access to abortion.

The third wave, which spanned the 1990s to the early 2000s, emphasized intersectionality and inclusivity, aiming to address criticisms of the second wave. This wave focused on uninhibited sexual freedom, with "consent" as the sole benchmark for sex to be considered lawful. The fourth wave, which began in the mid-2000s, continues the trajectory of the third wave, utilizing digital platforms for activism and highlighting issues such as online activism, the #MeToo movement, reproductive justice, and transgender rights. Notably, the fourth wave has made significant progress in challenging the notion that being a "woman" is inherently tied to biological femaleness, instead embracing gender diversity.

While each "wave" of feminism was built upon the achievements and critiques of its predecessors, there were also significant ruptures. The first wave, which was politically and ideologically conservative, laid the groundwork for the subsequent waves. However, the second, third, and fourth waves were characterized by a more ideological and

---

6. Favale, *Into the Deep*.

norm-critical approach. Favale argues that the fourth wave has eroded the very foundation of feminism, transforming the concept of "woman" into an identity that can be freely adopted by men, regardless of material or physiological reality.[7]

The ideological underpinnings of gender studies are particularly relevant to this study, and both Favale's work and a report from the Christian Medical and Dental Association in Norway provide valuable insights into how these underpinnings have shaped the development of radical sexology and feminism.[8]

We Are All Hermaphrodites

The idea of an inherent connection between a person's biological and psychosocial gender was seriously challenged by the emergence of modern sexology and the treatment of transsexual individuals.

John Money, a pioneering endocrinologist from New Zealand (1921–2006), played a significant role in shaping the language of gender. His work was influenced by behaviorist theories, which propose that individuals can be socialized into a gender different from the one they were born with. Money believed that our gender roles and orientation are primarily shaped during the first two years of life, within what he referred to as a "gender gate" or "window." During this period, gender orientation is entirely malleable and can develop in either direction, towards either male or female. This means that, in principle, everyone can be "born in the wrong body." Furthermore, Money's theory suggests that we are all, at least psychologically, born as "hermaphrodites." This idea has sparked a discourse surrounding the "assignment" of gender at birth through genital inspection. The notion is that this allocation of biological sex is inherently somewhat arbitrary and may not necessarily align with the identity that emerges later in life.

Robert Stoller, an American psychiatrist, introduced the concept of "gender identity" in 1964. Gender identity refers to the internal feeling or perception of being one gender or another. Stoller distinguished this concept from "gender role," emphasizing that they are not the same. Radical feminists from the late 1960s onwards used the gender theories of Money and Stoller to challenge the idea that societal norms and biological

---

7. Favale, *Genesis of Gender*, 55.
8. Heggheim et al., "Kjønn," 7–13.

factors shape gender. Stoller placed significant emphasis on psychological factors in the development of gender identity. In his influential book *Sex and Gender* (1968), he linked the emergence of gender incongruence in some men to a hypothetical Freudian scenario where they received excessive care from their mothers in infancy and correspondingly little contact with their fathers. According to Stoller, this scenario can lead to the establishment of a gender identity that is contrary to an individual's biological sex.

Frankensteinian Composites

A significant philosophical foundation for today's gender theory is found in postwar radical feminism. This feminism is closely tied to the sexual revolution, which entailed a transformation of traditional notions of gender and sexuality in Western countries. The groundwork for this revolution was laid in the interwar years and emerged into mainstream culture in the late 1960s. After sexuality lost its culturally and religiously conditioned place within family life and the institution of marriage between man and woman, it became the subject of the individual's identity-shaping project and, thus, something malleable. This shift has had enormous consequences for how we conceptualize gender and sexuality.

Radical feminism was critical of norms and aimed to dismantle existing gender norms, seeking to liberate women from oppressive societal structures. Central to this was the rejection of the idea that biological sex should dictate normative guidelines for a woman's role in family and society. This rejection finds its classic formulation in the work of the French philosopher Simone de Beauvoir (1908–1986). In her seminal work *Le Deuxiéme Sexe* from 1949, she writes, "On ne naît pas femme: on le deviant," that is, "One is not born, but rather becomes, a woman."[9] This formulation creates a distinction between biological sex (sex) and psychosocial gender (gender), which has become canonical in our culture. Beauvoir's book contributed to the ongoing debate since the Romantic era about nature and culture, or whether humans are "born that way or become that way." Beauvoir suggests that a woman "is" nothing more than the social role assigned to her by society based on her gendered biology.

However, she goes a step further than many of her predecessors in the women's movement by directing her criticism at culture and nature.

---

9. Beauvoir, *Deuxième Sexe*; *Second Sex*, 267.

The first part of *Le Deuxiéme Sexe* critiques women's reproductive biology. While man is unhindered by his biology, the potential for pregnancies and childbirth keeps women bound in social patterns that hinder their freedom. An essential inspiration for Beauvoir was her lifelong partner Jean-Paul Sartre's atheistic existential philosophy. It rejects the idea that humans have a nature and assigns humans to be their own project: "Existentialism's first move is to make every man aware of what he is and to make the full responsibility of his existence rest on him."[10] In existentialism, as Favale describes it in contrast to biblical essentialism, "existence precedes essence. Essence refers to the 'whatness' of a thing, a stable nature that defines what something is. Genesis 1–2 describes the human person as a body-soul. What a human being *is* in its very nature is before the fact of my particular existence. Existentialism insists that I am not a human being because I exist; I must *become* a human being through my creative action in the world. Humanness becomes something I achieve rather than something I am given."[11] Beauvoir applies this perspective to gender. However, if humans are nothing but their self-determining freedom, it also raises the question of what it means to be a woman and, therefore, what it means to be a man. This problem has haunted all subsequent feminism. If a woman is simply a variant of a man, the rationale for feminism loses some of its foundation. It also becomes difficult to identify relevant differences between the genders. As Favale notes,

> Too often, freedom for women is cast as freedom from femaleness. "Autonomy" is envisioned according to male parameters, and women are expected to use invasive chemical and surgical means to conform their bodies to that ideal. Women are not valued simply for being; they must prove their value by doing ... Gone is the ancient view that meaning exists inherently in the world and can be recognized by humans. Gone is the understanding of a shared human flourishing or eudaimonia that is achieved by living by our nature. Gone, in fact, is the idea of human nature altogether. The only telos is an open-ended freedom, an endless journey of self-creation with no particular destination. One's telos, is to find one's telos.[12]

No wonder Albert Camus's famous existentialist manifesto *L'Etranger* concludes *pessimistically* with the protagonist Meursault's

---

10. Sartre, *Existentialism Is a Humanism*, 32.
11. Favale, *Genesis of Gender*, 61–62. Emphasis original.
12. Favale, *Genesis of Gender*, 69.

acceptance of the absurdity of life and his realization that he, as an isolated and alienated individual in an indifferent world, must find meaning and purpose within himself! Or, in Sartre's words, man is nothing but a "useless passion," and humans are "nothing other than what they make themselves."[13]

Although the question of gender incongruence and transsexuality was outside her horizon, Beauvoir laid some of the groundwork for the distinction between biological and psychosocial gender that would characterize later feminism and gender theory. For some of her radical followers, this becomes the main issue.

The Norwegian report mentioned above also points to the groundbreaking book by the American radical feminist Kate Millett (1934–2017), *Sexual Politics* from 1970, in which the term "gender" is used to undermine what Millett perceives as the patriarchate's self-perpetuation through purported "natural" gender categories. Her feminist gender theory builds on the gender concept of Money and Stoller. Their scientific findings, she writes, prove that gender identity is something learned and not something that exists at birth. Therefore, the gender identity of individuals can be completely different from their biological sex. The existence of transsexual and intersex individuals allegedly demonstrates this. Millett saw the subversive potential in Money's and Stoller's gender theory for the radical women's movement. If gender identity is demonstrably something other than biological gender, then it's up to the individual woman to define her own identity.

This idea was further developed by the American philosopher and gender studies scholar Judith Butler (1956–), the most critical contributor to today's transgender movement and queer theory. Butler views the notion of humankind being divided into two biologically complementary sexes as a social construct rather than an empirical truth and is equally influenced by existentialist theory, not least the Foucauldian perspective of power: In one of the most influential works, the three-volume *The History of Sexuality*, Michel Foucault understands sexuality as closely tied to power structures and argues against a singular, reductive understanding of sexuality, emphasizing its multiplicity and the diversity of sexual experiences and identities.[14] Foucault also points to another significant development, namely the "personification" of sexual practices:

---

13. Sartre, *Existentialism Is a Humanism*, 22.
14. Foucault, *History of Sexuality*.

> As defined by the ancient civil or canonical codes, sodomy was a category of forbidden acts; their perpetrator was nothing more than the judicial subject of them. The nineteenth-century homosexual became a personage, a past, a case history, and a childhood, in addition to being a type of life, a life form, and a morphology, with an indiscreet anatomy and possibly a mysterious physiology. Nothing that went into his total composition was unaffected by his sexuality . . . Homosexuality appeared as one of the forms of sexuality when it was transposed from the practice of sodomy onto a kind of interior androgyny, a hermaphrodism of the soul. The sodomite had been a temporary aberration; the homosexual was now a species.[15]

Butler agrees: "The question of who and what is considered real and true is apparently a question of knowledge. But it's also, as Michel Foucault makes plain, a question of power. Having or bearing 'truth' and 'reality' is an enormously powerful prerogative within the social world, one way that power dissimulates as ontology."[16] When Butler speaks of "dissimulates," she is referring to the idea that what we commonly perceive as "real" is a construct, a fiction manufactured and upheld by institutional power. In 1988, she introduced her theory of gender as an involuntary, socially enforced performance that generates the illusion of an essence,[17] and in *Gender Trouble* from 1990, she continued to elaborate on the idea that gender is *only* performance, that there is no "real" man or woman below or behind the cultural expressions. She recognizes distinctions between the sexes yet contends that the body is a blank canvas, lacking inherent meaning, upon which social conventions are inscribed. For Butler, there is no such thing as a naturally given and "pre-discursive" body. The gendered body is always part of a discourse; in other words, it's politically and linguistically constituted. Gender identity is thus not something given but something we enact ourselves. There is no inherent gender identity in humans independent of how we express it. It's the political and linguistic enactment of our gender that defines our identity. Butler writes:

> If gender is the cultural meaning that the sexed body assumes, then gender cannot be said to follow a sex in any one way. Taken to its logical limit, the sex/gender distinction suggests a radical discontinuity between sexed bodies and culturally constructed

---

15. Foucault, *History of Sexuality* 1.43.
16. Butler, *Undoing Gender*, 27.
17. Butler, "Performative Acts and Gender Constitution," 519–31.

genders. Assuming for the moment the stability of binary sex, it does not follow that the construction of "men" will accrue exclusively to the bodies of males or that "women" will interpret only female bodies. Further, even if the sexes appear to be unproblematically binary in their morphology and constitution (which will become a question), there is no reason to assume that genders ought also to remain as two. The presumption of a binary gender system implicitly retains the belief in a mimetic relation of gender to sex whereby gender mirrors sex or is otherwise restricted by it. When the constructed status of gender is theorized as radically independent of sex, gender itself becomes a free-floating artifice, with the consequence that man and masculine might just as easily signify a female body as a male one, and woman and feminine a male body as easily as a female one.[18]

In *Gender as Love*, Felipe Vale notes that there is a certain ambiguity in Butler's concept of social construction as it is unclear whether gender and sex are constructed or the notions of sex and gender themselves. The best reading of Butler's views, Vale suggests, is that the constructivist element refers to the latter. In this reading, Butler should be seen as "a kind of creative anti-realist" since our concepts on sex and gender "do not *bring to light* their basic features; they *bring about* those basic features."[19] In other words, our variable *concepts* define gender and sex. What Butler thus rejects is the existence of an inherent gender identity in humans, and she focuses strongly on the subversive potential in how we *stage* our gender. In several places in *Gender Trouble*, she refers to drag performances, which are meant to "parody" the traditional two-gender model. While drag may lean on stereotypical gender roles, it also serves a political function by demonstrating that gender does not exist independently of our performance.[20] Butler also understands "trans" as a politically destabilizing category. Trans people must take control over the assignment of their gender in a continuous drag performance.

Butler uses a Nietzsche quote to support her performative gender theory: "There is no 'being' behind doing [. . .] doing is everything."[21]

18. Butler, *Gender Trouble*, 6.
19. do Vale, *Gender as Love*, 64. Emphasis original.
20. Butler, *Gender Trouble*, 31–32, 94–96, 141–42.
21. "Es gibt kein 'Sein' hinter dem Thun, Wirken, Werden: 'Der Thäter' giebt das Sein dem Werden, er hängt das Werden um seinen Willen, um seinen Sinn, er giebt den Dingen, die werden, ihren Sinn, ihren Zweck, er giebt ihnen ein 'Wozu', das heisst einen Blick in's Fernste, Einige.—Alles Sein ist Werden." Nietzsche, *Die Fröhliche Wissenschaft*, 276.

With this, she means that each person "is" nothing but what they create themselves to be. In this sense, she continues a premise from Beauvoir and Sartre, who argued that humans are nothing other than their self-determining, transcendent freedom.

It should, therefore, come as no surprise that Butler and other existentialists drew the logical consequence of their ontology and argued for the legalization of both incest and pedophilia. In 1977, Foucault petitioned the French government to decriminalize consensual sex with minors, and later the same year, he wrote a letter to *Le Monde* pleading for the release of three convicted pedophiles. The letter was signed, among others, by Simone de Beauvoir, Jean-Paul Sartre, Jean-François Lyotard, and Roland Barthes![22]

This philosophy has its roots in Nietzsche's nihilistic philosophy. After declaring the death of God, Nietzsche realized that we must create ourselves and all our values. Nothing is given. Harvey Mansfield has characterized modern feminism on this basis as a specific form of nihilism.[23] This nihilism is primarily a rejection of the idea that humans have a gendered nature. Instead, we must create our own gender identity entirely ourselves. Harvey Mansfield, in a discussion on womanly nihilism, points to a more profound paradox in this nihilism's perpetual quest for identity (the ability to be who one is) and freedom (the ability to do what one wants): "If you have an identity, you cannot do everything; if you can do everything, you have no identity. . . . Feminism has no understanding of womanhood; it leaves women without a guide and even tries to convince them they need no guide."[24] Mansfield has, unsurprisingly, been severely criticized for misreading Beauvoir. For example, Robyn Marasco argues, "For Mansfield, womanly nihilism is what happens when feminism becomes anti-essentialist and post-foundationalist in theory and oversexed in practice. I am suggesting that womanly nihilism, for Beauvoir, is what happens when women mistake solitary satisfaction for collective liberation, when they confuse their private ambitions for political struggle, when they substitute having everything for becoming someone."[25] Although Beauvoir "occasionally" appeals to "heroic indi-

---

22. See references in Favale, *Genesis of Gender*, 77.
23. Mansfield, *Manliness*, 160, 240.
24. Mansfield, *Manliness*, 240, 276.
25. Marasco, "On Womanly Nihilism," 58–59.

viduality or spontaneous will-formation," her philosophy avoids, according to Marasco, "the familiar pitfalls of existentialism."[26]

> For Beauvoir, the existentialist, freedom is an anguished affair. But unlike Sartre, who casts the anguish of freedom in terms of fragile subjectivity, Beauvoir links this anguish to inescapable human finitude and the requirements of collective action. Individual freedom, absent social conditions for its practice in concert with others, is at best fictitious. At worst, an ideology of sovereign subjectivity reproduces orders of oppression and paradoxically encourages retreat from the world. Female narcissism, erotomania, and mysticism indicate pathologies of the subject who neglects the worldly character of her existence—her deep dependency on objects and others and her ineluctable entanglement in the given order of things.[27]

Be that as it may, Mansfield's critique of the inconsistencies of existentialist and anti-essentialist philosophy still stands. Identity presupposes continuity with who one is over time. The freedom to continually "perform" who one is thus appears as an unstable and contradictory foundation for identity. It's unstable because the resulting "intersectional feminism" erases both the existential anchor of the *universal* and the *individual*. Favale writes:

> We can no longer appeal to a shared human nature or condition that is intrinsic and cross-cultural. Neither can we turn our attention to the individual; we must instead look at people through the lens of identity categories in order to discern whether their perspective has value. Human beings are defined or "constituted" by their position on the grid of interlocking forces of oppression. We are not unique individuals; we are Frankensteinian composites, stitched-together hubs of group membership. These group affiliations are hierarchically ordered and awarded varying degrees of social capital in an attempt to reverse oppressive power dynamics, to recenter the marginalized, to privilege the underprivileged. The attempt simply to reverse power dynamics, however, does nothing to undo an underlying preoccupation with power and domination. Claiming an oppressed identity itself becomes a mode of power.[28]

---

26. Marasco, "On Womanly Nihilism," 59.
27. Marasco, "On Womanly Nihilism," 59.
28. Favale, *Genesis of Gender*, 80–81.

Furthermore, it is also contradictory since the right to "be who we are" presupposes a normative foundation beyond simply deciding for ourselves ("doing is everything"). Butler's theory is problematic, therefore, not only for what she understands as the heteronormative majority but also philosophically eroding for traditional feminism, queer theory, and the transgender movement. If there is no inherent gender identity in humans, but instead, gender is a performance that we stage, and no one is a "natural" woman or man, it is difficult to argue that some people are born in the "wrong" body while others are in the "right" body. Or, as Vale has it:

> Statements about women *as such* are impossible, for that label may or may not apply in different contexts. But if feminist theology is anything at all, it is an attempt to talk about women *as such*... If no single description of women's lives is correct and all are equally valid, what standards are available for assessing harm or the nature of justice and injustice in women's lives? ... Rather, the best we can do, morally speaking, is to provide guidelines external to gendered concepts; the normative claims attached to masculinity and femininity are restricted to their contexts, with the result that there can be neither good or bad *men* nor *women's* rights, for those normative evaluations are produced by the social constructs constitutive of their gender.[29]

The one immortal (essentialist) head of Hydra has also been severed!

Sexologist Anne Fausto-Sterling, in *Sexing the Body*, argues that culture affects the way we view biology because nothing in nature decides whether XX and XY chromosomes or testicles and ovaries should be categorized as male or female or something else altogether. Humans create categories and then determine what is within the range or normal for a particular category. Responding to a question about what nature tells us through the existence of intersexuals, Fausto-Sterling replies, "That nature is not an ideal state. It's filled with imperfections and developmental variation. We have all these Aristotelian categories of male and female. Nature doesn't have them. Nature creates a whole lot of different forms."[30] In other words, male and female are what we make of them, and this erodes the very foundation of feminism, as noted by Favale, by turning "woman" into an identity that can be freely appropriated by men, regardless of material or physiological reality. Susannah Cornwall argues

---

29. do Vale, *Gender as Love*, 45, 54. Emphasis original.
30. Dreifus, "Conversation with Anne Fausto-Sterling."

in the same anti-realist and social-constructivist vein that by its very existence, the intersex condition "shows that human sex is *not* a simple binary; since any exception to a dualistic model necessarily undermines the model in its entirety, this makes essentialist assumptions about what constitutes 'concrete facts' even more precarious."[31]

The development in recent gender identity theory, where gender identity is anchored psychologically, must be seen in this context as an attempt to address this erosion of traditional feminism and gender theory. Austen Hartke, for example, distinguishes between biological, psychological, and sociological parts of being transgender and states on the psychological: "We don't choose our gender identity; rather, it's something that has innate seeds within us and develops as we grow ... Gender identity can't be changed by other people."[32] Our gender, in other words, is a psychological given; the *sociological* part is about expression or performance, and the *physiological* aspect is random and has no necessary correlation with the psychological. In other words, the incidental or external body is secondary to the inherent psychological gender. Favale contends that this perception of gender consequently involves devaluing the body "because *the body itself is a limit*. The concrete reality of the body and sexual difference puts a limit on choice, a limit on self-improvisation, and a limit on social construction. The gender paradigm ultimately holds a negative view of embodiment."[33] The dramatic increase in tattoos and the popularity of *Avatar* should be seen, according to Favale, as symptoms of this malleability of the body. This denigration of the body is already apparent in Butler's work: "The body is not a 'being,' but a variable boundary, a surface whose permeability is politically regulated, a signifying practice within a cultural field of gender hierarchy and compulsory heterosexuality."[34]

Despite its attempts to solve the problem of radical social constructivism, the new "Gender Paradigm," as Favale dubs it, has its problems. It's another contradiction to say that gender and sexual orientation are innate *and* biological (physiological) sex is a social construct arbitrarily assigned at birth! "How is it possible to have an *innate* attraction to something that is merely a social construct?"[35]

31. Cornwall, *Sex and Uncertainty*, 125. Emphasis original.
32. Hartke, *Transforming*, 26–27.
33. Favale, *Genesis of Gender*, 83. Emphasis original.
34. Butler, *Gender Trouble*, 189.
35. Favale, *Into the Deep*, 123. Emphasis original.

Genderbread Bending

The development of gender theory may be illustrated by the fact that two of the most common infographics are no longer sufficient for understanding gender identity. In both "The Gender Unicorn"[36] and "The Genderbread Person,"[37] it is only "Sex Assigned at Birth" that has fixed categories, whereas "Gender Identity" is illustrated as fluid with no "right side." "The Gender Unicorn" breaks down sexuality into five distinct factors, each of which can potentially conflict with the others: "Sex Assigned at Birth," "Gender Identity," "Gender Expression", "Physical Attraction," and "Emotional Attraction." By adding a sixth variable, "Anatomical Sex," "The Genderbread Person" only explains the reductive and denigrating view of the body that is latent in "The Gender Unicorn" and most fully expressed in the understanding of gender as psychologically and—if such thing as a brain gender can be identified—even anatomically innate. To visualize this development, the "Gender Identity" category in these educational tools would also have to be fixed categories, but they are not.

Butler only dismantled the relation between *three* variables, namely sex, gender, and sexuality; adding two further variables in these infographics is based on a natural *sequitur* of the social-constructivist legacy from Beauvoir and Butler. In this light, Butler and the feminist movement have *undermined* their position, and it comes as no surprise, therefore, that both feminists and proponents of the latest "Gender Paradigm" have reacted. The reactions are very dissimilar, however. Whereas feminists seek to rehabilitate the body and biological sex as a stable, scientifically knowable aspect of us, proponents of the "Gender Paradigm" go even further in the denigration of the body by locating an innate gender identity in brain anatomy. As an example of the former feminist reaction, Nancy Pearcey refers to feminist philosopher Carol Bigwood, who already, in 1991, wrote:

> It is important to realize, for example, that the body's organization, though not fixed, is far from being completely contingent and arbitrary. It is not that the body's phenomenological

---

36. "The Gender Unicorn" is an educational tool designed by Landyn Pan and Anna Moore for Trans Student Educational Resources (TSER) in 2014 to help explain concepts related to gender identity and expression. It provides a visual representation of various aspects of gender and sexuality (https://transstudent.org/gender).

37. "The Genderbread Person" is a teaching tool developed by Sam Killermann to illustrate concepts related to gender identity, gender expression, biological sex, and sexual orientation (https://www.itspronouncedmetrosexual.com).

structure depends only on what we decide to make significant or that we can manipulate and construct it as we want. The sexual body's phenomenal organization is seen as arbitrary only if we take an abstract biological view of the body, regarding its parts as isolatable fragments of matter and ignoring their living function... nature is a codetermining force in the constitution of our bodies. A specific phenomenology of the female body must recognize and begin with this earthy significance of the body that is so quickly repressed in our eco-destructive world. The female body has indeterminate natural structures that noncausally motivate womanly ways of being in the world-earth-home.[38]

Proponents of the "Gender Paradigm," on the other hand, follow a completely different trajectory by insisting that gender identity *is* innate, albeit psychologically and possibly anatomically in the brain, and that the body, therefore, is entirely malleable. A good example is the prominent ancient Near Eastern scholar Julia Assante, who, as an introduction to her website on the afterlife, writes: "Each person is born with a spiritual and biological faith that is personal, intimate, and optimistic. Real faith springs from an innate awareness of our connectedness with all living beings, with nature, and with All That Is. It requires only that we retrieve the childlike part within each of us that knows the universe is good. Not good and evil, not even good and bad. Just good. It is knowing that every consciousness is uniquely meaningful and charged with purpose. That survival beyond the body is the only possible outcome."[39] Though Assante clearly distinguishes between her ancient Near Eastern scholarship and her explorations in the afterlife, the welcome message nonetheless displays an approach to gender identity that is biologically rooted *not* in the body but *beyond* the body in an "innate awareness" that only waits to be discovered.

---

38. Bigwood, "Renaturalizing the Body," 67–68; cf. Pearcey, *Love Thy Body*, 208.
39. Assante, *The Last Frontier*, 136.

DECONSTRUCTING GENDER STUDIES

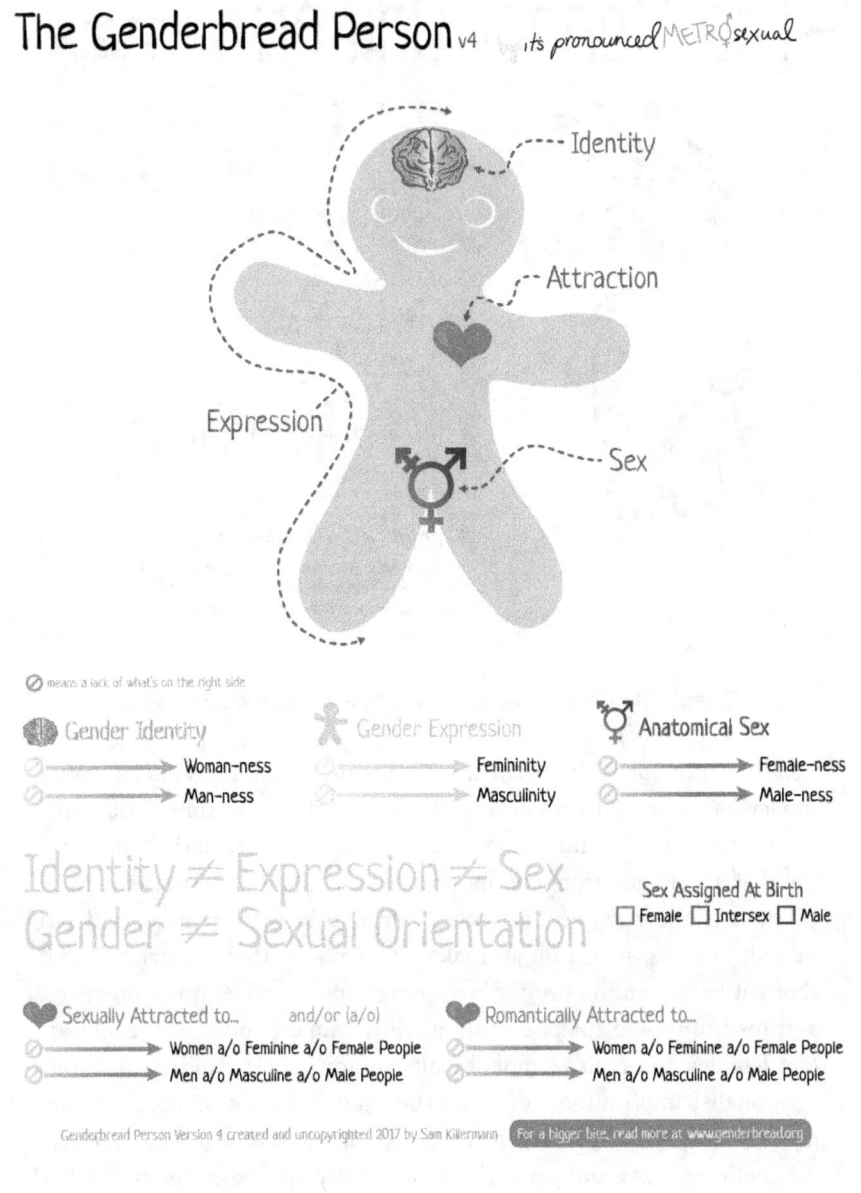

Figure 1: The Genderbread Person Version 4. Credit: Sam Killermann

Figure 2: The Gender Unicorn. Credit: Landyn Pan and Anna Moore

It is not surprising that this development within gender identity theory has been met with criticism. Much of the more substantial criticism comes from feminists and the LGBT+ community, and it's noteworthy that arguments from common sense are mainly predominant. Mari Mikkola is one example. She writes: "Ordinarily, women are considered human females, men human males. As a result, their *existence* is not thought to depend on productive, human social conventions, practices, and institutions so that we could abolish women and men leaving intact females and males simply by altering our social landscapes. Conventionalist implications, then, are unintuitive ... These problems are generated by a clash between the paradigmatic feminist and everyday conceptions of sex and gender."[40] And slightly later, she argues that her own trait/norm covariance model is more in alignment with common sense: "I contend that feminists should use the term 'woman' as ordinarily as possible ... The model I am proposing deals roughly with the same

40. Mikkola, "Ontological Commitments," 69.

phenomena that the sex/gender distinction does. It just understands that phenomena in a different way that is, I submit, more fruitful in being more congenial to everyday thinking."[41] Instead of maintaining Judith Butler's paradigmatic distinction between sex and gender, Mikkola opts for a more commonsensical distinction:

> In my view, we redraw the boundaries of the sets of gender traits and sex traits giving up the labels "sex" and "gender" to denote those traits. Instead, the traits are divided into sets of descriptive traits and evaluative norms. The former (in a sense) describe "the way the world is" and include physical and anatomical traits (e.g., chromosomes, ovaries, testes, genitalia, body shape and size), one's appearance (e.g., one's clothing, makeup, haircut, amount of body hair), roles (e.g., whether one undertakes caretaking roles, engages in childrearing tasks) and self-conceptions (calling oneself a woman or a man). These are features of which there are "facts of the matter"—it isn't in any sense mysterious or down to value judgements, whether one has ovaries, undertakes childrearing tasks, or calls oneself a woman . . . Evaluative norms are to do with stereotypical judgements: whether one is judged to be, to appear to be and/or act in "feminine," "masculine" or "neutral" ways. Evaluative norms attributed reflect value judgements and cultural norms.[42]

According to Mikkola, the advantage of this model is that it "avoids unintuitively taking the existence of women and men as a mind-dependent matter. It further avoids the implication that gender justice would or must do away with women and men: bluntly put, severing links between descriptive traits and evaluative norms can provide a way to dismantle social hierarchies without doing away with women and men."[43]

Another interesting reaction to the consequences of radical social constructivism has arisen within the LGBT+ community itself. This resistance led to the establishment of the Danish Rainbow Council in June 2022, which, in its press release about its founding, stated:

> There is a serious existential threat to all of us—and to the continued goodwill towards lesbians, gays, bisexuals, and transgender persons. The LGBT world has, catastrophically, created the threat itself: an ideological gender extremism that in recent

---

41. Mikkola, "Ontological Commitments," 76.
42. Mikkola, "Ontological Commitments," 76–77.
43. Mikkola, "Ontological Commitments," 82.

years has attacked everything from the rights of biological women to the mental well-being of our children. The extremists deny established science and suppress our freedom of speech—the phenomenon is called "wokeness." In the Danish Rainbow Council, we call it madness. The fight against this "politically correct," deeply intolerant ideology will be the next major battle of values. It's not just about LGBT people—it's about all of us. About you. About your children. About truth and lies. And about what vision of humanity Denmark should be guided by in the future . . . Let us finally make it clear for those who are a bit doubtful: There are only two genders. It's a biological fact, and it should be entirely uncontroversial to say so—but suddenly it's not. We at this moment challenge intolerance, cancel culture, and politically correct madness through our new association. We want extreme, socially harmful, ruthless gender ideology gone and humanity, tolerance, reason, and fairness back to the benefit of all—especially Denmark's many rainbow citizens.[44]

In addition to the press release's critique of ideological gender extremism, the council's website launches a frontal attack on the fluid gender identity that characterizes the work of organizations such as LGBT+ Denmark, *Sex & Samfund* [Danish Family Planning Association], and *Normstormerne* [The Norm Stormers]. The council advocates directly to the organizations above that "the words 'woman' and 'man' should be protected terms. Neither women nor men should be reduced to 'birthing persons' or 'persons with a penis,' etc. Words like 'mother' and 'father' should not be erased but rather respected for their meaning. Our language should not be reduced out of misguided concern for, for example, trans people."[45] The establishment of the Danish Rainbow Council shows that there is also internal dissent within the LGBT+ community, seeking to challenge the consensus that characterizes the media landscape and, by extension, public opinion. While the current study is based on a different set of values, specifically the Bible, and leads to broader conclusions, there is still a shared goal: searching for, and articulating, a foundational value system. This aims to counter the dissolution of values and the somewhat existentially rootless individualism often associated with extreme social constructivism in how individuals perceive their gender identity.

44. Dansk Regnbueråd, "Pressemeddelelse."
45. Dansk Regnbueråd, "12 opgør med wokeness."

It's in the Brain

We have already touched on the issue of an innate anatomical brain gender, and the anchoring of gender identity as psychologically innate is paralleled by neuroscience's research in the gendered brain. If it were possible to identify and describe a female or male brain, the term "intersex," for example, could be expanded to include conditions where a person experiences a mismatch between the biological brain and the biological (physiological) sex, thereby supporting the argument that physiological sex is subordinate to the biological brain sex. However, neuroscientists are divided, and studies that support such a conclusion are disputed because they are contradictory and due to neuroplasticity, that is, the brain's ability to *reflect* the experience of gender identity, for example. Nancy Pearcey, in her discussion on neuroplasticity, admits that studies have found differences in the size of various regions of the brain in homosexual-identified men compared to heterosexual-identified men but also point to research demonstrating brain differences as influenced by experience: "The part of the brain that deals with navigation is enlarged in London taxi drivers, as is the region dealing with the movement of the fingers of the left hand in right-handed violinists."[46]

An excellent example of the inconclusive character of studies is the summary in a recent article published in the *Journal of Neuroendocrinology*:

> The data summarized in the present review suggest that both gender identity and sexual orientation are significantly influenced by events occurring during the early developmental period when the brain is differentiating under the influence of gonadal steroid hormones, genes and maternal factors. However, our current understanding of these factors is far from complete, and the results are not always consistent. Sexual differentiation of the genitals takes place before sexual differentiation of the brain, making it possible that they are not always congruent. Structural and functional differences of hypothalamic nuclei and other brain areas differ in relation to sexual identity and sexual orientation, indicating that these traits develop independently. This may be a result of differing

---

46. Pearcey, *Love Thy Body*, 158. The Bible itself is not without "psychosomatical" insights; our thoughts and feelings affect the body: "A bright look brings joy to the heart, and good news gives health to the body"; "A cheerful heart brings good healing, but a crushed spirit dries up the bones" (Prov 15:30; 17:22).

hormone sensitivities and/or separate critical periods, although this remains to be explored. Most findings are consistent with a predisposing influence of hormones or genes, rather than a determining influence. For example, only some people exposed to atypical hormone environments prenatally show altered gender identity or sexual orientation, whereas many do not. Family and twin studies indicate that genes play a role, but no specific candidate genes have been identified. Evidence that relates to the number of older brothers implicates maternal immune responses as a contributing factor for male sexual orientation. All of these mechanisms rely on correlations and our current understanding suffers from many limitations in the data, such as a reliance on retrospective clinical studies of individuals with rare conditions, small study populations sizes, biases in recruiting subjects, too much reliance on studies of male homosexuals, and the assumption that sexuality is easily categorized and binary. Moreover, none of the biological factors identified so far can explain all of the variances in sexual identity or orientation, nor is it known whether or how these factors may interact. Despite these limitations, the existing empirical evidence makes it clear that there is a significant biological contribution to the development of an individual's sexual identity and sexual orientation.[47]

A 2016 report by physician Lawrence Mayer and psychiatrist Paul McHugh published in *The New Atlantis* concludes their comprehensive review of brain imaging studies. They argue that the studies "show inconclusive evidence and mixed findings regarding the brains of transgender adults. Brain-activation patterns in these studies do not offer sufficient evidence for drawing sound conclusions about possible associations between brain activation and sexual identity or arousal. The results are conflicting and confusing."[48]

Francis Collins, director of the Human Genome Project, agrees: "An area of extreme public interest is the genetic basis of homosexuality. Evidence from twin studies does in fact support the conclusion that heritable factors play a role in male homosexuality. However, the likelihood that the identical twin of a homosexual male will also be gay is about 20 percent (compared with 2–4 percent of males in the general population), indicating that sexual orientation is genetically influenced but not hardwired by DNA and that whatever genes are involved represent

---

47. Roselli, "Neurobiology of Gender Identity," 9.

48. Mayer and McHugh, "Special Report," quoted from Favale, *Genesis of Gender*, 133.

predispositions, not predeterminations."[49] Also critical is Kristina Olson, director of the TransYouth Project and associate professor of psychology at the University of Washington, who summarized the current state of gender identity studies, arguing:

> Similarly, although some neuroscience studies have shown that brain structures of trans people resemble those of individuals with the same gender identity, rather than people with the same sex at birth, these findings have often involved small samples and have not yet been replicated. Further complicating the interpretation of neuroscience results is the fact that brains change in response to experience, so even when differences appear, scientists do not know whether structural or functional brain differences *cause* the experience of a particular gender identity or *reflect* the experience of gender identity. Muddying the already murky waters, neuroscientists continue to debate whether even among people who are not transgender, there are reliable sex (or gender) differences in brains . . . Thus, whereas the topic is an active line of work in many research laboratories around the world, definitive conclusions about genetic and neural correlates of gender identity remain elusive.[50]

Favale seems to be on solid ground, therefore, when she concludes:

> First of all, there is no solid evidence for an association between brain structure and trans-identification. The neuroimaging studies that exist are small and very limited and generate inconclusive and contradictory results. Secondly, *even if* we had solid evidence for these structural and functional brain differences, due to neuroplasticity, the causal relationship would remain unclear. In other words, it would be impossible to tell if such differences were congenital and led to trans-identification or if trans-identification and transition had rewired the brain. Thirdly, *even if* we had solid evidence for this association *and* evidence that it is congenital like an intersex condition, we still arrive at another problem: Why should sex be defined according to neuroanatomy rather than the presence of a healthy reproductive system, when sex is fundamentally a reproductive category? Redefining sex according to brain structure and function would mean that *any* woman or man whose neuroimages deviate from the norm is not "really" a woman or a man at all. What I (Favale) am disputing is the idea of "brain sex," which

49. Collins, *Language of God*, 260.
50. Olson, "When Sex and Gender Collide."

is not supported by evidence and contradicts a basic biological understanding of what sex is.[51]

I'm getting ahead of myself, of course, since I have not yet argued that biblical creation theology correlates brain sex with "healthy reproductive organs." The argument is pending presentation, but the critical point concerning brain gender remains that neuroscience has not conclusively shown that physiological and psychological gender is innate and not influenced by the brain's neuroplasticity. We shall return to the implications of the possibility of an innate brain gender for a biblical theology in our discussion on transgenderism.

Binaries Breakdown

As we shall see below, many recent contributions to the discussion are an explicit deconstruction of the binary framework that has traditionally been the basis for assessing the fluctuating behaviors evident in the texts. Methodologically, it's entirely justified to challenge such a binary framework if it does not exist in the texts. However, the crux of the matter is that the opposite viewpoint is equally legitimate: the nonbinary as an interpretative framework should be challenged if it does not exist in the texts. Therefore, the significant question becomes, what criteria do we use to describe such a framework within the text—if it exists at all? When adopting a deconstructionist approach, one is confronted with the dilemma posed by Derrida's "transcendental signifiers," which constrain any search for stable and normative concepts behind the text by the very text itself. The normative, text-independent aspect must be relinquished in favor of the reader's experience or event when the reader discovers the conflicting forces of meaning, contradictions, or gaps within the text. It involves a "reversal" when conceptual pairs are turned upside down, favoring the marginalized or subordinate element in binaries, not necessarily to make that "reversal" a new starting point, privileging the opposite part, but with a view to "shifting" the discussion from focusing on the valuations of the elements to their significance as binary constructs.

In the context of the discussion on gender identity—for example, within modern feminism and queer theory—it has meant a shift in focus from the concepts of man/woman to the question of gender identity.

---

51. Favale, *Genesis of Gender*, 134; cf. the similar conclusion by Eddy and Beilby, "Understanding Transgender Experiences and Identities," 33.

Judith Butler, as we have seen, has argued that neither women nor men should be categorized or identified based on their biological sex because it implies a contradictory binary that forces the individual to remain within a given category. Instead, Butler points to social gender that arises through the individual's actions: "Performativity constitutes the identity it is purported to be ... There is no gender identity behind the expressions of gender; that identity is performatively constituted by the very 'expressions' that are said to be its results."[52] In other words, gender identity is not related to something essential but is performative.

However, the methodological problem with deconstructive approaches runs even deeper as they often tacitly assume that, since we cannot provide precise and exhaustive definitions of words, we must abandon categorization entirely. Applied to the discussion of concepts like man and woman, it tends to lead to the idea that because it's impossible to give an almost mathematically precise definition of the terms "man" and "woman," they must be abandoned as a valuable reference to reality. And when "man" and "woman" can no longer be categorized essentially, it's only through the performative that we can describe gender identity. Here, one must question whether there is something fundamentally flawed with the category concept. Suppose a category, such as "man," can encompass elements (i.e., concrete men) with attributes that deviate from the stereotype or "norm" (for example, not liking football) without excluding the element from the category. In that case, it does not necessarily follow that the category itself must be abandoned. Instead, the different elements contribute to a deeper, broader, and more nuanced understanding of what, for example, a "man" is.[53] Noreen Giffney aptly describes how these ideological foundations of queer theory result in the dissolution of categories and biological essentialism:

> Queer theory is an exercise in discourse analysis ... Queer is all about excess, pushing the boundaries of the possible, showing up language and discursive categories more specifically for their inadequacies ... There is an unremitting emphasis in queer theoretical work on fluidity, über-inclusivity, indeterminacy, indefinability, unknowability, the preposterous,

---

52. Butler, *Gender Trouble*, 25.

53. I owe my colleague Nicolai Techow a great deal of thanks for his input on the question of categorization and—as will become clear in the next section—the need to formulate a thesis on what in the analysis is expected to support or refute this. The specific wording, of course, is my own responsibility.

impossibility, unthinkability, unintelligibility, meaninglessness and that which is unrepresentable or incommunicable ... The erotics of thinking, speaking, writing, listening, and reading are a chief concern.[54]

When deconstruction is mentioned as a methodological challenge right from the beginning, it's connected to the fact that such a "reversal" and "shift" of the binary man/woman operates with assumptions that themselves must be open to criticism. Fundamentally, questions must be raised about rejecting the transcendent, normative, and categorical: whether language and texts can refer to a reality that transcends or exists independently of language and texts and whether categorization must be abandoned altogether because it is impossible to describe elements with mathematical precision. A theistic understanding of reality or an alternative language understanding would typically argue the opposite. But even if we limit ourselves to the literary level, a deconstructive reading still stands for discussion. This is not so much about the legitimate objection that if the text's logic must be deconstructed, and the reader must reconstruct the text's meaning, then everything can mean anything, but about the reading that a priori restricts the analysis to source texts that describe the performative. Suppose gender identity in ancient Middle Eastern cultures was performatively determined, and performatively determined gender identity was not understood and evaluated within a normative framework. In that case, it must at least be required that these texts, and other texts, do not suggest that the performative or social gender was understood and assessed within a normative binary framework. The problem, in other words, lies in the too-narrow criteria for the selection of relevant source texts. In a deconstructive analysis, the narrow criterion of the performative is a methodological *sequitur*. With other epistemological or literary a priori, it must entail a broader selection of texts, including, most notably, sources that describe gender polarity at the level of creation. The problem naturally becomes even worse if the categorization itself is problematized or abandoned because it's no longer about which source texts one selects but about the binary categorization of man/woman being abandoned in advance; therefore, no texts can be used to argue that "man" and "woman" should be understood within such a binary framework.

---

54. Giffney, "Introduction," 7–9, quoted from Beilby, *Understanding Transgender Identities*, 10–11.

FALSIFICATION

The principle of falsification is not explicitly addressed in the referenced discussion. Still, it is essential to consider because the arguments against interpreting performative testimonies in source texts within a normative binary framework seem to rely on a version of the falsification principle that contradicts its original intended use. This is related to the deconstructive approach discussed earlier. Karl Popper developed falsification for use in the natural sciences. While it may be suitable as a criterion for robust hypotheses in these disciplines, it may not apply within the humanities, such as literature and religious studies, where, at most, arguments for degrees of probability can be made. Nonetheless, many require nearly mathematical precision in argumentation to avoid falsifying the hypothesis that the binary framework existed, regardless of whether the discussion is about the existence of transcendent norms or only immanent mentalities. Suppose the falsification principle is applied in a literary or religious scientific analysis of the view of gender identity in ancient Middle Eastern cultures. In that case, it must first consider the distinction between quantifiable data in the natural sciences and the more modest "probabilistic substantiation" that applies to analyzing sources or data in the humanities. Secondly, which source texts should be included in such falsification or probabilistic substantiation must be determined. It is scientifically valid to work with deconstructive a priori in such an analysis and to insist that falsification or substantiation must be based on texts that focus on the performative. However, if that is the case, it must be done with openness to these assumptions and acknowledging the legitimacy of falsifying or substantiating based on other a priori assumptions. For both parties—those arguing for and against binary gender norms—a thesis must be formulated, including what such a thesis expects to find in the texts. This also includes what would make the thesis unlikely if found in the texts. The following analysis of biblical and comparative texts expects to find texts that support the present work's thesis, and it will pose a problem for the thesis if texts are found that are inconsistent with this assertion. Regarding the comparative material, this work does not operate with its thesis as the analysis of these sources serves as a backdrop for discussing the actual subject of the work, namely the biblical texts. Instead, in the presentation, there will be questions about the thesis that other interpreters—implicitly or explicitly—seek to substantiate in their analysis.

CARDS ON THE TABLE

The approach of this work stands in contrast to existentialist, nihilist, and social constructivist views on sex and gender. It is grounded in an ontology rooted in the teachings of the Bible, asserting that God defines reality and being as the ultimate reality. According to this perspective, human beings are creations of God, each with a defined purpose. Morality, truth, and meaning are absolute and are grounded in God's nature and commands. Unlike existentialism, nihilism, and social constructivism, biblical ontology asserts an external, divine source for meaning and reality.

Instead of relying on our understanding, the Bible encourages us to base our sense of reality on God's word: "Trust in the Lord with all your heart and do not rely on your understanding. Acknowledge him in all your ways; he will make your paths straight. Do not be wise in your estimation; fear the Lord and turn away from evil. This will bring healing to your body, and refreshment to your inner self" (Prov 3:5–8).

In essence, I adhere to both ontological realism and essentialism. I affirm an objective reality independent of human thought or perception, believing in entities, properties, or relations independent of our knowledge or understanding. Furthermore, I hold that objects possess a set of attributes that are inherent and unchangeable, serving as defining characteristics of the object.

With regards to the biblical text, this worldview emphasizes that God creates reality in Gen 1, and in Gen 2, man names and identifies a preexisting reality. As Favale argues:

> Throughout this account [Gen 2], naming is depicted as a linguistic response to that which is being named. Reality, then, exists before our naming it, and our language is true and meaningful when it corresponds to what exists. The understanding of language portrayed in Genesis contrasts starkly with the view that dominated contemporary debates about gender. Most gender theories hold that what we think of as "reality" is a linguistic and social construction . . . the constructionist view of language is a complete inversion of the correspondence view depicted in Genesis. In this divinely revealed origin story, our language does not project meaning onto things. Rather, meaning intrinsically exists in what God creates. Moreover, this meaning is intelligible to us, and language, a mark of God's image in us, enables human beings to proclaim that inherent meaning.[55]

---

55. Favale, *Genesis of Gender*, 43.

The premise of this work is that gender identity and sexual orientation are objectively defined and created realities. Embracing an essentialist and realist ontology does not preclude acknowledging that an individual's gender expression is culturally influenced and shaped by personal choices. An essentialist and ontological realist reading of the biblical texts posits that gender identity and sexuality, including culturally influenced and personally chosen elements, should be understood and assessed within the framework of an objective, created order. This viewpoint establishes an intrinsic connection between biological gender and its associated sexuality. Ideally, this perspective should guide both individuals and society in understanding the dynamic relationship among gender, the body, and sexuality. This is currently a foundational postulate, which naturally requires substantiation through the analysis of relevant biblical texts and comparative material from ancient Mesopotamia.

Part Two

Comparative Material on Gender Identity and Sexuality

MESOPOTAMIA

COMPARATIVE MATERIAL IS CRUCIAL for understanding whether the biblical authors adopted, adapted, or polemicized against the cultural and social context they and their listeners and readers were a part of. As we will see, the most relevant focus for our analysis of comparative material is the Mesopotamian Inanna/Ishtar cult and its North-West Semitic syncretism. In her analysis of four Greco-Roman period Ishtar temples, Kristina Michelle Wimber argues for a "macro-cultural" and millennia-long structure within this cult. Despite transplantation to other contexts and regardless of the Hellenization that prevailed in the Orient from the third century BCE, Wimber shows that the cult around Sumerian Inanna and Akkadian Ishtar largely retained its uniqueness in a Greco-Roman context: "[A]s the temple architecture is considered in the context of the cult it shows more clearly the effects of Hellenization on Near Eastern fertility religions. The temples at Hierapolis, Delos, Dura Europos, and Khirbet et-Tannur reveal the enduring nature of Oriental religions amidst the strong cultural influence of Hellenism."[1] Gary Beckman similarly states that the "Ishtar/Šawuška cult endured for at least fifteen centuries at Nineveh" and "extended its influence to the ends of the civilized

---

1. Wimber, "Four Greco-Roman Era Temples," 125.

world."[2] Max Dashu also writes about the many "faces" of the Ishtar cult, noting significant synchronic and diachronic continuity in its spread and transplants:

> Under succeeding dynasties and epochs, the temples of Ishtar were rebuilt again and again, retaining the traits of the earlier shrines, at Agade, at Nineveh, and in new countries that adopted her worship. In these places, Ishtar sometimes ceded pride of place to the local goddess, as she absorbed traits of Shaushka among the Hurrians and Hittites, or was paired with a new consort, as with the weather-god Hadad in Syria. The Ishtar temples took on place-specific characters. She of Babylon is the most famous because of the Ishtar Gate, but there are others: Ishtar of Shamukha, the very martial Ishtar of Arbela, an Ishtar of the Battlefield, and probably the most celebrated, Ishtar of Nineveh ... There were also Syrian Ishtars of Mari and Ebla, and at least 25 different Hittite Ishtars identified by towns and mountains, especially in the southern, Hurrian country.[3]

Inanna and Ishtar

Evidence from ancient Middle Eastern cultures of gender fluctuation or gender-bending is particularly associated with the cult of Sumerian Inanna and Akkadian Ishtar, the goddess of sex, war, and justice. For example, Bahrani writes about Ishtar:

> Ishtar is the place of all extremes; she is all that is in excess or out of control. Therefore, she functions as a sign not only of the essence of femininity, but of that which is outside societal norms, against whose image Mesopotamian masculine identity defined itself, and Mesopotamian patriarchal culture delineated its boundaries. Thus it seems that in Mesopotamian culture, alterity and chaos were gendered females. Ishtar can destroy civilized man using violence, as well as the power to destroy masculinity by turning men into women and beasts. Since culture was configured as a male domain and functioned according to patriarchal values, such a transformation of man into beast or man into woman is effectively a destruction of the cultural order itself. In psychoanalytic terms, Ishtar is therefore like a symptom, that is, a sign that emerges out of repression that fails.

2. Beckman, "Ištar of Nineveh Reconsidered," 8.
3. Dashu, "Goddess Temples in Western Asia."

As such, she becomes the signifying locus of displaced meanings. Unconscious meanings and associations, desires, and fears are displaced and appear in a disguised manner.[4]

Max Dashu points in the same direction, referring to Wimber and Joanna Stuckey's article on the "Hittite" Ishtar Shaushka: "The goddess herself had androgynous traits (including a bearded aspect associated with Venus as the male morning star, while her evening star aspect was female). She had transgender priests (male-to-female) who underwent castration. Nothing is mentioned about female-to-male trans folk participating. As usual, crossing the gender border from the female side is nearly invisible historically, and very possibly less socially accepted, or at a minimum, not institutionalized. Both Wimber and Stuckey highlight the cross-dressing, gender-switching, sex-altering powers of Ishtar."[5] Dashu illustrates this with relief from the temple at 'Ain Dara (in use from 1300 to 600 BCE) depicting Shaushka "in a diaphanous gown with clearly marked pubic triangle, and one leg bared in the Hittite style."[6] The first naturally represents her female, biologically sexual side, while the latter—the so-called "marching Hittite leg"—marks her male, warrior side.[7] Stephanie Lynn Budin, who otherwise strongly criticizes the "Victorian" sexualization of ancient Near Eastern cultic practice, also agrees:

> Ištar really should be a gender-bending goddess. Her Semitic name derives from the mixing of Inanna (Sumerian) with the Semitic astral-warrior god Aštar (male). So she is male and female combined, with a name that's grammatically masculine, lacing the feminizing –t of the Semitic and Hametic languages. Technically, Ištar should be Ištart, much as her western cognate is Athtart/Aštart, a.k.a. Astarte. This led to some considerable gender ambiguity/confusion in the Syrian city of Mari, a city located on the upper Euphrates and a natural melting pot between Mesopotamian and West Semitic cultures.

---

4. Bahrani, *Women of Babylon*, 159–60.

5. Dashu, "Goddess Temples in Western Asia"; Stuckey, "Shaushka and 'Ain Dara," 1–8.

6. Note John Monson's remark, however: "A stele from the temple's outer corridor depicts a goddess dressed in a semi-transparent gown. If the temple is indeed dedicated to Ishtar, this stele may represent the goddess, who took a mountain god as her lover. But the fact that this figure wears shoes, and the footprints in the temple threshold are bare, calls into question this identification." Monson, "New 'Ain Dara Temple," 20–35, 67.

7. Dashu, "Goddess Temples in Western Asia."

Several 3rd-millennium inscriptions from two temples reveal both "male" and "female" Ištars.[8]

If these scholars are correct in their description, the Inanna/Ishtar cult must be understood as an expression of failed repression and an outlet for nonconforming identities. This is supported, of course, by primary texts.

The same fluctuating gender identity is also found in other descriptions of the cultic personnel. In the poem "Passionate Inanna" from the twenty-third century BCE, where Enheduanna, Inanna's high priestess, addresses Inanna, "cross-dressing" is a significant part of worship (though the "cross-dressing" only applies to one side of the body):

> The people of Sumer parade before you.
> The male prostitutes[9] comb their hair before you.
> They decorate the napes of their necks with colored scarves.
> The women adorn their right side with men's clothing.
> The men adorn their left side with women's clothing.
> The ascending kurgarra priests raise their swords before you.[10]

The same phenomenon is mentioned in the twentieth century BCE "Hymn of Iddin-Dagan," in which the *male* cultic official SAR.UR.SAG (Akkadian *assinnu*) is described as follows:

> The SAG.UR.SAG comb their hair before her,
> they walk before pure Inana.
> They decorate the napes of their necks with coloured bands,
> they walk before pure Inana.
> They place upon their bodies the cloak/skin of divinity,
> they walk before pure Inana.
> The righteous man/king and the first lady, the woman of the great wise women,
> they walk before pure Inana.
> Those who are in charge? Of beating? The soothing balag,
> they walk before pure Inana.
> They gird themselves with the sword belt, the arm of battle,
> they walk before pure Inana.
> The spear, the arm of battle, they grasp in their hand,

---

8. Budin, *Gender in the Ancient Near East*, 200.

9. The translation "male prostitutes" of Sumerian SAG.UR.SAG (Akkadian *assinnu*) is highly contested. Cf. Budin's rendering of the same term in the Iddin-Dagan Hymn below.

10. Foster, *Age of Agade*, 115–31, quoted from Morgan, "Evidence for Trans Lives in Sumer."

they walk before pure Inana.
Fourth kirugu
They adorn their right side with male clothing
they walk before pure Inana
To the great lady of heaven, Inana, I would cry "Hail!"
they place female clothing on their left side
they walk before pure Inana
To the great lady of heaven, Inana, I would cry "Hail!"[11]

The Akkadian Erra poem from the beginning of the first millennium BCE mentions the male *kurgarrû* and *assinnu*, "whose maleness Ishtar turned female, for the awe of the people,"[12] while the priestess Enheduanna, in the somewhat older poem "Passionate Inanna" and the older poem by high priestess Enheduanna, says about Inanna:

> Without your consent, no destiny is determined, the most ingenious solution finds no favor.
> To run fast, to slip away, to calm, to pacify are yours, Inanna.
> To dart aimlessly, to go too fast, to fall, to get up, to sustain a comrade are yours, Inanna.
> To open high road and byroad, safe lodging on the way, helping the worn-out along are yours, Inanna.
> To make footpath and trail go in the right direction, to make the going good are yours, Inanna.
> To destroy, to create, to tear out, to establish are yours, Inanna.
> To turn a man into a woman and a woman into a man are yours, Inanna.[13]

Budin contests the "transgender" interpretation of the Erra Epic since the term "femininity" is almost entirely restored but acknowledges, nonetheless, that, as far as the "Hymn of Iddin-Dagan" is concerned, "there may well be transvestitism taking place here. Or at least some kind of half-body transvestitism."[14] Kelsie Ehalt mentions in connection with the "transformation" of the *assinnu* that it's not just a binary fluctuation between man and woman but a gender identity that breaks the binary. Ehalt supports this with the alternative logographic way of writing *assinnu* found in lexical lists where the syllabic as-sin-nu (or is-sin-nu-u) is

---

11. Budin, *Gender in the Ancient Near East*, 191–92; cf. Peled, *Masculinities and Third Gender*, 263.

12. Cagni, *Poem of Erra*, quoted from Morgan, "Evidence for Trans Lives in Sumer."

13. Quoted from Morgan, "Evidence for Trans Lives in Sumer."

14. Budin, *Gender in the Ancient Near East*, 189, 192.

equated with the logographic ˡᵘUR.MUNUS. The different components of the logogram are LÚ, which is the Sumerian word for "person" and is used in Akkadian as a determinative marker, while UR and MUNUS are the Sumerian words for "man" and "woman." An example of this is mentioned by Ilan Peled, namely a Neo-Assyrian manuscript of the list igi.tuḫ.a (= *tāmartu*) with the following entries that identify the *assinnu* (and the much lesser attested *kulu'u*) as a "man-woman":

> 265 lú [ur-munus] ku-lu-'
> 266 lú ur-munus as/i-sin-nu
> 265 [man-woman] kulu'u
> 266 man-woman assinnu/isinnu[15]

The combination indicates that the person *assinnu* is neither a man nor a woman but a combination that breaks the binary. Ehalt concludes that "this combination of gendered words indicates that *assinnu* do not fit neatly into either category, and their gender is more complicated than simply normatively masculine or feminine."[16] Ehalt goes too far, however. We only read about *males* turning into women, and these male cultic functionaries only bend their gender *ritually*. As Budin remarks, as a *cultic* identity, it "does not indicate that transvestitism was a part of any of the participants' *personal* identities."[17]

The role played by the *assinnu* (Sumerian SAG.UR.SAG), *kalû* (Sumerian GALA), and *kurgarrû* is highly contested. Budin argues, for example, that the *kalû* was a musician and singer of laments, whereas "much as with the *kurgarrû*, the *assinnu* was a cultic warrior of some kind, and one relevant for the performance of purification/healing rituals" and "[he] had a martial character, either as a warrior, the fife-and-drum band, or both. He is far closer to depictions of hegemonic masculinity than third gender."[18] As for the *kurgarrû*, "rather than a 'third' or 'non-normative' gender, the *kurgarrû*'s role in cult seems to have been to play out the idea of hegemonic masculinity, either as an aspect of Ištar herself or as something that the goddess found entertaining. Or both."[19] Budin and others may very well be correct in this description of their gender-bending

---

15. Peled, "Kula'ūtam Epēšum," 753.
16. Ehalt, "Assumptions About the Assinnu," 19.
17. Budin, *Gender in the Ancient Near East*, 192. Emphasis original.
18. Budin, *Gender in the Ancient Near East*, 185, 194, 196.
19. Budin, *Gender in the Ancient Near East*, 190.

ritual roles. Their performance in the Ištar cult functioned as a deliberate provocation against established binary gender identity.

The critical question, however, is whether it's tenable to completely desexualize the activities that occurred in the temples. Recent research appears to push back against this notion, presenting a more nuanced picture. Firstly, there are primary texts that link the temple with sexual services. The poem "Erra and Ishtum" (ca. the eighth century BCE) seemingly legitimizes, either positively or ritually, both men and women taking on the receptive role in binary and same-sex temple/sacred sex.

> Even Uruk the dwelling of Anu and Ishtar,
> city of prostitutes [*ḫarimtu*'s], courtesans [*kezertu*'s], and call-girls [*šamḫatu*'s],
> Whom Ishtar deprived of husbands and kept in her (lit. their) power:
> Sutean men and women hurl their abuse;
> They rouse Eanna, the party-boys and festival people
> Who changed their masculinity into femininity to make the people of Ishtar revere her.[20]

Describing it negatively, a Babylonian proverb from the collection "Councils of Wisdom" from the second millennium BCE refers to temple/sacred prostitution in a warning against specific marriages:

> Do not marry a harlot [*ḫarīmtu*] whose husbands are six thousand.
> An Ishtar woman [*ištarîtu*] vowed to a god,
> A sacred prostitute whose favors are unlimited,
> Will not lift you out of your trouble.[21]

In addition to warnings and laws, texts related to the Ishtar cult also suggest the involvement of the cultic officials in sexual acts. However, as Nissinen points out, "there are some ambiguous hints they were involved in sexual acts with male persons; however if such acts actually took place, they should not be interpreted as a case of same-sex interaction since the *assinnu* were not considered male on society's gender spectrum."[22] Jack Lundbom states in the same vein about the text from the collection "Councils of Wisdom" mentioning the *Ishtar woman*: "Lamberts translates *ištarîtu* as 'temple harlot,' but says regarding cultic prostitution: 'No

---

20. Dalley, *Myths from Mesopotamia*, 305.
21. Quoted from Pritchard, *Ancient Near Eastern Texts*, 427.
22. Nissinen, "Homosexuality," 295.

one doubts its prevalence, especially with the cult of ISHTAR, but little is known of its functioning."[23]

Regardless of whether sex with cultic functionaries may or may not be defined as same-sex sex, there is no doubt that it existed in temple/sacred contexts. This is evident from a series of texts about various cultic functionaries referred to by Nissinen, where the middle one strongly suggests that it involved prostitution:

> When the *kalû* wiped his anus, (he said): "I must not excite that which belongs to my lady Inanna"
> When a [*sinnišānu* "man-woman"] entered the brothel [*bīt aštammi*], he raised his hands and said:
> "My hire goes to the promoter. You are wealth, I am half"
> Men take into their houses *kurgarrûs* who deliver them children[24]

The meaning of the middle text is debated. Phillys Bird writes as follows: "Sexual encounters (with men and women) seem to have taken place in the *bīt aštammi* (variously translated as 'tavern,' 'hostel,' and 'brothel'), which was apparently attached to some temples, under the patronage of Ishtar."[25] For the meaning of *bīt aštammi*, see more below. Bird, referring to an essay by Gernot Wilhelm, also mentions the occurrence of the Sumerian KAR.KID and the Babylonian equivalent *ḫarimtu*, "prostitute," in temple complexes but simultaneously concludes that "the evidence is scant and indirect, however, and falls short of establishing a generally recognized institution of temple prostitution."[26] Despite this reservation, the texts quoted above can hardly be interpreted differently than that it was common knowledge that both women and men (voluntarily or under coercion) were initiated into prostitution as part of the cult. This practice served both ritual purposes, as was the case in the Ishtar cult, and economic purposes, with the proceeds from prostitution going to the temple treasury.

Many scholars question whether the KAR.KID/*ḫarīmtu* designates "a prostitute" in the first place. Assante has argued, for example, that KAR.KID/*ḫarīmtu* refers to the legal category of the single woman properly

---

23. Lundbom, *Deuteronomy*, 658.

24. Nissinen, *Homoeroticism in the Biblical World*, 33–35, quoted from Gagnon, *Bible and Homosexual Practice*, 49.

25. Bird, *Faith, Feminism, and the Forum*, 162; cf. Silver, *Sacred Prostitution*, 248–50.

26. Bird, "Of Whores and Hounds," 357n15.

belonging outside the patriarchal system.[27] Referring to the Semitic root *ḥrm*, which means "outside," Assante argues that "she lives on the street," the commonly used phrase when mentioning the *ḥarīmtu* in the texts, should not be taken literally but rather as a common ancient Mesopotamian metaphor signifying that the person is outside the community and outside the laws that apply to the community. Joan Goodnick Westenholz also avers that KAR.KID/*ḥarīmtu* designates "eine Frau, die sich außerhalb der gesellschaftlich akzeptierten Grenzen geregelter Sexualität befindet."[28] In Egyptian sources, there is also mention of women who live "outside" of society due to adultery and who, as a result of their economic hardship, may have turned to prostitution and had to leave their hometowns.[29] Budin takes this definition for granted when she, in a footnote to a discussion on the *ḥarīmtu* Šamḫat from the "Epic of Gilgamesh," argues that "this word is typically mistranslated as 'prostitute, harlot' in most modern translations. That is not, in fact, the definition of *ḥarīmtu*. The word designated a woman who is not under patriarchal authority insofar as she has neither father nor husband and is not dedicated to a deity. As such, she has a degree of sexual liberty not available to 'normal' Mesopotamian females, and thus, as with Shamhat here, was available to have sexual relations with a strange man on request. Request, not payment."[30] Assante admits, in later texts, *ḥarīmtu* came to designate a prostitute since some *ḥarīmtu*'s became prostitutes; Silver criticized this view: "Perhaps Assante is suggesting that in 'late' times, *ḥarīmtu* came to have the meaning 'prostitute' because many prostitutes were *ḥarīmtu*'s (= single women). Any such suggestion would be problematic because prostitutes would have been drawn from the ranks of single women/women without a husband in much earlier times."[31] Silver argues instead that KAR.KID/ *ḥarīmtu* indeed designates a "prostitute" and criticizes Assante for putting forward an extremist "desexualized" vision of ancient societies by arguing that "there are no cuneiform words for hierodule, prostitute, or prostitution; nor is there any evidence for sacred prostitution."[32]

27. Assante, "Kar.Kid/Harimtu, Prostitute or Single Woman," 5–96.
28. Westenholz, "Heilige Hochzeit," 59.
29. Westenholz, "Tamar, Qĕdēšā, Qadištu," 251.
30. Budin, *Gender in the Ancient Near East*, 113n120.
31. Assante, "Kar.Kid/Harimtu," 63; Marsman, *Women in Ugarit and Israel*, 418; Silver, *Sacred Prostitution*, 240–41.
32. Silver, *Sacred Prostitution*, 234; Assante, "Erotic Reliefs of Ancient Mesopotamia," 9; Assante, "From Whores to Hierodules," 33.

COMPARATIVE MATERIAL ON GENDER IDENTITY AND SEXUALITY

The most obvious example of the relationship between *harīmtu* and prostitution is in the Gilgamesh Epic, where Shamhat the *harīmtu* trades her sexual favors for material valuables:

> May no soldier [be slow] to undo his belt for you!
> May he [give you] obsidian, lapis lazuli, and gold,
> Multiple ear-[rings] shall be you gift!
> To a man whose household [is well off],
> whose storage bins are heaped high,
> To the man who is secure, whose granaries are full,
> may Ishtar, [the most able] of the gods, send you in![33]

Enkidu's blessing, Silver argues, "portrays Shamhat as a woman who will trade sex for gifts. Clearly, she is viewed as a prostitute."[34] Hennie Marsman concurs though she accepts Assante's argument that the text reflects a late development in the use of *harīmtu* as a "non-judgmental term for a woman who uses her sexuality to support herself."[35] Silver argues contra Assante and Marsman, however, that Shamhat the *harīmtu* was a *professional* prostitute because Shamhat's favors to Enkidu clearly take place in the temple of Ishtar, who herself is designated a *harīmtu* (in other texts; see below):

> "Enkidu spoke to the harlot"
> 'Come, Shamhat, take me along
> to the sacred temple, the holy dwelling of Anu and Ishtar
> where Gilgamesh is perfect in strength.'"[36]

Silver concludes that "the status of professional prostitute explains Shamhat's willing participation and ties in well with Enkidu's blessing. Enkidu's [later] curse 'The shadow of a wall shall be your station' reinforces the conclusion that Shamhat is a prostitute."[37]

Two other Sumerian texts mention the KAR.KID is remarkable. In "Inanna and Enki," it's described that three of the ME (elements of civilization) that Inanna took from Enki to the world were sex, the (kissing of the) penis (fellatio?), and the office of the KAR.KID. The KAR.KID is

---

33. George, *Babylonian Gilgamesh Epic*, 1:643; GE 7, 156–60.
34. Silver, *Sacred Prostitution*, 239.
35. Marsman, *Women in Ugarit and Israel*, 418–19.
36. George, *Babylonian Gilgamesh Epic*, 1:551; GE 1, 215–18.
37. Silver, *Sacred Prostitution*, 239.

described in a Sumerian love poem as "the maid, the daughter of Inanna, who frequents the tavern."[38]

Another relevant text is the Babylonian proverb mentioned above, which, in Lambert's translation, reads:

> Do not marry a *harīmtu*, whose husbands are legion [literally 3600],
> A temple harlot [*ištarītu*] who is dedicated to a god,
> A courtesan [*kulmašītu*] whose favours are many.
> In your troubles, she will not support you,
> In your dispute she will be a mocker;
> There is no reverence or submissiveness with her.
> Even if she dominates your house, get her out,
> For she has directed her attention elsewhere.
> Variant: She will disrupt the house she enters, and her partner will not assert himself.[39]

Assante explains the text by arguing that all three categories of women, i.e., the *harīmtu*, *ištarītu*, and *kulmašītu*, are bad marriage choices because they, for different reasons, will not give their primary attention to their husbands. The *harīmtu* has a reputation for multiple sexual partners, the quintessential sign of her unmarried state, and her full attention will not go to her husband, nor can she be counted to be faithful. The *ištarītu* is also independent of her husband but because she is dedicated to a god, and the *kulmašītu* is dedicated to the betterment of her family members, not to her husband. What these women have in common in this text that makes them undesirable as wives is their shared emotional, not physical, infidelity.[40]

Assante's explanation, according to Silver, is unsatisfactory since it's difficult to understand the *harīmtu*'s legion of husbands as "the quintessential sign of her unmarried state." If the category designates single women "properly belonging outside the patriarchal system," there must have been such women who were *not* involved with a "legion of husbands." If this is the case, Assante is begging the question of why the *harīmtu* is not a prostitute. Contra Assante, Hennie Marsman also points to a text from Emar mentioning a father making his KAR.KID daughter into the "father

---

38. Quoted from the chapter on *harīmtu* in Budin, *Freewomen, Patriarchal Authority*.
39. Lambert, *Babylonian Wisdom Literature*, 103.
40. Assante, "Kar.Kid/Harimtu," 54.

and mother" of his house,⁴¹ and whatever this means, she is *not* a "single woman properly belonging outside the patriarchal system."

Texts describe both Inanna and Ishtar as *ḫarīmtu*'s. Silver mentions the Epic of Lugalbanda, in which Inanna is "the KAR.KID [= *ḫarīmtu*], setting out toward the *éšdam* ["tavern"], who makes the bed sweet," and the Sumerian Hymn to Inanna-Ninegalla, in which the goddess departs from the tavern, her "dwelling place," in search for men in a sexy outfit and wearing the beads of the KAR.KID.⁴²

The same characterization is found of Ishtar on an Old Babylonian (ca. 1900–1600 BCE) bilingual literary tablet (IM 013348) from Ur.⁴³ Martin Stol points to the so-called Burney Relief, which is often interpreted as figuring Ishtar as a whore since several elements point in that direction: "Under her horned crown we see a fringe of hair, and hair was a sign of a woman's sex appeal. A stone model of a woman's 'wig' is inscribed 'female sex appeal' . . . Around her neck she wears a necklace, possibly made from particular egg-shaped jewels. A Sumerian text says these are the gems that hang round the neck of a whore."⁴⁴

Silver, furthermore, points to an Old Babylonian Akkadian composition from Nippur called "Ishtar Will Not Tire" in which "numerous husbands" are invited to have sex with "Ishtar."

> "Since I'm ready to give you all you want,
> Get all the young men of your city together,
> Let's go to the shade of a wall!"
> Seven for her midriff, seven for her loins,
> Sixty then sixty satisfy themselves in turn upon her nakedness.
> Young men have tired, Ishtar will not tire⁴⁵

Also relevant is a Sumerian text in which Inanna herself is described as a KAR.KID and "one who knows the penis," a description most compatible with being involved with a "legion of husbands."⁴⁶

---

41. Marsman, *Women in Ugarit and Israel*, 416.

42. Silver, *Sacred Prostitution*, 249; cf. "The harlot who goes out to the tavern, who makes the bed a delight"; Vanstiphout, *Epics of Sumerian Kings*, 115:174.

43. Matuszak, "Don't Insult Inana!," 365.

44. Stol, *Women in the Ancient Near East*, 429–30.

45. Foster, *Before the Muses*, 678.

46. Quoted from Matuszak, "Don't Insult Inana!," 365; cf. Silver, *Sacred Prostitution*, 242; Cuneiform Digital Library Initiative, "CDLI Literary 000771"; Oppenheim, "Ḫarīmtu."

> When I'm sitting in the alehouse,
> I'm a woman, I'm a proud young man.
> When I'm witnessing (lit., standing at the place of) a quarrel,
> I'm the one who revives the weak.
> When I'm sitting in the gate of the tavern,
> I'm a prostitute who knows the penis.
> A man's friend, a girlfriend to the woman.

Though it may be argued that it's Ishtar who prostitutes herself, it's more likely that Ishtar functions as a role model or that the invitation refers to temple prostitutes who *represent* Ishtar in "the shade of the wall," an acknowledged euphemism for prostitution.

Silver provides substantial additional evidence and concludes that "the sexualized nature of the *harīmtu*/kar-kid has been established. There is sufficient reason to believe that she was a prostitute."[47] In particular, Silver mentions two texts describing women's consignment to Ishtar/the temple of Ishtar.

The first is a text from Nuzi (SMN1670) in which a man, due to debt, pledges a woman to Ishtar Shaushka *ana harīmūtu* "for whoredom, prostitution."[48] The second is a curse made on the statue of Kapara, king of the Aramean kingdom of Tell Halaf (1000–850 BCE):

> Let him burn his seven sons before the god Adad.
> Let him consign (*luramme*) his seven daughters to Ištar as whores (*ana harīmtu*).[49]

Assante argues that the "force of the curse relies wholly . . . on the importance Mesopotamia placed on continuing the patrilineal line. Destroying the sons and turning one's daughters into *harīmtu*'s effectively end the house, for neither dead sons nor estranged *harīmtu* daughters could produce legal heirs to carry his life."[50] Silver mentions that, though Assante's argument taken in isolation has merit, the many texts describing *harīmtu*'s as prostitutes means that the apparent translation of the consigning of the seven daughters "*ana harīmtu*" would be to render it, as CAD does, "for prostitution."[51] The fact that, according to CAD, *bit aštammu* ("tavern") may refer to a building in the temple complex likely

---

47. Silver, *Sacred Prostitution*, 245.
48. Silver, "Temple/Sacred Prostitution in Ancient Mesopotamia Revisited," 640.
49. Menzel, *Assyrische Tempel*, 27–29.
50. Assante, "Kar.Kid/Harimtu," 23.
51. Oppenheim, "Harīmūtu."

refers to *temple* prostitution. Silver mentions two texts about the relationship between the "tavern" and the temple. The Assyrian ruler Adadnārāri I boasts in a stela from the second half of the second millennium that he "restored the storeroom of the goddess Ishtar of the courtyard which is called the 'Inn of the Goddess Ishtar,'" and an Old Babylonian letter from the Ur-Utu archive refers to "the taverns lying next to the temple."[52] Silver also points to a version of an Old Babylonian Sumerian dialogue hymn (CBS 8530) in which "Nanaya, an Inanna-like goddess, explicitly offers to sell sexual serviced at the door or her *papāḫum* 'cella, sanctuary, chapel, bedroom'" and even "quotes prices for sexual acts."[53] "Given the evidence suggesting that *ḫarīmūtu*'s were prostitutes and the absence of a reasonable alternative explanation of the *ḫarīmūtum*-payments," Silver argues, "it is fair to accept as a working hypothesis that the income originated in the prostitution industry."[54] Based on several Old Babylonian texts, Silver, a specialist in ancient economies and the role of ancient religions in facilitating economic growth, concludes that "the Inanna/Ishtar cult was involved, directly and/or by means of agents, in the production and sale of sexual services . . . Sexually explicit hymns and myths of goddesses served to advertise and to increase the demand for the services of cultic prostitute s. . . Taverns/Inns in temple precincts housed brothels . . . The *ḫarīmtu*/KAR.KID was a professional prostitute with cultic connections."[55]

Silver dismisses Assante's conclusions as being at odds with significant evidence and ultimately asserts that the Inanna/Ishtar cult, either directly or through intermediaries, played a role in the creation and distribution of sexual services.[56] It's also proposed that sexually explicit rituals, myths, and hymns involving goddesses were employed to boost the demand for the services provided by cultic prostitutes.[57] It should be noted that Silver's analysis finds comparative support from an extensive study, which argues that there is substantial evidence from ancient Greece and Rome that the sexual services offered at temples were systematically organized, promoted through various methods to the general public, occasionally outsourced to semi-independent religious entrepreneurs,

52. Silver, *Sacred Prostitution*, 250.
53. Silver, *Sacred Prostitution*, 254.
54. Silver, *Sacred Prostitution*, 257.
55. Silver, *Sacred Prostitution*, 258–59.
56. Assante, "Kar.Kid/Harimtu," 10; Assante, "From Whores to Hierodules."
57. Silver, *Sacred Prostitution*, 233.

financially lucrative, and endorsed as a religious ritual.[58] The women engaged in providing these services were not merely priestesses or prostitutes individually; instead, they were a unique category known as *priestess prostitutes*. Like certain other priestesses, they had specific roles and functions. In some cases, celibate priestesses specialized in handling administrative and financial aspects to support the work of the temple's prostitutes. Additionally, male religious agents often acted as intermediaries between groups of female prostitutes and their male clients.[59] This matters not only because Morris criticizes recent studies on Greek and Roman evidence, which argue that sacred or temple prostitution in the ancient world is a myth, but also, as we have seen, because he brings the evidence to bear on ancient Mesopotamia with the same conclusion.

In his *Women in the Ancient Near East*, Marten Stol argues that texts suggest that the *ḫarīmtu* in Sippar and *kezertu* in Kish were involved in sacred prostitution. From Sippar, Stol mentions a list of eleven prostitutes (*ḫarīmtu*) supervised by the so-called First Lamentation Singer. Stol remarks on this supervisor that "the women who organized this were respectable women who participated in these temple services, providing them with a source of income, a kind of benefice."[60] Stol also mentions a proverb that most likely refers to sex for money in a temple context:

> Let me lie with you. Let the deity enjoy his share.[61]

This is supported by archaeological evidence. In the Etruscan city of Pyrgi, north of Rome, a temple dating back to the second century BCE dedicated to Ashtoreth, one of Ishtar's synchronisms, was discovered. It contained seventeen small rooms that were very likely used for temple prostitution, as mentioned by the contemporary Roman satirist Gaius Lucilius.[62] The same holds in Dura-Europos near the Euphrates, where up to a dozen small rooms with low benches were found before a temple dating back to the first century CE, dedicated to the Aramaic goddess Atargatis. Although these rooms could have been used for sacrificial meals, excavations at the Apollo temple in Bulla Regia, near present-day Jendouba in Tunisia, showed that such rooms were also used for sexual

---

58. Silver, *Sacred Prostitution*.
59. Silver, *Sacred Prostitution*, 5.
60. Stol, *Women in the Ancient Near East*, 423–24.
61. Lambert, *Babylonian Wisdom Literature*, 227; 2.27, 231, quoted in Stol, *Women in the Ancient Near East*, 427.
62. Lipiński, "Cult Prostitution," 25–26.

services provided by men and women dedicated to or held captive for temple prostitution. In the temple, a woman was found buried with the inscription "Adulteress. Prostitute. Seize (me) because I fled from Bulla Regia."[63]

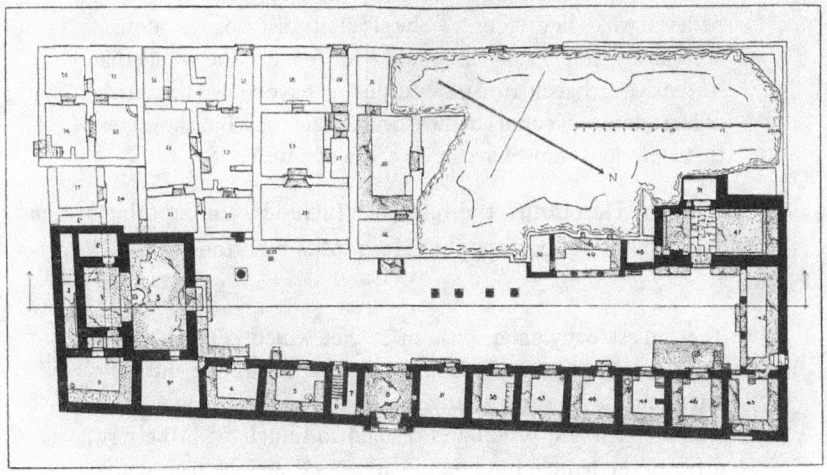

Figure 3 Building attached to the temple for Atargatis at Dura-Europos

The overall conclusion reached above is shared by Clay Jones, who criticizes Stephanie Lynn Budin's allegation that cultic prostitution didn't exist at all in antiquity.[64] The criticism is worth repeating in its entirety since it not only refers to classical sources (Herodotus) but also to descriptions of such a practice by Paul and the church fathers Clement, Athanasius, and Augustine:

> What Budin means is that sacred prostitution never ever happened in all of the ANE. Not even once. But to make the case that the world's oldest profession was never involved where sexual practices and greed abounded is almost beyond comprehension. The only way one can argue that sacred prostitution never occurred is to discount absolutely every report of it, and the only way one could do that is to already know that it never happened and thus argue in a circle. But Budin does this. She disregards the early Christian testimony from Paul to Clement to Athanasius and Augustine as no more than self-interested polemic

63. Lipiński, "Cult Prostitution," 26.

64. Budin, *Myth of Sacred Prostitution in Antiquity*; cf. Glinister, "Rapino Bronze, the Touta Marouca," 18–38.

presenting paganism "in the worst possible light" and therefore concludes that "references to sacred prostitution" are not "historical evidence" but "condemnatory rhetoric." "I doubt that many of the authors who contributed to the sacred prostitution myth entirely believed what they wrote... But in the end, what is more important for the rise of the myth is that their readers believed what they wrote..." She similarly discards Herodotus's account by simply asserting that he made it up. She grants that "extensive archaeological excavations... have shown that many of Herodotos's accounts to have been correct..." But she argues that Herodotus must have made some of it up.[65]

Regarding Herodotus, the reference includes, among other things, the Babylonian rite of passage that Herodotus mentions in his *Histories* 1.199:

> The foulest Babylonian custom is that which compels every woman of the land to sit in the temple of Aphrodite and have intercourse with some stranger once in her life. Many women who are rich and proud and disdain to mingle with the rest, drive to the temple in covered carriages drawn by teams, and stand there with a great retinue of attendants. But most sit down in the sacred plot of Aphrodite, with crowns of cord on their heads; there is a great multitude of women coming and going; passages marked by lines run every way through the crowd, by which the men pass and make their choice. Once a woman has taken her place there, she does not go away to her home before some stranger has cast money into her lap and had intercourse with her outside the temple; but while he casts the money, he must say, "I invite you in the name of Mylitta" (that is the Assyrian name for Aphrodite). It does not matter what sum the money is; the woman will never refuse, for that would be a sin, the money being by this act made sacred. So she follows the first man who casts it and rejects no one. After their intercourse, having discharged her sacred duty to the goddess, she goes away to her home; and thereafter there is no bribe however great that will get her. So then the women that are fair and tall are soon free to depart, but the uncomely have long to wait because they cannot fulfill the law; for some of them remain for three years or four. There is a custom like this in some parts of Cyprus.[66]

---

65. Jones, "We Don't Hate Sin," 59n20.
66. Herodotus, *Herodotus I*, 250–53.

The fact that it concerns a rite of passage rather than a more general practice is emphasized by the texts that confirm what Herodotus referred to back in his time. Lipiński argues that the so-called *rēdûtum* rite, performed only once in a woman's lifetime, underlay the custom Herodotus mentions. Lipiński notes that although the so-called *rēdûtum* at the temple of Ishtar-Annunītum in Sippar were primarily married women, they were married at such a young age that it could represent a rite of passage marking their sexual debut.[67]

A similar custom existed in Phoenicia, as described in Lucian's *The Syrian Goddess* 6.25, where women "stand for a single day in readiness to expose their person for hire. The place of hire is open to none but foreigners, and out of the proceeds of the traffic of these women, a sacrifice to Aphrodite is paid."[68] Lipiński also remarks regarding Lucian's wording that "the custom of submitting to a stranger in the service of a goddess points to a rite of passage, performed only once, not 'for a single day,' as Lucian has misunderstood his informant."[69]

Eva Anagnostou-Laoutides and Michael B. Charles, in analyzing Herodotus's mention of the Babylonian custom, note that, while cultic prostitution undoubtedly existed, many of the texts have generally been misunderstood as literal descriptions. This is because "explicit sexual language" is often used figuratively to describe "religious devotion," and these different descriptions are better understood in that light. They state, "Our interpretation does not discount the fact that prostitution was a widespread phenomenon of the ancient world, often practiced around temples that attracted numerous visitors, especially during festive days; yet, by drawing attention to the use of explicit sexual language to describe religious devotion in antiquity, from the most sensual near eastern examples, discussed above, to the survival of the trend in Greek cultic titles, we seek to challenge the prevailing historical appreciation of the institution of 'sacred prostitution,' which is based, by and large, on a rather inflexible reading of a handful of ancient texts."[70] This more reserved acknowledgment of cultic prostitution aligns with the consensus that has emerged in research in recent decades, which we will revisit when discussing the so-called *qᵊdēšîm* in the Old Testament.

---

67. Lipiński, "Cult Prostitution in Ancient Israel?," 49–56, 70.
68. Quoted from Lipiński, "Cult Prostitution," 13.
69. Lipiński, "Cult Prostitution," 13.
70. Anagnostou-Laoutides and Charles, "Herodotus on Sacred Marriage," 22.

Greenberg also mentions that "lesbianism is also mentioned in a divinatory apodosis, in a context that suggests that it may not have been unusual."[71] The Mesopotamian warning from the collection "Šumma izbu" ("If a city is elevated") states, "If one male dog mounts another, women will copulate."[72] Nissinen suggests that this occasional mention of same-sex female sex may be because "sexual contacts between women did not threaten the sexual hierarchy of the patriarchal social space."[73] Same-sex female sex existed, albeit sparsely documented.

Relevant to our analysis, another category of texts is narrative or epic literature. The relationship between Gilgamesh and Enkidu in the Epic of Gilgamesh has been interpreted as a same-sex sexual relationship. In the epic, Gilgamesh is portrayed as the great virile king of Uruk; Enkidu is described as a primitive wild man who, after days of sex with the seductress Shamhat, loses his primitive animality and gains reason and intellect. Enkidu goes to Uruk to confront the great king Gilgamesh, who has seen him coming in dreams. Gilgamesh's mother interprets the dreams: "You will love him [Enkidu] as a wife and embrace him, and I will make him your equal."[74] Gilgamesh subsequently defeats Enkidu but forms a close relationship with him. While the epic never explicitly mentions sexual intercourse between them, the prediction of Gilgamesh's mother and Gilgamesh's lamentation over Enkidu's death hint at such a possibility. For example, Gilgamesh is described as covering Enkidu's face "like a bride," and he circles over him "like an eagle."[75]

It is also interesting to note that in the description of Gilgamesh and Enkidu, there seems to be a wordplay involving *kezertu* and *assinnu*, both of which are terms for cultic functionaries.[76] The extent to which their relationship was a close friendship or a sexual one depends on how much one reads between the lines. Interpretations vary, with David Greenberg viewing the relationship as a homosexual one: "Though Enkidu was certainly not effeminate, he is analogized to a female prostitute under the subordinate sexual role he played after being defeated by Gilgamesh."[77] Nissinen, on the other hand, argues that "they do not

---

71. Greenberg, *Construction of Homosexuality*, 127n12.
72. Leichty, *Omen Series Šumma Izbu*, 24:33.
73. Nissinen, *Homoeroticism in the Biblical World*, 186.
74. Søndergaard and Helle, *Gilgamesh*, 25.
75. Søndergaard and Helle, *Gilgamesh*, 90.
76. Gagnon, *Bible and Homosexual Practice*, 50.
77. Greenberg, *Construction of Homosexuality*, 113.

form a 'homosexual' partnership in modern terms but, rather, a mutual bonding of two equal men based on love and with no division of sexual roles resembling those between men and women in the patriarchal society."[78] Nissinen does not exclude the possibility that the relationship also—or at least initially—had a same-sex sexual aspect. However, he emphasizes that if such a dimension existed, it evolved into "an accentuated masculine asceticism." In this case, the resulting equal relationship between individuals "exemplifies less a homoerotic than a homosocial type of bonding, which is often seen in societies in which men's and women's worlds are segregated."[79]

David Instone-Brewer argues along similar lines, stating that the erotic element in the context of the story's plot is expected because "his people arranged for him to meet handsome Enkidu to distract him from his overenthusiastic use of *droit du seigneur*. That is, they hoped to protect the city's virgins by distracting him in other directions. However, the text never actually states that they had a sexual relationship."[80]

Canaan

In the northwest Semitic, Syro-Palestinian, or Canaanite religion,[81] the cult of the Ugaritic ʿAthtart, *ʿṯtrt* and the Phoenician ʿAshtart, *ʿštrt* (Hebrew עַשְׁתֹּרֶת, *ʿaštōret*,[82] "Astarte" in 1 Kgs 11:5 and 2 Kgs 23:13) and the Greek Ἀστάρτη, *Astártē*, corresponded with the Mesopotamian Ishtar cult. Lists of god names from Ugarit show that ʿAshtart was considered analogous to the Mesopotamian Ishtar. Although there are descriptions

78. Nissinen, "Homosexuality," 294.
79. Nissinen, *Homoeroticism in the Biblical World*, 24.
80. Instone-Brewer, "Are There Two Types of Men," 42.

81. The term "Canaanite" in sources from the ancient Near East denotes someone or something from the region of Canaan and can therefore refer to any person or group from the area that encompasses modern Lebanon, southwestern Syria, Israel, western Jordan, and the Palestinian territories. Our textual knowledge of Canaanite religion primarily comes from the epics, god lists, and descriptions of rituals found since 1928 in Ugarit and since 1972 in Emar, as well as the biblical texts, which—albeit in strongly negative terms—also provide information on this subject. Although geographically Israel was part of Canaan, biblical sources are treated separately as they are inherently biased descriptions of the Canaanite religion that was not Israelite.

82. It has been suggested that the consonants are vocalized with the vowels from the Hebrew term בֹּשֶׁת (*bōšet*, "shame"). The ETCBC transcription as documented at https://annotation.github.io/text-fabric/tf/writing/hebrew.html is used in transcription of Hebrew words.

of cultic practices in many Ugaritic texts (ca. 1400–1200 BCE), none of them, like the descriptions of the so-called *assinnu* in the Mesopotamian material, describe a corresponding role for the cultic personnel in the Ugaritic cults. According to Alan Cooper, a category of priests or cultic personnel called *qdšm* is mentioned, which may have had the same role as the Hebrew *qᵃdēšîm* mentioned in 1 Kgs 15:12 and 2 Kgs 23:7, among others.[83] However, the term only appears in administrative texts, and there is no information about their function. Since the 'Athtart cult corresponded with the Mesopotamian Ishtar cult, it's not unlikely that the fluctuating gender identity was also expressed in the Canaanite context. Kurt Noll mentions in this regard that even though Ugaritic gods sometimes had sex in myths (e.g., KTU 1.4.v. 38–39; 1.5.v. 18–22; 1.11; 1.12; 1.23; 1.24), the texts do not provide grounds to believe that such relationships reflected or encouraged similar sexual relationships between humans in the temple. One text even prohibits any ritual that "brings shame" upon a woman (without defining this further).[84]

The so-called "Aqhat Epic" should also be mentioned in connection with the Northwest Semitic material. The epic is about the hero Danel's son Aqhat, who receives a fantastic bow that costs him his life when he refuses to give it to the goddess Anat. Subsequently, Aqhat's sister *Pūġatu* decides to "strike down him who struck down my brother, so that I may finish off him who finished off the (most important) child of my family."[85] Before encountering the murderer Yatpan, she disguises herself as both a man and a woman: "She washed herself, [hand] and shoulder; She rouged herself with 'husk of the sea,' which ranges a thousand furlongs in the sea. She [. . .], she puts on the outfit of a warrior, she put [a knife in] her NŠG, a sword she put in [her] sheath."[86] It is unclear in the text what purpose this gender-mixed attire serves, but Cyrus Goron remarks on the prohibition of cross-dressing in Deut 22:5 that "this act is described in the Epic of Aqhat as well. After the hero is slain, his sister *Pūġatu* seeks revenge against Anat for the murder. To do so, *Pūġatu* disguises herself as a male, replete with rouge (the coloration of males, especially warrior heroes), man's clothing, and weaponry . . . No doubt, the average

---

83. Cooper, "Canaanite Religion"; for the texts see Gordon, *Ugaritic Textbook*; 81:2; 113:73; 114:1; 169:7.

84. KTU 1.4.iii.15–24; Noll, "Canaanite Religion," 61–92, quoted from https://people.brandonu.ca/nollk/canaanite-religion.

85. COS 1.103, line 196.

86. COS 1.103, lines 203–8.

Canaanite male or female dressed in proper fashion throughout most of his or her life. But since Canaanite epic literature describes transvestism in a noble manner, we may conclude that this act not only was practiced but also was countenanced."[87] However, it must be noted that such a conclusion is not necessarily sustainable since, as per the methodological considerations regarding ethics and morals in the mythological space, we could just as well conclude that Canaanite epics describe transsexuality in the divine realm as an anti-norm. This is mentioned as a methodological caveat since it's challenging to arrive at a more precise understanding based on the sparse material from Ugarit.

Kurt Noll also notes about the goddess Anat that she appears "sexually compelling . . . and bloodthirsty in battle," and her behavior "reverses Canaanite society's patriarchal norms, in which males do the fighting and women are sequestered in private quarters to 'protect' their sexuality. Or perhaps Anat represents the military subculture in Canaanite society, where foremost on the minds of young male soldiers are love and war."[88] The depiction of Anat can thus be seen as an attempt to destabilize the stereotypes associated with the "masculine" and "feminine" adjectives rather than necessarily an expression of fluid gender identity.

Arguing from iconography and closer to ancient Israel, Yitzhak Paz, Ianir Milevski, and Nimrod Getzov have suggested that a cultic scene depicted on a third-millennium-BCE cylinder seal impression from Bet Ha-Emeq in western Galilee, Israel, enables us to reconstruct a Canaanite sacred marriage ritual:

> Considering the major role Inanna/Ishtar had as the inspiration for the "sacred marriage" ceremony, one can now connect all loose rope ends together: the scene depicted on the impression from Bet Ha-Emeq reflects one stage of the "sacred marriage," which involves the employment of a musical instrument. That this activity is sacred is well illustrated by the depiction of priest women, one priestess and her accompanied helpers, or three priestesses. The main figure, possibly dressed and defined by a stylized three-tress hairdo, is playing the lyre. Hovering above is the emblem of the goddess, and one may wonder if the relation between the lyre (musical instrument)—Lyra (astral constellation)—Gula and Inanna/ Ishtar (fertility and healer goddesses)—the "sacred marriage" are co-incidental. What is clear is that the scene depicted on the impression from Bet Ha-Emeq

87. Gordon and Rendsburg, *Bible and the Ancient Near East*, 160.
88. Noll, "Canaanite Religion."

is closely connected to "cultic scenes" that were known from impressions from sites like Bet Yerah, Giv'at Rabi, Tel Dan, and Tamra, all depict male and female figures and the sacred hovering symbol of the goddess.[89]

Based on the mentioned impressions, Paz, Milevski, and Getzov offer a tentative reconstruction of the ritual (fig. 4 below) with ritual dance (1a) and music (1b), meeting scene (2, based on the impressions from Tamra, Giv'at Rabi, Tel Qashish and Bet Yerah), and intercourse (3, based on the impression from Kh. Ezek-Zeraqon). However, the performance of a (royal) sacred marriage is highly debated.[90] Some scholars argue that texts such as the Sumerian "Inanna and Dumuzi" hymns and similar compositions depict a sacred marriage ritual between a deity and a human king, symbolizing fertility and divine sanction of the king's rule. Other scholars contend that these texts are more symbolic or literary rather than descriptions of actual rituals. They suggest that the sacred marriage was a symbolic or mythological concept rather than a regularly performed ceremonial practice. Suppose the interpretation of "the depiction of priest women, one priestess, and her accompanied helpers, or three priestesses" is correct. In that case, the impression is, at a minimum, evidence of intercourse in a temple context—regardless of whether the impressions refer to *hieros gamos*.

Other iconographical evidence is sparse and, not surprisingly, also contested. Worth mentioning, however, is an MB IIB (1700–1550) scarab described by Silvia Schroer as possibly reflecting ritual sex: "Whether, as in Mesopotamia, the representation of sexuality in Palestine/Israel was also expected to have amulet powers or whether intercourse was ritually 'performed' to encourage the weather god to impregnate his partner, remains uncertain. The fact that the figures are clothed supports the latter interpretation."[91] Keel, however, does not mention the ritual interpretation in his latest publication and dates the MB IIB slightly later to 1650–1500.[92] On the other hand, Keel mentions another MB IIB scarab

---

89. Paz et al., "Sound-Track of the 'Sacred Marriage'?," 249–50.
90. Lapinkivi, "Sumerian Sacred Marriage and Its Aftermath," 7–41.
91. Schroer and Keel, *Ikonographie Palästinas*, 256. My translation of "Ob wie in Mesopotamien auch in Palästina/Israel von der Repräsentation der Sexualität Amulettkräfte erwartet wurden ode rob der Koitus rituell 'gespielt' wird, om den Wettergott zur Befruchtung sener Partnerin zu animieren, bleibt offen. Für Letzteres spricht, dass die Figuren bekleidet sind."
92. Keel, *700 Skarabäen*, 158.

depicting a *coitus a posteriori* with more apparent ritual association: "The blossom or the branch seen in the hand of one or the other of the two figures confirms the association of the scene with the cultic events of the autumn festival."[93]

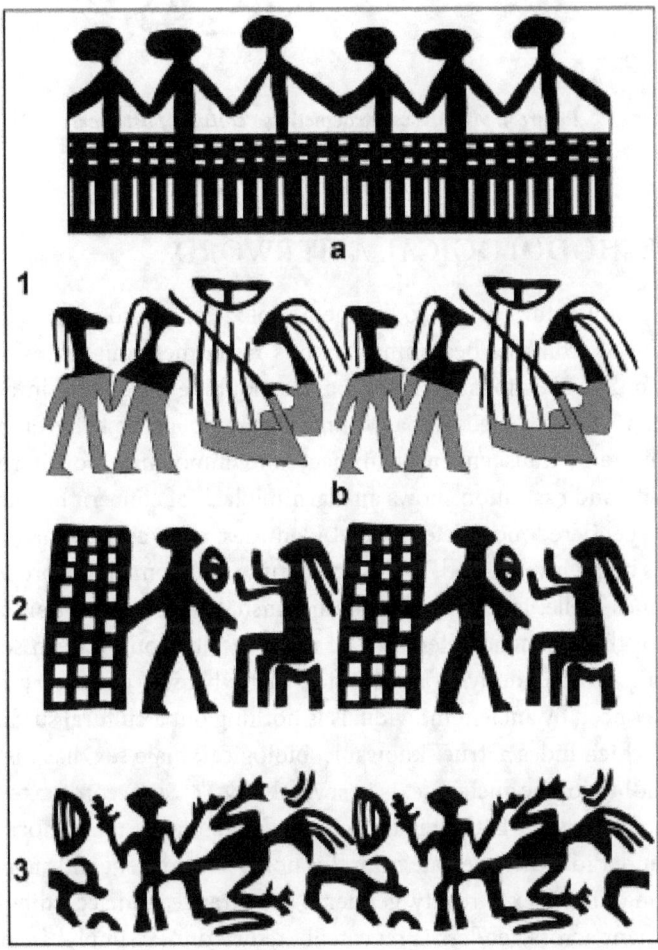

Figure 4: Reconstruction of Sacred Marriage Scenes. 4.1.a: The Ritual Dance, after an Impression from Rosh Ha-Niqrah. 4.1.b: The Music Scene, Lyre Players. 4.2: The Meeting Scene, Based on Impressions from Tamra, Giv'at Rabi, Tel Qashish, and Bet Yerah. 4.3: The Intercourse, Based on the Impression from Kh. Ezek-Zeraqon.

93. Keel, *700 Skarabäen*, 160–61. My translation of "Die Blüte bzw. Der Zweig, die der in der Hand der einen oder der anderen der beiden Figuren zu sehen ist, bestätigt die Zugehörigkeit der Szene zum Kultgescheben im Rahmen des Herbstfestes."

Figure 5: MB IIB scarab depicting a *coitus a posteriori*

A METHODOLOGICAL AFTERWORD

We will now return briefly to the methodological considerations that we introduced from the beginning. Sophus Helle mentions in his deconstructionist reflections on taxonomy to nonbinary genders in ancient texts that "the repeated slippage in modern scholarship between homosexuality and transgender, effeminacy and impotence, non-normative sexuality and castration shows an alarming lack of concern for different non-cisgendered, non-heterosexual identities, even as these are exactly what is being investigated."[94] This "multitude of incompatible proposals," continues Helle, is mainly due to an "unshakeable assumption, across most of the secondary literature, of a binary division between sex and gender... The underlying assumption that whatever nonbinary behavior is evinced by ancient individuals is nothing but a cultural surface beneath which hides a 'true,' knowable, biological, male sex, has distorted the readings of the ancient texts in several ways."[95] So, according to Helle, the main problem is the binary; biological gender is made normative, and gender identities deviate from this norm and consequently appear as abnormalities: "Sex is reality, gender is appearance, and accordingly any movement across genders is repeatedly reduced to a 'simply,' an 'only,' a temporary 'role-play.' It's, in the end, of no consequence because what matters is the underlying biological reality. This division serves both to obfuscate the effects of gender transitivity and to set it apart from ahistorical sex that is supposedly stable and nonnegotiable."[96] Therefore,

94. Helle, "Only in Dress?," 42.
95. Helle, "Only in Dress?," 42–43.
96. Helle, "Only in Dress?," 43.

according to Helle, the problem is not just that later cultures' binary understanding of gender and identity is imposed on the texts but also that we only have texts as sources, which is a problem. The cuneiform script that we decipher to understand the ancient Mesopotamians' understanding of gender identity (i.e., gender) provides valuable information about cultural norms, prevailing perceptions, and gender identity ideology, according to Helle. However, nothing about an underlying, static "bedrock biology" is revealed.[97] Helle's initial intention is not to be normative but to liberate the texts from a normativity that the texts may not necessarily share. Concerning the texts mentioned above describing a procession for Inanna, where participants on the left are dressed as women and those on the right as men, Helle points out the methodological problem in modern interpreters' attempts to understand the relationship between the participants' biological gender and their "gender performance" within the binary man/woman spectrum:

> But taking a different view of gender, there is no true and false side. The effect of this "gender performance" does not lie in one side of the body presented as other than what it truly is, but in the doubt that both sides produce as to what is appearance and what is reality. There is no way of determining which is which—not for us today and not for the ancient audience of the parade. It brings us into doubt, and that is the key effect of this performance. We are made to understand the reversibility of gendered signs such as "male" and "female" clothing. The swapping of these cultural markers reveals the extent to which we rely on straightforward correspondences between body and dress when assigning genders to individuals, but there is no inherent stability to be found in these cultural markers. They can be effortlessly reversed. Rather than searching for a biological truth beneath the performance, we should accept the doubt it engenders as a core statement about how gender is constructed.[98]

A similar or even severer criticism of the traditional understanding of the relationship between biology and gender can be found in Julia Assante's work. She writes about Ishtar's "transformation" of masculinity into femininity in the cult personnel as follows: "It is scholarship, not Ishtar, who has emasculated [male functionaries in the cult], turning them into passive 'homosexuals,' prostitutes, transvestites, eunuchs,

---

97. Helle, "Only in Dress?," 44.
98. Helle, "Only in Dress?," 46.

hermaphrodites, and self-lacerating masochists, circulating like minor moons around a celestial fetish."[99] Although neither Helle nor Assante openly present their a priori assumptions, it's clear that the deconstructionist perspective heavily influences their analysis. This includes the fundamental a priori rejection of binary categorization, a clear focus on the performative aspect, and problematizing the texts as access to the normative. This does not mean Helles's subsequent reconstruction of the meaning of source texts is irrelevant. But it *does* mean that if Helles's assumptions are untenable—or replaced with others—then there could just as quickly be an argument that the texts' testimony of cross-dressing should be understood within the binary framework. After deconstructing the influential approach to the relationship between "sex" and "gender," the text suggests that the solution lies in "the study of culturally conditioned patterns, that is, consistently recurring associations in our texts between a given gendered identity and a set of cultural images, figurative positions, and social roles."[100] Such a study, according to Helle, shows "a consistent association in cuneiform texts between Ishtar's followers and a position at the threshold—both literal thresholds and figurative borders between binaries. This association recurs across genres and periods, and besides shaping how the gender of these individuals is portrayed, it also applies to their social status, ritual role, and cultural significance."[101] Being placed in such a "threshold," Helle argues, "implies the ability to manipulate that intersection. The most important binary these ritual practitioners traverse is that between humanity and divinity. Associated as they are with the goddess Ishtar, their role is to mediate between humans and gods."[102] Based on an analysis of the previously cited Erra Epic, where the so-called *assinnu* are described as those "whose maleness Ishtar turned fe[male] for the awe of the people; carriers of swords, carriers of razors, scalpels, and blades, who break [taboos?] to Ishtar's delight," Helle argues that "the gender of *kurgarrû*'s and *assinnu*'s is here described not as either male or female, as such, but as residing in the very transition between the two. The two groups are not identified through either category in itself... With such considerations in mind, it becomes untenable to claim that this passage from Erra reveals a specific biological state of one kind

99. Assante, "Bad Girls and Kinky Boys?," 24.
100. Helle, "Only in Dress?," 48.
101. Helle, "Only in Dress?," 48.
102. Helle, "Only in Dress?," 49.

or the other beneath the cultural signifiers."¹⁰³ A similar criticism is made by Ken Stone against—somewhat surprisingly—Martti Nissinen, who, in *Homoeroticism in the Biblical World: A Historical Perspective*, argues like Ken Stone that the comparative material shows that "ancient attitudes toward same-sex relations cannot be separated from assumptions about gender role, social status, and active/passive positions in intercourse," and that the negative judgment of these attitudes in the biblical texts is based on "presuppositions about gender, power and penetration that are less widely accepted today than they were in ancient Mediterranean and Near Eastern cultures."¹⁰⁴ Thus, the critique is not about Nissinen's conclusions but rather the very question that Nissinen seeks to answer, as it reflects a "heteronormative bias," revealing that the discussion of homosexuality is still taking place within the framework of a binary gender understanding.¹⁰⁵ Stone, therefore, encourages a "queering of biblical studies" where the historical and culturally conditioned gender perception of the comparative material and the challenges it poses to modern binary gender identity are used to destabilize heteronormativity so that neither the comparative material nor the biblical texts are read within such a dichotomy but rather liberated to allow new interpretations to emerge.¹⁰⁶

Helles's and others' warnings against imposing later or different cultures' categories onto ancient Mesopotamian texts are essential and relevant. This applies to both gender stereotypes and the understanding of the relationship between biological and social gender. Helle's observation of the frequent association between Inanna's/Ishtar's cult personnel and liminal contexts is also an essential contribution to understanding the role played by the cult personnel in the cult. However, this does not necessarily lead to the conclusion that gender manipulation in the texts should be understood within a nonbinary framework. Suppose the categories of "man" and "woman" in the relevant source texts are understood as essential and not performative and are based on the idea that the categories "man" and "woman" can encompass elements that deviate from stereotypes. In that case, gender manipulation makes perfect sense

---

103. Helle, "Only in Dress?," 50.

104. Stone, "Homosexuality and the Bible or Queer Reading?," 110–12.

105. Stone, "Homosexuality and the Bible or Queer Reading?," 112–15; cf. Heacock, "Wrongly Framed?"

106. Stone, "Homosexuality and the Bible or Queer Reading?," 115–18; cf. Ehalt, "Assumptions About the Assinnu," 12–17.

within a binary framework. Arguably, this perspective can also be applied to a lesser extent if there are no clear poles to manipulate.

Linguistics

The binary nature of biological sex is, as already mentioned, most clearly illustrated in the ideograms used to represent human beings: essentially, they depicted images of genitalia. In Sumerian, the UŠ/NITA sign depicting an ejaculating penis was used to designate a human male. In contrast, a human female was rendered by the SAL/MUNUS sign depicting a vulva. "Woman," in other words, equals "human with vulva" and "man" is a "human with penis."

Figure 6: Old Babylonian sign for woman

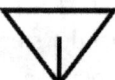

Figure 7: Abstract rendering of sign for woman rotated 90 degrees right

Regarding whether language allows us to identify a biologically grounded, binary man-woman category more generally, the latest research, as already mentioned, is characterized by a deconstructive and skeptical trend. Helle, for example, argues that "we do not have any access to a pre-cultural body. Theoretical, methodological, and philological concerns conjoined bar us from assuming that, with nothing but cultural sources to go on, we may speak confidently of non-cultural bodies. Apart from anything else, maintaining that gender is 'simply a surface' while sex is 'actual reality' misconstrues the kind of reality we have at our disposal . . . Even if a recourse from textual to biological reality were possible, one could not expect to necessarily find, beneath the ambiguities of cultural terms, a stable, univocal, and binary biological state."[107] So, according to both Helle and others, even at the most basic lexical and grammatical level, it's methodologically problematic to operate with the category of "man (human)." Joan Goodnick Westenholz and Ilona Zsolnay argue in their analysis of the Sumerian language that even though "sexual dualism is encoded in the Sumerian cultural system," one cannot conclude from that that there was an underlying and static "bedrock biology" defining a binary *gender* understanding. Even though "the lexeme nita could be used adjectivally (male) or as a substantive (generic man), attestations of the latter are rare and meant more for clarification, thus continuing to serve a more adjectival function." The examination of various lexemes shows that "there seems to have been no true generic category 'male human,' that is, one devoid of social status with an accompanying generic construct of masculinity. From the Archaic period onward, the southern Mesopotamian writing system demonstrates a complex system for designating men that is dependent upon social class, age, text type (e.g., lexical versus ration list), and period in which it was written."[108] Referring to Westenholz and Zsolnay, Kelsie Ehalt makes a similar point, namely that even though MUNUS and NITA, from their earliest pictographic origin, refer to "a vulva, the genital configuration which modern English speakers label as female," and "a penis and is translated into English as 'male or man,'" one cannot conclude from this that there was a necessary connection between the biological and the experienced/lived gender: "Even though these signs pictographically represent anatomy and sex, their semantic meaning is broader and also refers to gender; a normative NITA might have a penis, but not all NITA necessarily do; instead, they could be seen as fulfilling the NITA societal role no matter their anatomy."[109] It's different from Akkadian, which distinguishes between grammatical masculine and feminine, where the grammatical binary system can only be moderated or bypassed adjectivally, i.e., by attaching adjectives that describe the other gender to a grammatical masculine or feminine lexeme. Ehalt notes regarding this "bypass" that it might be due to a cognitive dissonance between the original coding of the language and reality: "Perhaps the lived experiences of people simply did not fit into the semantic system, so they were forced into one category

---

107. Helle, "Only in Dress?," 45.
108. Westenholz and Zsolnay, "Categorizing Men," 13, 38–39.
109. Ehalt, "Assumptions About the Assinnu," 12.

or the other in order to preserve grammar rules."[110] This observation is interesting because it could be argued that the language—in the case of Akkadian, at least—actually reflects an "original" binary understanding of human sex *and* gender and that the "adjectival" bypass of such a binary understanding, as Ehalt points out in both Akkadian and "other mostly ungendered languages," nevertheless has the binary as a starting point and reference framework.[111]

Both Helle and Ehalt argue for a separation between biological sex and gender identity. Gender, according to Helle, is symbolized not only with bodily features but *primarily* with material objects:

> The description of the ritual relies on the assumption that one can tell baby boys from baby girls just by looking at them: the text presupposes that it will be clear to the ritual practitioner whether it's male or female. But the practice also relies on the notion that gender had to be constructed through other means than one's body, reinforced by items that made gender manifest. The text identified the axe given to the boy as the "force of his manliness," but for a mewling newborn child, that force cannot be anything but symbolic—it was not something that could have sprung from his strength or behavior alone. Gender was thus not just a property of the body, but also had to be actualized and made visible by other means.[112]

These objects, according to Helle, are *mutable*. "Gender," to Helle, "refers to that process of 'making visible by other means,' whereby a supposedly inherent bodily property is exteriorized, symbolized, and made socially apparent," and "because gender did not emanate from an unchanging property of the body, but had to be constantly performed and made visible, it also became possible to negotiate gender through symbolic means. Gender could be reinforced, as in the birth ritual, or misperformed."[113] As evidence of such "misperformance" or "manipulation of gender," Helle points to many texts in which weapons and

---

110. Ehalt, "Assumptions About the Assinnu," 12–13.

111. It is also telling that in languages where grammatical gender is an original and fundamental element, efforts are being made to develop pronouns that reflect a more fluid gender identity. This is the case, for example, with the Nonbinary Hebrew Project, where it is stated that "we are building a bigger tent for nonbinary Jews through a third-gender grammar systematics for Hebrew, guided by our Torah and Talmud that teach us to rejoice that which cannot be neatly categorized." Nonbinary Hebrew, "Nonbinary Hebrew Project."

112. Helle, "Weapons and Weaving Instruments," 106.

113. Helle, "Weapons and Weaving Instruments," 106–7.

weaving instruments were used in several ways to construct and reshape the gender of ancient individuals. Concluding his analysis of the text *The Elevation of Ishtar*, Helle argues:

> Since gender identity was represented through items, it became possible to manipulate gender by moving those items around. Masculinity and femininity could be reinforced, impaired, reversed, or even subverted through the transfer of symbols ... Men could become less male by wearing spindles, women could wear weapons while remaining women, men could be turned into women while wearing swords, and the same individuals could wear spindles in one context and daggers in another ... It could even be difficult to tell which items counted as weapons and which as weaving instruments since one could pierce with spindles and weave with swords. In The Elevation of Ishtar, this symbolic confusion is employed to highlight the power of Ishtar, who plays with chaos as with knucklebones. All rules can be overturned at her decree, and mortals can do nothing but bow to her might.[114]

Admitting the influence of Helle's work on her thesis, Ehalt goes even further and argues that these objects are "completely separate from the body."[115] That is, the categories of biological sex and gender identity are entirely disconnected.

Theology and Anthropology

Although Westenholz, Zsolnay, Helle, and others have convincingly demonstrated how a grammatical, binary understanding of gender is often modified in various ways, including towards gender fluidity, and that such modification should be considered a reflection of reality, the question remains as to whether it still reflects an original, natural connection between biological and lived gender. Such a question cannot be answered solely by the presence of a binary grammatical system but must be supplemented by texts that can support such an original connection. This is especially true for texts dealing with human origins or revealing a more fundamental theology and anthropology.

Regarding the first point, material from both Mesopotamia and Egypt initially seems ambivalent as there are examples of gods

---

114. Helle, "Weapons and Weaving Instruments," 114.
115. Ehalt, "Assumptions About the Assinnu," 14–15, 17.

transcending the binary. This is evident in Mesopotamia with Inanna/Ishtar. However, Inanna/Ishtar is neither a creator nor a fertility goddess but a *manipulator* of creation. We turn, therefore, to a brief discussion of human gender in ancient Near Eastern *creation* texts.

In both Sumerian and Akkadian texts, the purpose of creating humans is primarily to alleviate the workload of the lower-ranking gods, as expressed in the Sumerian "The Song of the Hoe" (lines 28–34) and the Akkadian Atrahasis epic (1.4.192–97; 7.337–39). However, later in the same Atrahasis epic, we also find another account of human creation that views it from a different aspect than purely labor-related, focusing instead on fertility and sexuality. In this version, humans initially exist in seven pairs, allowing them to multiply seven times faster. The text emphasizes multiple times that humans were created in pairs:

> While the wise and knowledgeable were gathered,
> the seven and seven womb goddesses,
> seven create males
> seven create females
> (For) the womb-goddess (is) creator of destiny.
> They will crown(?) them in pairs,
> they will crown(?) them in pairs in her presence.[116]

The epic continues without hesitation to describe how these pairs, when both the woman and the man show signs of sexual maturity, come together, copulate, and thus fulfill the reproductive purpose for which they were created. The birth goddess Nintu says as follows:

> [. . .] her breasts.
> A beard can be seen(?)
> On a young man's cheek.
> In gardens and wayside
> a wife and her husband choose each other.[117]

> When beds are laid out [in their houses],
> a wife and her husband shall choose each other.
> Ishtar shall rejoice in the wife-husband relationship
> In the house of [. . .]
> Celebration shall last for nine days.[118]

---

116. *Atrahasis* 1.5.261–67, quoted from Kvanvig, *Primeval History*.
117. *Atrahasis* 1.5.272–76, quoted from Kvanvig, *Primeval History*.
118. *Atrahasis* 1.6.299–303, quoted from Kvanvig, *Primeval History*.

COMPARATIVE MATERIAL ON GENDER IDENTITY AND SEXUALITY

In this context, Helge Kvanvig notes, there is a connection between the initial destiny of humans and their everyday lives. Humans were created as sexual beings with the purpose of procreation and rapid multiplication. This aspect of human nature is evident every time a man and a woman choose each other for sexual union. The creation occurs in "bīt šīmti," which translates to "the house of destiny."[119] Nintu, the birth goddess, *uṣurāti ša nišī uṣṣar*, literally draws "the drawings for the people," creating the fundamental conditions and determining destinies.[120] The same concept of "destiny" is also reflected in the advice given by the taverner to Gilgamesh in his quest for eternal life. She tells him, "But you, Gilgamesh ... Look proudly upon the little one who holds your hand, and let a woman delight in your arms. That is the fate of mortals." This advice underscores the idea that mortal humans are destined to find joy and fulfillment in companionship, love, and procreation rather than seeking eternal life."[121]

At the same time, the early creator gods are consistently described as heterosexual. For example, "The Theogony of Dunnu" states, "In the beginning, Ha'rab married Earth."[122] Similarly, the text "Erra and Ishum" mentions, "When Anu, king of the gods, impregnated Earth, She bore the Seven Gods for him, and he named them Sebitti."[123]

Turning to Ugarit, the discussion about material from Ugarit, including the Ba'al Cycle, revolves around whether it describes the creation of the world order by the gods or the restoration/maintenance of it through kingship. Loren Fischer argued (1965) that the cycle represents a "creation of the Ba'al type."[124] More recently, Marjo Korpel and Johannes de Moor have suggested that several texts attest to what Fischer calls the "creation of the El type." Korpel and de Moor argue as follows:

> El created in various manners. His main wife was Ashera, mother of his seventy children and a creatress in her own right. Creation by word or thought alone is attested for both of them. However, like other creators in the ancient Near East, El also "created" by impregnating other goddesses and earthly women. On other occasions he creates by molding clay like a potter (cf.

119. *Atrahasis* 1.5.249, quoted from Kvanvig, *Primeval History*.
120. Kvanvig, *Primeval History*, 31.
121. Søndergaard and Helle, *Gilgamesh*, 109.
122. *COS* 1.113, line 1.
123. *COS* 1.113, tablet 1, lines 28–29.
124. Fischer, "Creation at Ugarit," 313–24.

Gen. 2:7). El creates not merely at the beginning of the cosmos, but many times after. So the Canaanites believed in a continuous process of creation, as did some biblical writers—a fact often disregarded by theologians. Some lesser deities in the Ugaritic pantheon were also able to create, be it on a lower level.[125]

Korpel and de Moor argue that, based on several texts from Ugarit dating from the late thirteenth century BCE, it's possible to reconstruct the so-called "Adamic myth." This myth supposedly parallels the biblical text in Ezek 28 and the much later Enoch tradition. In their reconstruction, Adam is one of the gods sent to earth to rectify the chaos caused by the rebellious god Ḥôrānu when he was cast down to the Syrian desert region of Hauran after his rebellion against the high god El. Similarly, in Greek tradition, Adam's wife is one of the Ugaritic goddesses, later known as the Magna Mater, Cybele.[126]

An alternative reconstruction, proposed by Alberdina Houtman, suggests that Adam was originally an androgynous divine being sent to rescue the world from the harm done by Ḥôrānu. Houtman argues that this androgynous nature is reflected in the Jewish tradition, such as in Genesis Rabbah, which suggests that Adam was created as an androgynous being before being split into male and female. According to this perspective, the general monotheistic trend in the Tanakh led to the perception of Adam as a male of flesh and blood: "In the ancient Canaanite Adamic myth, Adam was originally an androgynous divine being, who was sent to the earth to rescue the world from the harm done by Ḥôrānu. Although the Genesis accounts do not contradict his divine origin or his androgyny, the general monotheistic line in the Tanakh gave rise to our modern perceptions of him as a male of flesh and blood." Houtman exemplifies this tradition by quoting from Genesis Rabbah 8:1:

> R. Jeremiah ben Leazar said: When the Holy One, blessed be He, created the first human/Adam, He created him androgynous, for it's said, "male and female He created them" (Gen 5:2).[127] Said R. Shmuel bar Naḥman: When the Holy One, blessed be He, created the first human/Adam, he created him two-faced. Then he split him and made him two backs, one for this side and one for that. They answered him: has it not been

---

125. Korpel and de Moor, "Adam, Eve, and the Devil," 3; cf. Korpel, "Adamic Myth from Canaan," 21–35; Korpel and de Moor, *Adam, Eve, and the Devil*.

126. Korpel and de Moor, "Adam, Eve, and the Devil," 5.

127. All Bible translations are taken from ESV, unless otherwise noted.

COMPARATIVE MATERIAL ON GENDER IDENTITY AND SEXUALITY

written "He took one of his ribs" (מצלעתיו, Gen 2:21)? He said to them: [one] of his sides, as you say "and for the other side of the Tabernacle, etc." (ולצלע, Exod 26:20).[128]

Of particular interest to the discussion is the idea that Ḥôrānu's revenge involved making the Tree of Life inaccessible to the gods, including Adam, by positioning himself in the tree as a snake whose venom turned it into the Tree of Death, causing the world to wither. In this reconstruction, Korpel and de Moor argue, "after Adam has received the lethal bite, the Ugaritic sun goddess seems to promise him 'a good-natured woman' to start the eternal cycle of procreation with her, thus ensuring the preservation of human life despite the inevitable death of every individual."[129]

Notably, these reconstructions are based on fragmented texts and involve a degree of speculation. However, suppose Korpel and de Moor's interpretation of the texts is accurate. In that case, it suggests a connection between the creation of the first (divine) humans and "the eternal cycle of procreation," emphasizing the reproductive intent in the creation or emergence of the binary human.

Without denying the culturally contingent character of gender roles, these texts nonetheless provide a basis for distinguishing between innate gender identity and self-chosen, constructed, or manipulated gender identity. Manipulations of gender symbols, as seen in the cult of Inanna/Ishtar, do not necessarily imply that gender identity was *initially* fluid.

The creation texts suggest that procreation was inextricably linked to binary sex and that procreation—that is, motherhood and fatherhood—was a given an element of gender identity. Manipulations with this procreative role run counter, therefore, to the binary framework for sex *and* gender in the creation texts. A few objections to this conclusion could be made, of course. We don't know, for a start, whether creation texts were considered more foundational than texts describing the Inanna/Ishtar cult. It could also be argued that the silence in the creation texts about other identities does not preclude the existence and acceptance of such identities. What they do show, however, is a different weighing of the texts, that is, making the explicit combination of sex and gender in the creation texts foundational and texts on transgression, subversion, and "misperformance" derivative and *reactionary*.

---

128. Houtman, "Development of the Adamic Myth," 37, with reference to Korpel and de Moor, *Adam, Eve, and the Devil*, 26, 57.

129. Korpel and de Moor, "Adam, Eve, and the Devil," 6.

Conclusion

The comparative analysis reveals that many interpreters of source texts do not explicitly express their inherently deconstructionist a priori, and such approaches often assume that the texts do not presuppose norms and/or categories. Instead, they rely solely on testimony regarding the performative aspects when determining how the texts reflect contemporary views on gender identity. Conversely, arguments have been made that if such an approach is replaced with other scientifically and epistemologically legitimate assumptions, the texts appear to reflect a binary framework equally, and the contrary is not necessarily the case.

With this alternative starting point, the texts suggest that it could be argued that there was an original binary approach to the question of gender identity and that this binary understanding is linked to procreation. This is evident in both the heterosexual relationships characterizing the gods in various pantheons and the connection between the creation of humans as biological males and females and their primary purpose or "destiny," which is copulation for reproduction. The texts also have no universal prohibition or criticism of same-sex relationships. Instead, the texts indicate that different forms of manipulation of the relationship between biological and lived gender existed in other contexts but did not necessarily challenge the fundamental binary understanding of gender.

Part Three

Gender and Body in Biblical Creation Theology

If I set the sun beside the moon,
And if I set the land beside the sea,
And if I set the town beside the country,
And if I set the man beside the woman,
I suppose some fool would talk about one being better.

—G. K. Chesterton[1]

LORD-OF-THE-RINGS-THEOLOGY

IN GENERAL, SOCIAL CONSTRUCTIVISM, and specifically queer ideology, find it irrelevant what biblical texts say about gender identity and sexual orientation. Such an attitude is reflected, for example, in an interview in the newspaper *Information* in 2011 when the Danish government considered allowing homosexuals to be married in church. Søren Sønderstrup expressed an understanding that "some homosexuals want to get married in a church for religious or cultural reasons" but also emphasized that "it is natural for him and other homosexuals to look for norms

---

1. Quoted from Wilson, *Future Men*, 16; originally published in Chesterton, *Poems*.

for relationships elsewhere than in the state church."[2] The reasoning is that "now that the church can admit homosexuals to its congregation, homosexuals become subject to the dogmas that the church stands for. Monogamy, family, and traditional gender roles—are all things that the homosexual environment has dispensed with. Part of what's great about being gay is that you could turn off the norms."[3]

However, those who defend a different view of gender and body than presented in this book, using *biblical* texts, adopt two different hermeneutical strategies. The first strategy attempts to demonstrate that the relevant biblical texts do not exclude multiple genders and do not address contemporary consenting same-sex relationships between two free adults in their ethical guidance. A representative example from a Danish context is a report from the Methodist Church in which it's noted that "there are few biblical texts that deal with homosexuality" and that "the selection of texts to form the basis for a study is significant."[4] When it comes to criteria, attention is drawn to "the classic Wesleyan guidelines for theological work" as expressed in the Wesleyan Quadrilateral, which consists of the following: "The Methodist Church seeks God's will as revealed in the Bible, illuminated by the Christian tradition, vivified in personal experience, and confirmed by the right use of reason."[5] The study gives considerable attention to the Bible, even though the biblical texts are few and not directly compatible with contemporary questions. As a summary and conclusion, it's stated that:

> Examination of the biblical statement makes it difficult to argue that there is biblical support for maintaining a rejection of people because of their homosexual identity, orientation, or practice. It is also problematic in the Bible to find direct and specific support for homosexual orientation and practice ... Apart from the biblical texts that deal with homosexual practice in the context of idolatry, syncretism, rape, and prostitution, there are no biblical texts that deal with the type of homosexuality where two parties voluntarily choose each other and build a relationship that includes mutual love and declared commitment.[6]

---

2. Elmelund, "Er kirkebryllup virkelig."
3. Elmelund, "Er kirkebryllup virkelig."
4. Metodistkirken i Danmark, "Kirken og homoseksualitet."
5. Metodistkirken i Danmark, "Kirken og homoseksualitet," 30.
6. Metodistkirken i Danmark, "Kirken og homoseksualitet," 30–31.

The same strategy is found in the Danish Baptist Church's paper "On the Place of Homosexuals in the Congregation" from 2012, which states that "the church's attitude toward homosexuality has traditionally been based on several texts that condemn homosexual practice. As we have seen, homosexual acts are relatively few places in the Bible, and these places do not deal with homosexuality in the sense that many understand it today."[7] In both of these examples, the conclusion and the associated possibility of a changed attitude and practice are based on a different *interpretation* of the biblical texts that have traditionally been used to support a binary understanding of gender identity and same-sex intercourse.

When it comes to the "relatively few texts" that mention homosexuality, we shall return to the validity of the interpretation below. However, the argumentation, namely that the texts do not address the type of homosexuality we are discussing today, is the same as that of Robert Gnuse, who, based on his interpretation of "Seven Gay Texts," concludes that "I believe that there is no passage in the biblical text that truly condemns a sexual relationship between two adults, free people, who truly love each other."[8]

A variant of the first strategy is to point to the sheer number of texts addressing homosexuality as an indication that the question of homosexual practice is a marginal concern for the Bible's ethical guidance. One example is John J. Collins, who argues in his *What Are Biblical Values?* that "the most striking thing about the Hebrew Bible about same-sex relations, however, is how little it has to say on the subject. The Prophets have nothing to say about it. Neither do the sages who compiled the Wisdom Literature, or the scribes who edited Deuteronomy and the Deuteronomistic History. The fact that the subject is addressed explicitly in only two verses, in a distinctive strand of Priestly Law, shows that it is a marginal concern in the Hebrew Bible."[9]

The second strategy is to acknowledge several biblical texts' binary, heterosexual perspectives to set them aside or subordinate them to other texts that are allegedly more significant. This applies, for example, to Luke Timothy Johnson, who writes:

> I have little patience with efforts to make Scripture say something other than it says through appeals to linguistic or cultural

---

7. Teologisk Forum, "Om homoseksuelles plads i menigheden," 19.
8. Gnuse, "Seven Gay Texts," 85.
9. Collins, *What Are Biblical Values?*, 74.

subtleties. The exegetical situation is straightforward: we know what the text says. But what are we to do with what the text says? . . . I think it important to state clearly that we do, in fact, reject the straightforward commands of Scripture, and appeal instead to another authority when we declare that same-sex unions can be holy and good. And what exactly is that authority? We appeal explicitly to the weight of our own experience and the experience thousands of others have witnessed to, which tells us that to claim our own sexual orientation is in fact to accept the way in which God has created us. By so doing, we explicitly reject as well the premises of the scriptural statements condemning homosexuality—namely, that it is a vice freely chosen, a symptom of human corruption, and disobedience to God's created order.[10]

It's not the critical views of these biblical texts on nonbinary gender identity and same-sex intercourse Johnson rejects, but their *authority*. Instead of grounding Christian ethics on the biblical texts, the *experience* of being created as homosexual is made the authority. In other cases, authority is not moved outside the Bible but is shifted to other texts that are privileged about texts that have such a critical view. Helen Savage, who completed her dissertation at Durham University in 2006 with the thesis "Changing Sex?: Transsexuality and Christian Theology," writes about such privileging of texts that it "presents no challenge to the literal meaning of the offending text, but its message or meaning is qualified or even canceled by a text of prior significance."

It usually leads to a "sidelining of major sections of biblical material," and "the significance of the Old Testament, in particular, may be downgraded."[11] Or as the American transgender individual Lee Frances Heller writes: "When I discovered the books of Exodus, Leviticus, Numbers, and Deuteronomy were laws designed to keep Israel in check and to prevent them from going after pagan gods and then discovered in Col 2:14 that Christ nailed all of these laws and ordinances to His cross, taking them out of the way by canceling them, I was released from that load of guilt and was born-again a second time! There is no need to carry all of that guilt brought on because of cross-dressing."[12] Along with Rom 5:9 and 8:2, these texts, Heller claims, show that the "release" that takes

---

10. Johnson, "Homosexuality and the Church."
11. Savage, "Changing Sex?," 135–36.
12. Heller, "Is God Against Us?," 120.

place "when you take Christ as your Lord and Saviour" includes liberation from the "bondage" expressed by the Pentateuchal laws.[13] The same conclusion is reached by the late Danish professor of dogmatics, Theodor Jørgensen, in a column in *Kristeligt Dagblad*. When the Bible considers homosexuality a sin, according to Jørgensen, the apostles, on the one hand, "could not have known better" since they did not know that homosexuality "is a congenital disposition, according to well-founded research-based knowledge," while Paul, if he had known this, on the other hand, "would have expanded his statement in Gal 3:27–28 as follows: 'All of you who are baptized into Christ have clothed yourselves with Christ. Here there is no longer Jew or Greek; there is no longer enslaved person or free; there is no longer male or female, homosexual or heterosexual, for you are all one in Christ Jesus.'"[14] Here, "freedom texts" are privileged. Otherwise, in this strategy, "love texts" like 1 John 4:8 are often privileged and used in practice to annul or set aside any text critical of nonbinary gender identity and same-sex intercourse. An example could be from Professor of Systematic Theology Niels Henrik Gregersen's statement in 2010 in favor of introducing a marriage ritual for homosexuals in the Danish State Church, where he says, "For the State Church, it must, in my opinion, be crucial that a ritual is based on the Christian message of love."[15] Also, an article in the newspaper *Politiken* could be mentioned where Irene Larsen, a lecturer at the Teacher Education College Metropol, and State Church pastor Anne-Birgitte Zoëga write that "it is a mistake to read the Bible completely literally. It was written in a completely different time, and the core message is precisely love."[16] The same Irene Larsen writes in an article published in connection with the bill presented in the Danish Parliament in 2010 to allow religious communities to perform marriages of homosexuals—and entirely in line with the aforementioned second strategy—that "there is [no] doubt that the Bible condemns sex between two of the same sex," but that the essential thing is to interpret the Bible from its center, namely, "the revelation of salvation in Jesus Christ," defined further in the article as a love that should make the church inclusive to homosexuals.[17] According to Larsen, such

13. Heller, "Is God Against Us?," 120.
14. Jørgensen, "Er bøsser og lesbiske"; cf. Nielsen et al., *Forkynd evangeliet for al skabningen*.
15. Lind, "Folkekirken ønsker tænkepause."
16. Larsen and Zoëga, "Præst og teolog."
17. Larsen, "Homoseksualitet og kristendom." According to the website, the article

a hermeneutics is demanding but necessary: "It requires its woman and its man to transform the text and the text's impact from a 'Text of Terror' to a text about the preaching of God's love," and "it is high time" for such an interpretation to gain influence in the Evangelical Lutheran Church of Denmark.[18]

The US-American queer theologian Robert Goss also borrows the term "texts of terror" from feminist theologian Phyllis Trible to describe biblical narratives depicting oppression against women, applying it to texts about sexuality to highlight their use as a form of biblical terror against queer individuals.[19] Goss, in his seminal *Jesus Acted Up: A Gay and Lesbian Manifesto*, argues that Jesus himself would have supported queer liberation movements and addressed issues of sexuality, identity, and social justice from a queer perspective.[20] Goss argues that Jesus's teachings and actions align with principles of inclusion, love, and social justice, which are central to queer theology. He suggests that Jesus's radical message of love and acceptance transcends conventional boundaries of gender, sexuality, and identity. Goss interprets Jesus's interactions with marginalized individuals, such as the outcasts and the oppressed, as evidence of his solidarity with those on the margins of society, including LGBTQ+ individuals. Additionally, Goss contends that Jesus's emphasis on compassion and liberation underscores his support for queer liberation movements. Overall, Goss presents Jesus as a figure who embodies the values and principles of queer theology, advocating for a vision of Christianity that embraces diversity, affirmation, and equality for all.

Referring to Goss's work, Copenhagen pastors Mia Rahr Jacobsen and Viggo Julsgaard Jensen argue that LGBTQ+ people often don't see their lives reflected in the biblical texts and that this prompts a queer strategy to rediscover queer voices within the Bible.[21] The story of Lazarus, they argue, is interpreted as illustrating a journey from shame to acceptance, resonating with many LGBTQ+ individuals. Martha's role in the Lazarus story is emphasized, highlighting her transformation and

---

was originally published on the Ministry of Children and Education's digital learning portal at www.emu.dk/sem/fag/kre/tema/homoseksualitet.html, but the page is no longer available—perhaps because it violated the editorial guidelines, which are available in a version from 2021 at https://www.emu.dk/sites/default/files/2021-11/Redaktionelle percent20retningslinjer_emu_15.11. percent202021.pdf.

18. Larsen, "Homoseksualitet og kristendom."
19. Trible, *Texts of Terror*.
20. Goss, *Jesus Acted Up*.
21. Jacobsen and Julsgaard Jensen, "Køn Og Bibellæsning."

faith journey. West also emphasizes themes of coming out and transformation in the narrative, relating them to the personal experiences of LGBTQ+ individuals. Ultimately, these interpretations challenge heteronormativity and offer a new perspective on biblical narratives for queer individuals seeking affirmation and inclusion.

Most recently, in *The Widening of God's Mercy*, Christopher and Richard Hays have argued that the Bible often reveals a progressive, expanding vision of mercy that extends beyond rigid family or national ties. This expanding view shows God adjusting his relationship with humanity in ways that question earlier limitations or traditions. The authors underscore examples where God's covenant reaches those once seen as outsiders, such as gentiles and eunuchs, indicating a trajectory of growing inclusion and compassion. This "trajectory" perspective suggests that divine mercy in the Scriptures gradually encompasses a broader array of people, stepping beyond conventional social and ethnic lines. Through this lens, the authors propose that long-standing interpretations of God's intentions might shift to emphasize mercy in new, relevant contexts—a perspective they believe applies to current discussions on inclusion and belonging of sexual minorities. Their overall conclusion is that "the many biblical stories of God's widening mercy invite us to re-envision how God means us to think and act today with regard to human sexuality. The biblical narratives throughout the Old Testament and the New trace a trajectory of mercy that leads us to welcome sexual minorities no longer as 'strangers and aliens' but as 'fellow citizens with the saints and also members of the household of God' (Eph 2:19)."[22]

If one accepts the hermeneutical assumptions for such selective and reader-oriented readings, the interpretation—borrowing a term from social science—is path-dependently correct. However, it's incumbent upon the interpreter to argue for the acceptability of privileging specific texts over others. Suppose the argument is purely reader-oriented, meaning that it's solely the reader's decision about what to privilege and disregard. In that case, it doesn't make sense to discuss which interpretation is correct as every reader's interpretation on this hermeneutical basis is legitimate. It's different if one argues that the texts themselves suggest such prioritization. In this case, the arguments can be pretty diverse.

For instance, in the cited passage, the argument is that "the books of Exodus, Leviticus, Numbers, and Deuteronomy were laws designed to

---

22. Hays and Hays, *Widening of God's Mercy*, 206.

keep Israel in check and to prevent them from going after pagan gods," and that "Christ nailed all of these laws and ordinances to His cross, taking them out of the way by canceling them." Hence, they are no longer binding "when you take Christ as your Lord and Saviour." However, this is essentially a nonargument that is reader oriented. Neither the near nor the far context is used as an argument; therefore, it does not explain why Paul would have such an understanding.

An example from the Danish context is Evangelical Lutheran Church of Denmark pastors Steffen Ringgaard Andresen and Ulla Salicath, who, in a debate in the newspaper *Kristeligt Dagblad* in 2010, argued that "it seems as if the common theology has forgotten to read the Scriptures with the new spirit that comes into the world through Christ," and that Paul in Gal 3:28–29 allows "the spirit to annul the order and difference between ethnicity, gender, and status."[23] Furthermore, it's argued that a typological reading of "family solidarity" in the Old Testament is replaced by "spiritual solidarity" in the New Testament. The latter results in a blessing in the New Testament reality, which homosexual partners share.[24] In addition, when God's children are "not born of blood, nor of the will of the flesh, nor the will of man, but of God" (John 1:13), it leads to "a new way of understanding humanity," making all humans equal in relation to God and thus transcending the created differences and orders in a way that also allows new arrangements like same-sex partnerships to be blessed.[25] Therefore, texts about "the spirit" in the New Testament are given such weight that they override Old Testament texts about "ethnicity, gender, and status."

Revealing her anti-realist presuppositions, Susannah Cornwall, in a similar manner, argues that redemption in Christ and the "nascent new order" erases boundaries and categories of the current old order: "A realized temporal world where there is no male and female—or where biological maleness and femaleness are not the only available options—has seemed too unrealistic or utopian for most theologians to take seriously... The Galatians text implies that there is something about participation in Christ, about *perichoresis* between Christ and the church and between humans, which means that even such self-evident concepts as sexed nature are not to be taken as read in the nascent new order."[26]

23. Andresen and Salicath, "Når Det Gamle Testamente."
24. Andresen and Salicath, "Forfejlet kætteranklage."
25. Andresen and Salicath, "Nej til splittelsens retorik."
26. Cornwall, *Sex and Uncertainty*, 72.

Cornwall, because of the anti-realist metaphysics she assumes, can take the "literal" reading of Gal 3:28 and therefore maintain that, in Christ, the categories of Gen 1 and 2 are removed. They are neither fixed nor limiting categories; we can create new realities due to redemption. "For the normally sexed male and female to truly take account of differently sexed bodies, it will be necessary to move to an understanding that the dichotomously-sexed world is not the 'only' or 'real' world."[27]

The problem with prioritizing New Testament texts and abrogating commandments in the Pentateuch differs from the prioritizing itself. In practice, everyone prioritizes specific texts over others. The issue, instead, lies in what Esau McCaulley has termed a "Lord-of-the-Rings theology," where there is no consideration for the embeddedness of individual passages within the Bible's overall canonical structure and logic, permitting "one verse to rule them all."[28] We will soon revisit the significance and requirement of a canonical approach, and we will also allocate a significant portion of our discussion to examining the hermeneutical criteria for prioritizing texts. This will be about the pastoral implications of the forthcoming analysis of biblical sexual ethics.

GENDER HERMENEUTICS

In the first part, I outlined my general assumptions: ontological realism and essentialism. Based on these, it's now time to develop a gender hermeneutics based on biblical texts.

The general assumptions are reflected in the biblical texts in the form of what Pope John Paul II called a prescientific hermeneutics, which insists that ontology precedes biology, sociology, anthropology, etc., and a "hermeneutics of the gift," which describes the ontology of man and woman as "a given," not a social construct.

When it comes to more specific biblical hermeneutics, my reading of the texts will be based on the principles that John Webster lays out in his definition of Christian theology in the introduction to *God and the Works of God*. The triune God is the primary object and the key to understanding the biblical narrative as the divine economy. We will revisit this after examining how the biblical text can support the general assumptions.

---

27. Cornwall, *Sex and Uncertainty*, 178.
28. McCaulley, "Esau McCaulley," 21:36.

Before Science

In *Before Nature*, Francesca Rochberg demonstrates how the ancient Mesopotamians did not conceive of nature as a separate and distinct entity from the divine or the cosmos. Instead, they saw the natural world as interconnected with heavenly forces, continually in flux and subject to divine will: "In the cuneiform record, one finds no ancient equivalent of our term 'nature,' no contrast between 'natural' and 'supernatural,' no natural laws of the sort that would come to be articulated by the Greeks. In their place, one finds instead a notion of the cosmos as a world that is endlessly dynamic, that is, continually changing as it is moved and transformed by forces both within and outside of itself."[29] Although there is much monotheistic polemic against this polytheistic worldview in the Old Testament, the latter shares the idea that what we call nature is inseparably connected with and can only be understood in relation to the divine. In Mesopotamia, it is the gods; in the Old Testament, it is God. And even though the Old Testament also polemicizes against the idea that the cosmos is "endlessly dynamic" and subject to the whims of the gods by insisting on the reliability of natural laws (e.g., Ps 19:1–4; Jer 33:25; Job 38:33), the texts nevertheless insist that the study of nature—what we call "natural science"—is not sufficient if we are to understand human existence. From a philosophical perspective, the texts diverge from the viewpoint of materialism and physicalism, which assert the nonexistence of immaterial or nonphysical entities and propose that all phenomena, including mental states, can be explained by physical processes.

This is clearly expressed in Old Testament anthropology. As for the *physical* aspect of humans, עֶצֶם (*ʿeṣem*) refers to the "bones" or "skeleton," whereas בָּשָׂר (*bāśār*), which means "flesh" or "body," stands as an antonym to *nefeš*. In biblical Hebrew, נֶפֶשׁ (*nefeš*) can signify both that which has the breath of life, encompassing both animals (Gen 1:20, 24, 30; 9:12, 15, 16; Ezek 47:9) and humans (Gen 2:7) and "the self" or "personality," which is exclusively applied to humans. Although *nefeš* is often translated as "soul," it does not mean "immortal soul." The term רוּחַ (*rûaḥ*), most often translated as "spirit," is used to describe humans in the sense of "an independent, invisible, conscious existence," essentially in the same way as *nefeš* when used for humans. The lexeme נְשָׁמָה (*nᵉšāmāʰ*), meaning "blowing, breath," is used both of God's creative in-breathing of life (Job 32:8; 33:4) and of that creative breathing's result, namely חַיִּים נִשְׁמַת

---

29. Rochberg, *Before Nature*, 3.

(*nišmat ḥayyîm*), man's "breath of life" (Gen 2:7). In Job 34:14 and Isa 42:5, both expressions are used interchangeably:

> If God were to set his heart on it and gather in his spirit and his breath [רוּחוֹ וְנִשְׁמָתוֹ, *rûḥô wᵉnišmātô*], all flesh [בָּשָׂר, *bāśār*] would perish together and human beings would return to dust. (Job 34:14 NET)

> This is what the true God, the Lord, says—the one who created the sky and stretched it out, the one who fashioned the earth and everything that lives on it, the one who gives breath [נְשָׁמָה, *nᵉšāmāh*] to the people on it and life [רוּחַ, *rûₐḥ*] to those who live on it. (Isa 42:5 NET)

The problem is that נֶפֶשׁ (*nefeš*), רוּחַ (*rûₐḥ*), and נְשָׁמָה (*nᵉšāmāʰ*) can also refer to the breath of life in animals. Therefore, the distinction between the conscious, personal life of humans and the "unconscious" life of animals does not stem from a difference in the meanings of *nefeš*, *rûₐḥ*, and *nᵉšāmāʰ*. Instead, according to the creation story, humans are unique, as they are the only creations made in the image of God. Animals are created male and female and possess "the breath of life" in the same manner as humans, but it's only humans, by being made in the image of God, who possess a conscious, personal spiritual life. And humans are the only creatures made accountable to their Creator.

The ontological primacy and superiority of humankind are also underscored by the specification of the content of the image of God as summed up in two interrelated aspects: procreation (Gen 1) and vocation (Gen 2). Man is created in the image of God as the apex of the created order and as God's vice-regents to honor the Creator by procreation and sustainment/expansion of world order. This is especially evident in the account of the creation in Gen 1, where the creation of humans is marked in various ways as the climax of creation. Firstly, it is only the creation of humans that is explained using the deliberative plural form: "Let us create mankind in our image, in our likeness" (Gen 1:26). Second, man, by God's kingly rule, is given dominion in the ensuing explanation of the *imago Dei*: "so that they may rule over the fish in the sea and the birds in the sky, over the livestock and all the wild animals, and over all the creatures that move along the ground" (Gen 1:26). This is further elaborated in Gen 9:1–7, where animals are now also provided to serve humans as food. The following apocryphal texts confirm that Gen 1 has been understood in this way throughout history:

> He allotted to them their appointed times and the limits of their life and gave them authority over the things upon the earth. He endowed them with strength like his own and made them in his own image. He placed the fear of them in all living beings and granted them dominion over beasts and birds. (Sir 17:2–4)

> O Lord, the God of my ancestors, the God of mercy, who have made all things by your word, and by your wisdom have formed humankind to have dominion over the creatures you have made, to rule the world in holiness and righteousness and to pronounce judgment in uprightness of soul [לְבָב, 'heart']. (Wis 9:1–3)

> It was she [Wisdom] who preserved the first-formed father of the world when he alone had been created; she delivered him from his transgression and gave him strength to rule all things. (Wis 10:1–2)

Regarding the subsequent narrative of "the generations of the heavens and the earth" in Gen 2, humans are also central. Instead of the (analogically) chronological structure of Gen 1, the long introductory clause in Gen 2:5–6 indicates that creation is incomplete if there is no human to till the earth. Similarly, the description of the garden of Eden leads to its purpose: that it's meant to be cultivated and cared for by humans. Cory Barnes has also argued that when the source of water in Gen 2 is not rain but a spring, it further emphasizes the central role humans play in the creation:

> Whatever the appropriate translation of 'ēd, the word denotes an otherness to the initial way in which the earth was irrigated. The presence of the 'ēd rising from the earth highlights the lack of vegetation in the fields (agriculture) mentioned in Gen 2:4–5, which comes from the absence of man and not the absence of God creating a fecund world ready to produce agriculture. The presence of the 'ēd contributes to the ethical force of the narrative of Gen 2–3 by demonstrating that the lack of agriculture upon the earth is due to the absence of humankind, not the absence of water or any other non-human element. The vital role of humanity in the appropriate ecology of creation is essential in orienting the ethical force of the narrative of Gen 2–3 in terms of the relationship between humans and the rest of creation. Creation without humanity does not constitute a fully functioning ecology. Humanity is dependent upon all other elements of

creation, but the other elements are equally as dependent upon humanity to achieve their intended role.[30]

Besides human vocation, human solitude must also be understood as an expression of the image of God and, therefore, as something that distinguishes humans from animals. As Eirik Steenhoff explains concerning Pope John Paul II's *Catechesis of Human Love* (CHL):[31]

> The pope elaborates, in Aristotelian terms, that man "cannot identify himself essentially with the visible world of the other living beings (*animalia*)," because of his specific *differentia* that distinguishes his animal nature (as a *proximate genus*) from that of the others (CHL 5:5). While this difference—namely, that man is a *rational* animal and not just any animal—is a crucial characteristic, John Paul II points out that it is "not yet a complete definition." "Solitude also signifies man's subjectivity, which constitutes itself through self-knowledge. Man is alone because he is "different" from the visible world, from the world of living beings" (CHL 5:6). But he is different not simply in virtue of being a rational animal, but in virtue of possessing a self-consciousness that leads to the "*first delineation* of the human being *as* a human *person*, with the proper subjectivity that characterizes the person."[32]

In addition to these texts where creation is explicitly described as being created for and intended for humans, several other texts emphasize the qualitative difference between humans and animals:

> Before I formed you in the womb I knew you, before you were born, I set you apart; I appointed you as a prophet to the nations. (Jer 1:5)

> Your eyes saw my unformed body; all the days ordained for me were written in your book before one of them came to be. (Ps 139:16)

> But no one says, "Where is God my Maker, who gives songs in the night, who teaches us more than he teaches the beasts of the earth and makes us wiser than the birds in the sky?" (Job 35:10–11)

---

30. Barnes, "Curious Setting of Eden," 5–6.

31. While Steenhoff refers to CHL, we will refer to and quote from the published version of *Man and Woman He Created Them. A Theology of the Body* (TOB).

32. Steenhoff, "Body That Reveals the Person(s)," 10.

Furthermore, as emphasized in Ps 8, humans are made "a little lower than God," and this position is precisely an expression of God's desire to privilege humans:

> What is mankind that you are mindful of them, human beings that you care for them? You have made them a little lower than the angels and crowned them with glory and honor. You made them rulers over the works of your hands; you put everything under their feet. (Ps 8:4–7 NIV)

In the New Testament, the same distinction is expressed:

> So don't be afraid; you are worth more than many sparrows. (Matt 10:31 NIV)

Biblical anthropology is, therefore, not only "physical" by referring to man's בָּשָׂר (*bāśār*, "flesh" or "body") but also *meta*physical in its reference to man's נֶפֶשׁ (*nefeš*, "self") and רוּחַ (*rûaḥ*, "spirit") as crucial for understanding the image and likeness of God. The image of God—that is, God himself—is the decisive framework for understanding what a human being is, and even though biblical anthropology, as we shall see below, has a distinctly positive view of the body and the physical world, the body must be understood within this metaphysical framework. In Pss 32 and 51, the explanation for David's *somatic* atrocities is *metaphysical*:

> When I refused to confess my sin, my whole body [עֲצָמָי, *ʿaṣāmāy*] wasted away, while I groaned in pain all day long. (Ps 32:3 NET)

> Grant me the ultimate joy of being forgiven! May the bones [עֲצָמוֹת, *ʿaṣāmôt*] you crushed rejoice! (Ps 51:10 MT)

> O God, you are my God. I long for you. My soul thirsts for you, my flesh yearns for you, in a dry and parched land where there is no water. (Ps 63:1 NET)

> Do not let them depart from your sight, guard them within your heart; for they are life to those who find them and healing to one's entire body. (Prov 4:21–22 NET)

To avoid a reductionistic approach to biblical sexual ethics, it's paramount, therefore, to begin with what Pope John Paul II has called a prescientific approach, which rejects modernity's distinction between nature and person in favor of biblical creation theology's insistence on humans as a psychosomatic unity with ontology as the defining basis for understanding biology, sociology, anthropology, etc.[33] John Paul II writes concerning the modernist scientific analysis of the *compositum humanum* that it does not reach "man's integrum." Therefore, its descriptions will be helpless, reductionist, and clinically objectifying. As helpful as an analysis and description of man as an "object" may be, within the framework of a creation theological framework, it must begin with and be informed by the holistic and subjectivizing focus that characterizes the biblical texts on the creation of man:

> We know hardly anything about the interior structures and the regularities that reign in the human organism. However, at the same time, perhaps precisely because of the antiquity of the text, the truth that is important for the total vision of man is revealed in the most simple and full way. This truth concerns the meaning of the human body in the structure of the personal subject. Subsequently, reflection on those archaic texts enables us to extend this meaning of the whole sphere of human inter-subjectivity, especially in the perennial man-woman relationship. Thanks to that, we acquire with regard to this relationship a perspective which we must necessarily place at the basis of all modern science on human sexuality, in the bio-physiological sense. That does not mean that we must renounce this science or deprive ourselves of its results. On the contrary, it can teach us something about the education of man, in his masculinity and femininity, and about the sphere of marriage and procreation. If it is to do so, it is necessary—through all the single elements of contemporary science—always to arrive at what is fundamental and essentially personal, both in every individual, man or woman and in their mutual relations.[34]

The problem with the modernist scientific foundation is, as Eirik Steenhoff formulates it,

> the good, the beautiful, life, consciousness, love, freedom, man and woman, and so on: none of these can be comprehended from the concepts of mathematics, nor from the new natural sciences that make empirical observation the only valid method. Because they cannot be measured or weighed, or tested in the laboratory, they lose scientific validity. Everything that is personal, truly human, is in danger of being reduced to

---

33. I owe Eirik Steenhoff a great deal of gratitude for introducing me to Pope John Paul II's work and its implications for a biblical gender identity hermeneutics.

34. John Paul II, *Redemption of the Body*, 59.

purely subjective phenomena. At best, they receive a reductionist explanation from the new natural science, and later from the social sciences. We can no longer say anything about what these things are in themselves, only about how they function, how they appear from empirical observation. This becomes, of course, an enormous problem when one is to understand living things, and above all, man, who in Greek and Christian philosophy had a unique position in the universe.[35]

This is crucial not only for understanding the psychosomatic compositum of human beings but also for describing biblical sexual ethics. Commenting on Pope John Paul II's *Man and Woman He Created Them: A Theology of the Body*,[36] often referred to informally as the "Catechesis of Human Love" (CHL), Eirik Steenhoff writes:

> "But in and of itself such *science does not yet develop* the consciousness of the body as a sign of the person, as a manifestation of the spirit. The whole development of contemporary science of the body as organism has rather the character of biological knowledge, because it is based on the disjunction between what is bodily and what is spiritual in man" (CHL 59:3). The body has become a mere "*object of manipulations*," so that "man no longer identifies himself subjectively, so to speak, with his own body, because it is deprived of the meaning and dignity that stem from the fact that his body is proper to the person." If the sciences only account for the human person according to what Wojtyła [Pope Paul II] called its cosmological definition, they end up dehumanizing him. The "adequate anthropology" or "integral vision of man" of the *Catechesis*, which is its method and goal, is radically opposed to such a reduction. Put simply, the body, in its twofold exterior and interior dimensions, reveals man to himself; that is, it is able to reveal man both as a personal *suppositum* and as a self-possessing subject.[37]

We shall return to the primacy of the metaphysical in the discussion on the relation between the anatomical or physiological and psychological gender below. Still, it should now be clear that it potentially has significant implications if the inseparable connection between the human

---

35. Steenhoff, "Om det nye synet," 3. Emphasis original.

36. John Paul II, *Man and Woman He Created Them*; original catecheses of Pope John Paul II delivered to general audiences from September 5, 1979, to November 28, 1984, where he delved deeply into the meaning of human love, marriage, and sexuality.

37. Steenhoff, "Body That Reveals the Person(s)," 8.

body and spirit, as described in the Bible, is broken. In other words, the Bible asserts that humanity's definition should precede that of science, chronologically and ontologically, before materialist and physicalist scientific perspectives.

For the same "prescientific" reason, it's essential to recognize that using modern terms such as "homosexuality," "transgender," "gender dysphoria," etc., in the context of texts from the ancient Near East can be anachronistic and may not accurately capture their understandings. Firstly, the terms "heterosexuality" and "homosexuality" are relatively modern concepts and are attributed to Richard von Krafft-Ebing, who used the terms coined by Karl-Maria Kertbeny in his 1891 psychiatric study on homosexuality.[38] The term "lesbian" did not emerge until the twentieth century when it was discovered that the female poet Sappho of Lesbos (ca. 615–570 BCE) wrote homoerotic poetry. Martti Nissinen begins a lexicon entry on homosexuality in the ancient Near East and the Old Testament by stating that "Eastern and biblical sources sometimes describe love and erotic-sexual interaction between people of the same sex. To bring all this under the rubric of 'homosexuality' is an anachronism, however, because the concept of homosexuality implies an interpretation of gender different from that of the ancient sources."[39] Modern and individualistic categories of homo-, bi-, and heterosexuality are the product of sexological research conducted since the late nineteenth century CE. Still, the underlying assumption of an individual's sexual orientation is unknown to the ancient sources, which do not categorize human gender and sexual behavior in such terms. Instead, they describe or presuppose same-sex interactions from various perspectives, reflecting the gender politics of their own cultures. The issue is not same-sex interaction per se but (masculine) gender hierarchy and appropriate sexual roles within the patriarchal social framework. Some forms of same-sex erotic-sexual interaction are portrayed as unconventional and/or objectionable while others are not subject to moral judgment.

The modern categories of homo-, bi-, and heterosexuality are based on the idea of "sexuality," which is the product of the sexological research conducted since the last part of the nineteenth century CE. The underlying assumption of an individual sexual orientation is unknown to the ancient sources, which do not categorize human gender and sexual

---

38. Krafft-Ebing, *Neue Forschungen*.
39. Nissinen, "Homosexuality," 289.

behavior accordingly. Instead, they describe or presuppose same-sex interaction from a variety of perspectives, reflecting the gender politics of their own cultures. The issue is not same-sex interaction as such but (masculine) gender hierarchy and appropriate sexual roles within the patriarchal social space. Some forms of same-sex erotic-sexual interaction are presented as queer and/or reprehensible, while others do not feature as a matter of moral judgment.[40] Nissinen's reservations are indicative of timely methodological diligence. The absence of these terms does not necessarily mean that the phenomenon they refer to was unknown; the analysis of the sources may demonstrate that the phenomenon existed under different designations.

Secondly, it must be acknowledged that while the modern concept of "homosexuality" can refer both to sexual orientation and the practice of this orientation, there is no such distinction in the texts from ancient Mesopotamia, which exclusively focus on practice. This also applies to Rom 1, which may describe an orientation or disposition but mentions it solely in connection with practice.[41]

Thirdly, it is evident that biological gender is timeless. Therefore, it's methodologically sound to use the term "fluctuating gender identity" to describe instances where the experienced or expressed gender deviates from the binary, biological gender. To what extent was such fluctuation considered a norm or not? This is another question, and the ethical evaluation of such fluctuation must be placed within the broader culturally determined gender framework reflected in the texts. That is, how was the relationship between biological and experienced gender understood and assessed in the contemporary context? The difficulty reflects a significant methodological weakness that seems to characterize many discussions of source texts, namely, the reliance on deconstructive readings and a methodologically problematic application of the falsification principle to determine whether such fluctuation was acceptable.

A final "prescience" consideration concerns whether one can infer from the performative actions in ritual space to real-life reality. In social practice, rituals often assert the status quo and affirm it, while in literature, they can usually provide opportunities to challenge or even dismantle it. Vassiliki Panoussi, for instance, discusses women's rituals in Roman literature, stating:

---

40. Nissinen, "Homosexuality," 290–91.
41. Taylor, "Bible and Homosexuality," 4.

For Roman authors, women's religious activity becomes a useful medium onto which ideological debates are mapped. In social practice, ritual usually asserts the status quo, yet in literature it often provides opportunities to challenge or even dismantle it ... Roman authors use ritual as a medium through which they contemplate ideological propositions. Although those alternatives are often eventually suppressed or defeated, nevertheless they express notions of cultural identity that complicate or even oppose traditional Roman norms and suggest a more dynamic process of cultural and ideological formation than is indicated by previous analyses of women's roles in literature.[42]

Suppose Panoussi's conclusion applies to Roman literature regarding the use of rituals. In that case, it's not inconceivable that something similar applies to the way rituals are depicted in literature from ancient Near Eastern cultures. Therefore, it must be considered in the analysis of source texts whether the rituals are part of such a literary context or if they are merely more or less accurate representations of social practice, that is, purely descriptive in relation to what took place ritually within or outside the temples.

The Chicken and the Egg

Regarding the more specific biblical hermeneutics, I find the principles laid out in John Webster's theological thought especially sensitive to the Bible's insistence on understanding the human psychosomatic *compositum* in the light of God's image. At the center of Webster's theological thought is a deep focus on the nature and character of God. Theology, for Webster, is primarily about God's self-revelation and the study of God's being, attributes, and works. Webster advocates for a theological interpretation of Scripture. This means that reading Scripture is not merely an academic exercise but a theological one. It involves understanding the text considering the Christian tradition and the doctrines it has developed. Still, it's first and foremost "a work of regenerate intelligence," awakened and illuminated by the divine, revelatory instruction of the Bible. Webster's work often focuses on the doctrine of the Trinity. He explores the implications of the triune nature of God for theology, including how God's triunity shapes our understanding of salvation, creation, and the Christian life: "Christian theology is a work of regenerate

---

42. Panoussi, *Brides, Mourners, Bacchae*, 3.

intelligence, awakened and illuminated by divine instruction to consider a twofold object. This object is, first, God in himself in the unsurpassable perfection of his inner being and work as Father, Son, and Spirit and in his outer operations, and second and by derivation, all other things relative to him. Christian divinity is characterized both by the scope of its matter—it aims at a comprehensive treatment of God and creatures and by the material order of that treatment, in which theology proper precedes and governs economy."[43] In "Life in and of Himself," Webster, in a similar way, describes the two dimensions of God's *aseity*: "First, it indicates the glory and plenitude of the life of the Holy Trinity in its self-existent and self-moving originality, its underived fullness. In every respect, God is of himself God. Second, it indicates that God's originality and fullness constitute the ground of his self-communication. He is one who, out of nothing other than his own self-sufficiency, brings creatures into being, sustains and reconciles them, and brings them to perfection in fellowship with himself."[44]

In *God and the Works of God*, Webster explores how the Christian doctrine of the Trinity involves a "disturbance of order" in how we think about God and God's economy (God's activities in relation to the world, especially in salvation history). This disturbance occurs because the doctrine of the Trinity challenges conventional philosophical categories and requires us to think beyond our natural understanding. God's economy refers to the divine actions and works in the world, particularly in salvation history. This includes God's creation, redemption, and sanctification of humanity. Webster argues that the doctrine of the Trinity disturbs our typical understanding of God's economy because it reveals an inherent relationship between God's eternal being (*ad intra*, within the Trinity) and God's external works (*ad extra*, in creation and redemption). This disturbance challenges the idea of a God who simply acts in history according to preexisting categories or rules. Instead, the Christian understanding of the Trinity suggests that God's actions in history flow from the very being of God as the Trinity. In "On the Matter of Christian Theology," Webster writes: "The divine Agent of revelatory acts is not fully understood if the phenomenality of those acts is treated as something primordial, a wholly sufficient presentation of the agent. God's outer works bear a surplus within themselves; they refer to the

---

43. Webster, *God Without Measure*, 3.
44. Webster, *God Without Measure*, 13.

divine Agent who exceeds them."⁴⁵ God's being as Trinity is not just a theory about God's inner life, but it has direct implications for God's actions in the world. The triune God is not only the source of creation but also the one who enters the depths of human existence in the incarnation of Christ. This disturbance challenges attempts at neatly separating God's being from God's actions. Instead, the doctrine of the Trinity suggests that God's being and actions are intimately related and cannot be fully understood apart from each other. The Trinity reveals that God's being as Father, Son, and Holy Spirit is inseparable from God's works in creation and redemption, challenging any attempt to compartmentalize or separate these aspects of God's nature and activity. In Webster's thought, as Tom Greggs explains it, "Christian theology done properly should concern first God's life *in se* in the immanent trinity with reflection on divine processions and missions; and then (and strictly then) all things in relation to God—including the divine economy, Christology, creation, history. Order here is the key: God in God's own complete plenitude first and then *and only then* everything related to God; the divine life *in se* first and only subsequently the divine life *ad extra*."⁴⁶

Webster's insistence on God's *self*-revelation in Scripture prior to the explanation of creation is in many ways parallel to Ryan Peterson's approach to the image of God as "identity."⁴⁷ In his work *The Imago Dei as Identity*, Peterson emphasizes that being created in the image of God bestows upon humans a unique and intrinsic dignity, independent of external factors or societal norms. This identity is not merely a static characteristic but a dynamic aspect of our relationship with God, challenging conventional notions of identity formation. Understanding ourselves as image bearers also gives us a sense of purpose and meaning as our lives are imbued with significance by reflecting God's character in the world. This includes a moral responsibility to live by God's love, justice, and compassion values. Furthermore, the *imago Dei* highlights the relational nature of human identity, drawing parallels to the relational existence of God in the Trinity. Humans are designed for relationships—with God and one another. This relational aspect influences our understanding of community, love, and interconnectedness. Peterson suggests that recognizing the image of God is not merely a theoretical concept but a transformative

---

45. Webster, *God Without Measure*, 8.
46. Greggs, "Call to Focus on God," 659. Emphasis original.
47. Peterson, *Imago Dei as Human Identity*.

call. As we grow in understanding and living out our identity as image bearers, we are shaped and transformed to become more Christ-like and represent the perfect image of God. The human person is thus simultaneously being and becoming the image of God. Overall, Peterson's exploration of the *imago Dei* as the foundation of human identity invites individuals to consider themselves from a divine perspective, offering a profound sense of dignity, purpose, moral responsibility, and a call to relational living. Peterson, in a similar way to Webster, insists that though the actual *outworking* of the image as both essential, functional, and relational is *internal*, of course, to humans, the image as such is *external* in that it's rooted in and defined by God's Trinitarian relational existence.

Neither Webster nor Peterson are without critics. Tom Gregg, for example, in a very personal review of his late long-time friend and colleague's *God Without Measure*, argues that Webster's distinction between God *in se* and creation may be too rigid:

> Surely, that very distinction is meaningful only in its relationality? There is no Creator without a creature, no creature without a Creator: there is as much relationality as distinction in the principle of creation ex nihilo as creation comes from nowhere but from God's free and gracious act. Although God is free to be a se, the reality that we can even speak in this way determines that God is not: there is now never a time when God is without God's creature. To speak of God as Creator implies not only God's infinite otherness to creation and creation's dependence on God's grace, but also God's relationship to God's creature.[48]

That Webster was not ignorant of this critique is evidenced by a remark on man's access to God *in se*. Man's knowledge is *ectypal*; it derives from God's archetypal understanding of himself and all things. And though man has no *direct* access to this archetypal knowledge, "the limitations of the intellect, rendered vicious by the fall," Webster argues, "do not sever created intellect's natural connection to God, or place it beyond the reach of providence, regeneration, and revelation. Theological science is a graced enterprise: not perfect, but mortified and vivified, caught up in the Spirit's work of sanctification, its deficiencies sufficiently repaired so that fulfilling its vocation to know God can be a matter of prayerful confidence in divine instruction."[49]

---

48. Greggs, "Call to Focus on God," 660.
49. Webster, *God Without Measure*, 10.

One critique raised by Gregg is that the argument is more systematic theologically than exegetically based. Acknowledging that "the focus of systematics is always going to be the sensus plenior of Scripture as we seek to offer light codas to aid the reading of Scripture—codas which themselves arise from reading Scripture together with the tradition rationally for today's church and world," Gregg questions "how much Scripture's message is presumed in its univocity rather than argued for" and "how much the impetus of Webster's dominant principle is borne out by the Scriptures which testify to God's relationship to creation far more in terms of proportion than to God's life in se."[50] The same critique could be applied to Peterson, who imports an *etic* concept of identity in his reading of Gen 1. Peterson is heavily influenced by Richard Bauckham, who distinguishes between identity, function, and ontology in his work on monotheism in Second Temple Judaism. Peterson uses this distinction to argue that identity precedes and is separate from man's ontology or functions.[51] Just as it's difficult to discuss "Creator without creature," man's identity cannot be determined without reference to creation, especially when considering Scripture's creaturely-embedded revelation about the Creator.[52] As Fellipe do Vale argues, "What we have in Scripture, then, is the norming norm of theology, that which provides theology with its subject matter precisely because it reveals God and the divine economy. Holy Scripture is not a mere repository of facts but something that enables the reader to encounter God when read with the right Spirit-produced virtues. Thus, Scripture both discloses the divine economy and plays a pivotal role within it."[53] While critics are right that we do not have access to knowledge of God's essence a se detached from natural and special revelation, Webster and Peterson correctly assert that God's essence logically precedes God's actions, including the creation of humanity and our understanding of it. Combined with the knowledge of God's economy (Webster) and the possibility of becoming the image of God post-regenerationem (Peterson), their theology is—at least by implication—fundamentally Christological, since the incarnated Christ reveals to us most fully the image of God.

50. Greggs, "Call to Focus on God," 662–63.

51. Peterson, *Imago Dei as Human Identity*, 63–65, and references to Bauckham there.

52. I owe Anders Landkildehus for pointing me to Peterson's dependence on Bauckham's concept of identity.

53. do Vale, *Gender as Love*, 16.

All these hermeneutical deliberations matter for biblical sexual ethics, by implication, because the realization of the image of God in personal ethics can never occur in contradiction to God's essence. Suppose the biblical understanding of gender and sexual ethics is, in other words, grounded in who God is. In that case, it cannot simply be understood as mere situational ethics or casuistry. Likewise, it would require a process-oriented understanding of God's essence to argue that the knowledge of gender and sexual ethics changes with Christ.

A Radical Gift

Just as fundamental to the work of describing a biblical understanding of gender identity should be what John Paul II calls a hermeneutics of the gift: "It is a fundamental and 'radical' giving, that is, a giving in which the gift comes into being precisely from nothingness;"[54] a hermeneutics of the gift that, as an a priori, views life as a gift and therefore insists that life—whether human life or life in all its forms—should be interpreted as a gift. Contrary to the insistence in gender identity theory on reality as a construct, a hermeneutics of the gift insists that reality is not something we create but receive. In the words of Steenhoff: "The most basic ontological and anthropological reality is that we are created out of nothing by a personal God who loves us and has created us in His image, giving us the ability to understand this creation. This gift is the underlying structure for everything that exists, and everything must be interpreted in its light."[55] What the Bible's texts about the creation of humanity say about what it means to be male and female must, in other words, be understood within the framework of this prescientific hermeneutics of the gift, which insists, as one of its trajectories, that the gift is expressed and experienced relationally, bodily, and in binary terms. "The image of God," according to John Paul II, "constitute[s] two different ways of the human 'being a body' in the unity of that image," and the prelapsarian gift of life "speaks of the grace that made it possible for man to experience the meaning of the primary donation of the world. In particular, it concerns the meaning of the mutual donation of one to the other through masculinity and femininity in this world."[56] The narrative of human

---

54. John Paul II, *Redemption of the Body*, 34–35.
55. Steenhoff, "Om det nye synet," 7.
56. John Paul II, *Redemption of the Body*, 34, 43.

creation in Gen 2 describes the primordial experience of loneliness ("It is not good for the man to be alone"), unity ("Therefore a man shall leave his father and mother and hold fast to his wife, and they shall become one flesh"), and nakedness ("The man and his wife were both naked and were not ashamed"), which, despite the fall, remains fundamental to understanding the relational and binary gift that human life is: "Speaking of original human experiences, we have in mind not so much their distance in time, but rather their basic significance. The important thing is not that these experiences belong to man's prehistory (to his 'theological prehistory'), but that they are always at the root of every human experience. That is true even if little attention is paid to these essential experiences during the evolution of ordinary human existence. They are so intermingled with the ordinary things of life that we do not generally notice their extraordinary character."[57] When a man and a woman come together in such a complementary relationship or marriage, nakedness is "[a] fundamental experience, in which man expresses himself as a person according to his own specific structure." In the relationship between the man and the woman, it is an expression of "an extraordinary fullness in their mutual communication."[58] Moreover, even though this experience is no longer as straightforward and pure as in the garden of Eden, Jesus affirms with his reference in Matt 19:4–6 and Mark 5–9 to this relational order as created that it still should be pursued because longing for it is inherent in human beings from the beginning. It is about, as Steenhoff puts it, not loneliness in the psychological sense but ontological "aloneness." Therefore, it is also a theological point that אָדָם (ʔādām, "human") first becomes אִישׁ (ʔîš, "man") and אִשָּׁה (ʔiššāʰ, "woman") after and because of this primordial experience, not because we should understand the first human in Gen 2:7 as androgynous,[59] but because הָאָדָם (hāʔādām, "hu-

---

57. John Paul II, *Redemption of the Body*, 29.

58. John Paul II, *Redemption of the Body*, 31, 75.

59. Though the midrash Genesis Rabbah (8:1) suggests that God created Adam double-faced and sawed him in two, it has no basis in the biblical text and may be inspired by the androgyne in Plato's *Symposion*: "For our original nature was by no means the same as it is now. In the first place, there were three kinds of human beings, not merely the two sexes, male and female, as at present: there was a third kind as well, which had equal shares of the other two, and whose name survives though the thing itself has vanished. For 'man-woman' was then a unity in form no less than name, composed of both sexes and sharing equally in male and female; whereas now it has come to be merely a name of reproach. Secondly, the form of each person was round all over, with back and sides encompassing it every way; each had four arms, and legs to match these, and two faces perfectly alike on a cylindrical neck. There was one head

man")—even though he is a biological man—is not yet complete, whole, or complementary at this point.⁶⁰ It is the not-yet-gender-differentiated human (i.e., the man without the woman) who is "alone," and it is only when the entire human (i.e., the man and the woman) is created and lives together as a man and a woman that the fellowship of togetherness arises, which is the destiny of humanity. Thus, Steenhoff states,

> There is an identity between the two; they are part of the same human nature. They are both persons, created for fellowship with God, which is a reality that in this sense is more fundamental than that they are created for fellowship with each other. Original loneliness points to this. Loneliness lies at the bottom, we can say, precisely because we are persons created for fellowship with other persons. Nevertheless, we always exist as either male or female, called to live out God's love in the world in the life-giving fellowship of the family. So in other words: Adam and Eve are called to acknowledge to each other that they are created for God and have their origin and purpose in Him. From there, we derive our dignity. The love between man and woman is meant to reflect this in the world.⁶¹

Steenhoff goes on to describe how this distinction between original loneliness and unity has two important implications for a Christian understanding of gender and sexuality, namely that "the fellowship between man and woman can be said to be a part of being created in God's image" and that "the distinction between Adam and 'isj' and 'isja' means that a person is not identical with their gender or their sexuality."⁶² However, we are preempting further exegetical and biblical theological analysis, so we shall only note that, although these hermeneutical a priori statements

---

to the two faces, which looked opposite ways; there were four ears, two privy members, and all the other parts, as may be imagined, in proportion. The creature walked upright as now, in either direction as it pleased and whenever it started running fast, it went like our acrobats, whirling over and over with legs stuck out straight; only then they had eight limbs to support and speed them" (Plato, *Plato in Twelve Volumes*, 189d–190a). It is more likely, however, that the interpretation should be understood more as an attempt to explain what צֵלָע, ṣēlāʕ, means in the description of the creation of the woman in Gen 2:21—"God the Lord took אַחַת מִצַּלְעֹתָיו, ʔaḥat miṣṣalʕōtāʸw, and closed it with flesh"—and where the interpretation thus understands צֵלָע, ṣēlāʕ, as (the whole) one side of the originally androgynous man.

60. The understanding of the first human as androgynous was common in rabbinic exegesis, possibly under the influence of the so-called androgynous myth in Plato; cf. Rothenberg, *Wisdom of Love*, 13–58.

61. Steenhoff, "Om det nye synet," 8; cf. John Paul II, *Redemption of the Body*, 15.

62. Steenhoff, "Om det nye synet."

must initially stand as assertions, it will become apparent that they are not systematic-theological eisegesis but can indeed be argued for based on the text.

Fall, Fix, and Finish

One last hermeneutic observation revolves around Webster's emphasis on Scripture reflecting the divine economy. This means that Scripture possesses a chronological and theological framework, and understanding where a particular text fits within this framework is essential. John Webster explores Scripture as the divine economy by highlighting its significance within God's comprehensive design for creation and redemption. He does not view Scripture merely as a collection of writings but as an essential component of God's governance of all things—an aspect he terms the *divine economy*. According to Webster, Scripture participates in this divine economy by serving as a medium through which God reveals himself and communicates his intentions to humanity. Within this framework, Scripture acquires its significance and authority. Webster underscores the interactive relationship between God, Scripture, and the Christian community, wherein Scripture reflects God's self-disclosure and continues to serve as a means through which God communicates with his people. Ultimately, Webster's perspective on Scripture as the divine economy emphasizes its pivotal role in God's plan for creation and salvation. It is the authoritative testimony to God's self-revelation and redemptive activity in the world.

According to John Webster, Christ is indispensable in the divine economy. Webster sees Christ as the focal point of God's plan for creation and redemption, serving as the definitive revelation of God's nature and will to humanity. Christ embodies God's self-disclosure in human form, making the divine accessible to humanity. In the divine economy, Christ is not merely a historical figure or a moral teacher but the very Son of God incarnate—the Word made flesh. He is the culmination of God's redemptive purposes, the fulfillment of God's promises, and the source of salvation for humanity. Through his life, death, and resurrection, Christ reconciles humanity to God, restores what was broken by sin, and inaugurates the kingdom of God. Christ's role in the divine economy is as the mediator between God and humanity and as the perfect revelation of God's character and purposes. As the mediator, Christ bridges the gap between the divine and the human, offering reconciliation and salvation to all who believe in him. As the perfect revelation, Christ reveals the fullness of God's love, justice, mercy, and grace, inviting humanity into a restored relationship with God. In essence, Christ's role in the divine economy is to bring about God's purposes for creation and redemption, reconciling humanity to God and revealing God's love and salvation to the world. He is the cornerstone of God's plan, the embodiment of divine grace, and the hope of humanity for eternal life.

One of the critical implications of considering the placement of texts in the divine economy concerns the crucial distinction between what belongs to the *definition* of what it means to be human (in creation), the *properties* of fallen humanity, and the redemptive *hope* of restoration. Man is not sinful. He was not created as such. However, after the fall, sin becomes one of humanity's properties. Through Christ, the "representation of his (God's) essence [χαρακτὴρ τῆς ὑποστάσεως αὐτοῦ]," fallen man is "conformed to the image of his Son" (Rom 8:29) and "clothed with the new man that is being renewed in knowledge according to the image of the one who created it" (Col 3:10). Regarding gender identity, this consideration of the divine economy situates the fallen human's experience of their identity within a framework that not only exposes the "fall" but also enables the fallen individual, by the Spirit, to initiate a regenerative process. As Fellipe do Vale puts it with reference to Sarah Coakley: "The way beyond the simple alternative of secular gender theory and unreflective Christian positions lies with the 'theological concepts of creation, fall, and redemption which place the performances of gender in a spectrum of existential possibilities *between* despair and hope.' When one allows one's theological vision for gender to be impacted by these concepts, 'the fallen, 'worldly' view of gender relations is open to the future and to change; it is set in an unfolding, diachronic narrative both of individual spiritual maturation and societal transformation.'"[63]

While Scripture, on the one hand, insists that the realization of God's image in personal ethics can never occur in contradiction to God's essence, a consideration of the divine economy entails a reminder that this realization is a process that exclusively takes place with the help of the Spirit and does not reach its ultimate goal, namely conformity with Christ, in the present dispensation of God's economy.

---

63. do Vale, *Gender as Love*, 21–22. Emphasis original.

CREATED MATTER MATTERS

The theological subtheme of body theology makes a strong argument for a created and, therefore, inseparable connection between "sex" and "gender"—that is, between outer, biological sex and inner, experienced gender. This theme involves three central Christian doctrines: the goodness of material creation, the incarnation, and the resurrection.

Soul Stuff

Before delving into the biblical theology of the body, we should examine what Scripture says about the relationship between body and spirit—that is, how the texts address the relationship between the physical and spiritual parts of the human being.

As we have argued above, man's psychosomatic *compositum* must be understood within the metaphysical framework of his createdness in the image of God. The question, however, is how we should understand these parts, as their ontology has implications for their relationship to each other. Are body and soul independent entities? Moreover, is there a mutual or asymmetric dependency relationship concerning their origin? Questions are fundamental to the present discussion because, by implication, they also address the question of the relationship between biological and psychological gender identity.

Specific biblical texts describe body and soul as separate substances or entities. In Ecclesiastes, man is going to his "eternal home" means that "the dust returns to the earth as it was, and the life's breath [הָרוּחַ, *hārûₐh*] returns to God who gave it" (12:7), and Job 34:14–15 states that "if God were to set his heart on it and gather in his spirit [רוּחוֹ, *rûhô*] and his breath [נִשְׁמָתוֹ, *nišmātô*], all flesh [בָּשָׂר, *bāśār*] would perish together, and human beings would return to dust." In Ezek 13:20, the Lord "releases the people's lives [הַנְּפָשׁוֹת]," and in 1 Sam 28, Saul approaches an אֵשֶׁת בַּעֲלַת־אוֹב, *ʔēšet baʕᵃlat-ʔôv*, "a woman who is a medium," that is, a necromancer (from the Greek words νεκρός, "dead," and μαντεία, "divination, prophetic utterance") to bring up the deceased Samuel's spirit.[64] In the New Testament, Jesus teaches the same distinction when he says, "Do not be afraid of those who kill the body [τὸ σῶμα] but cannot kill the soul [τὴν δὲ ψυχὴν]. Instead, fear the one who is able to destroy both soul

---

64. See also the prohibition in Lev 20:27: "A man or woman who has in them a spirit of the dead or a familiar spirit must be put to death."

and body [καὶ ψυχὴν καὶ σῶμα] in hell" (Matt 10:28). When the criminal on the cross next to Jesus asks him to "remember me" *postmortem* in his kingdom, "me" cannot mean anything else than his soul (Luke 23:42–43). In Acts 7:59, Stephen believed that his spirit would be with Christ after his body had died. In Luke 9:28–36, the pre-resurrection spirits of Moses and Elijah appear to Jesus, and in Matt 22:31–32, Jesus (referring to Exod 3:6) identifies Abraham, Isaac, and Jacob with "the living," not "the remembered" or the "pending-resurrection."

Other texts, most clearly in the New Testament, teach that the separation between body and soul in these texts is temporary (more on this below); nonetheless, the body and soul are described as separate entities or substances. Such an understanding rules out monistic explanations that insist body and soul are the same. It leaves us with explanations that acknowledge body and soul as dual parts or substances that exist in some sort of relationship.

The major challenge regarding gender identity is, therefore, not so much about whether there should be a distinction between body and soul but what *kind* of distinction should be made and what it means for the relationship between the body and the soul. This applies both in terms of gender dysphoria: is the biological or psychological gender indicative of one's "true" gender when there *post lapsum* is a discrepancy between the body's and soul's gender? Nevertheless, it also applies to the view of the body itself, which, if the soul is given primacy, is degraded and can be manipulated without changing or destroying the soul. As Nancy Pearcey expresses it with a few apt quotes: "Feminist philosopher Susan Bordo writes, 'The training, toning, slimming, and sculpting of the body ... encourage an adversarial relationship to the body.' These practices express the will to conquer and subdue the body—and ultimately to be liberated from its constraints. The radical ethicist Joseph Fletcher declared, 'To be a person ... means to be free of physiology!' Nature is treated as a negative constraint to be overcome."[65]

In this context, within the fields of philosophy and neuroscience, there appears to be a renewed interest in the soul as an independent entity. For decades, scientists have considered this approach outmoded and expired, and new atheists like Richard Dawkins, Daniel Dennett, and Sam Harris only have contempt for it. Joshua Farris summarizes the story in his recent *The Creation of Self: A Case for the Soul*:

---

65. Pearcey, *Love Thy Body*, 32–33.

> For one to say that the soul has been under attack, would be an understatement. Since the rise of logical positivism, the attitude to the soul is likened to the attitude toward God. Logical positivism is the philosophical thesis that we can only know that which is empirically verifiable, which excludes the statement: "God exists," because it is not verifiable empirically, at least not directly. Logical positivism may not hold prime authority in philosophy and science anymore, but the shadow of logical positivism remains in some academic circles. Closely related to it is the belief in materialism of some sort, namely, the philosophical stance that the reality under investigation is wholly material in nature, mechanistic, and is governed solely by regular lawful events. And, it is often supposed that belief in the soul, if not in contradiction with it, is not supported by science.[66]

Farris continues to demonstrate, however, that cracks in the rock of logical positivism and physicalism are beginning to appear. Summarizing neuroscience in *The Ashgate Research Companion to Theological Anthropology*, philosopher Daniel Robinson argues, for example, that though "the brain has no motives and seeks no solace," there is more to motives than can be explained by the material brain: "That actual persons—possessed of brains and other anatomical structures—are, indeed, motivated and do, indeed, strive to find deeper meaning in an otherwise indifferent cosmos is beyond dispute. That such motives and longings are somehow enabled by the brain should be readily granted but not as a fact that would give the motives and longings to the brain or locate them in the brain. Such inferences might well trigger activity in the anterior cingulate cortex in any creature expecting propositions to be meaningful."[67] Farris concludes, "What we cannot say, along with so many scientists, is that the soul is a crazy idea. In fact, given the above, what has historically been considered an unusual and unwelcome guest deserves a place at the table of science. Even more, it deserves a place at the table of reality."[68] Due to the importance of the relationship between body and soul, a more systematic theological discussion seems in place.

In *An Introduction to Theological Anthropology*, Joshua Farris explains that our ontological presuppositions determine whether gender identity is anchored in the body, the soul, or a necessary correspondence

---

66. Farris, "Soul and Science."
67. Farris and Taliaferro, *Ashgate Research Companion*, 79.
68. Farris, "Maybe the Idea."

between the two. Regarding the gender-dysphoric choice between the physical and spiritual gender, Farris writes:

> It could follow that one person's metaphysical assumption of a distinct gendered body means either that that person's gender changes or simply that person experiences a mismatch with his or her body. How one accounts for these contingencies depends on the underlying ontology of gender, and gender in relation to sex. Certainly, if we take some version of physicalism as our starting point, then it follows that when the sex of my physical part (i.e., the body) changes anatomically (along with the right sort of hormone supplements), then I am the sex/gender that is instantiated in my physical part because I am either my physical part (with higher-order neural properties) or I am constituted by my physical part in a way that my physical part determines my sexed nature. But, if I am my soul or a person who has a soul—a belief that I, along with much of the Christian tradition, take as true—then the ontological facts of gender and sex are more complicated. I might have difficulty imagining that I could become the opposite gender, but the conceivability or possibility of gender transformation depends on our ontology of gender.[69]

As for ontological presuppositions, we have already rejected physicalism as being contrary to biblical anthropology's insistence that man is a composite of the physical body and the metaphysical soul. Farris does the same. Therefore, according to Farris, the choice lies between various forms of hylomorphic dualism (Thomism) and substance dualism.

Regarding human beings, hylomorphic dualism posits that they are composed of two distinct substances: matter (ὕλη) and form (μορφή). According to this view, the body (matter) and soul (form) are intimately united in a composite being with the soul being the substantial form that gives life and organization to the body. This perspective emphasizes the holistic nature of human existence, recognizing the inseparable connection between humanity's physical and spiritual aspects. In Farris's words, "The two components, form and matter, are nonreducible to their respective parts and are somehow fitted to each other in a matter-form arrangement, which produces something distinct, a new substance."[70]

Substance dualism, according to Farris, is the view that "persons are identical not to the material body but to the immaterial parts (e.g.,

---

69. Farris and Cortez, *Introduction to Theological Anthropology*, 223.
70. Farris and Cortez, *Introduction to Theological Anthropology*, 28.

the soul, the spirit, the mind) or some compound configuration of both body and soul. On most versions of substance dualism, the carrier of personal identity is the soul."[71] Farris dubs the latter pure substance dualism and rejects it as incompatible with Scripture's view of the body. Farris's rejection is fully in line with the conclusion above that the biblical texts necessitate the correlation between זָכָר (zāxār, "[biological] male") (Gen 1:27; 5:2) and אִישׁ (ʔîš, "[complementary] man") on the one hand, and נְקֵבָה (nᵉqēvāʰ, "[biological] female") and אִשָּׁה (ʔiššāʰ, "[complementary] woman") on the other. Instead, Farris opts for *composite substance dualism*, in which humans are composed of two distinct substances: a material body and an immaterial soul. Unlike hylomorphic dualism, which emphasizes the unity of body and soul, composite substance dualism (COSD) views them as separate entities that interact but remain distinct. John Farris explains: "On composite substance dualism, the soul and the body are not individually substantial but rather compose one substance (possibly a form-matter arrangement). In this way, the soul informs the matter in question."[72] Man is, in other words, composed of both body and soul, and both are essential or necessary in establishing a person's identity.[73] Using the scholastic terms *ens per se* ("being in itself," denoting something that exists essentially or inherently, without dependence on anything else for its existence) and *ens per accidens* ("being accidental," denoting something that exists contingently or incidentally, not because of its own essence but because of some external factors or circumstances), Farris explains that "the composite dualist contends that the soul substance is properly unified with the body as a human person and the soul substance may have an *ens* per se kind of existence in a weak sense, yet more naturally is an *ens per accidens* as it's united substantially with the material organism."[74] In contrast to other variants of COSD that emphasize that the soul substance is not a proper substance and does not have any *ens* per se, Farris advocates for an understanding that less

---

71. Farris and Cortez, *Introduction to Theological Anthropology*, 29.

72. Farris and Cortez, *Introduction to Theological Anthropology*, 70.

73. Farris's composite substance dualism is in many ways similar to Nancey Murphy's holistic dualism, which emphasizes the integrated nature of body and soul, viewing the soul as an emergent property of the entire person. In contrast, Farris's composite substance dualism posits separate material and immaterial substances, with the soul playing a distinct role in human consciousness. While Murphy's view leans towards emergentism, highlighting interconnectedness, Farris maintains a traditional dualistic stance with distinct substances.

74. Farris, *Soul of Theological Anthropology*, 40.

considers the soul as emerging from complex physical processes and more emphasizes the interaction between God's supernatural creation of the soul and complex physical processes of the brain.

One of the advantages of composite substance dualism is that it both explains the substantial distinction between body and soul in the biblical texts and simultaneously describes the interdependency of the coming into existence of the physical brain and God's creation of the soul. Farris explains:

> One could understand the soul as having some direct relationship to God's action of bringing it about, but the soul's existence is somehow dependent on the whole of the human body/brain. Thus, the soul is a part of the body/brain and actualizes its normal or common properties respective of a naturally functioning human nature. One could say, then, that there are jointly necessary and sufficient conditions for the soul's coming into existence: (1) God acts, sufficiently, by way of bringing about the particular soul; and (2) the body/brain, at some sufficient complexity, is a necessary condition for the soul's origination.[75]

The same "interconnectedness" is argued by Gregg Allison. Though he omits the distinction between (or avoids the discussion on) primary and secondary causes, he nevertheless argues in the same vein:

> [God] is intimately engaged in each and every aspect, the minute and large details, of embodied creation, which include the following: (1) a mental component, associated with the intellect, cognition, mind, thinking, memory, and reasoning; (2) an emotional component, associated with feelings, sentiments, the heart, passions, motivations, and affections; (3) a volitional component, associated with the will, judgment, decision-making, purposing, and choosing; (4) a moral component, associated with the conscience, ethical awareness, scruples, a sense of right and wrong, feelings of guilt/innocence, shame/honor, and fear/power; (5) a physical component, associated with the body, action, agency, and effecting change. Importantly, these components cannot be sequestered into discrete parts of human nature, some pertaining to the soul, others to the spirit, and still others to the body. Indeed, rather than thinking in terms of isolation or even of influence (e.g., a bodily state influences one's mental state, and vice versa), we should think in terms of interconnectivity, with all these aspects inextricably linked

---

75. Farris and Cortez, *Introduction to Theological Anthropology*, 72.

together, dependent on one another, and together determinative for human existence, whether for suffering and misery, or for flourishing and happiness.[76]

Though composite substance dualism seems to describe precisely what the biblical texts argue about the correlation between biological and psychological gender in the *original* creation, composite substance dualism does not necessarily explain whether *gender dysphoria* should be resolved by respecting biological or psychological gender. A solution to this dilemma involves the century-long debate on when and how the soul comes into existence, as the two classical explanatory models could be taken to favor each part of the *compositum humanum* as indicative of gender.

A good way to illustrate the dispute is to point out the challenge that arises when the anthropology in Pss 51 and 139 is compared. In Ps 139 (NET), both body and soul are created by God: "Certainly you made my mind and heart; you wove me together in my mother's womb.... My bones were not hidden from you, when I was made in secret and sewed together in the depths of the earth. Your eyes saw me when I was inside the womb. All the days ordained for me were recorded in your scroll before one of them came into existence" (vv. 13, 15–16). The focus is clearly on the awesome, amazing, and unfathomable character of each human person's creation: "I will give you thanks because your deeds are awesome and amazing... How difficult it is for me to fathom your thoughts about me, O God! How vast is their sum total!" (vv. 14, 17). The same focus is found in Ps 8, where "honor and majesty," the explicit marks of God's image in Gen 1, are ascribed to humans *post lapsum*.

On the other hand, in Ps 51, the focus is on the psychosomatic consequences of original sin: "Look, I was guilty of sin from birth, a sinner the moment my mother conceived me... Grant me the ultimate joy of being forgiven! May the bones you crushed rejoice! Hide your face from my sins! Wipe away all my guilt! Create for me a pure heart, O God! Renew a resolute spirit within me!" (vv. 5, 8–10). If God, per Pss 139 and 8, creates the human soul or spirit awesomely, amazingly, and unfathomably not only in original creation but also *post lapsum*, how, then, is it affected by original sin once created? This question has marred theologians since the dawn of Christian theology.

---

76. Allison, "Four Theses Concerning Human Embodiment," 162–63.

Tradux or Creatio

The classical explanation models both have their advantages and weaknesses. According to creationist belief,[77] God directly and immediately creates the soul and immediately unites it to a body to comprise the full human nature. While the soul is supernaturally created by God, the parents generate the body of every new human. Scripture lends support to the argument that the soul exists at conception. David's words in Ps 51:5 (NET), "Look, I was guilty of sin from birth, a sinner the moment my mother conceived me," suggest the presence of the soul from the moment of conception. Additionally, we find evidence in the Gospel of Matthew, where an angel reassures Joseph about Mary's conception, stating, "Joseph, son of David, do not be afraid to take Mary as your wife, because the child conceived in her is from the Holy Spirit" (Matt 1:20), indicating the existence of Jesus in Mary's womb from the moment of conception. This presents the challenge of how God can accomplish this without simultaneously recreating sinful nature and bearing direct responsibility for placing a male soul in a female body or a female soul in a male body. The creationist answer is that God creates everyone immediately, subjecting that creation to the secondary causes inherent to the nature of that being. In the case of the descendants of Adam and Eve, this entails secondary causes deeply entrenched in the sinful nature. Sin is not *transmitted* by God, creating a sinful soul. The perfect soul, by subsequent imputation, inherits the original sin of Adam.

The term "traducian" originates from the Latin word *tradux*, which refers to a "branch of a vine." Thus, it implies that every human being is a "branch" derived from their parents. In contrast to creationism, which posits that God directly creates each individual soul at the moment of conception or birth, traducianism suggests that the soul is generated through the biological process of reproduction. According to traducianism, just as offspring's physical traits and characteristics are inherited from their parents, so is the spiritual aspect—the soul—transmitted from one generation to the next. Here, the issue of God's association with sinful nature is resolved. Sin is passed down to every individual in Adam's lineage. On the other hand, it becomes difficult to explain why sex is not sinful since the act of sexual intercourse transmits original sin.

---

77. Not referring to the creation of *cosmos* but to the creation of the soul in a narrow sense.

Scriptural support may be found in Gen 2:2, where it is stated that God ceased his work of creating at day six (cf. Heb 4:4). Creating souls anew would contradict this. And Gen 5:2–3 states that whereas God created the first humans in his image, Adam fathered a son "in his own likeness." Moreover, Rom 5:1–2 seems to imply that we all sinned "through one man," underscoring the interconnectedness of everyone to Adam and his initial transgression. In other words, both the fallen soul and body are generated by human parents. In the traducian view, the parents are only the instrumental cause of the new human soul. God is still the efficient cause.

There are other teams in the league, of course. We have already mentioned emergentism as distinct from Farris's version of COSD. The doctrine of emergence suggests that when the components of a system are organized in a specific way, their combined behavior gives rise to something entirely new. This emergent entity cannot be reduced to the individual parts from which it originated, as it possesses unique structure and causal abilities distinct from its components. In relation to the evolution of the soul, emergentism argues that the soul supervenes on the body and that the soul, at a certain stage of bodily complexity, comes into being. According to William Hasker, emergent causal powers are "already implicit in the physical 'stuff,'"[78] and "emergentism implies that consciousness, thought, rational volition, and so on make their appearance naturally as a result of the structure and functioning of the human brain and nervous system . . . emergentists do not view the mind and its powers as being, as it were, injected from outside into the human biological system. Instead, the soul appears naturally, given the appropriate physical organization and function of the body and brain."[79] This view should be rejected, however, because it does not consider that man, from the beginning, was matter *and* spirit.

The result? Probably a draw! Historically, prominent figures like Augustine and Luther were either indecisive or held different beliefs during their careers, and the reformed theologian Herman Bavinck notes in his *Reformed Dogmatics* that "the argument between traducianism and creationism remained undecided in Christian theology," and that "in the strength of their arguments traducianism and creationism are almost equal."[80] The same verdict is cast more recently by Oliver Crisp, who

78. Hasker, *Emergent Self*, 177.
79. Hasker, "Dialect of Soul and Body," 215–16.
80. Bavinck, *Reformed Dogmatics*, 580–81.

argues that it's not terribly surprising that "arguments against traducianism that are worthy of serious consideration are not easy to come by" since "the question of the origin of the soul has taxed some of the greatest minds in Christendom."[81]

It would be an act of hubris to attempt to resolve this dilemma here; the purpose, anyway, is only to highlight where different views are relevant to the discussion about the relationship between biological and psychological gender. Regardless of the more detailed differences between the explanatory models mentioned, the starting point must be the models that reflect the correlation between biological and psychological gender and the tension between the creation of the perfect soul and its influence by original sin, as described in the biblical texts.

The first relevant point concerns the difference that seems to exist regarding whether a person *is* both their soul and their body. According to the creationist perspective, man consists of or *is* a soul while possessing a body. Traducianists, however, would argue that man is a unified entity comprising both soul and body. Consequently, traducianists interpret the image of God to encompass both the soul and body, whereas creationists assert that only the soul bears the image of God. Based on our exegesis of the relevant biblical texts, it seems that, in this respect, the traducianist explanation is more in line with biblical anthropology. The explication of the image of God in Gen 1–2—i.e., procreation and vocation—would simply not make sense if the image only refers to the soul. As Gregg Allison writes with reference to Luke Timothy Johnson:

> Johnson notes, "Whereas there is some truth to the claim that I have a body, since I can in fact dispose of it in a number of ways, there is at least equal truth to the claim that I am my body. I cannot completely dispose of my body without at the same time losing myself. In strict empirical terms, when my body disappear, so do I." I would slightly modify Johnson's view by contending that the statement "I am my body" is the ground for the statement "I have a body." Illustrating Johnson's point, because I have a body, I can sacrifice certain parts of it for the sake of others. For example, I can donate one of my kidneys so that someone else whose kidneys are failing may, by organ transplantation, live. Or, if I suffer from body integrity identity disorder (BIID; apotemnophilia), I can request that part of my body—my left arm, for example—be amputated so that I feel whole once more. But if I sacrifice too much of my body, which

---

81. Crisp, "Pulling Traducianism out of the Shedd," 2.4.57.

I have—for example, if I donate both kidneys for the sake of others—or if I request that certain parts of my body—my head, for example—be amputated, then I (and I am my body) no longer exists (i.e., I'm dead). Thus, "I am my body" is the ground for "I have a body."[82]

Or as Carl Trueman has it, "There is no 'I' behind or before the body. There is no 'us' that exists (logically, let alone chronologically) independently of our flesh, and that is then randomly assigned to the bodies we have. Our bodies are an integral part of who we are. And I do not 'occupy' my body as I might occupy a house or a space suit or a deck chair at the beach. On the contrary, it's an integral part of me, inseparable from who I am."[83] For the same reason, the creationist interpretation is vulnerable to arguments by suggesting that if humans are their soul, but have a body, then humans can manipulate their body if it does not reflect their soul or personality. This is *not* what creationists argue, but it is, nevertheless, a weakness in their explanation model, and this aspect of the traducianist model should, therefore, be preferred. Farris points to another open flank in the creationist model, namely the (neo-Platonic) view that the soul is more important than the body.[84] The physical and corporeal aspects of image [צֶלֶם, ṣelem], likeness [דְּמוּת, dᵉmût] in Gen 1, and the creation of woman from man's צֵלָע (ṣēlāʕ) "side" in Gen 2 could be used to argue for the bodily aspect of God's being. This implies that the soul is not any closer to God than the body is. Caution must be exercised, however, due to the clear use of analogies elsewhere in Gen 1–2 (e.g., days in Gen 1 and, more indisputable, the "potter verb" וַיִּיצֶר, wayyîṣer, "and he formed [the man]," in 2:7). Taken as analogies, these texts do not, therefore, *exclude* the possibility that souls are ontologically closer than bodies to God's being. Besides, at least the New Testament teaches clearly that though God became "flesh" (John 1:14), God *is* "spirit" (John 4:24; 2 Cor 3:17). The Old Testament is more ambiguous, but the following texts may be understood accordingly: "Where can I go to escape your Spirit? Where can I flee to escape your presence?" (Ps 139:7 NET) and "The Spirit of God has made me, and the breath of the Almighty gives me life" (Job 33:4 NET). Though it is by way of the spirit man consciously *relates* to God, the body, as we have seen, is nevertheless a prerequisite for

---

82. Allison, "Four Theses Concerning Human Embodiment," 176n22.
83. Trueman, "Triumph of the Social Scientific Method."
84. Farris and Cortez, *Introduction to Theological Anthropology*, 70.

man's *expression* of the procreative and vocative aspects of the image of God, that is, who God *is*. And when Peter, in the New Testament, argues that "you do not see him [Jesus Christ] now, but you believe in him, and so you rejoice with an indescribable and glorious joy because you are attaining the goal of your faith—the salvation of your souls" (1 Pet 1:8–9 NET), he is using "soul" in the context of the resurrection (v. 3) to refer to the whole self, body included.[85] At least as far as salvation is concerned, the body seems just "as close to God!" Much more on that below.

A second and even more important issue regards how to understand gender dysphoria. On a Thomistic/hylomorphic account, Farris argues, the soul informs or configures the body, and there would be no mismatch, therefore, between biological sex and sexual gender. "The body is the matter that a soul informs. Some would call the soul the 'configured configurer.' On such an account, it is not clear that a soul could be mismatched with the opposing gendered body. Instead, the soul and the matter would simply be two constituents that constitute the person, and the gender is made manifest in the body."[86] Gender dysphoria must consequently be regarded as a delusion stemming from original sin, and since biological gender reflects the spiritual gender, biological gender is accurate.

Though traducianism, according to Farris, seems like a more likely possibility, it has its problems:

> Traducianism takes it that, on most accounts, God creates the first Adamic soul or the first pair, Adam and Eve, with a mechanism for splitting off potential souls at the moment of conception . . . Even if we assume that a mismatch between soul and body is possible, we could tell some story that the cause for the mismatch would be due to the problem of original sin somehow messing about with the biological process. What sort of origination story is needed to explain this possibility? To tell this story, one needs a plausible account of the origination process that separates the splitting off of future souls in that it is unaffected by the biological origins of the body.[87]

---

85. The word *soul* may, however, also be used in the more restricted sense in distinction from the body: "Do not be afraid of those who kill the body but cannot kill the soul. Instead, fear the one who is able to destroy both soul and body in hell" (Matt 10:28 NET). The focus here, however, is on the fragility and transience of the body, not that is only an external shell. The same point is made by Paul when he writes about "our earthly house, the tent we live in" being "dismantled" (2 Cor 5:1 NET). It is, after all, to be replaced by "our heavenly dwelling" (v. 2).

86. Farris and Cortez, *Introduction to Theological Anthropology*, 227.

87. Farris and Cortez, *Introduction to Theological Anthropology*, 227–28.

In other words, Farris suggests that according to traducianism, if the soul is generated along with the body at conception, then any mismatch between the soul and body would need to be explained in terms of the effects of original sin on the process of procreation. Farris then raises the question of what kind of explanation would be needed to account for this possibility within the framework of traducianism. He suggests that such an explanation would require a plausible account of how the process of soul generation (the "splitting off" of souls from the parents) is distinct from the biological origins of the body. In other words, if traducianism is to provide a coherent explanation for gender dysphoria, it would need to explain how the soul's development is affected by original sin independently of the biological development of the body. Here, creationism offers a simpler solution by arguing that while the body is created by God through secondary causes (procreation), the perfect and gendered soul (reflected in the biological gender) is immediately subject to original sin. Therefore, any discrepancy between biological and psychological gender should—in this model, too—be seen as a misconception stemming from original sin, with the biological gender reflecting the true gender.

Bodyology

A popular body-loathing pun in ancient times was σῶμα σῆμα, "the body is a tomb." In one of Plato's dialogues, Socrates says that the orphics were probably the inventors of this idea. Answering Hermogenes's question about the soul, Socrates states that

> I think this admits of many explanations, if a little, even very little, change is made; for some say it is the tomb [σῆμα] of the soul, their notion being that the soul is buried in the present life; and again, because by its means the soul gives any signs which it gives, it is for this reason also properly called "sign" [σῆμα]. But I think it most likely that the orphic poets gave this name, with the idea that the soul is undergoing punishment for something; they think it has the body as an enclosure to keep it safe, like a prison, and this is, as the name itself denotes, the safe [σῶμα] for the soul, until the penalty is paid, and not even a letter needs to be changed.[88]

---

88. Plato, *Cratylus*, 400b–c (cf. *Phaedrus*, 250c, *Gorgias*, 493a).

Epictetus, a Stoic philosopher from Greece in the first century AD and deeply influenced by Socrates, asks rhetorically: "But what says Zeus? Epictetus, if it were possible, I would have made both your little body and your little property free and not exposed to hindrance. But now be not ignorant of this: this body is not yours, but it is clay finely tempered."[89] In a similar manner, Seneca, a Stoic philosopher of Roman descent from the same era, articulates that the soul "is weighted down by a heavy burden and desires to be freed and to return to the elements of which it was once a part. For this body of ours is a weight upon the soul and its penance . . . I was born to a greater destiny than to be a mere chattel of my body, and I regard this body as nothing but a chain which manacles my freedom."[90]

In biblical anthropology, the body is not a tomb, a hindrance, a burden, or an addition to human identity but an integral part of it. The body is an essential part of the image of God. Both the physical and the spiritual, body and soul, are willed by God and therefore encompassed by God's assessment of the first creation: "And God saw everything that he had made, and behold, it was very good. And there was evening and there was morning, the sixth day" (Gen 1:31). And it still is in the sense that even after the fall, creation continues to display the Creator's magnificence, majesty, and glory (Pss 8; 19; 24), or as Paul summarizes it: "For every creation of God is good and no food is to be rejected if it is received with thanksgiving. For it is sanctified by God's word and by prayer" (1 Tim 4:4 NET). "Everything" obviously includes the body, and this idea is clearly expressed in Job 10:11, where Job says of God, "You clothed me with skin and flesh, and knit me together with bones and sinews." Likewise, it is stated in Ps 139:13 (NET) that "certainly you made my mind and heart; you wove me together in my mother's womb." And though the doctrine of resurrection is found only *in nuce* in the Old Testament, several passages more or less clearly expect the body to be part of the afterlife:

> Your dead will come back to life; your corpses will rise up. Wake up and shout joyfully, you who live in the ground! For you will grow like plants drenched with the morning dew, and the earth will bring forth its dead spirits. (Isa 26:19 NET)

---

89. Epictetus, *Discourses* 1.1.
90. Seneca, *Epistles* 65.16, 22.

> As for me, I know that my Redeemer lives, and that as the last he will stand upon the earth. And after my skin has been destroyed, yet in my flesh I will see God, whom I will see for myself, and whom my own eyes will behold, and not another. My heart grows faint within me! (Job 19:25–27 NET)
>
> So my heart rejoices and I am happy; My life is safe. You will not abandon me to Sheol; you will not allow your faithful follower to see the Pit. You lead me in the path of life; I experience absolute joy in your presence; you always give me sheer delight. (Ps 16:9–11 NET)
>
> Many of those who sleep in the dusty ground will awake—some to everlasting life, and others to shame and everlasting abhorrence. (Dan 12:2 NET)

Also relevant is the vision of the valley of dry bones, where Ezekiel prophesies to the bones, and they come together, are covered with sinews, flesh, and skin, and then receive breath to become a vast army. While this vision is often interpreted as a symbol of the restoration of Israel, it has also been seen as having broader implications related to resurrection. And though all these passages may not explicitly spell out the doctrine of resurrection as it is understood in Christian theology, they contain language and imagery that some interpret as pointing toward a hope for life after death or toward a future restoration. Furthermore, the passage from Ps 16 is directly quoted by the apostle Peter in his sermon on the day of Pentecost, as recorded in Acts 2:25–28, where he applies it to the resurrection of Jesus Christ. The apostle Paul also alludes to this passage in his sermon in Antioch of Pisidia (Acts 13:35–37), applying it to the resurrection of Christ and the fulfillment of God's promises.

Let us return, however, to the beginning. When in Gen 1:26 it says, "Let us make man in our image [צֶלֶם, ṣelem], after our likeness [דְּמוּת, dᵊmût]," both "visibility" and "corporeality" are part of the semantic fields of צֶלֶם, ṣelem, "image," and דְּמוּת, dᵊmût, "likeness." The former denotes a physical, carved, or sculpted statue or copy of something metaphysical. It is used in biblical Hebrew to describe various idols (e.g., 2 Kgs 11:18). When applied to God and humanity in Gen 1:26–27, it should be understood, as Marc Cortez formulates it, as "a declaration that God intended to create human persons to be the physical means through which he would manifest his own divine presence in the world."[91] Or, as Randall Garr has it, "The statue, then, is the vehicle through which a god resides

---

91. Cortez, *ReSourcing Theological Anthropology*, 109.

in the community, maintains a presence, receives worship and prayer, and can actively participate in society."[92] Our bodies are, in other words, tangible symbols or indicators of a divine mystery: "In fact, the *physical* body makes visible the *spiritual* realities of God's nature and covenantal love."[93] Or, as John Paul II phrases it, "The body, in fact, and only the body, is capable of making visible what is invisible: the spiritual and divine. It has been created to transfer into the visible reality of the world the mystery hidden from eternity in God, and thus to be a sign of it."[94] The body simply testifies to who I am, and without my body, Carl Trueman argues, it would be impossible to demonstrate that I am me: "[My body] is perhaps the foundational piece of evidence that, were I to claim that I am, for example, Attila the Hun or Nancy Pelosi, I would be talking nonsense, with my body as Exhibit A in the case for the prosecution. It is not simply instrumental to my identity; my identity is inseparable from it. To downgrade it to a mere incidental, or to set the real me in opposition to it, is a recipe for chaos."[95]

This understanding of the corporeality of humans is supported by comparative material showing that kings in both Egypt and Mesopotamia were considered physical images of the gods. For example, Tutankhamun's (1334–25 BCE) name means "Living Image of Amun," and on a stele erected in Amenhotep III's (1390–53 BCE) mortuary temple, the creator god Amun declares about Amenhotep:

> Speech of My son,
> of my body, my beloved Nebmare,
> my living image, my body's creation,
> Born of me by Mut, Lady of Ashru in Thebes,
> Mistress of the Nine Bows,
> Who nursed you to be the sole lord of peoples![96]

From Mesopotamia, an inscription from the time of Esarhaddon (681–68 BCE) describes the king as the embodied image of the deity Bel, thereby representing the power and grandeur associated with the god:

> What the king, [my lord] wrote to me: "I heard from the mouth
> of my father that you are a royal family, but now I know it from

---

92. Garr, *In His Own Image and Likeness*, 144.
93. Tennent and Fernando, *For the Body*, 17. Emphasis original.
94. John Paul II, *Redemption of the Body*, 19:4.
95. Trueman, "Triumph of the Social Scientific Method."
96. Lichtheim, *Ancient Egyptian Literature*, 46.

my own experience," the father of the king, my lord, was the very image of the god Bel, and the king, my lord is likewise the very image of Bel.[97]

Also, Amarna letter 19, titled "Love and Gold," describes the concept of humans being "images" of someone else. The letter discusses the gold trade from Egypt, the familial bonds between past monarchs, and the contemporary alliance between the king of Mitanni and the Pharaoh of Egypt. Responding to "my brother," i.e., the Egyptian king's request for his daughter in marriage, the king of Mittani replies:

> When my brother sent Mane, his messenger, saying, "Send your daughter here to be my wife and the mistress of Egypt," I caused my brother no distress and immediately I said, "Of course!" The one whom my brother requested I showed to Mane, and he saw her. When he saw her, he praised her greatly. I will l[ea]d her in safety to my brother's country. May Shaushka and Aman make her the image of my brother's desire.[98]

J. Richard Middleton further writes about the broader ancient Near Eastern background, stating:

> Various Egyptian and Mesopotamian kings were called "the image" of particular deities. In Egyptian and Mesopotamian royal ideology, the king was believed to be the royal representative of the gods on earth, a personal manifestation of divine presence and authority through whom the gods ruled the nation. Likewise, statues of the gods placed in temples were thought to be physical sites of divine power and presence on earth. These royal and cultic practices provide a conceptual background for understanding the human role in the cosmos as analogous to that of a king ruling over his nation: like a statue in a temple, the king was understood as a visible "image" of the gods, mediating their rule.[99]

The image of God, of course, is not limited to the corporeal, as Gen 2:7 emphasizes that נִשְׁמַת חַיִּים, "the breath of life," was a prerequisite for the physical human to become a נֶפֶשׁ חַיָּה, "living being." The same applies after the fall, where it is the same breath of life that keeps the body alive. In Ezekiel's vision of the dry bones, God repeats the

---

97. LAS 125 in Parpola, *Letters from Assyrian Scholars*, quoted from Gentry and Wellum, *Kingdom through Covenant*, 193.

98. EA 19.3.17–24, in Moran, *Amarna Letters*, 43–46.

99. Middleton, "Image of God," 518; cf. Middleton, *Liberating Image*, 104–22.

"reviving" from the morning of creation and says, "Come from the four winds, O breath, and breathe on these slain, that they may live ... and the breath came into them, and they lived" (Ezek 37:9–10, cf. Eccl 12:7; Wis 16:14). The breath of life is a prerequisite for the human body to live, but without corporeality, the human is not the human created in God's image. And without over-interpreting the order in Gen 2:7, God actually *first* "formed the man from the soil of the ground" *then* "breathed into his nostrils the breath of life" so that "the man became a living being."

In the New Testament, Paul encourages the Christians in Rome to offer their bodies "as a living sacrifice, holy and acceptable to God" (Rom 12:1). When Paul writes to the believers, "Do not present your members to sin as instruments for unrighteousness, but present yourselves to God" (Rom 6:13), he sees the body, referred to as "your members," and the personality, "yourselves," as inseparable. Moreover, believers don't just long for "the freedom that God's children will have in glory" but also for the eschatological redemption of their bodies: "[We], who have the Spirit as the firstfruits, groan inwardly as we eagerly wait for adoption as sons, the redemption of our bodies" (Rom 8:23). In his letters to the Corinthians, Paul reminds them that their bodies are the "temple of the Spirit" (1 Cor 3:16–17) and the "temple of the living God" (2 Cor 6:16). In 1 Cor 6:13–20, Paul uses the word σῶμα, meaning "body," eight times. Perhaps this emphasis is due to the presence of Christians in Corinth who were influenced by a dualistic thinking that separated the positive spiritual from the negative physical aspect of existence. Paul counters this by portraying the body unequivocally as a "body for the Holy Spirit" (v. 19). He stresses that "the body is for the Lord, and the Lord for the body" (v. 13). While Paul is concerned about warning against sexual immorality in this passage, his argument is not solely moral but also anthropological. This is because both the body and the spirit are created and positively willed by God, and because the male and female bodies are created to become one flesh, "the immoral person sins against his own body" (v. 18). Therefore, what we do with our bodies is never ethically neutral, as the body belongs to the Lord. Hence, Paul concludes with an exhortation to the Corinthian Christians: "So glorify God in your body" (v. 20).

In Paul's theology, there is no division between the external body and the inner person regarding the identity of the believer. As Preston Sprinkle puts it, "It doesn't seem that Paul's logic would support the notion that one's internal sense of self is more important for identity than their bodies are, or that there is an essential 'I' without a body. A disembodied 'you' is not a more real part of 'you' than your embodied 'you.'"[100]

The strongest argument for a positive view of the body and the body as inseparable from or integral to the soul comes, of course, from the incarnation. Christ's becoming flesh is never described in pejorative "Platonic" terms or as an accommodating concession. John, in his Gospel prologue, begins by stating that all things physical or material are created "through him, and without him was not anything made that was made" (1:3). And the unmistakable allusion to the creation account in Gen 1 makes it clear that all these physical "things" were "good." The embodied humans are even "very good." Furthermore, becoming *flesh*, according to verse 14, was a means of displaying God's glory: "And the Word became flesh and dwelt among us, and we have seen his glory, glory as of the only Son from the Father, full of grace and truth." Christ's "flesh" not only displays God's glory, however. The repeated emphasis on the *incarnate* Christ serves to emphasize that the restoration of man accomplished by Christ's work included the restoration of the body. This is clear from Heb 2:14–18, where it is "the offspring of Abraham," i.e., humans with body and soul, not non-corporeal angels, who made it *necessary* for Christ to become human "in every respect":

> Since therefore the children share in flesh and blood, he himself likewise partook of the same things, that through death he might destroy the one who has the power of death, that is, the devil, and deliver all those who through fear of death were subject to lifelong slavery. For surely it is not angels that he helps, but he helps the offspring of Abraham. Therefore, he had to be made like his brothers in every respect, so that he might become a merciful and faithful high priest in the service of God, to make propitiation for the sins of the people. For because he himself has suffered when tempted, he is able to help those who are being tempted. (Heb 2:14–18)

It was "in his body of flesh by his death" that he reconciled those "who once were alienated and hostile in *mind*, doing evil deeds" (Col 1:22 NET). And since doing evil deeds requires a *body*, Christ's reconciliation was *holistic* in that it encompassed the whole human person, that is, both body and soul.

Adding Paul's assertion that Christ "is the image [εἰκών cf. LXX Gen 1:26] of the invisible God, the firstborn of all creation," and that "by him

---

100. Sprinkle, "Sex, Gender, and Transgender Experiences: Part 7."

all things were created" (Col 1:15–16) to the equation, Christ arguably was the template for אָדָם (*ʔādām*, "humanity") in the beginning just as the *incarnate* Christ is a template for restored humanity. And just as first man as body and soul was a reflection of God's image, Christ restores man to reflect his image by both body and soul, "for in him all the fullness of deity lives in bodily form" (Col 2:9 NET). It is by "beholding the glory of the Lord" displayed in the *incarnate* Christ, believers "are being transformed into the same image from one degree of glory to another" (2 Cor 3:18). They are "predestined to be conformed to the image of his Son, in order that he might be the firstborn among many brothers" (Rom 8:29). It is Christ, the only *incarnated* image of God, who is "firstborn," followed by "many brothers" who are "born" or restored in the image of Christ and after his likeness. Paul makes it very clear later in his letter to the Romans (with my italics) that it is both body and soul (or mind) that is the result of this "birth" and affected by the restoration: "I appeal to you therefore, brothers, by the mercies of God, to present your *bodies* as a living sacrifice, holy and acceptable to God, which is your spiritual worship. Do not be conformed to this world, but be transformed by the renewal of your *mind*, that by testing you may discern what is the will of God, what is good and acceptable and perfect (12:1–3). It is in perfect congruency with the incarnation. Therefore, reconciliation through "his body of flesh by his death" is followed by bodily resurrection. Having explained that Jesus appeared to Cephas, the twelve, five hundred brothers, James, the apostles, and finally Paul himself, Paul asserts that "if Christ has not been raised"—as he appeared!—"your faith is futile and you are still in your sins" (1 Cor 15:5; 8:17). Or, as John puts it, "By this you know the Spirit of God: Every spirit that confesses Jesus as the Christ who has come in the flesh is from God" (1 John 4:2 NET). The body thus receives its greatest value and honor from the *incarnate* Christ and his bodily resurrection. That's why "we," as Paul phrases it "who have the firstfruits of the Spirit, groan inwardly as we eagerly await our adoption as sons, the redemption of our bodies" (Rom 8:23).

The passage in 1 Cor 15:42–44 is sometimes used to argue for a degrading of the body, but this would be a misunderstanding of the Greek term σῶμα πνευματικόν. Nancy Pearcey writes, "The term *spiritual body* is often misunderstood to mean something ghostly and intangible. But the adjective does not tell us what the body is made of or, rather, what powers it. By analogy, a gasoline engine is not made of gasoline but powered by it. The great church father Augustine explains, 'They will be spiritual not because they will cease to be bodies, but because they will be sustained by a quickening Spirit.' In the resurrection from the dead, our bodies will be fully powered and sustained by God's Spirit."[101] In a similar manner, when Paul distinguishes between flesh and spirit, "flesh" refers to the whole person—body and soul—cut off from God's "in-spiration," from his Holy Spirit.

> Moreover, if the Spirit of the one who raised Jesus from the dead lives in you, the one who raised Christ from the dead will also make your mortal bodies alive through his Spirit who lives in you. (Rom 8:11 NET)

> But I say, live by the Spirit and you will not carry out the desires of the flesh. For the flesh has desires that are opposed to the Spirit, and the Spirit has desires that are opposed to the flesh, for these are in opposition to each other, so that you cannot do what you want. (Gal 5:16–17 NET)

In Galatians, Paul clearly distinguishes between *living by* or being *led by* the Spirit or the flesh, and the body clearly plays a crucial role in both ways of living.

> Now the works of the flesh are obvious: sexual immorality, impurity, depravity, idolatry, sorcery, hostilities, strife, jealousy, outbursts of anger, selfish rivalries, dissensions, factions, envying, murder, drunkenness, carousing, and similar things. I am warning you, as I had warned you before: Those who practice such things will not inherit the kingdom of God! But the fruit of the Spirit is love, joy, peace, patience, kindness, goodness, faithfulness, gentleness, and self-control. Against such things there is no law. (Gal 5:19–23 NET)

In this terminology, the "flesh counts for nothing" (John 6:63), but when a person opens up to God's Spirit, the body becomes a dwelling place for the Spirit, "mak[ing] your mortal bodies alive," and enables the whole human being to carry out the desires of the Spirit!

Such a positive view is reflected in the earliest readings of the Bible. The early Christian apologist and philosopher Justin Martyr, for example, argues that

> we must now speak with respect to those who think meanly of the flesh, and say that it is not worthy of the resurrection nor of the heavenly economy, because, first, its substance is earth; and

---

101. Pearcey, *Love Thy Body*, 42. Emphasis original.

besides, because it is full of all wickedness, so that it forces the soul to sin along with it. But these persons seem to be ignorant of the whole work of God, both of the genesis and formation of man at the first, and why the things in the world were made. For does not the word say, *"Let Us make man in our image, and after our likeness?"* What kind of man? Manifestly He means fleshly man, For the word says, *"And God took dust of the earth, and made man."* It is evident, therefore, that man made in the image of God was of flesh. Is it not, then, absurd to say, that the flesh made by God in His own image is contemptible, and worth nothing? But that the flesh is with God a precious possession is manifest, first from its being formed by Him, if at least the image is valuable to the former and artist; and besides, its value can be gathered from the creation of the rest of the world. For that on account of which the rest is made, is the most precious of all to the maker.[102]

Based on Paul's distinction between σῶμα "body" and σαρκὸς "flesh," St. Francis reputedly called his body "Brother Ass" as an expression of his humility and his view of the body as a humble and sometimes stubborn creature that must be tamed and disciplined in service to the soul and God. He did this because he held the belief that the body should be treated with asceticism, providing it only with the essential sustenance necessary for physical function, akin to the treatment of a humble donkey used as a beast of burden. He would provide it with the minimal nourishment required for sustenance and occasionally administered self-inflicted blows when he felt he was sluggish, lazy, or deserving of physical discipline. However, upon his death, St. Francis expressed remorse for these extreme austerities and sought forgiveness from his body for the undue hardships he had imposed upon it. C. S. Lewis, in *The Four Loves*, draws attention to the dual description of the body as "brother" and "ass" as a precise expression of biblical anthropology:

> Man has held three views of his body. First there is that of those ascetic Pagans who called it the prison or the "tomb" of the soul, and of Christians like Fisher [Bishop John Fisher's head was chopped off by King Henry VIII in 1535] to whom it was a "sack of dung," food for worms, filthy, shameful, a source of nothing but temptation to bad men and humiliation to good ones. Then there are the Neo-Pagans (they seldom know Greek), the nudists and the sufferers from Dark Gods, to whom the body is glorious.

---

102. Justin Martyr, *On the Resurrection 7*. Emphasis original.

> But thirdly we have the view which St. Francis expressed by calling his body "Brother Ass." All three may be—I am not sure—defensible; but give me St. Francis for my money. Ass is exquisitely right because no one in his senses can either revere or hate a donkey. It is a useful, sturdy, lazy, obstinate, patient, lovable and infuriating beast; deserving now a stick and now a carrot; both pathetically and absurdly beautiful. So the body.[103]

Commenting on Lewis's (and John Piper's) "Christian hedonism," David Mathis notes that while the term "ass" may be attention-grabbing and difficult to overlook, it highlights our inherent tendency towards laziness and stubbornness, portraying us as the "infuriating beast" deserving of correction: "But I don't want you to miss the affection and warmth in the word *Brother*. I don't think Lewis says 'Brother' lightly. Just as Jesus doesn't say 'brother' lightly. I don't say it lightly. *Brother* accents the usefulness, sturdiness, patience, and lovability of these bodies, which are, Lewis says, 'absurdly beautiful.' And he steers a careful course between reverence and beauty—they are not to be revered but acknowledged and appreciated as 'absurdly beautiful.'"[104]

The Gnostic Connection

In biblical thinking, "the human mind is more deceitful than anything else" (Jer 17:9), whereas the body is reliable as it was designed to serve as the residence of both God incarnate and the Holy Spirit (John 1:14; 1 John 4:2; 1 Cor 6,19–20). Such thinking, according to James Nelson, is a fatal blow to all dualistic piety:

> That stunning prologue to the Fourth Gospel begins, "In the beginning was the Word . . ." The Word—God's own creative meaning and energy. And when the Word came to dwell with us, it became—what? A book? A creed? A theological system? A code of morality? No. To the everlasting embarrassment of all dualistic piety, it became flesh—full of grace and truth. Warm-blooded sexual flesh. And it still does. When we meet God in and through our sensuous, urinating, defecating, menstruating, lubricating, orgasmic, ejaculating, youthful, aging, frail, vigorous, hungry, and vulnerable human flesh, there is incarnation.[105]

103. Lewis, *Four Loves*, 65.
104. Mathis, "Brother Ass." Emphasis original.
105. Nelson, "Embracing the Erotic"; cf. Nelson, *Body Theology*, 108; Nelson, "On Doing Body Theology," 47.

As far as dualism is concerned, we have already contrasted biblical anthropology with the Platonic and Stoic denigration of the body, and in the early church, one had to continue the apologetic work that the New Testament had already begun regarding what we today call Neoplatonism, gnosticism, and docetism. Neoplatonism and gnosticism share similarities in their dualistic worldview, hierarchical understanding of reality, emphasis on asceticism and spiritual salvation, focus on knowledge as a path to salvation, and rejection of the material world. Both systems prioritize spiritual enlightenment and liberation from the constraints of physical existence, though they have distinct philosophical and historical contexts.

Docetism originated in early Christianity, likely in the first century CE. The term "docetism" comes from the Greek word δοκέω, which means "to seem" or "to appear." Docetism emerged as a theological viewpoint within certain Christian communities, particularly those influenced by gnostic thought and dualistic philosophies prevalent in the ancient Mediterranean world. The precise origins of docetism are not fully clear, but it likely arose as a response to questions about the nature of Jesus Christ's humanity and divinity. Docetists believed that Jesus only appeared to have a physical body and suffer on the cross, but he was purely divine and, therefore, not subject to physical suffering or death. This belief may have been influenced by various philosophical currents of the time, including dualistic views that denigrated the material world and exalted the spiritual realm. Early Christian writers, such as Ignatius of Antioch and Irenaeus, vigorously opposed docetism as a heresy, emphasizing the genuine humanity of Jesus Christ as essential to the Christian faith. Despite these condemnations, docetism persisted in various forms within certain Christian circles for several centuries before eventually fading from prominence.

Unlike the fading of docetism, Platonic and gnosticist denigration of the body has reappeared and continues to pose a threat to biblical anthropology. The malleability of the body in contemporary gender theory should, according to a controversial letter from N. T. Wright to the editor of *The Times*,[106] be seen as a modern counterpart to (proto)gnostic, dualistic texts like the Gospel of Thomas (second–third century):

> Sir, The articles by Clare Foges ("Gender-fluid world is muddling young minds," July 27) and Hugo Rifkind ("Social media

---

106. Hailes, "N. T. Wright Attacks 'Fashionable Fantasy.'"

is making gender meaningless," Aug 1), and the letters about children wanting to be pandas (July 29), dogs or mermaids (Aug 1), show that the confusion about gender identity is a modern and now internet-fueled, form of the ancient philosophy of Gnosticism.

The Gnostic, one who "knows," has discovered the secret of "who I really am," behind the deceptive outward appearance (in Rifkind's apt phrase, the "ungainly, boring, fleshly one").

This involves denying the goodness, or even the ultimate reality, of the natural world. Nature, however, tends to strike back, with the likely victims, in this case, being vulnerable and impressionable youngsters who, as confused adults, will pay the price for their elders' fashionable fantasies.

The Rt Rev Prof Tom Wright
St Mary's College, St Andrews

The gnostic roots of "gender-meaninglessness" are clear in Saying 22 of the Gospel of Thomas, where it is stated that "when you make the two one, and when you make the inside like the outside and the outside like the inside, and the above like the below, and when you make the male and the female one and the same so that the male not be male nor the female when you make eyes in place of an eye, a hand in place of a hand, a foot in place of a foot, an image in place of an image, then you will enter [the kingdom]."[107] Herbert Christian Merillat comments on this:

> The core message of the Gospel of Thomas appears in Saying 22 and the other logia that ring changes on the theme of two-becoming-one, looking back toward the androgynous unity that existed before the diversity found in worldly creation. Sayings 11, 16, 22, 61, 87, 106, and 114 bear on this theme of unity, and some readers find a similar message in sayings that give the "solitary" or "single one" a special status. Some, who agree that the two-becoming-one theme is at the heart of the Gospel, regard it principally as part of an early baptismal rite. It can be seen as a dramatization of "the initiate's putting off the body, putting on light, and returning to sexual oneness"—to the androgynous primal Adamic human being. It was, in this view, a mystery rite ensuring the initiate of oneness with God and with one's heavenly mate.[108]

---

107. Giversen, *Thomasevangeliet*, 36.
108. Merillat, "Gnostic Apostle Thomas."

We find a similar idea in the Gospel of the Egyptians, which was in use during Egypt in the second and third centuries CE and today known only fragmentarily from quotations in other works. According to Clement of Alexandria (ca. 150–ca. 215 CE), Jesus says in the gospel to Salome, "I came to destroy the works of the female," and in response to Salome's question about when this will happen, Jesus states that it will happen "when you trample on the garment of shame, when the two become one and the male with the female neither male nor female."[109] Ron Cameron comments on these fragments of the Gospel of the Egyptians:

> Each fragment endorses sexual asceticism as the means of breaking the lethal cycle of birth and of overcoming the alleged sinful differences between male and female, enabling all persons to return to what was understood to be their primordial and androgynous state. This theology is reflected in speculative interpretations of the Genesis accounts of the Creation and the Fall, according to which the unity of the first man was disrupted by the creation of woman and sexual division. Salvation was thus thought to be the recapitulation of Adam and Eve's primordial state, the removal of the body and the reunion of the sexes.[110]

When the Gospel of Thomas and other (proto)gnostic texts are seen as an intellectual background for the constructivist idea that our inner or personality defines our social or true gender, regardless of our external, biological sex, it is about the dissolution of boundaries and distinctions, which, according to biblical creation theology, is a prerequisite for a functional and blessed act of creation. If humanity was originally androgynous, as gnostic texts argue, then male and female genders are to be understood as just two "carnal" or "bodily" manifestations of a potentially infinite range of ways in which the male and female principles can manifest themselves.[111] It is not difficult to find examples of how the same line of thought emerges in modern perspectives on God-ordained sexuality. For instance, Robert Song writes in his book *Covenant and Calling: Towards a Theology of Same-Sex Relationships* that "sexual differentiation is therefore justified within marriage, but it is only justified

---

109. Quoted from James, *Apocryphal New Testament*, 11.

110. Cameron, *Other Gospels*, quoted from Kirby, "Gospel of the Egyptians."

111. The idea that man was originally androgynous is not only gnostic. As mentioned above, Genesis Rabbah 8:1 also reflects such an understanding with its quote from Rabbi Samuel bar Nahman: "When the Lord created Adam He created him double-faced, then He split him and made him of two backs, one back on this side and one back on the other side."

because marriage in creation is oriented to procreation. There are no other grounds that can provide the theological weight needed to require that marriage be sexually differentiated. However, this also implies that if procreation is no longer eschatologically necessary, then there are no grounds for requiring all committed relationships to be heterosexual."[112] The argument that the command to procreate itself is an argument for binary gender differentiation within heterosexual marriage is, of course, very biblical. The second part of Song's argument is problematic. Here, Song argues that since there will be no procreation in the resurrection, there is no longer a basis for requiring all "committed" relationships to be heterosexual. And since Christians are called to live the resurrection life here and now, it is not a biblical requirement that current "committed" relationships be exclusively heterosexual. Such thinking closely resembles the gnostic belief that, just as humans were originally androgynous and could manifest the "male" and "female" binary, they should be able to manifest this potential in regeneration. The limitation of this potential to male/female and heterosexual relationships is, in this understanding, a consequence of the fall. According to this perspective, the new life that Christians live becomes a liberation from this limitation, allowing them to realize the original, God-created potential, which can be realized other than in heterosexual marriage.

We have already mentioned Ignatius of Antioch and Irenaeus's critique of docetism; the latter especially played a crucial role in the early church's rejection of Neoplatonic and gnostic beliefs. The gnostics argued that reconciliation entailed a departure from the creation of the physical realm. The gnostic *Treatise on Resurrection*, according to Fellipe do Vale, articulates this perspective, which

> makes this particularly clear: just as the savior exchanged the corruptible world for the incorruptible one, we, in union with him, die, rise, and ascend. Yet, as with his resurrection and ascension, the flesh is not included: "For you will not pay back the superior element when you depart. The inferior element takes a loss, but what it owes is gratitude . . . What is the meaning of resurrection? It is the uncovering at any given time of the element that has "arisen." This is a direct result of the transience of material creation: "All changes, the world is an apparition . . . Resurrection is not of this sort, for it is real." But if resurrection does not require the body, only the ascension of the soul into that

---

112. Song, *Covenant and Calling*, 48.

which is incorruptible, resurrection is already available insofar as one does not live "according to (the dictates of) this flesh," for anyone "rushing toward this outcome (that is, *separation from the body*)" already possesses resurrection.[113]

Irenaeus's rejection of the gnostics' negative view of the body is an early expression of John Webster's insistence that God's actions in history flow from the very being of God as Trinity. Paraphrasing Vale's presentation of Irenaeus's argument, Irenaeus initiates his discourse with the concept of *pleroma*, or fullness, which resembles a central tenet in gnostic ideology.[114] However, he interprets this fullness as indicative of God's inner triune existence. Within the Father, Son, and Spirit resides perfect love and goodness, and the impetus for creation stems from an outward expression of the blessedness already inherent within God. Unlike the gnostic portrayal of creation, where God's act is motivated by arrogance or excess, Irenaeus posits creation as an extension of God's desire to share the abundance of presence in his immanent life. He asserts that God formed Adam not out of necessity but to bestow his blessings upon him. Before the creation of Adam and all things, the Word glorified the Father and was glorified by him. This contrast in motivation significantly impacts the resulting creation, transforming matter from a source of instability and wretchedness into an avenue for partaking in God's goodness. God creates to enable creation to share in his glory and goodness, which are eternally shared among the Father, Son, and Spirit and exemplified through the Son's incarnate relationship with the Father in the economy of salvation. This concept is vividly depicted by Irenaeus's analogy of God's creation through the Father's "two hands," namely the Son and the Spirit, who supersede the lesser gnostic deities as mediators of divine action. Consequently, what we witness in material creation is the result of a craftsman's loving workmanship, as intra-Trinitarian love and goodness manifest as external Trinitarian acts of love and goodness. Secondly, and crucial for biblical ethics, Irenaeus maintains that the divine plan must maintain internal consistency, portraying creation as the initial phase of a seamlessly unfolding whole. Material creation is טוֹב (*ṭôv*, "good") because it is an externalization of intra-Trinitarian love in which all entities have purposes for which they were created. And despite distortions arising after the onset of sin, it still holds the categories of

---

113. do Vale, *Gender as Love*, 183, quoting from Layton et al., *Gnostic Scriptures*, 455–56. Emphasis original.

114. do Vale, *Gender as Love*, 184–85.

creation. It provides insight into what it means to be a properly functioning example of that particular entity, even in the aftermath of sin. The unfolding of material creation follows a teleological path, aiming toward eschatological perfection *by* its initial purpose and function. In Martin Buber's words, "Creation is not a hurdle on the road to God; it is the road itself."[115] The implication for sexual ethics is obvious. If "the proper function of a being within a system is its fittingness, what it ought to do to a system of other beings doing what they ought to," the goodness of *binary* creation means that "sexed bodies also have a proper function, along with all other natural human traits, like our sociability and our ability to love."[116] For this reason, biblical ethics regarding gender and sexuality must start from the role and function assigned to man and woman in the original creation. Texts describing gender and sexuality in the fallen creation must then be read and interpreted on this basis, just as the corresponding ethical counseling must be "teleological," that is, in correspondence with and as an unfolding of the role and function of man and woman in original creation. As Vale puts it, "The proper function of a sexed body, in conjunction with its ability to love and its tendency toward sociability, is to organize and appropriate social goods to manifest itself socially. When it does so, gender emerges."[117]

The eschatological perfection of this "teleology" is expressed in incarnation and resurrection. Jesus was born, lived, and died a fully human life as God in the flesh, yet without sin. His resurrection was a bodily resurrection as a human being, the first fruits of all those whom God will raise (1 Cor 15:20–23). Jesus lived with all the experience of a human body and all the differentiation a human body possesses in comparison with other human bodies.[118] Similarly, the resurrection confirms the fundamentally positive view of the biological, physical body. In Luke 24:34–47 and John 20:20–27, one of the points is that the risen Jesus is not a revived corpse or a ghost, and that Jesus is not less incarnate than the resurrected one. The idea of bodily resurrection—the reunification of the soul with the body—will not be weakened considering Jesus's words in Matt 10:28: "Do not be afraid of those who kill the body [τὸ σῶμα] but cannot kill the soul [τὴν ψυχὴν]. Rather, be afraid of the One who can

---

115. Buber, *Between Man and Man*, 60.

116. do Vale, *Gender as Love*, 189.

117. do Vale, *Gender as Love*, 190.

118. Cf. The General Presbytery, Assemblies of God, "Transgenderism, Transsexuality, and Gender Identity."

destroy both soul [ψυχὴν] and body [σῶμα] in hell." Although the soul is briefly separated from the body, they are so inseparable that they will be reunited in heaven and hell, or as Robert Smith expresses it, "The soul is the soul of the body, as the body is the body of the soul."[119] Though Paul is clear about the intermediate state with its temporary disembodiment of the soul, he also, in 2 Cor 5:1–5, envisions the reembodiment of the soul in the resurrection:

> For we know that if our earthly house, the tent we live in, is dismantled, we have a building from God, a house not built by human hands, that is eternal in the heavens. For in this earthly house we groan, because we desire to put on our heavenly dwelling, if indeed after we have put on our heavenly house, we will not be found naked. For we groan while we are in this tent, since we are weighed down because we do not want to be unclothed, but clothed so that what is mortal may be swallowed up by life. Now the one who prepared us for this very purpose is God, who gave us the Spirit as a down payment. (2 Cor 5:1–5 NET)

Just as the evangelists describe both continuity and discontinuity in Jesus's resurrection body, Paul emphasizes in 1 Cor 15 that the difference between the natural and the glorified body is about mortality, not corporeality (though the character of that corporeality is only enigmatically described in the New Testament).

It is interesting that testimonies about near-death experiences (NDEs) also include experiences of having a body and thus reflect the New Testament's testimony on eschatological anthropology.[120] Some critics argue that the disparity between NDEs and the New Testament accounts warrants closer examination. Instead, it is argued that cultural expectations frame our visualizations of what will happen when we are near death. Cultural expectations could also be explained neurologically as a coping mechanism.[121]

In any case, the New Testament clearly explains that reconciliation is not complete without bodily resurrection, and true humanity is achieved by rising both spiritually and bodily with Christ. Whether the body and gender are also connected in the resurrection is a matter of debate, as there are texts that can be interpreted to suggest that there will

---

119. Smith, "Responding to the Transgender Revolution."

120. Cf., e.g, the NDE and Conversion Testimony by Dr. Donald Whitaker Kiraxes, "Amazing NDE and Conversion Testimony by Dr. Donald Whitaker (RIP)."

121. Marsh, *Near-Death Experiences*.

GENDER AND BODY IN BIBLICAL CREATION THEOLOGY

be no gender differentiation in the resurrected bodies. This includes Gal 3:28, but especially Mark 12:25 // Matt 22:30 // Luke 20:36, where Jesus says to the Sadducees that "in the resurrection, people will neither marry nor be given in marriage; they will be like the angels in heaven." However, several factors suggest that gender differentiation will also apply in the resurrection and that Jesus's response to the Sadducees does not necessarily exclude this. Ian Paul mentions that angels in both the Old and New Testaments are consistently male, not genderless, so Jesus's response does not rule out gender differentiation in the resurrected human body.[122] Paul also cites the early church theologian Jerome as representative of the Church Fathers' insistence that gender differentiation is inseparable from the resurrection of the body: "If the woman shall not rise again as a woman nor the man as a man, there will be no resurrection of the body for the body is made up of sex and members."[123] According to Ian Paul, Thomas Aquinas expresses the same idea in the *Compendium Theologiae*:

> Although risen men will not occupy themselves with such activities (as nutrition and reproduction), they will not lack the organs requisite for such functions. Without these organs, the risen body would not be complete. But it is fitting that nature should be completely restored at the renovation of risen man, for such renovation will be accomplished directly by God, whose works are perfect. Therefore all the members of the body will have their place in the risen, for the preservation of nature in its entirety rather than for the exercise of their normal functions.[124]

In addition, Preston Sprinkle points out that Jesus only says that we will not marry but not become sexless, and even though we do not explicitly hear about Jesus's gender after the resurrection, the New Testament authors consistently refer to him using masculine pronouns. The biblical material and early church theology conclude: "Our sexed embodied existence will carry on into the new creation and be part of our eternal state. This bears ethical significance as we think about male and female-embodied sex differences. If we were created male and female, and if this creation was deemed 'very good,' and if our future, glorified existence will be in a sexed body, then it would seem reasonably consistent that

---

122. Paul, "Male and Female in the Resurrection?"
123. Paul, "Male and Female in the Resurrection?"
124. Aquinas, *Light of Faith*, 178–79, quoted from Paul, "Male and Female in the Resurrection?"

we should honor and celebrate our embodied sex now."[125] Fellipe do Vale reaches the same conclusion by pointing to consummation as the eschatological goal of the teleological unfolding of initial creation. Grace redeems and perfects gender, and "eschatology ... does not abolish gender to remedy the influences of sin. Because 'all of [us] are one in Christ Jesus' (Gal 3:28), we await a world in which we will be gendered in ways that do not define our worth. In the new heaven and earth, mysterious as they remain, we will be women and men who know perfect justice in accordance with our worth."[126]

It's time to focus on the biblical texts relevant to formulating a theology of gender identity and sexuality, beginning with Gen 1 and 2.

MAN, MALE, AND MATE

In Gen 1 and 2, various terms describe different aspects of humanity, including notably the relationship between the generic, binary, and complementary aspects of humans. All three aspects derive their ontological and existential meaning from the image of God.

Being Human

In Gen 1, both אָדָם (ʔādām, v. 26) and הָאָדָם (hāʔādām, v. 28) are used in the generic sense of "humankind," and defined, ontologically, in relation to the image of God. The same is true in Gen 5:2, where God, having created "male and female," named *them*, that is, man *and* woman, אָדָם (ʔādām, "humankind" [וַיִּקְרָא אֶת־שְׁמָם אָדָם]). The lexeme אָדָם (ʔādām) is not used indisputably as a personal name until Gen 4:25 where it is stated euphemistically that "Adam knew his wife." The reason for this is that in Gen 2–3, the Hebrew אָדָם (ʔādām) is used with a prefixed, definite article, and since Hebrew never fronts personal names with the definite article, it should be translated either as "(generic) man" or "the not-yet-complete biological male human"—but *not* as the personal name for the individual person *Adam*. In Gen 3:8, the expression הָאָדָם וְאִשְׁתּוֹ (hāʔādām wəʔištô) could be taken—in isolation—to mean "the individual Adam and his wife," but again, since Hebrew never fronts personal names with the

---

125. Sprinkle, "Sex, Gender, and Transgender Experiences: Part 7"; Sprinkle, *Embodied*, 105–6.

126. do Vale, *Gender as Love*, 234.

definite article, it is better to understand it as an unusual mix of the generic הָאָדָם (*hāʔādām*) as a representative of humankind (including אִשְׁתּוֹ [*ʔištô*, "his woman"]) and אִשְׁתּוֹ (*ʔištô*) as either his (individual) wife or as a representative of her part of humankind. It could be argued, for the same reason, that the lexeme behind the translation "Eve" is also not used as a personal name, since "she" is referred to as "helper" (עֵזֶר [*ʕēzer*]; Gen 2:18) and "woman" (אִשָּׁה [*ʔiššāʰ*], Gen 2:22). Although the name חַוָּה (*ḥawwāʰ*) given by "man" to his "woman" in Gen 3:20 may be transliterated (roughly) as "Eve," its meaning is "life." This is clear from the subsequent explanation "because she was the mother of all living" in Gen 3:20, and illustrated by Gen 4:1, where "man" impregnated this "[mother of] life" with Cain. And though the expression וַיִּקְרָא (*wayyiqrāʔ*) + שֵׁם (*šēm*) is the normal way of describing the giving of a personal name, the use of the expression in Gen 5:2 to categorize man *and* woman generically as "humankind" cautions us to conclude that Eve is *only* a personal name. To this could be added that "Eve's" name חַוָּה (*ḥawwāʰ*) does not appear anywhere else in the Old Testament as a personal name. Further usage of אָדָם (*ʔādām*) and חַוָּה (*ḥawwāʰ*) demonstrate, however, that they are *also* used as personal names. In the patrilineal genealogy of Gen 5:1, 3–4, the lexeme אָדָם (*ʔādām*) is used as a personal name for the individual "Adam":

> This is the record of the family line of Adam [אָדָם, *ʔādām*]. When God created humankind [אָדָם, *ʔādām*], he made them in the likeness of God. He created them male and female; when they were created, he blessed them and named them "humankind" [אָדָם, *ʔādām*]. When Adam [אָדָם, *ʔādām*] had lived 130 years he fathered a son in his own likeness, according to his image, and he named him Seth. (Gen 5:1–3 NET)

The case of חַוָּה (*ḥawwāʰ*) in Gen 3:20 is more ambiguous. On the one hand, it has an etiological flavor that speaks in favor of understanding it generically or archetypically as "(mother of) life" or "life(giver)." This understanding is reflected in the Septuagint's *translation* with the substantive Ζωή (*Zoe*, "life", or Symmachus's translation with a participle "life-producer"). On the other hand, the same expression with וַיִּקְרָא (*wayyiqrāʔ*) + שֵׁם (*šēm*) followed by an explanatory כִּי (*kî*) "because" in Gen 4:25 (NET) indisputably refers to the individual Adam's wife, just as the explanation describes how "she" (third-person singular) names their son:

And Adam had marital relations with his wife [אִשְׁתּוֹ, ʔištô] again, and she gave birth to a son. She named him Seth [וַתִּקְרָא אֶת־שְׁמוֹ, wattiqrāʔ et-šᵉmô], saying, "God has given me another child in place of Abel because Cain killed him."

In the New Testament, 2 Cor 11:3 and 1 Tim 2:13–14 use Εὕα "Eve" regarding the name-giving in Gen 3:20, and the most natural understanding of those passages would be to take "Eve" as a personal name, and that, in Jewish conception, Adam and Eve were the first people, the parents of everyone (whether genealogically and/or genetically in the modern scientific meaning of the words). Though we have a generic or archetypical use of אָדָם (ʔādām) as "humankind" in Gen 2–3, חַוָּה (ḥawwāʰ) seems to be used as a personal name with an archetypical *explanation*. This is reflected in the Vulgate's *transliteration* of חַוָּה (ḥawwāʰ) as (the name) "Hava."

Male and Female

It is only subsequently that we hear about the creation of humanity with the binary gender polarity זָכָר (zāxār, "male") and נְקֵבָה (nᵉqēvāʰ, "female"): "God created humankind in his own image, in the image of God he created him; male and female he created them" (Gen 1:27). That Gen 1 describes a "subsequence" becomes clear if the narrative in Gen 2 is read as an explication of God's creation of man on day 6. Man is created first (הָאָדָם, hāʔādām; 2:7), and the binary gender is only established with the creation of the woman in verses 21–22 (אִשָּׁה, ʔiššāʰ).

The Bible mentions only these two *biological* genders: זָכָר, (zāxār), meaning "male," and נְקֵבָה, (nᵉqēvāʰ), meaning "female." The concept of intersexuality, as understood today, was not recognized during biblical times. Rabbinic sources use the terms "eunuch" (born or castrated), "androgynous" (with both male and female sexual characteristics), *tumtum*, (a person with no discernible masculine or feminine genitalia), and *'aylonith* (a barren woman, wombless or otherwise incapable of conception). Genesis Rabbah 8:1 describes Adam as created androgynous—an interpretation accepted by the Medieval Jewish commentator Rashi. *Tumtum* appears 17 times in the Mishna, 23 times in the Tosefta, 119 times in the Babylonian Talmud, 22 times in the Jerusalem Talmud, and hundreds of times in midrash and commentaries. One example is the medieval text Sefer HaChinukh 606:2–5 in which it is stated (regarding Mishnah Bikkurim 1:5) that "the obligation of the commandment of the recital of the first fruits is not upon all that bring first-fruits to the Temple, as there are those that bring [them] but do not recite. And these are them: a woman; a *tumtum* [טֻמְטוּם] and an *androginos* [אַנְדְּרוֹגִינוֹס] (the latter two being those the sex of which is in doubt)—since these are not able to say, from 'the land that the Lord gave me,' as the land was only distributed to definite males."[127] The term *'aylonit* occurs in the Talmud, where it is stated that "we too will say: *Ailonit* [אַיְילוֹנִית], a sexually underdeveloped woman, is a term meaning: Like a ram [*dukhranit*], because like a male sheep [*ayyil*] she does not bear children" (Ketubot 11a, 1), and in Mishna, where it is said that "a woman who is twenty years old who did not grow two pubic hairs and was never classified as a young woman shall bring proof that she is twenty years old, and from that point forward she assumes the status of a sexually underdeveloped woman [אַיְילוֹנִית], who is incapable of bearing children" (Niddah 5, 9).[128]

The *modern* term "intersex" is a broad term encompassing diverse situations where certain aspects of an individual's physical anatomy deviate from typical expectations for either male or female. This can result in ambiguity regarding the individual's biological sex. Medical literature tends to use the terms "disorders or sexual development" or "differences of sexual development (DSDs)," "variations of sexual development" (VSD), and "congenital conditions of sexual development" (CCSDs). Some intersex persons might combine both male and female biological categories, but this does not entail that they constitute a third gender. Intersex conditions are considered biologically based variation *within* maleness or femaleness. Though Anne Fausto-Sterling, the "fairy godmother of the intersex gambit,"[129] argues that biological sex should be understood as a continuum rather than a binary, this is not supported by the medical definitions. Instead of Fausto-Sterling's 1.7 percent intersexed births, the real number is 0.018 percent: most individuals often categorized as intersex are unambiguously male or female. As Preston Sprinkle reminds us: "No intersex person has an innovative new sex organ called a 'plankerton' (or whatever) that's neither penis nor vagina, neither male nor female. They may have atypical features in their male or female anatomy, or they might have a blend of male and female parts, but

---

127. Nataf, "Sefer HaChinukh."

128. Quotations from The William Davidson digital edition of the Koren Noé Talmud, with commentary by Rabbi Adin Even-Israel Steinsaltz at https://www.sefaria.org.

129. Favale, *Genesis of Gender*, 126.

this doesn't mean there are more than two biological sexes. It seems more accurate to say that some people exhibit a combination of both—the only two—biological sexes."[130] Another point mentioned by Sprinkle is that intersex persons are different from persons who experience a mismatch between their biological sex and gender identity. Interpersons "factually *are* intersex... The claims of their ontological reality—*that* their biological sex is ambiguous or blended—are indisputable and objectively verifiable. Claims about gender identity, in contrast, carry a whole different set of ontological assumptions about human nature."[131] In a binary framework, a true interperson would have to choose, ideally, either a male or female gender identity. In contrast, a person's choice of gender identity in contrast with his or her undisputed biological sex involves a discussion on brain gender. Notably, Stephanie Lynn Budin, who otherwise questions the application of modern notions of masculinity and femininity to the ancient world, agrees. Quoting a different study from 2000, Budin writes that "true hermaphrodites constitute 0.0117 per 1,000 live births worldwide" and that "very few humans are hermaphroditic/intersex, that is, *both* female and male. There are no neutered humans because of the effect of the indispensable X chromosome that will automatically turn anybody female without an intervening and fully functional Y chromosome 'patch.' And the most common 'intersexing' genetics only manifest in the cells, not on the bodies."[132]

To return to זָכָר (zāxār, "male") and נְקֵבָה (nᵊqēvāʰ, "female"), the former is used in approximately 10 percent of the cases where the Hebrew Bible refers to a "man," that is denoting male in contrast to the female. There are no instances of זָכָר (zāxār) where maleness is not the dominant meaning, and the binary approach to biological gender is so strong that even etymology supports it.[133] Brettler acknowledges Barr's warning that the original meaning of a word does not necessarily carry over into its later usage. Still, in this case, it makes sense to consider etymology. The word נְקֵבָה (nᵊqēvāʰ) is etymologically "unusually transparent," Brettler claims, as it originates from the root *nqb*, meaning "to penetrate." Therefore, it must be understood, as Brettler argues, as "a biological term similar to the cuneiform munus sign of the female pubic

---

130. Sprinkle, *Embodied*, 122.
131. Sprinkle, *Embodied*, 124. Emphasis original.
132. Budin, *Gender in the Ancient Near East*, 8.
133. Cf. the discussion on the etymology in the cognate expressions in Sumerian, Akkadian, and Egyptian.

triangle."¹³⁴ Even though the etymological background of זָכָר (zāxār) is more debated, according to Brettler, there are good arguments to understand it in the light of the Semitic root zkr, which, as a noun, means "phallus." Brown-Driver-Briggs (BDB) also mentions a cognate Arabic word that denotes the male genitalia.¹³⁵ While this root is not attested in this sense in biblical Hebrew, the fact that זָכָר (zāxār), specifically, is used in the context of (male) circumcision (e.g., Exod 12:48) supports this interpretation. Thus, in this interpretation, the terms זָכָר (zāxār) and נְקֵבָה (nᵊqēvāʰ) would mean "one with a penis" and "one who is penetrated," respectively. Brettler emphasizes that the users of these biblical Hebrew terms probably did not have these etymological meanings in mind. Still, they nevertheless used them consciously to mean "a biological male" and "a biological female."¹³⁶ This "biological" meaning is also underlined by the fact that the description in Gen 1:26–27 is followed by the "reproduction command" פְּרוּ וּרְבוּ וּמִלְאוּ (pᵊrû ûrvû ûmilʔû), meaning "be fruitful and multiply and fill [the earth]." It is also supported by the fact that these terms are not only used for humans but also for the biological gender differentiation in animals (e.g., Gen 7:3), and that Jeremiah uses it to describe what a man can physically do and what a woman cannot. The rhetorical question "Can a man [זָכָר, zāxār] give birth to children?" is followed by a statement about the biological difference between a man and a woman: "Why do I see every man with his hands on his waist as a woman in labor [כַּיּוֹלֵדָה, kayyôlēdāʰ]?" (Jer 30:6). Therefore, the command and reference to reproduction would not make sense if the lexemes זָכָר (zāxār) and נְקֵבָה (nᵊqēvāʰ) exclusively referred to "brain gender," that is, psychological or social gender.

It has been objected to the linkage between the image of God and gender polarity in the understanding of זָכָר (zāxār, "male"), and נְקֵבָה (nᵊqēvāʰ, "female"), that since it also applies to animals, and animals are not created in the image of God, gender polarity cannot be associated with the image of God in Gen 1:26–27. However, even though gender polarity is also a characteristic of animals and thus not unique to humans, it is still linked to the image of God. When Gen 1:27 says, "So God created mankind in his own image, in the image of God he created him; male and female he created them," the last clause, "male and female

---

134. Brettler, "Happy Is the Man," 199; cf. the discussion on Sumerian MUNUS above.

135. BDB, 271.1.

136. Brettler, "Happy Is the Man," 199.

he created them," should be understood as explanatory or clarifying in relation to the preceding "in his own image God created mankind." The same applies to circumcision. Although זָכָר (*zāxār*), when paired with נְקֵבָה (*nᵊqēvāʰ*), can denote the masculine in both humans and animals, it refers exclusively to the male human when the context is circumcision. Karl Barth writes in response to the objection that "every other differentiation and agreement will continually prove to be preliminary or supplementary as compared with the fact that they are male and female. And this strictly natural and creaturely factor, which is held in common with the beasts, is not in any sense an animal element in man but the distinctively human element—not in itself but because it has pleased God to make man in this form of life an image and likeness, a witness, of His own form."[137] What makes maleness and femaleness a distinct human feature is not, therefore, their maleness or femaleness in itself, but the way gender differentiation should reflect the image of God. Quoting Heather Looy, Mark Yarhouse suggests that the relationship between male and female should reflect God's *genderfulness*: "The 'genderfulness' of God [may have been] deliberately separated into female and male by God in the creation of humankind as a way of structuring into creation a basic need for us to be in a relationship, so that is it in community, not individually, that we most fully reflect God's image and are most fully equipped for the tasks to which we are called."[138] That this is not merely an exotic idea is underscored by the fact that Scripture regularly depicts God with gendered characteristics. Although God reveals himself in the "masculine" and was incarnated in the *man* Jesus Christ, both are also described with feminine traits:

- God comforts his people like a mother comforts her child (Isa 66:13).
- Like a woman would never forget her nursing child, God will not forget his children (Isa 49:15).
- God is like a mother eagle hovering over her young (Deut 32:11).
- God cares for his people like a midwife that cares for the child she just delivered (Ps 22:9–10; Ps 71:6; Isa 66:9).

---

137. Barth, *Church Dogmatics* 3.1, quoted from Meadowcroft, "Vive La Différence!," 199.

138. Yarhouse, *Understanding Gender Dysphoria*, 38; cf. Looy, "Male and Female God Created Them," 17.

- God experiences the fury of a mother bear robbed of her cubs (Hos 13:8).
- God seeks the lost like a housekeeper, trying to find her lost coin (Luke 15:8–10).
- Jesus longed for the people of Jerusalem like a mother hen longs to gather her chicks under her wings (Luke 13:34).

Anselm famously captured this "genderfulness" at the end of a prayer to St. Paul, composed ca. 1070 CE:

> And you, Jesus, are you not also a mother?
> Are you not the mother who, like a hen,
> gathers her chickens under her wings?
> Truly, Lord, you are a mother;
> for both they who are in labour
> and they who are brought forth
> are accepted by you.
> You have died more than they, that they may labour to bear.
> It is by your death that they have been born,
> for if you had not been in labour,
> you could not have borne death;
> and if you had not died, you would not have brought forth.
> For, longing to bear sons into life,
> you tasted of death,
> and by dying you begot them.
> You did this in your own self,
> your servants, by your commands and help.
> You as the author, they as the ministers.
> So you, Lord God, are the great mother.
>
> Then both of you are mothers.
> Even if you are fathers, you are also mothers.
> For you have brought it about that those born to death
> should be reborn to life—
> you by your own act, you by his power.
> Therefore you are fathers by your effect
> and mothers by your affection.
> Fathers by your authority, mothers by your kindness.
> Fathers by your teaching, mothers by your mercy.
> Then you, Lord, are a mother
> and you, Paul, are a mother too . . .
>
> And you, my soul, dead in yourself,

> run under the wings of Jesus your mother,
> and lament your griefs under his feathers.
> Ask that your wounds may be healed
> and that, comforted, you may live again.
>
> Christ, my mother,
> you gather your chickens under your wings;
> this dead chicken of yours puts himself under those wings.
> For by your gentleness, the badly frightened are comforted,
> by your sweet smell the despairing are revived,
> your warmth gives life to the dead,
> and your touch justifies sinners.
> Mother, know again your dead son,
> both by the sign of your cross and the voice of his confession.
> Warm your chicken, give life to your dead man, justify your sinner.
> Let your terrified one be consoled by you;
> despairing of himself, let him be comforted by you;
> and in your whole and unceasing grace
> let him be refashioned by you.
> For from you flows consolation for sinners;
> to you the blessing for ages and ages. Amen.[139]

The Bible unequivocally states that God is spirit (John 4:24), so he is not gendered. When we refer to him as "Father," we are not suggesting, Eric Naus argues, that he possesses male characteristics akin to human fathers.[140] Rather, we are acknowledging that he interacts with us like a human father. He cares for, protects, guides, and even disciplines us, much like the best human fathers, though he does so with perfect wisdom and love (Matt 6:25–30; 6:7–11; Heb 12:7–10). Likewise, when the Bible depicts God as a husband, it is not suggesting that God is male; instead, it conveys that God passionately safeguards his relationship with his people, reflecting the way a faithful husband loves and protects his wife (Hos 2:16, 19). At the same time, all these traits nevertheless portray who God *is*. They are his attributes, and in this light, there is good reason to use the term "genderfulness" about God.

---

139. Anselm, *Prayers and Meditations*, 152–56.
140. Naus, "God's Feminine Attributes."

Man and Woman

Where הָאָדָם (hāʔādām) denotes humans generically and זָכָר (zāxār) and נְקֵבָה (nᵊqēvāʰ) describe the biological binary of humans, the terms אִישׁ (ʔîš) and אִשָּׁה (ʔiššāʰ) indicate the binary gender's functional and existential complementarity. Functional, because the two genders have different roles in the task of being fruitful, numerous, filling the earth, and subduing it (Gen 1:28); existential, because in relation to each other, they are the most complete reflection of the divine image. Complementarity, because the binary gender is the solution to the "aloneness" that the human experienced before becoming אִישׁ (ʔîš, "man") and אִשָּׁה (ʔiššāʰ), "woman"). And though neither of the lexemes זָכָר (zāxār, "male") nor נְקֵבָה (nᵊqēvāʰ, "female") is used in Gen 2, a canonical reading necessitates the correlation between זָכָר (zāxār, ["biological"] male) (1:27; 5:2) and אִישׁ (ʔîš, "[complementary] man") on the one hand, and נְקֵבָה (nᵊqēvāʰ, "[biological] female") and אִשָּׁה (ʔiššāʰ, "[complementary] woman") on the other. Both because Gen 2, in its canonical or literary setting, functions as an explanation of Gen 1, and because Jesus, in Matt 19:4–5, *combines* the expressions from Gen 1 and 2: "Have you not read that from the beginning the Creator made them male and female [ἄρσεν and θῆλυς = זָכָר (zāxār, "male") and נְקֵבָה (nᵊqēvāʰ, "female")], and said, 'For this reason, a man [ἄνθρωπος = אִישׁ (ʔîš, "[complementary] man")][141] will leave his father and mother and will be united with his wife [γυνή = אִשָּׁה (ʔiššāʰ, "[complementary] woman")], and the two will become one flesh?'"

As for complementarity, it is reflected in the human's reaction to the creation of the woman:

> Then the man said, "This one at last is bone of my bones and flesh of my flesh; this one will be called 'woman,' for she was taken out of man." (Gen 2:23 NET)

Where "for Adam, no companion who corresponded to him was found" among the animals (Gen 2:20), his first encounter with the woman was a moment of mutual recognition: the man is not only naming the woman *'ishshah* but also renaming himself *ish*. In Gen 2, it is emphasized that even though man and woman are different, they are created for and to complement each other. The woman is described as

---

141. The Septuagint uses ἀνδρός for אִישׁ (ʔîš) in 2:23, but Matthew's use of ἄνθρωπος is probably due to the interchangeable use of ἄνθρωπος for ἀνδρός in 2:24: "That is why a man [MT: אִישׁ (ʔîš); LXX: ἄνθρωπος] leaves his father and mother and unites with his wife, and they become a new family."

an ʕēzer kᵉnegdô, "a helper corresponding to him" (2:18). The English word "helper" is ambiguous, however, since the Hebrew term denotes allied soldiers who "help" in battle (e.g., Josh 1:14; 1 Chr 12:1–22) or God who "helps" Israel (e.g., Gen 49:25; Exod 18:4; Deut 33:29; 1 Sam 7:12; Isa 41:10–14; Ps 10:14; 20:2; 33:20; 70:5; 124:8; 2 Chr 32:8). It can refer to both a superior and an equal, but never, in its over ninety instances, designate what subordinates or servants do for their superiors.[142] Furthermore, the qualification kᵉnegdô—literally "corresponding to the front of him"—should be preferred: "a companion for him who corresponds to him." Robert Chisholm points out that arguments in favor of the intended concept of male headship are based on uncertain or unstable foundations.[143] Indeed, when a name is "called over" an object, it often signifies authority.[144] However, names are also commonly given based on the apt and fitting descriptions of the object itself.[145] Chisholm writes, "Any idea of ownership or authority must be derived from the context (as when a conqueror renames a town, Judg 1:17); it is not inherent in the expression itself... Yet, the context views them as a unified entity (1:26–28) and focuses on the correspondence between them (2:18).[146]

Also worth mentioning is the fact that the woman was created from אַחַת מִצַּלְעֹתָיו (ʔaḥat miṣṣalʕōtāʸw, "a part of man's side") (Gen 2:21). Given that, in ancient Hebrew anthropology, the rational and emotional faculties were believed to reside in the internal organs, it is likely that this suggests that the woman shared in man's capacities for understanding, reason, and agency.

The enigmatic expression נְקֵבָה תְּסוֹבֵב גָּבֶר (nᵉqēvāʰ tᵉsôvēv gāver, "a woman encircles a man") in Jer 31:22 probably also adds to this understanding. The "enigmatic" character is evidenced both by the BHS editors' rearrangement of the Hebrew consonantal text (they suggest the reading *maledicta mutatur in dominam*, "the cursed are turned into a lady/queen") and the various translations of Jeremiah as it stands:

---

142. God or the Lord, for example, is often described as an ʕēzer: Exod 18:4; Deut 33:29; 1 Sam 7:12; Ps 20:2; 33:20; 70:5; 124:8.

143. Chisholm, "Male and Female," 68–69.

144. Cf. Deut 28:10; 2 Sam 12:28; 1 Kgs 8:43; 2 Chr 6:33; 7:14; Isa 4:1; 63:19; Jer 7:10–11, 14, 30; 15:16; 25:29; 32:34; 34:15; Dan 9:18–19; Amos 9:12.

145. Cf. Gen 16:13; Ruth 4:17; 1 Sam 9:9; 2 Sam 18:18; Prov 16:21; Isa 1:26; 32:5; 35:8; 62:4, 12; Jer 19:6.

146. Chisholm, "Male and Female," 69.

> How long will you vacillate, you who were once like an unfaithful daughter? For I, the LORD, promise to bring about something new on the earth, something as unique as a woman protecting a man! (NET; cf. RSV)
>
> How long will you waver, O faithless daughter? For the LORD has created a new thing on the earth: a woman encircles a man. (ESV)
>
> How long will you go here and there, You rebellious daughter? For the LORD has created a new thing on the earth: A woman will encompass a man. (NASB)
>
> How long will you waver, O rebellious daughter? For the LORD has created something new on earth: A woman courts a man. (JPS)
>
> How long will you waver, O faithless daughter? For the LORD has created a new thing on the earth: a woman protects a man. (RSV)

In this passage, Jeremiah speaks metaphorically of Israel as a wayward daughter who has turned away from God and needs to return to him. He urges the people to cease their wandering and recommit to their faith. Though the phrase "a woman shall compass a man" is cryptic and open to interpretation, it suggests a reversal of traditional roles. It may allude to significant events like the virgin birth of Jesus or the restoration of Israel's fortunes under divine protection. John Yates remarks that the difficult expression is followed by the promise of the new covenant in vv. 31–34, and that "it seems to mean that previously rebellious Israel will now cling tenaciously to the LORD. Ultimately this speaks of the church as the Bride holding fast to Christ her Head (Eph 5:23). Since the word for 'encircle' in Jeremiah is the same used in Deut 32 for the work of the Spirit in the glory cloud, it points to the church entering into the glory of God in the Spirit as it is penetrated by the Word."[147] Deborah Sawyer's take on the text is also worth mentioning:

> The Jeremiah passage (31:15–22) uses tropes from the creation narratives to describe the new thing that God is doing. The reference to the woman grieving over her children recalls the punishment of Eve related to her childbearing (Gen 3:16) and the violent loss of her son, Abel (4:25). The punishment is being reversed in an act of God that will bring missing children home. In 31:22, God sums up the reversal by alluding to a new creation with the conscious use of the verb used with God as subject in the creation narrative: ברא. The passage ends with

147. Yates, "New Vision of the Father."

this verse: נקבה תסובב גבר ("a woman encircles a man") which may allude to Gen 3:16 where the fraught woman/man relationship, marked by notions of longing and rule, gives way in Jeremiah's image to a union of great intimacy. The sexual imagery of the encirclement of the man reverses the usual imagery of (male) penetration. It is an image from a woman's perspective, conjuring ideas of nourishment and protection of a vulnerable figure. The inversion of expected female/male power relations provides a striking picture of Israel's eschatologically renewed life with God.[148]

This is a far cry from descriptions of the woman as "defective" or important only as far as procreation is concerned! In his "literary" commentary on Genesis, Augustine argues that "I do not see, therefore, in what other way the woman was made to be the helper of the man if procreation is eliminated."[149] Thomas Aquinas, in a similar vein, notes that the only aspect in which the woman is not "defective" and "misbegotten" is her role in reproduction: "As regards the individual nature, woman is defective and misbegotten, for the active force in the male seed tends to the production of perfect likeness in the masculine sex; while the production of woman comes from a defect in the active force or from some material indisposition, or even from some external influence. On the other hand, as regards human nature in general, woman is not misbegotten but is included in nature's intention as directed to the work of generation."[150] In *Paradise Lost*, John Milton presents Eve and women as potentially weak and morally compromised in several passages, particularly in Book 9. For instance, Eve's temptation and fall in the garden of Eden, where she yields to the serpent's persuasion and eats the forbidden fruit, portrays her vulnerability to deception and temptation. Additionally, Milton describes Eve's desire for independence and knowledge as leading to her disobedience to God's command, suggesting a moral weakness in her character. Reflecting on her own desires and inclinations, Eve, in Milton's words, withdraws from Adam's hand and associates herself with nature instead of the image of God by comparing herself to a wood nymph, a supernatural being associated with nature. The mention of Delia, another name for the moon goddess Artemis in Greek mythology, adds to the imagery of divine grace and beauty. Eve's demeanor is likened to that of

---

148. Sawyer, "Gender-Play and Sacred Text," 99–111.
149. Augustine, *Literal Meaning of Genesis* 9.7.
150. Aquinas, *Summa Theologica* I, Q92, A1, ad. 1.

a goddess, even though she lacks the weapons typically associated with deities. Instead, she is depicted with simple gardening tools, highlighting her innocence and closeness to nature. The comparison to Pomona and Ceres, goddesses of fruitfulness and agriculture, further emphasizes Eve's connection to the earth and fertility:

> Thus saying, from her husband's hand her hand
> Soft she withdrew; and, like a Wood-Nymph light,
> Oread or Dryad, or of Delia's Traine,
> Betook her to the Groves; but Delia's self
> In gait surpassed, and Goddess-like deport,
> Though not as she with Bow and Quiver arm'd,
> But with such Gardening Tools as Art yet rude,
> Guiltless of fire, had form'd, or Angels brought.
> To Pales, or Pomona, thus adornd,
> Likelist she seem'd, Pomona when she fled
> Vertumnus—or to Ceres in her Prime,
> Yet virgin of Proserpina from Jove.[151]

Such an understanding of the woman, as persistent as it may be in later interpretation, cannot be supported by the biblical text. Abigail Favale, quoting philosopher Edith Stein, even goes as far as to argue that, instead of portraying the woman as weak, her role in the fall narrative indicates her influence: "One can see a similitude between the narrative of the Fall and the Annunciation, when Mary is approached by a divine messenger ... Philosopher Edith Stein puts it this way: 'As woman was the first to be tempted, so did God's message of grace come first to a woman, and each time woman's assent determined the destiny of humanity as a whole.' The woman's temptation indicates not her weakness but rather her influence: a woman's assent has the power to shape and reshape humankind."[152] In any case, there is no idea of defection or "misbegottenness" in the text, which precisely underscores the equal complementarity. The difference or "inequality" between man and woman in the text must be understood in the context of the correlation between male/man and female/woman and the ontological significance it holds in light of the fundamental nature of being created as human in the image of God. As Katie McCoy phrases it, the difference constitutes a "'polaric complementarity,' a corresponding oppositeness that reflects

---

151. Milton, *Paradise Lost*, Book 9, lines 385–96.
152. Favale, *Genesis of Gender*, 45–46.

interdependence and congruence."[153] Favale borrows the term "polaric complementarity" from James Stoner Budziszewski, who, in *On the Meaning of Sex*, explains it by arguing that "men and women aren't just different, but different in corresponding ways. They are complementary opposites—alike in their humanity, but different in ways that make them natural partners."[154] Whereas the terms "male" and "female" obviously point to the corresponding *biological* difference, the lexemes "man" and "woman" explain how their likeness gives ontological meaning to their difference. Sam Allberry writes: "What first leaps out at Adam is not all the things that are *different* between Eve and him but the very fundamental way in which she is *like* him. There are differences. He's not oblivious to that—evidenced by the one-flesh union they quickly enter into. But more fundamental than the obvious differences between men and women is the more fundamental likeness. Our human commonality precedes our sexual difference."[155] The "likeness," expressed through the assonant terms אִישׁ (*ʔîš*, "man") and אִשָּׁה (*ʔiššāʰ*, "woman") are explained as *kinship*. The woman "is bone of my bones and flesh of my flesh." In anthropological terminology, "kinship" refers to the social relationship between individuals or groups based on blood ties, marriage, or adoption. It encompasses the various ways in which people are related to each other through familial connections, including biological relatives such as parents, siblings, and cousins, along with relationships formed through marriage or other social arrangements. Kinship systems vary across cultures and societies, influencing patterns of family structure, inheritance, and social organization, and to understand the "biblical variation" of the term, we need to situate the expression in its ontological context and the light of other instances of the expression. In other parts of Scripture, expressions such as "you are my flesh" are employed to denote familial connections. For instance, Laban refers to Jacob, his cousin, as "my own flesh and blood" (Gen 29:14), Abimelech reminds his supporters that "I am your own flesh and blood" (Judg 9:2), and the tribes of Israel remind David that "we are your own flesh and blood" (2 Sam 5:1; cf. 16:11; 19:12–13). In all of these instances, the kinship bond referred to is *not* a sexual or marital relationship between man and woman but relationships

---

153. McCoy, "What It Means," 146.
154. Budziszewski, *On the Meaning of Sex*, 42.
155. Allberry, *What God Has to Say*, 72. Emphasis original.

(mostly male) through biological relatives or connections through marriage or other social arrangements.

In queer interpretation, it is argued that the kinship formula refers to the *primal* bond between "the man" and his "helper," whereas the *sexual* bond constituted through man and woman becoming לְבָשָׂר אֶחָד (*lᵊvāśār ʔeḥād*, "one flesh," or, as the NET Bible has it, "a new family") is tied to the preceding explanation: "That is why a man leaves his father and mother and unites with his wife" (Gen 2:24). An example is Terrence Diggory, professor emeritus of English at Skidmore College, who has held roles as a ruling elder in the Presbyterian-New England Congregational Church in Saratoga Springs, New York, and as moderator of Albany Presbyterian Rainbow, an inclusive organization within Albany Presbytery. Diggory argues, for example, that "the initial bond between Adam and Eve is not described as sexual," and that "a sexual bond, if it is implied at all, attaches more clearly to the 'father and mother,' because they produced the man who leaves them behind in order to 'cling to' his wife.'"[156] The "clinging" (דָּבַק, *dāvaq*), according to Diggory, "invokes a feeling of kinship rather than a sexual act, as when Ruth 'clung to' [*dabaq*] her mother-in-law, Naomi (Ruth 1:14). Even the terms 'man' and 'wife,' as they are used in Gen 2:24, refer to the primal bond embodied in Adam and Eve rather than the sexual bond of 'father and mother.' . . . *The translation* 'wife,' in Gen 2:24, hinges on the attachment of a grammatical possessive form: 'his woman' is taken to mean 'his wife.' But in the context of this story, it could just as well mean 'the helper that is perfect for him.'" Diggory concludes that "Gen 2:24 does not appear to me to offer unequivocal authority for declaring heterosexual intercourse to be a necessary condition of marriage," not because the text explicitly condones same-sex marriage, but because "it opens the door in two important respects," by, firstly, describing "one flesh" as the primary condition for marriage, and, secondly, by establishing the "archetype" for a larger pattern, in which someone is sent out to embrace a stranger. As for the first "opening," Diggory takes the expression "one flesh" as meaning "meant for each other," that since "homosexual as well as heterosexual couples report the joy of recognizing each other in these terms," such an interpretation "may bring the law of the church closer to God's intention." Regarding the second "opening," Diggory explains that "in response to questions about marriage, the human authors of the Bible kept getting answers that were much broader in

---

156. Diggory, "Reading the Bible."

scope. Finally, Jesus brought the message that all of the nations (gentiles) were to be included in the new covenant that was early on understood in terms of marriage (Eph 5:32)."[157]

Associate Professor of Christian Ethics at the University of San Diego Emily Reimer-Barry argues the kinship bond in Gen 2:23–24 refers to the marital partner's shared humanity, not to their biological binaries:

> The human creature does not praise his new partner's difference and complementarity to himself. The man does not say "This one at last is different from me! Our genitals fit together! I am naturally masculine, and she is naturally feminine, and we are as different as night and day!" On the contrary. The man instead focuses on sameness, their common humanity. "This one, at last, is bone of my bones, flesh of my flesh!" This one, unlike the previous animals, is a true partner. But our interpretation of sexual ethics need not zero in on sexual complementarity too quickly. What is celebrated is the miracle of finding someone to love, someone to share one's life with, someone to share the struggles of life. At this point in the story, their partnership is rooted in their shared humanity.[158]

These interpretations have several issues. To begin with, it is illogical to conclude that the kinship terms אִישׁ (*ʔîš*, "man") and אִשָּׁה (*ʔiššāh*, "woman") in Gen 2:23, which denote shared humanity and "human" complementarity, are unrelated to the subsequent etiological explanation of marriage in Gen 2:24. There *is* a focus on "likeness" in these terms. This likeness should be understood as "their shared humanity." At the same time, the "mutual recognition" expressed by the human's reaction to the creation of the woman cannot be seen as anything other than a relief of the "aloneness" experienced by the human prior to the creation of the woman. The question is, therefore, what *kind* of "aloneness" is relieved? If only "existential," queer interpretations may be correct, of course, that it "opens the door" for nonbinary "shared humanity" being the primary condition for marriage. Such an interpretation cannot be sustained when the text is read in context. As previously discussed, within the framework of Gen 1 and 2, the essence of humanity must be comprehended within the context of the divine image. In Gen 1, this image is explained functionally through humanity's role in procreation and stewardship of the earth. While this functional interpretation does not

---

157. Diggory, "Reading the Bible." Emphasis original.
158. Reimer-Barry, "Queer Reading of Genesis."

fully encapsulate the significance of the divine image, it remains a crucial aspect, especially considering that procreation is a recurring theme in Gen 1–2 and the canonical perspective. The "aloneness" relieved is thus not only "existential" but also functional vís-a-vís procreation. Adding the correlation between male/man and female/woman, the human's reaction in Gen 2:23 cannot be understood otherwise as recognition of "polaric complementarity"—that is, a recognition of the couple's likeness in humanity. It must be the difference "in ways that make them natural and necessary partners" in expressing the image of God. Read in context, the narrator's following etiological remark on a man leaving his father and mother and uniting with his wife makes perfect sense. It is not a disconnected remark that has nothing to do with the intended bond between the human and his (female) helper but describes a crucial aspect of that bond, namely becoming "one flesh" in order to most fully express their humanity and secure procreation. Moreover, the common denominator in the uses of the kinship formula referred to above is clearly that the parties are offspring of a common ancestor—in other words, the result of a marriage. The combination of shared humanity and marital unity is also exemplified in the Song of Solomon, where the bride is a sister, a fellow human, one who shares the same humanity:

> You have stolen my heart, my sister [אֲחֹתִי, *ʔaḥōtî*], my bride [כַּלָּה, *xallāʰ*]! You have stolen my heart with one glance of your eyes, with one jewel of your necklace. How delightful is your love, my sister, my bride! How much better is your love than wine; the fragrance of your perfume is better than any spice! (Songs 4:9–10 NET)

Combining the existential and functional, Robert A. Gagnon mentions that "only a being made from *'ādām* longs to reunite in sexual intercourse and marriage, a reunion that not only provides companionship but restores *'ādām* to his original wholeness. The woman is not just '*like* himself' but '*from* himself' and thereby a complementary fit to himself. She is a complementary sexual '*other*.'"[159]

Marriage

The text, therefore, continues not surprisingly to specify this created complementarity as the rationale and basis for what we now call

---

159. Gagnon, *Bible and Homosexual Practice*, 60–61.

marriage. It is thus (ʿal-kēn, v. 24a)—because of the created complementarity—that these two pieces of the same "flesh" are destined for each other: "[he] clings to his wife, and they become one flesh" (v. 24b–c). And with "one flesh," in light of the text's juxtaposition with the narrative in Gen 1, it no longer refers solely to the essential but also to the functional aspect of complementarity, namely procreation. Gagnon describes it this way: "The sexual union of man and woman in marriage, of two complementary beings, in effect makes possible a single, composite human being. So great is the complementarity of male and female, so seriously is the notion of 'attachment' and 'joining' taken, that the marital bond between man and woman takes precedence even over the bond with the parents that physically produced them. A descriptive statement about the creation of woman thus provides etiological justification for prescriptive norms regarding marriage."[160] And this "marital" joining into "one flesh" is so strong that when a man uncovers the nakedness of his father's or brother's wife (with the intention of sexual intercourse), it is equally an uncovering of his father's or brother's nakedness (ʿerwāʰ, "nudity, genitals").

> You shall not uncover the nakedness of your father's wife; it is your father's nakedness. (Lev 18:8)

> You shall not uncover the nakedness of your brother's wife; it is your brother's nakedness. (Lev 18:16)

It is the same conjunction that Jesus refers to in Matt 19:4–6 and its parallel in Mark 10 (NET): "Have you not read that the Creator from the beginning made them male and female and said, 'Therefore a man shall leave his father and mother and be joined to his wife, and the two shall become one flesh?' So, they are no longer two, but one flesh. What God has joined together, let no one separate." Even though the Hebrew verbs יַעֲזָב (yaʿazov), דָּבַק (dāvaq), and הָיוּ (hāyû) in Gen 2:24 could technically be translated more descriptively as "leaves," "cleaves," and "becomes," Jesus's reference to them shows that they do not merely state what de facto happened with the first man and woman but that it should also be understood normatively for every relationship: man and woman were created to enter into such a relationship with each other and not with others. It is worth noting that Jesus not only refers to Gen 1 and 2 but also links the texts by combining "created them male and female" and "therefore a man

---

160. Gagnon, *Bible and Homosexual Practice*, 61.

GENDER AND BODY IN BIBLICAL CREATION THEOLOGY

shall leave." As Joel Marcus formulates it in his commentary on the parallel in Mark 10:6–8, "These passages [Gen 1:27; 2:24] speak of Adam and Eve as beings whose complementary sexual equipment proves that they were designed for each other (10:6, citing Gen 1:27) and whose resultant sexual union (10:7–8, citing Gen 2:24) is part of an indelible marital bond created by God (10:9)."[161] We find the same reasoning in Paul in 1 Cor 6:16 (NASB): "Do you not know that the one who joins himself to a prostitute is one body with her? For He says, 'The two shall become one flesh.'" The problem is that the conjunction is "wrong" because it is not an inseparable, monogamous (and heterosexual) relationship that is being entered. In other words, when one becomes "one body" and "one flesh" with a prostitute the very first time, it is akin to separating what God has joined together if one does not "stick to"—that is, marry—that person. It is worth considering whether the same principle of marriage as a God-created and God-ordained "joining arrangement" also underlies Paul's words in 1 Cor 7:13–14, where he advises that even when a woman is married to an unbelieving man and vice versa, the believer should not separate from the unbelieving spouse because "an unbelieving husband is sanctified by the wife, and an unbelieving wife is sanctified by the husband." In that case, it would be the fact that they have already become "one flesh" which means not even an unbelieving spouse is reason enough to break this unity. More certainly, this conjunction is the overarching framework for Paul's characterization of same-sex intercourse as incompatible with Christian living. The argument in 1 Cor 6 is thus that the cleansing and "joining" of the believers with Christ has made them a temple for the Holy Spirit. The vices in verses 9–10—including same-sex intercourse—must therefore be seen as a breach of this conjunction: "You were washed clean, you were made holy, you were justified in the name of the Lord Jesus Christ and by the Spirit of our God . . . Therefore, glorify God in your body!" (1 Cor 6:11, 20 NLT). In addition, Paul's and John's use of the believer and the church's joining with Christ as an analogy for the heterosexual marital union of man and woman is also a (pre)view of same-sex intercourse: "Husbands, love your wives, just as Christ loved the church and gave himself up for her to make her holy, cleansing her by the washing with water through the word, and to present her to himself as a radiant church, without stain or wrinkle or any other blemish, but holy and blameless" (Eph 5:25–27 NIV; cf. John 3:29; Rev 19:7; 21:2).

---

161. Marcus, *Mark 8–16*, 710.

Another Old Testament text, the inseparable unity of the heterosexual couple, thematizes the inseparable unity of the heterosexual couple as a creation order. Despite its obvious textual transmission and syntactic challenges, it must be included.

> You also do this: You cover the altar of the Lord with tears as you weep and groan, because he no longer pays any attention to the offering nor accepts it favorably from you. Yet you ask, "Why?" The LORD is testifying against you on behalf of the wife you married when you were young, to whom you have become unfaithful even though she is your companion and wife by law. No one who has even a small portion of the Spirit in him does this. What did our ancestors do when seeking a child from God? Be attentive, then, to your own spirit, for one should not be disloyal to the wife he took in his youth. "I hate divorce," says the LORD God of Israel, "and the one who is guilty of violence," says the LORD who rules over all. "Pay attention to your conscience, and do not be unfaithful." (Mal 2:13–16 NET)

This applies to Mal 2:15, where Malachi in the preceding verse 14 explains the Lord's rejection of the people's sacrifices by using marriage as an image of the broken relationship:

> Because the LORD has been a witness
> between you and the wife of your youth,
> with whom you have dealt treacherously;
> yet she is your companion and your wife by covenant. (Mal 2:14 NASB)

While it is obviously marriage that is introduced as an image in the explanation, the challenge is in how verse 15 should be understood as a continuation of the argument in verse 14. Karl William Weyde has provided a useful overview article of the different solutions to the challenges.[162] The Masoretic text reads וְלֹא־אֶחָד עָשָׂה וּשְׁאָר רוּחַ לוֹ וּמָה הָאֶחָד מְבַקֵּשׁ זֶרַע אֱלֹהִים, and the various translations Weyde mentions (with the addition of ESV and the perhaps most divergent solution in DO92) clearly illustrate the aforementioned challenges.

> *Revised English Bible* (REB): "Did not the one God make her, both flesh and spirit? And what does the one God require but godly children?"

---

162. Weyde, "Does Mal 2:15a Refer," 73–90.

New Jerusalem Bible (NJB): "Did he not create a single being, having flesh and the breath of life? And what does this single being seek? God-given offspring!"

New Jewish Publication Society Translation (NJPS): "Did not the One make [all] so that all remaining life-breath is His? And what does that One seek but godly folk?"

Einheitsübersetzung der Heiligen Schrift: "Hat er nich eine Einheit geschaffen, ein lebendiges Wesen? Was ist das Ziel dieser Einheit? Nachkommen von Gott."

New Revised Standard Version (NRSV): "Did not one God make her? Both flesh and spirit are his. And what does the one God desire? Godly offspring."

English Standard Version (ESV): "Did he not make them one, with a portion of the Spirit in their union? And what was the one God seeking? Godly offspring."

NET Bible: "No one who has even a small portion of the Spirit in him does this. What did our ancestor do when seeking a child from God?"

The challenges are many, and it would take too long to discuss them all. Still, in relation to our discussion, they mainly concern whether the opening sentence is to be understood interrogatively, even if it is not indicated explicitly with the interrogative pronoun in the Masoretic text, and whether אֶחָד is to be understood as subject with the translation "the one [God]" or as object of the verb עָשָׂה with the implicit subject "he" (implied God), and where the translation thus becomes: "Did he (not) create [them] as one?" Most interpreters agree that the Hebrew text is corrupt. Weyde, along with Markus Zehnder,[163] rejects the translation that probably makes the best sense of the Masoretic text, namely "And no one, who has done this, has a remnant of spirit. But what does the One require? Godly seed!" because it is elliptical and assumes an original "this," which is alleged to have slipped out in the transmission of the text. Based on a few changes to the Masoretic text, Zehnder suggests two possible translations of 2:15a: "Has he (the One) not made him one, He who has spirit," or "Has not the One made (him) one, He who has spirit," where the meaning (according to Weyde) is: "Because this One, who alone possesses spirit in the full sense of the word, has created man in the mutual relationship of man and woman as a unity, this creational

---

163. Zehnder, "Fresh Look at Malachi II 13–16," 224.

unity that is realized in the marriage covenant must not be attacked by the dissolution of the marriage bond."[164] Weyde agrees with Zehnder, for example, that Malachi alludes to God's creation of both man and woman in Gen 2:4–25 but also argues for an understanding of the text that involves fewer changes to the Masoretic text than Zehnder suggests. By re-vocalizing שְׁאָר (šᵊʾār, "remnant") from the root שאר I to שְׁאֵר (šᵊʾer, "flesh") from the root שאר II, according to Weyde, the verse can be translated as "Not one (not only man) did he (God) make, but flesh with spirit (woman) for him (man)." According to Weyde, this means that "God made not only man but also woman for him, as his partner, and they were (are) a unity. This interpretation makes sense as part of the argument in the literary context, and it also provides a clear allusion to Gen 2:18, especially in the phrase 'make for him,' which takes up the first words of YHWH's speech in the Genesis passage. 'I will make (for) him a helper as his partner.'"[165] Weyde further points out that when Malachi chooses to use שְׁאֵר (šᵊʾer) instead of the source text's בָּשָׂר (bāśār), it may be related to the fact that שְׁאֵר (šᵊʾer) is used in the Holiness Code to denote "near of kin" and "their own flesh" (Lev 18:6 and 25:49) and that the lexeme is therefore particularly well suited to describe the central idea in Mal 2:15a, namely "the close relationship between husband and wife, and the close relationship of both of them to God, which is also emphasized in Gen 2:18."[166] Weyde concludes by pointing out that

> the above-suggested interpretation of Mal 2:15a implies that the creation account in Gen 2:4–25 is used as an argument against divorce, which is one of the two central themes in Mal 2:10–16. The argument in v. 15a is that God created not only man but also woman, and she is for him, which echoes the phrases "a helper, his partner" in Gen 2:18, perhaps also the man's words "flesh of my flesh" in Gen 2:23. This allusion to the creation account includes the idea that they—husband and wife—should belong to each other and be one flesh for the rest of their lives.[167]

Thus, both Zehnder and Weyde argue—along with a number of translations—that Malachi also understood the heterosexual relationship or marriage in Gen 2:4–25 as a God-created and God-ordained "joining arrangement":

164. Weyde, "Does Mal 2:15a Refer," 78–79.
165. Weyde, "Does Mal 2:15a Refer," 86.
166. Weyde, "Does Mal 2:15a Refer," 87.
167. Weyde, "Does Mal 2:15a Refer," 87.

> The passage presumes the complementary, and distinct, sexes of male and female as necessary conditions for marriage and sexual intimacy—"the man who hates and divorces his wife." Other notes in the passage are sufficient for establishing the fact that the "biological" condition for "productivity" in procreation is nonreductionistic in the covenantal relation, but in fact, it extends to social realities between the male and female. Both male and female are joined in such a way that the relationship is permanent and not intended to be broken. The relationship extends to the whole of the persons—"You belong to him in body and spirit." This points in the direction of a "comprehensive" relationship that is conditioned by biological complementarity.[168]

In early reception history, it is interesting that the Wisdom text 4Q416 from Qumran specifically refers to the limits and conjunctions of creation regarding the unbreakable bond in marriage. Jesper Høgenhaven writes in his analysis of the text that

> the exclusiveness of the marital relation remains in focus in l. 6, which states that any other man apart from the mebin/husband who attempts to exercise authority over the wife is a transgressor, one who removes the "boundary of his life" (חיהו גבול). The expression draws on Deut 19:14, 27:17, and Prov 22:28, which prohibits the moving of boundaries. The addition of the nomen regens חיהו adds weight and importance to the expression and also establishes a close connection with creation. The "boundary of one's life" is intimately associated with the basic conditions of life as shaped by the creator.[169]

Høgenhaven further points out that the text has a "close connection to the material in Gen 2–3."[170] Although the Wisdom text otherwise argues for male dominance over the woman, which is not present in Gen 2, it is still interesting that the text's ethics of marriage draws on the boundaries and conjunctions found in Gen 1–2.

Procreation

In addition to the intended lifelong union in Gen 2, we also have the context in Gen 1 between the creation of humans as biological men and

---

168. Farris and Cortez, *Introduction to Theological Anthropology*, 218.
169. Høgenhaven, "Adam in Qumran Wisdom Literature," 207.
170. Høgenhaven, "Adam in Qumran Wisdom Literature," 208.

women and the primary task or function of humans, namely, sexual intercourse for procreation. Gordon Wenham writes about this connection:

> When Genesis comes to man's creation, it states that God deliberately created mankind in two sexes in order that he should "be fruitful and multiply." This is the first command given to man and is repeated after the flood; contrast the gods of Babylon who introduced various devices to curtail man's reproduction. In that homosexual acts are not even potentially procreative, they have no place in the thinking of Gen 1. Nor do they fit in with Gen 2. There the lonely Adam is provided not with a second Adam, but with Eve. She is the helper who corresponds to him. She is the one with whom he can relate in total intimacy and become one flesh. It therefore seems most likely that Israel's repudiation of homosexual intercourse arises out of its doctrine of creation. God created humanity in two sexes so that they could be fruitful and multiply and fill the earth. Woman was man's perfect companion, like man created in the divine image. To allow the legitimacy of homosexual acts would frustrate the divine purpose and deny the perfection of God's provision for two sexes to support and complement one another.[171]

Jacob Milgrom mentions in his notes on Lev 18:6–23 that "the common denominator of all the prohibitions, I submit, is that they involve the emission of semen for the purpose of copulation, resulting in either incest and illicit progeny or, as in this case [v. 22], lack of progeny. In a word, the theme (with Ramban) is procreation."[172] Here, procreation as the creation-theologically intended purpose of copulation is emphasized. Milgrom notes in his application of the law that "a consolatory and compensatory remedy is at hand for Jewish gays (non-Jews, unless they live within the boundaries of biblical Israel, are not subject to these laws): if gay partners adopt children, they do not violate the intent of the prohibition."[173]

> It is not a coincidence that the author places procreation and dominion together. Instead, these are integrally related to the human story and central to God's covenantal blessing of life to the world. For it is by dominion through the means of procreation that God gives life and blesses the life of his creation. The male-female formula of procreation is positively fitting for how God chooses to bless his creation . . . The use of "image"

---

171. Wenham, "Old Testament Attitude to Homosexuality," 363.
172. Milgrom, *Leviticus 17–22*, 1567.
173. Milgrom, *Leviticus 17–22*, 1567.

and "likeness" are reintroduced [in Gen 5:1–3], thus pointing us back to Gen 1:26–28. It is through the "family" predicated on the "He created them male and female" that God's purposes are carried out through the family line. In other words, what we have here is a dynasty, a royal family, the line for which God carries out his plan to give life and bless his creation. Dominion is satisfied through the dynasty that God created and "blessed." The image described in the early chapters of Genesis is transmitted through the dynasty that God will later expand to the rest of the earth. But it is here in this formula of male-and-female complementarity that God reveals to us the interrelated nature of sexual identity, sexual activity, and the creation of culture.[174]

The creation of humans as biological man and woman is thus linked both functionally and relationally so that the blessing of humans—or the blessed human life—is found where biological gender is complemented and lived out through the relationship with the opposite biological gender, with procreation as one of the purposes.

Before summing up our discussion, we need to note regarding אִישׁ (ʔîš), "man," and אִשָּׁה (ʔiššāʰ), "woman," that the former is used not only in the sense of "man" but also for "human" and a group of people that can consist of both men and women (e.g., Exod 35:21). However, when these words appear together, they denote the binary human as a whole (Lev 13:29; 1 Sam 27:11; Jer 44:7). Unlike זָכָר (zāxār, "male") and נְקֵבָה (nᵊqēvāʰ, "female"), אִישׁ (ʔîš, "man,") is also used for social gender. This applies, for example, in 1 Kgs 2:2, where the dying King David tells his son: חָזַקְתָּ וְהָיִיתָ לְאִישׁ (ḥāzaqtā wᵊhāyîtā lᵊʔîš, "be strong and become a man!"). David Instone-Brewer notes that while זָכָר (zāxār) can refer to both boys and adult men, אִישׁ (ʔîš) is rarely used for children.[175] When it is, it is exclusively to emphasize the masculine aspect in relation to circumcision (e.g., Gen 17:10, 12, 23; Exod 12:48), the redemption of the firstborn (Exod 13:15; Lev 27:5, 6; Num 3:15, 22, 28, 34, 39, 40, 43; 26:62), impurity periods after the birth of a boy or girl (Lev 12:2, 7), and the birth of a boy rather than a girl (Isa 66:7; Jer 20:15). It is also used for young animals, but only, as Instone-Brewer notes, "when emphasizing their maleness, for offerings where a female animal was not appropriate: Exod. 12:5; 13:12; Lev. 1:3, 10; Deut. 15:19; Mal. 1:14."[176]

---

174. Farris and Cortez, *Introduction to Theological Anthropology*, 213–14.
175. Instone-Brewer, "Are There Two Types of Men," 38.
176. Instone-Brewer, "Are There Two Types of Men," 38.

A final term used for both biological and social gender is גֶּבֶר (*gever*), meaning "strong man" or "young man." Unlike אִישׁ (*ʾîš*), it has no corresponding feminine form, but interestingly, it occurs in two instances together with other feminine terms.[177] Judg 5:30 describes how the warriors took spoils after the death of the Canaanite general Sisera in the form of רַחַם רַחֲמָתָיִם (*raḥam raḥᵃmātayim*), which can be translated as "a girl or two" or, more literally, "a uterus or two." In Jer 31:22, it co-occurs with נְקֵבָה (*nᵉqēvāʰ*), "woman." Brettler notes that this strongly suggests that גֶּבֶר (*gever*) may be a sex term (and the phrase לְרֹאשׁ גֶּבֶר [*lᵉrōʾš, gever*], literally "to the head of a *geber*," may include a euphemism for the penis). In the abovementioned text from Judg 5, the spoil, "a uterus or two," is dedicated to לְרֹאשׁ גֶּבֶר [*lᵉrōʾš, gever*], and it would make sense to translate the expression as Brettler suggests with the meaning that the uterus was "spoiled" by penetration. Jer 30:6 uses גֶּבֶר (*gever*) in parallelism with זָכָר (*zāxār*) and as the opposite of a female giving birth. Prov 30:19, though part of a somewhat cryptic unit, speaks of "the way of a גֶּבֶר (*gever*) with a young woman," another clearly sexual use of the term.[178] If this etymological understanding of גֶּבֶר (*gever*) is correct, there is a strong connection between gender and the body in this case as well. Brettler summarizes his semantic analysis in saying that "the pairs *zakar* and *neqebah* and *ʿish* and *ʿishshah* also suggests that each of these pairs is dichotomous: a person is either a *zakar* or a *neqebah* and a person is seen by culture as either a *ʿish* or a *ʿishshah*. This contrasts with modern gender theory, which sees male and female as poles with many options in between, rather than an absolute dichotomy."[179]

The biblical texts clearly describe the man-woman gender polarity as a dichotomy (where a whole is divided into two equal parts), excluding an understanding of polarity as endpoints in a spectrum. Therefore, the interpretation that some intersex persons might be both male and female and thus bear God's image as much as those who are either male or female, as suggested by Preston Sprinkle from *The Center for Faith, Sexuality & Gender*, is a perspective imposed on the use of these terms. There is no support for it in their meanings: "Some intersex persons might be both male and female and therefore bear God's image just as much as

---

177. The feminine form is, interestingly enough, found in modern Hebrew, where *geveret* is used as the address "Mrs." or "Miss." See Muchnik, *Gender Challenge of Hebrew*, 35n37.

178. Brettler, "Happy Is the Man," 202.

179. Brettler, "Happy Is the Man," 202.

those who are either male or female. After all, the author says, 'male and female he created them' and not 'male or female he created them.'"[180]

In addition to the etymological argument for such a God-intended and God-created dichotomy in the original state, several biblical texts show that it also applies after the fall. This includes texts where the gender of newborn children is determined immediately after birth (Gen 4:25; cf. 21:2; 30:21; Hos 1:6) and texts that show that if one has a body designed to menstruate and become pregnant, then one is, by definition, a woman (Exod 21:22; Lev 12:2; 15:29; Jer 4:31; 1 Tim 5:14), just as everyone who has a seminal emission is, by definition, a man (Lev 15:16; 22:4–6; Deut 23:11) (Vigilius 2019, 47–48). Furthermore, the following, far from an exhaustive list,[181] also shows that other Hebrew terms are based on the binary:

> son (בֵּן) and daughter (בַּת)
> boy (יֶלֶד) and girl (יַלְדָּה)
> brother (אָח) and sister (אָחוֹת)
> young man (נַעַר) and young woman (נַעֲרָה)
> bridegroom (חָתָן) and bride (כַּלָּה)
> father (אָב) and mother (אֵם)
> father-in-law (חָם) and mother-in-law (חָמוֹת)
> uncle (דּוֹד) and aunt (דֹּדָה)
> male servant (עֶבֶד) and female servant (אָמָה)
> prophet (נָבִיא) and prophetess (נְבִיאָה)
> prince, leader (שַׂר) and princess (שָׂרָה)
> king (מֶלֶךְ) and queen (מַלְכָּה)

Summing up our discussion on the interrelationships between the lexemes translated as "human," "male"/"female," and "man"/"woman," we have seen that Scripture describes the ontological primacy and superiority of humankind through the specification of the content of the image of God, as outlined in Gen 1 and 2. Man is created in the image of God as the apex of the created order and as God's vice-regents with the purpose of honoring the Creator by procreation and sustainment/expansion of world order. Since the creation of mankind precedes the creation of *gendered* mankind, it suggests that the generic term is ontologically primary to the gendered human. The human being is, in other words, not its gender. To be human is more than being male or female. At the same time, the correlations between "male"/"man" and "female"/"woman" show that embodied sex and the marital bond between "male"/"man" and "female"/"woman"

---

180. Sprinkle, "Sex, Gender, and Transgender Experiences—Part 7."
181. Adapted from Smith, "Responding to the Transgender Revolution."

is a crucial expression of the image of God, that is, what it means to be human. This is beautifully summarized by Katie McCoy:

> The creation account reveals the human body is neither incidental nor accidental to gender identity. Genesis 1 uses the Hebrew terms *zakar* (male) and *neqebah* (female) to depict their sexual differentiation, while Gen 2 includes the words *ish* (man) and *ishah* (woman) to reflect their gender differentiation. These pairs of terms relate *zakar* to *ish* and *neqebah* to *ishah*. To be a *zakar* makes one an *ish*. To be a *neqebah* makes one an *ishah*... To be sure, biological sex and gender are not *identical* aspects of one's humanity—sex is a primarily reproductive descriptor, while gender is a relational one—but they are indeed *correlative* aspects... one's biological sex indicates and corresponds to one's gender such that both are binary. The sexed body is indivisible from gendered self.... We are more than our embodied sex, yet we cannot be separated from our embodied sex. Christianity gives us the framework to affirm that our bodies and reproduction are good yet not ultimate. Andrew Walker clarifies, "Maleness isn't only anatomy, but anatomy shows that there is maleness. And femaleness isn't only anatomy, but anatomy shows that there is femaleness. Men and women are more than just their anatomy, but they are not less."[182]

SOLITUDE, UNITY, NAKEDNESS

Before we turn to the connection between binary creation and the "leaving" and "cleaving" of Gen 2, we need to dwell a bit more on Pope John Paul II's theology of the body. We have already mentioned how human solitude leads to the "first delineation of the human being as a human person with the proper subjectivity that characterizes the person," and this subjectivity is inextricably linked to the body. Quoting the later (and late) pope Karol Wojtyła's essay "The Person: Subject and Community," Steenhoff writes: "'Being a subject (a *suppositum*) and experiencing oneself as a subject occurs on two entirely different dimensions. Only in the latter do we encounter the actual reality of the human self. Consciousness plays a key and constitutive role in the formation of this latter dimension of personal human subjectivity.'" Steenhoff continues with a quote from the abovementioned catechesis: "Man 'belongs to the visible

---

182. McCoy, "What It Means," 149, 152–53.

world; he is a body among bodies' (CHL 6:3). But he possesses that body in such a way as to make him aware of being 'alone.' Man is distinguished from the animals because he is a *person*, and that personhood is revealed through his body."[183] What the human person says "subjectively," therefore, is not (only) "I think, therefore I am," but *sum incarnatus, ergo sum*, "I am embodied, therefore I am!" This qualification of the human person's subjectivity is crucial for the "second delineation" mentioned by the pope. Paraphrasing Steenhoff's explanation, the second meaning of original solitude is that man is "alone" in the sense of lacking a "helper." God addresses this by creating the woman, and their union forms the original unity. To answer the question of how man could know what it meant to be alone before he had experienced this unity, the pope makes a significant interpretative move by connecting the narratives on the trees and the creation of the woman. In Gen 2:16–17, Adam is warned not to eat from the tree of the knowledge of good and evil or else he will die. But how could man, who only knows the experience of existing and, therefore, of life in his original consciousness, understand what it means to die? The pope suggests that since these words "appeared on the horizon of man's consciousness without his ever having experienced the reality," he "had to find their truth in the inner structure of his own solitude." According to this view, Adam had not yet experienced death so that it couldn't be an object of his understanding in metaphysical terms. Nor could it be known through what Wojtyła calls "mirroring consciousness," which presupposes a previously recognized object. The only type of consciousness we can discuss is an entirely internal consciousness like a form of spiritual self-awareness.[184] Whereas, in Gen 1, man is male and female from the beginning, Gen 2 "authorizes us," John Paul II asserts, "to think first only about man inasmuch as, through the body, he belongs to the visible world while going beyond it," and *then* "lets us think about the same man, but through the duality of sex."[185] John Paul II continues: "Although in its normal constitution, the human body carries within itself the signs of sex and is by its nature male or female, *the fact that man is a 'body' belongs more deeply to the structure of the personal subject than the fact that in his somatic constitution he is also male or female.*" Solitude is, therefore, "substantially prior to the meaning of original unity; the latter is based on masculinity and femininity, which are, as it were, two

---

183. Steenhoff, "Body That Reveals the Person(s)," 11.
184. Steenhoff, "Body That Reveals the Person(s)," 11–12.
185. John Paul II, *Man and Woman He Created Them*, 8:1.

different 'incarnations,' that is, two ways in which the same human being, created 'in the image of God' (Gen 1:27), 'is a body.'"[186] What Gen 2 describes, therefore, is that "man (ʔādām) falls into that 'torpor'[187] in order to wake up as 'male' (ʔîš) and 'female' (ʔiššāʰ)," and that "despite the diversity in constitution tied to the sexual difference, *somatic homogeneity* is so evident that the man, on waking up from genesis sleep, expresses it immediately when he says, 'This time she is flesh from my flesh and bone from my bones. She will be called woman because from man has she been taken' (Gen 2:23)."[188] The significance of the Hebrew terms is even stronger, however, than John Paul II suggests. As already mentioned, the "likeness" expressed through the assonant terms אִישׁ (ʔîš, "man") and אִשָּׁה (ʔiššāʰ, "woman") are explained as *kinship*, stressing that more fundamental than the obvious differences between men and women is homogeneity. Our human commonality precedes our sexual difference, and instead of translating the terms as "male" and "female," as John Paul II does, it catches better the meaning of the terms to distinguish between זָכָר (zāxār, "male") and נְקֵבָה (nᵊqēvāʰ, "female") in Gen 1 (common to all creatures) and translate אִישׁ (ʔîš) and אִשָּׁה (ʔiššāʰ) as "man" and "woman," since this characteristic is specific to humankind. By reading Gen 1 and 2 together (as Jesus does in Matt 19), we may conclude that man (ʔādām) fell asleep to awaken as "man" (ʔîš) and "woman" (ʔiššāʰ), experiencing their *kinship* or *somatic homogeneity* and the subsequent one-flesh union as both a "bodily" and "spiritually" experience of that homogeneity. John Paul II writes, "When they unite with each other (in the conjugal act) so closely so as to become 'one flesh,' man and woman rediscover every time and in a special way the mystery of creation, thus returning to the union in humanity ('flesh from my flesh and bone from my bones') that allows them to recognize each other reciprocally and to call each other by name, as they did the first time."[189] At the same time—as being זָכָר (zāxār, "male") and נְקֵבָה (nᵊqēvāʰ, "female")—they fulfill the roles and functions assigned to man and woman in creation, namely being fruitful, multiplying, and filling the earth. The "one-flesh" union, therefore, is not solely defined by kinship, as some argue. The discussion is important, of course, since kinship alone would allow for same-sex marriages. James Brownson, for example, asserts that

186. John Paul II, *Man and Woman He Created Them*, 8:1. Emphasis original.
187. I.e., a state of physical or mental inactivity, lethargy, or sluggishness.
188. John Paul II, *Man and Woman He Created Them*, 8:3–4. Emphasis original.
189. John Paul II, *Man and Woman He Created Them*, 10:2.

the language of "one flesh" refers not to complementarity but to kinship. The relationship of kinship is not based on complementarity, but on similarity and mutual obligation. Kin are those who have something essential in common with each other, and who accept the obligation to help and support each other in distinctive ways. Moreover, nowhere in Scripture is the notion of anatomical or biological complementarity of male and female explicitly portrayed or discussed. The absence of confirming texts calls into question whether this vision of gender complementarity truly underlies the antipathy Scripture shows toward the same-sex erotic relationships it addresses.[190]

We shall return to a discussion of the rationale behind passages in Scripture with "antipathy... towards the same-sex erotic relationship it addresses." Suffice it here to mention that such a reading of Gen 2 is unfounded if Gen 1 and 2 are read together as proposed above. Without complementarity between male/man and female/woman, the blessing of Gen 1 is simply not present. It is *the sexually differentiated body*, that is, their shameless, naked "maleness" and "femaleness," that enables them to enter into that union, recognize their mutual humanness, and fulfill their assigned role and function. Though interpreters disagree whether the description of the first humans' shamelessness עָרוֹם (*ʕārôm*) (Gen 2,25) refers to external or internal "nakedness," it is most likely a combination of the two. This is because, in its sixteen attestations, עָרוֹם (*ʕārôm*)—in contrast with the other biblical Hebrew term for nakedness עֶרְוָה (*ʕerwāʰ*)—never relates to (illicit) *sexual* nakedness or activity. Though it *does* refer to physical nudity, the emphasis is on what nudity symbolizes, namely being stripped of something or having no barrier/ protection against something or somebody. In Isa 58:7, it is argued, for example, that "when you see someone naked, clothe him! Don't turn your back on your own flesh and blood!" The naked is nude, of course, but his nudity symbolizes his lack of protection from wind and weather. The LXX counterpart γυμνός carries the same meaning as the Hebrew lexeme.[191] Thus understood, the first couple's shameless, *external* nudity symbolized their internal "shalom," blessed unity, and created "fittingness." Steenhoff summarizes:

> Original solitude was "portrayed as the 'non-identification' of his own humanity with the world of the living beings (*animalia*)

---

190. Brownson, *Bible, Gender, Sexuality*, 260.
191. Brannan, *Lexham Research Lexicon*; Liddell, *Lexicon*, 362.

that surround him" (CHL 12:3), a non-identification that, in turn, lets man discover his full humanity with the help of the woman. This discovery happens through the body. "For this reason, it is not difficult to understand that nakedness corresponds to that fullness of consciousness of the meaning of the body that comes from the typical perception of the senses. One can think about this fullness in categories of the truth of being or reality"—that is, in metaphysical categories—and this immediate "participation in the perception of the world" must come before any "critical" complication of knowledge and experience, "and it seems to be strictly linked with the experience of the meaning of the body." . . . Ultimately, the words "they did not feel shame" signifies "an original depth in affirming what is inherent in the person" as "visibly" feminine and masculine.[192]

Finally, we come to the most fundamental and *teleological* significance of their union, namely the inherent significance of the human body in its capacity to express love and communion. According to Pope John Paul II, this "spousal" or "nuptial" meaning of the body means that the body is not merely a physical entity but carries profound spiritual and relational significance. The term "nuptial" emphasizes the connection between the body and the marital union, suggesting that the body is designed by God to participate in and reflect the divine plan for human love and communion, particularly within the context of marriage. It underscores the idea that the body is meant for self-giving love and free mutual fulfillment in interpersonal relationships, echoing the biblical imagery of marriage as a union of one flesh: "The human body, with its sex—its masculinity and femininity—seen in the very mystery of creation, is not only a source of fruitfulness and of procreation, as in the whole natural order, but contains 'from the beginning' the 'spousal' attribute, that is, *the power to express love: precisely that love in which the human person becomes a gift* and—through this gift—fulfills the very meaning of his being."[193] Seen as a mutual gift, the union of sexually differentiated human bodies in marriage is a profound expression of the image of God as the perfect Giver and life as the ultimate gift. For the same reason, marriage is teleological in the sense that it refers back to God's gift of life in original creation but also, due to the fall, forward to the gift of new and everlasting life through incarnation and consummation. Christopher West, in a most

---

192. Steenhoff, "Body That Reveals the Person(s)," 15–16.
193. John Paul II, *Man and Woman He Created Them*, 15:1. Emphasis original.

helpful presentation of John Paul II's theology of the body, writes that the "giving" is both eternally *internal* to God and revelationally external in creation: "Within the Trinity, the Father eternally 'begets' the Son by *giving himself* to and for the Son. In turn, the Son (the 'beloved of the Father') eternally receives the love of the Father and eternally gives himself back to the Father. The love they share *is* the Holy Spirit, who 'proceeds from the Father and the Son' (Nicene Creed)."[194] Creation of man in *this* image means, specifically, that man in marriage is called to reflect God's internal "giving" and "creating." By complementing each, "in the normal course of events, their reciprocal 'giving' enables sperm and ovum to meet, and a 'third' comes into existence."[195] As Herman Bavinck has it: "God made two out of one so that he could then make the two into one ... The two-in-oneness of husband and wife expands with a child into a three-in-oneness," with the family together "unfolding the one image of God ... From conception onward, a human being is a product of fellowship; every person is born from, and in, fellowship; persons are cared for and nurtured in the context of fellowship, and continue in some kind of fellowship throughout life, all the way to one's final breath."[196] In this light, Eve's enigmatic outbreak after the conception and birth of Cain makes sense: "I have created a man just as the Lord did!" (Gen 4:1). And it is telling, also, that the Hebrew word for "oneness" is the same in reference to God and to marriage: "The Lord our God, the Lord is one [אֶחָד, *ʔeḥād*]" and "they shall become one [אֶחָד, *ʔeḥād*] flesh" (Gen 2:24 ESV).

SPOUSAL BOOKENDS

As you gave the ring to one another and have now received it a second time from the hand of the pastor, so love comes from you, but marriage from above, from God. As high as God is above man, so high are the sanctity, the rights, and the promise of love. It is not your love that sustains the marriage, but from now on, the marriage that sustains your love.

—Dietrich Bonhoeffer, "A Wedding Sermon from a Prison Cell"[197]

---

194. West and Metaxas, *Our Bodies Tell God's Story*, 34–35. Emphasis original.
195. West and Metaxas, *Our Bodies Tell God's Story*, 39.
196. Bavinck and Eglinton, *Christian Family*, 7–8.
197. Bonhoeffer, *Letters and Papers from Prison*, 7.

> The third incomparable benefit of faith is this: that it unites the soul with Christ, like a bride with a bridegroom. By this "mystery" (as Paul teaches), Christ and the soul are made one flesh. For if they are one flesh and if a true marriage—indeed by far the most perfect marriage of all—is culminated between them (since human marriages are but weak shadows of this one), then it follows that they come to hold all things, good and bad, in common. Accordingly, the faithful soul can both assume as its own whatever Christ has and glory in it, and whatever is the soul's Christ claims for himself as his own.
>
> —Martin Luther, "The Freedom of a Christian"[198]

On this basis, it is not surprising that one of the central images of the relationship between God and Israel, Christ and the Church, is the "binary" relationship between the bridegroom and the bride, the beauty that characterizes the bridegroom and the "joinedness" that characterizes the church as the body. Reading forward from Gen 2, the Bible discloses itself a basically a *marital* story. It commences in Gen 2 with the marriage of the first couple, and it ends in Revelation with the "wedding of the Lamb" (Rev 19:7), the marriage of Christ and the church. And like all other *inclusio* instances, these "bookends" point to the key theme of the "in-between": God wants to marry us! N. T. Wright combines the binary and complementary aspects in the Bible's view of gender and body in the following concise statements:

> The last scene in the Bible is the new heaven and the new earth, and the symbol for that is the marriage of Christ and his church. It's not just one or two verses here and there which say this or that. It's an entire narrative that works with this complementarity so that a male-plus-female marriage is a signpost or a signal about the goodness of the original creation and God's intention for the eventual new heavens and new earth.[199]

> Heaven and earth, it seems, are not after all poles apart, needing to be separated forever when all the children of heaven have been rescued from this wicked earth. Nor are they simply different ways of looking at the same thing, as would be implied by some kinds of pantheism. No: they are different, radically different; but they are made for each other in the same way (Revelation is suggesting) as male and female. And, when they

---

198. Wengert, *Roots of Reform*, 499–500.
199. Quoted from Schmitz, "N. T. Wright on Gay Marriage."

finally come together, that will be cause for rejoicing in the same way that a wedding is: a creational sign that God's project is going forwards; that opposite poles within creation are made for union, not competition; that love and not hate has the last word in the universe; that fruitfulness and not sterility is God's will for creation.[200]

Turning to the "marital story," in Ps 45, the marriage of the blessed king to his bride, standing at his right hand, wearing jewelry made with gold from Ophir (v. 9), is described as a type of God's relationship with his people.

> My heart is stirred by a beautiful song. I say, "I have composed this special song for the king; my tongue is as skilled as the stylus of an experienced scribe." You are the most handsome of all men! You speak in an impressive and fitting manner! For this reason God grants you continual blessings ... Your throne, O God, is permanent. The scepter of your kingdom is a scepter of justice. You love justice and hate evil. For this reason God, your God has anointed you [the king] with the oil of joy, elevating you above your companions. (vv. 1–2; 6–7 NET)

In the Old Testament, it is probably the prophets Isaiah, Ezekiel, and Hosea who express God's "marital" commitment to Israel most succinctly:

> As a young man marries a young woman,
> so your sons will marry you.
> As a bridegroom rejoices over a bride,
> so your God will rejoice over you. (Isa 62:5 NET)

> I made you plentiful like sprouts in a field; you grew tall and came of age so that you could wear jewelry. Your breasts had formed and your hair had grown, but you were still naked and bare. Then I passed by you and watched you, noticing that you had reached the age for love. I spread my cloak over you and covered your nakedness. I swore a solemn oath to you and entered into a marriage covenant with you, declares the sovereign Lord, and you became mine. (Ezek 16:7–8 NET)

> I will commit myself to you forever; I will commit myself to you in righteousness and justice, in steadfast love and tender compassion. I will commit myself to you in faithfulness; then you will acknowledge the Lord. (Hos 2:19–20 NET)

200. Wright, *Surprised by Hope*, 105.

Numerous other passages describe God and Israel/the Church as bridegroom and bride:

> I will greatly rejoice in the Lord; I will be overjoyed because of my God. For he clothes me in garments of deliverance; he puts on me a robe symbolizing vindication. I look like a bridegroom when he wears a turban as a priest would; I look like a bride when she puts on her jewelry. (Isa 61:10 NET; cf. Jer 2,1–2; Song 4:8–12; 5:1; Wisd 8:2; Matt 9:15; 25:1–13; 1 Cor 12:24; Eph 5:21–29; Rev 19:7–8; 21:2; 9)

In the New Testament, Paul makes the point unequivocally: "For this reason, a man will leave his father and mother and will be joined to his wife, and the two will become one flesh. This mystery is great—but I am actually speaking with reference to Christ and the church" (Eph 5:31–32 NET). Similarly: "For I am jealous for you with godly jealousy, because I promised you in marriage to one husband, to present you as a pure virgin to Christ" (2 Cor 11:2 NET).

Answering the question "How does Gen 2:24 refer to Christ?," Christopher West notes—with reference to the apostolic letter *Muleris Dignitatem* of Pope John Paul II—that "Christ, the new Adam, 'left' his Father in heaven. He also left the home of his mother on earth. Why? To give up his body for his bride (the church) so that we might enter into holy communion with him. In the breaking of the bread, 'Christ is united with his *body* as the bridegroom with the bride. All this is contained in the letter to the Ephesians.'"[201] "The deepest meaning and purpose of human sexuality," West continues, "is to point us to the 'wedding supper of the Lamb' (Rev 19:9). In other words, God created us male and female right from the beginning to live a 'holy communion' that foreshadows the holy communion of Christ and the church."[202] A biblical theology of the body, therefore, leads us "from the body to the mystery of sexual difference; from sexual difference to the mystery of communion in 'one flesh'; from communion in 'one flesh' to the mystery of Christ's communion with the church; and from the communion of Christ and the church to the greatest mystery of all: the eternal communion found in God among Father, Son, and Holy Spirit."[203] And answering the question "Will there

---

201. West, "Our Bodies Tell God's Story," 24; John Paul II, *Mulieris Dignitatem*, 26. Emphasis original.

202. West and Metaxas, *Our Bodies Tell God's Story*, 18.

203. West and Metaxas, *Our Bodies Tell God's Story*, 4–5.

be sex in heaven?," West goes as far as stating that "in the marriage of the Lamb, 'penetration and permeation of what is essentially human by what is essentially divine will then reach its peak.'"[204]

Two issues in regard to sexual ethics should be mentioned. First, it is based on this approach to gender, body, and marriage that we must understand the radical prohibitions and severe penalties for homosexual sexual practices (Gen 19; Lev 18:22; 20:13; Rom 1:26–27; 1 Cor 6:9–10; 1 Tim 1:10). Such practices break (in the same way as bestiality) the binary distinction between man and woman and the complementary joining of man and woman.[205] Timothy Tennent writes:

> Sexual differentiation is a crucial and necessary feature of the privilege to procreate, a privilege God gave to marriage at creation. Without sexual differentiation, we disfigure the deeper, theological truth to which marriage points as an icon of Christ and his bride. The church cannot marry the church; nor can Christ marry himself. These two unique glories are binaries, Christ and his church, and they come together in a joyful unity . . . Marriage between one man and one woman must be protected because the man and woman united together to stand as icons representing Christ's unity with his church, the bride of Christ. Adultery, fornication, and gay marriage all erode one of the key markers of marriage: the exclusive, unitive sign of our union with Christ as the people of God. Alternative arrangements, though endorsed by the culture, cannot be embraced by the church since they serve as an antisacrament, a visible sign of our rebellion against God's design. They are the antithesis of what marriage is intended to be.[206]

We shall return to a more detailed discussion of these passages below and simply underscore here that, in biblical sexual ethics, they cannot be understood divorced from the theological context of creation, as has been outlined here.

Secondly, it is a *non sequitur* that because "the bride" in biblical bridal symbolism can be both a man and a woman, the Christ event

---

204. West and Metaxas, *Our Bodies Tell God's Story*, 85, quoted from John Paul II, *Man and Woman He Created Them*, 67:3.

205. When non-cultic prostitution, adultery, and polygamy are not prohibited and punished in the same radical way, it may be because in these cases, there is no breaking of the distinction but only of the joining. These actions take place within the framework of the binary gender concept and the associated sexual orientation and practice.

206. Tennent and Fernando, *For the Body*, 52–53.

annuls heterosexual marriage. This is, for example, what Elisabeth Gerle argues when she writes, "Christ as a bridegroom has gender-transgressing qualities. These slippages and mixed metaphors can be used against those who seek to cling to polarized notions about what it means to be a bride or a bridegroom. These are elements that extend the tradition further by making it available to the contemporary emphases provided by gender-transgressing and queer theologies."[207] It is true, of course, that Christ's reconciliation has "gender-transgressing" implications, since, as Paul argues, "there is neither Jew nor Greek, there is neither slave nor free, there is no male and female, for you are all one in Christ Jesus" (Gal 3:28). Paul's argument in both Gal 3, however, is that there is no distinction between men and women regarding *reconciliation and justification*; it does not imply the absence of differentiation between genders in other aspects. Similarly, in Eph 5, Paul's inclusive portrayal of the bride as comprising both men and women pertains to the union with Christ, who "loved the church and gave himself for her to sanctify her by cleansing her with the washing of the water by the word, so that he may present the church to himself as glorious—not having a stain or wrinkle, or any such blemish, but holy and blameless" (Eph 5:25–27 NET). Consequently, it would be incongruous for Paul, who is fundamentally faithful to Jesus, to distance himself from Jesus's teachings on heterosexual marriage in Matt 19 within the Ephesian context. Although the union with Christ extends to both genders and, in that sense, transcends gender norms, it remains that only the complementary marriage between a man and a woman can effectively symbolize this union.

Singleness

After such a thorough review and appreciation of biblical marriage and bridal symbolism, it is appropriate to comment on the meaning and importance of singleness. This is not only because the number of singles in a Western context appears to be increasing, but also because an unbiblical or overly one-sided appreciation of marriage contributes to the understanding of singleness as deficient and inferior, and not without reason. In the Babylonian Talmud, celibacy is likened to nothing short of homicide and tarnishing the divine image: "Anyone who does not

---

207. Gerle, *Passionate Embrace*, 143; cf. Pedersen, "Radical Incarnation and Creative Ambiguity," 4–22.

engage in the mitzva to be fruitful and multiply is considered as though he sheds blood, as it is stated: 'Whoever sheds the blood of man,' and it is stated near it: 'And you, be fruitful and multiply.' Rabbi Elazar ben Azarya says: It is as though he diminishes the Divine Image. Ben Azzai says: It is as though he both sheds blood and diminishes the Divine Image" (Yevamot 63b). And in my own tradition, Luther emphasized the exceptionality nature of celibacy: "Such persons are rare, not one in a thousand, for they are a special miracle of God. No one should venture on such a life unless he be especially called by God, like Jer [16:2], or unless he finds God's grace to be so powerful within him that the divine injunction, 'Be fruitful and multiply,' has no place in him" (LW 45:21). While Luther does not go as far as the Talmud, his emphasis on marriage in his thinking is so strong that there is little encouragement for singles who do not perceive themselves as "especially called by God" and who may still be waiting for "the one and only." Luther's *Stände*, that is, "estates" or "stations," for example, do not include singles. A significant part of the explanation is likely the Reformation's confrontation with the monastic movement's view of celibacy as a lifestyle particularly close to God. However, the emphasis on marriage is also biblically and exegetically grounded. In "The Estate of Marriage" from 1522, Luther writes:

> For this word which God speaks, "Be fruitful and multiply," is not a command. It is more than a command, namely, a divine ordinance [*werck*] which it is not our prerogative to hinder or ignore. Rather, it is just as necessary as the fact that I am a man, and more necessary than sleeping and waking, eating and drinking, and emptying the bowels and bladder. It is a nature and disposition just as innate as the organs involved in it. Therefore, just as God does not command anyone to be a man or a woman but creates them the way they have to be, so he does not command them to multiply but creates them so that they have to multiply. And wherever men try to resist this, it remains irresistible nonetheless and goes its way through fornication, adultery, and secret sins, for this is a matter of nature and not of choice. (LW 45:18)

Without in any way diminishing the significance of marriage in biblical creation theology, it is evident that the Bible presents a much more nuanced perspective on celibacy and singleness than what these quotes suggest.

The blessed life can indeed be found outside marriage! Jesus breaks with the marriage pattern. Further, he emphasizes to his disciples that it may mean giving up a normal family life if they follow him. Even though it may not necessarily involve physically leaving one's family when Jesus says that "he who loves father or mother more than Me is not worthy of Me, and he who loves son or daughter more than Me is not worthy of Me" (Matt 10:37; cf. Luke 14:26), discipleship clearly had the obvious cost that they, at least for extended periods, had to leave their families. Furthermore, Jesus—as we will see shortly—also acknowledges that a person's renunciation of fulfilling their sexual potential can be "for the kingdom of heaven's sake" (Matt 19:12). Paul also mentions celibacy as commendable. In 1 Cor 7, Paul seems to suggest that those who are married should live as though they were not, and those who are not should remain single as he is. Tim Keller summarized Paul's inner logic well: "We are to be neither overly elated about getting married nor overly disappointed about not being so—because Christ is the only spouse who can truly fulfill us and God's family the only family that will truly embrace and satisfy us. The Christian gospel and hope of the future kingdom dethrone the idolatry of marriage . . . This exalted view of marriage, however, shows us that marriage is only penultimate. It points to the true marriage that our souls need and the true family our hearts want. No marriage can ultimately give us what we most desire and truly need."[208] Or as Christopher West explains: "A eunuch is someone physically incapable of sexual relations. But a eunuch for the kingdom of heaven is someone who freely forgoes sexual relations in anticipation of the ultimate reality to which sexual relations point: the eternal union of Christ and the church. In this way, those who take up Christ's call to remain unmarried explicitly for the kingdom do not reject their sexuality. They're showing the rest of the world the ultimate purpose and meaning of sexuality: to point us to union with God."[209]

By pointing to "the true marriage that our souls need" and the "ultimate reality to which sexual relations point," it becomes clear that the blessing of the single life encompasses not only lifelong, dedicated celibacy but also includes the single individual who is currently living in celibacy—thus abstaining from sexual intercourse—but who is open to or longing for living with a man or woman in heterosexual marriage. Even though such a life entails sexual abstinence, the single individual

---

208. Keller, "Gospel and Sex," 8–9.
209. West and Metaxas, *Our Bodies Tell God's Story*, 81–82.

is just as capable of experiencing what marriage symbolizes, namely, the mutual giving of oneself to each other in faith in Christ as "bride" and "bridegroom." As Aimee Byrd articulates it with the Song of Solomon:

> The man and the woman in the Song mutually give themselves to one another and are a delight to one another. The whole Song is poetry of delight in one another's presence and longing when separated. It's dripping with anticipatory language like that of the mare among Pharaoh's chariots, "until the day breaks and the shadows flee" (2:17; 4:6). And that anticipatory language is for singles as well. So is the eros that goes with it. Singles tell the story of the virgin bride, waiting for that day to break. Waiting for the shadows to flee. Waiting for true eros to be consummated. And singles, as Paul said, have an opportunity for more single-minded devotion to the Bridegroom now (1 Cor 7:32–35).[210]

For the same reason, it would be incorrect to make a fundamental distinction between the love expressed through philia and eros, the devotion and affection expressed in friendship, and the love expressed sexually in marriage. As we have seen above, the longing for fellowship with God and others is "primordial," something that exists in the inner structure of man's solitude. Therefore the single individual is also—and perhaps even more so—capable of directing this "primordial drive" toward Christ, as the "erotically" loving individuals in marriage. Melinda Selmys states that "philia and eros are both expressions of the same primordial drive—not the biological drive to reproduce, but rather the spiritual drive to become one. Eros directs this drive towards physical expression, a 'one flesh' union. In contrast, philia directs it towards a union of souls, as expressed both in the Aristotelian formula of 'one soul in two bodies' and in the scriptural example of David and Jonathan, where 'Jonathan became one in spirit with David' (1 Sam 18:1)."[211] The "penultimate" character of "exalted marriage" means, in other words, that it is the *giving* and the *gift*, not the physical expression of eros, that is fundamental to marriage symbolism. And such a "covenantal love of self-giving" is not found only in marriage but is expressed both in marriage and in single life, in Christ, and in the congregation:

---

210. Byrd, *Sexual Reformation*, 135.
211. Selmys, "John Paul II, Intimate Friendship."

Paul radically breaks with the contemporary cultural narrative by saying that married couples are *not* free to do what they want with their own bodies. In contrast to a goal of self-fulfillment, Paul says, "The wife does not have authority over her own body but yields it to her husband. In the same way, the husband does not have authority over his own body but yields it to his wife" (1 Cor 7:4). In this both spouses are reflecting the Eucharistic language of Christ, when he says, "This is my body, given for you" (Mark 14:22–25; Luke 22:18–20; 1 Cor 11:23–25). In the Eucharist, Jesus is living out the sacrificial, self-giving love that marriage is designed to reflect and image. Thus, the spousal self-giving of marriage models Christ's sacrificial love. And corporately, the church of Jesus Christ is to model this sacrificial and self-giving posture to the world ... The church is a macrocosm; marriage is the microcosm. And both institutions are designed to reflect a covenantal love of self-giving (Phil 2:5–11; Eph 5:25).[212]

EROTICISM AND REPRODUCTION

Animal reproduction is *assumed*, but human sexuality is *celebrated*.
—Tennant and Fernando[213]

God gave us eros "in the beginning" to be the very power to express agape.
—Ortlund, Ortlund, and Pelt[214]

It is well documented that both in ancient Judaism and in the early church, there was a strong tradition that regarded eroticism or sexual pleasure as sinful desire. Intellectual historians typically point to Greek Platonism, which sharply distinguished between the body and the soul, as responsible for at least the early Christian approach to sexuality. Ambrose (340–397 CE) encouraged priests not to have sex with their wives and recommended celibacy instead, and Origen (185–ca. 254 CE) viewed sexual desires as a bodily hindrance to the growth of spiritual

---

212. Tennent and Fernando, *For the Body*, 56–57. Emphasis original.
213. Ortlund et al., *Marriage and the Mystery of the Gospel*, 18. Emphasis original.
214. West and Metaxas, *Our Bodies Tell God's Story*, 37.

or soulful life. Concerning the Christian interpretation of the Song of Songs, he wrote:

> But if an adult approaches this book in a carnal way, there is significant risk and danger for that person in encountering this biblical book. For if this person does not know how to listen to the name of love with chaste ears, it can happen that he turns everything he has heard from the inner person to the outer, carnal person and is lured away from the spiritual to the carnal. Then he will end up nourishing his carnal desire, and it will seem as if it is the Holy Scripture that incites and drives him toward carnal lust. Therefore, I warn and advise all those who are not yet free from the temptations of the flesh and have not yet freed themselves from bodily nature to refrain from reading this book and what is said about it.[215]

Regarding early Christian tradition, Greek Platonism to Parthian Manichaeism was a crucial source of inspiration. Paraphrasing my colleague Carsten Elmelund Petersen, Manichaeism posited that sexual intercourse was sinful even within the bounds of marriage, where it was not to be associated with pleasure. Abstinence was considered the ideal, with procreation being a last resort. Augustine adhered to Manichaeism prior to his conversion to Christianity. Upon his arrival in Rome in 383, he began to advocate for Christianity, heavily influenced by Neoplatonic thought, particularly regarding sexuality. Augustine asserted that sexual intercourse, although a forgivable sin, cast a shadow over marriage as an institution. Centuries later, the eminent Catholic theologian Thomas Aquinas maintained that all sexual acts outside the context of reproduction were sinful.[216]

Håkon Sunde Pedersen, in his dissertation "The Retributive and Suffering God of the book of Jeremiah," points out that the understanding of desire[217] and longing as expressions of a lack or an unmet need, as defined in Plato's *Symposium*, is adopted in Augustinian thought.[218] In the *Symposium*, both Aristophanes and Agathon define "eros" as a quest for what humanity lacks, and this understanding is employed by Augustine

---

215. Origen, *Prologue*, 218.

216. Petersen, "Samkønnet Sex i et Historisk Lys," 31.

217. Pedersen employs the English term "desire," whose semantic field encompasses both positive and negative connotations. In the following discussion, the term is used in the broader and mostly positive sense "wish; strong desire; longing; craving."

218. Pedersen, "Retributive and Suffering God," 48–53.

to describe both human positive divine need and negative sinful desire. The former is expressed in the famous dictum, "My heart is restless until it finds rest in you, O God," while the latter is described in *Confessions* from 397–401 CE, where he details how he was led astray by *concupiscentia carnis*, "the compelling desire of the flesh," including sexual or erotic libido.[219] Augustine juxtaposed this life-destroying libido with abstinent chastity, which was even seen as sinful to the commanded procreation within marriage. Thus, Augustine laid the foundation for the negative view of eroticism, which centuries later, in his essay "Jenseits des Lustprinzips," led Freud to connect eros with self-preservation and categorize eroticism alongside basic life-sustaining elements such as food, sleep, and so on.[220]

However, it is interesting that in the same *Symposium*, Plato presents an alternative understanding of desire. Socrates explains in his speech how Eros was born as the child of Poros (resource) and Penia (poverty), and theologians and philosophers have connected desire or attraction positively with abundance, generosity, and grace on this basis. This applies to the Neoplatonic Christian theologian Dionysius the Areopagite (Pseudo-Dionysius), who even called God Eros. According to Lisa Isherwood, Dionysius "could imagine a God who lacks nothing but desires everything, and who in the act of creation also creates desire."[221] What characterizes Dionysius's understanding of desire, according to Pedersen, is that it is "unmotivated and follows from the nature of the desiring subject (God)" and "rooted in excess rather than lack and need, and in continuity with that, a desire that seeks good for the desired—a desire to give rather than to have and receive."[222] Although this understanding is not explicitly found in biblical texts, it may be argued that if it is characteristic of God that his "needs" or "desires" must be understood in this way, then it makes sense from a theological perspective to understand human desire as reflecting precisely this aspect of the *imago Dei*. Eroticism, as desire, should not be seen negatively as a lack that renders the desiring subject incomplete but as a desire to give the object all the good that the subject also experiences as good.

Another significant intellectual historian who, based on Augustine's negative understanding of eroticism, criticized Christianity was Friedrich

219. Augustine, *Augustines Bekendelser*, 1.1.1; 2.2.2.
220. Freud, *Jenseits des Lustprinzips*.
221. Isherwood, "Impoverished Desire," 2.
222. Pedersen, "Retributive and Suffering God," 52–53.

Nietzsche, who, in *Jenseits von Gut und Böse* from 1886, claimed that "Christianity administered a dose of poison to eros. He did not die from it, but he degenerated into vice."[223] K. E. Løgstrup comments on this, stating that "from an intellectual history perspective, Judaism did not give eros poison. Hellenism did. If Christianity presupposes Judaism, as is the case in Jesus's preaching, deeds, and entire behavior, then Christianity did not give eros poison. If Christianity gave Hellenism domicile rights and effectiveness in Western culture, then Christianity gave eros poison."[224] Løgstrup emphasizes that while Jesus understood the Old Testament's theology of creation, Christianity, to the extent that it has been influenced by Hellenism (Platonism), misunderstood the texts. One of the trajectories of the aforementioned body theology is that a "toxic" understanding like Nietzsche's might be excusable in light of the early church's Augustinian and the Catholic (Thomistic) interpretive history but should nonetheless be rejected as a misreading of the texts.

There can be no doubt that, according to Gen 1:26-28, the prime command to man and woman is to rule over creation with procreation as the most important contributor. In v. 26, the nonconsecutive weyiqtol וְיִרְדּוּ (*wᵊyirdû*) is best taken as indicating purpose ("in order that they may rule") or result ("so that, as a consequence, they may rule"). Such an understanding is supported by at least three other examples of a cohortative followed by a jussive weyiqtol indicating intent or result in biblical Hebrew:

> Let me go [אִמָּלְטָה] there. It's just a little place, isn't it? Then I'll survive [וּתְחִי]. (Gen 19:20b)
>
> So let's consent to their demand [נֵאוֹתָה], so they will live [וְיֵשְׁבוּ] among us. (Gen 34:23)
>
> Let me leave [וְאֵלֲכָה] so that I may go [אָקוּמָה] and gather [וְאֶקְבְּצָה] all Israel to my lord the king so that they may make an agreement [וְיִכְרְתוּ] with you. (2 Sam 3:21)

In order to execute their rule, they need to "be fruitful [פְּרוּ] and multiply [וּרְבוּ] and fill [וּמִלְאוּ] the earth." For the same reason, God, as Robert Chisholm explains it, "imparts sexuality, and the procreative power inherent in it, to the first male and female (and, by extension, to their offspring) so they can fulfill their God-given commission to rule on his behalf," and "in this context, just prior to his command to reproduce,

---

223. Nietzsche, *Beyond Good and Evil*, 168.
224. Løgstrup, *Skabelse og tilintetgørelse*, 174.

'bless' means 'to endue with procreative power.'"[225] Or, as Tennant and Fernando have it:

> When God calls us to be "fruitful and multiply and fill the earth," he calls us to become co-creators with him by bearing children and thus creating a family unit that reflects the mystery of the triune God. The sexual act has the potential to produce new life, even as the intimate communion within the Trinity is fruitful in producing life. Because God's nature is inherently life-producing and fruitful, so the "sign" of his covenantal love should also be normatively life-producing and fruitful. The sexual act is, of course, exceedingly enjoyable, but its deeper purpose is to point to spiritual realities, and when sex is separated from these spiritual realities, fragmentation and brokenness occur.[226]

Whereas procreation undeniably is the most *explicit* explanation in Gen 1 of what it means for humans to be created in the image of God, other texts support a more comprehensive understanding of sexuality. Firstly, Gen 2, the most foundational text for understanding the creational purpose of marriage, does not mention multiplying. According to Sandra Glahn, this is a significant omission: "If procreation were the purpose of marriage, or even a primary purpose or a moral mandate for all time, one would expect to find reproduction at least mentioned in the husband-wife creation story. Certainly, part of God's design for marriage includes procreation. However, based on the Genesis text in which marriage is established, reproduction is certainly less emphasized than bearing God's image and partnering together to subdue the earth."[227] In contrast, Gen 1 focuses primarily on the functional aspect of the *imago Dei*; Gen 2, though mentioning the functional aspect of subduing the earth (v. 15), nevertheless emphasizes the existential "oneness" discussed above. This emphasis was acknowledged by both Jesus and Paul in the New Testament, where Jesus argues that in marriage, man and woman "are no longer two, but one flesh" (Matt 19:6), and Paul argues that "man . . . will be joined to his wife and the two will become one flesh" (Eph 5:31). This is significant not only for the understanding of eroticism but also as a qualifier of the reproduction mandate. Sons (and, by extension, daughters) are, as Ps 127:3–5 reminds us, "a gift from the LORD." That is, *a* gift, but—in the light of Gen 2—not a gift *required* for a marriage to be

---

225. Chisholm, "Male and Female," 66–67.
226. Tennent and Fernando, *For the Body*, 53–54.
227. Glahn, "Reproduction, Contraception, and Infertility," 198.

valid or successful. Sandra Glahn writes: "Procreation, while a wonderful part of God's design for married couples, is not mandated for all able married people in this age of grace. Ps 127 is not saying that godly people in all eras of human history must strive to have large families—nor that those who choose to have few or no children are somehow quenching the Spirit."[228] Secondly, the notion that romance and eroticism represent an expression of the previously mentioned "excess" suggests that the *imago Dei* is revealed not only through commanded sexuality, as seen in the "be fruitful" command of Gen 1:28 and 9:1, but also inherently through the recognition of human beauty and the experience of sexual longing. In Gen 26:8, we hear that "Abimelek, king of the Philistines" at one point "looked out of a window and saw Isaac, who was caressing his wife, Rebekah." In the "Song of Songs" in Ps 45:3, it is said of the king: "You are the most handsome among men; grace is poured upon your lips; therefore God has blessed you forever." Since the former statement appears in a narrative text and the comment in Ps 45 is probably more a royal trope than a physical description,[229] poetry is primarily where we find a description of eroticism for the sake of enjoyment. This applies to Prov 5:18–19, which with "her breasts" clearly refers to erotic pleasure:

> Let your fountain be blessed,
> and rejoice in the wife of your youth,
> a lovely deer, a graceful doe;
> let her breasts [דַּדֶּיהָ, *dadde*ᵛ*hā*] fill you at all times with delight;
> be intoxicated always in her love.

Another text where the erotic plays a role is the Song of the Vineyard in Isa 5. On the surface, it is about Israel and Judah, according to verse 7: "For the vineyard of the LORD of hosts is the house of Israel, and the men of Judah are his pleasant planting; and he looked for justice, but behold, bloodshed; for righteousness, but behold, an outcry!" However, beneath the surface are metaphors that any Israelite would have understood just as immediately. When the prophet's "song of my beloved" is parallel to "my beloved's song about his vineyard" (v. 1), it is obvious that the vineyard is a woman. And since women and their genitals have been

---

228. Glahn, "Reproduction, Contraception, and Infertility," 204.

229. Dexter Callender mentions that both in Isa 33:17 ("Your eyes will behold the king in his beauty; they will see a land that stretches afar") and in the Mesopotamian text VAT17019 ("form his feature harmoniously; make his body beautiful"), the designation "beauty" functions as a "royal attribute." Callender, *Adam in Myth and History*, 97–98.

described as gardens, fields, and vineyards everywhere in the ancient Middle East for millennia, it is this imaginative world that the prophet associates with. From Egypt, it can be exemplified with a text from the Harris Papyrus, which says:

> I am your favorite sister,
> I am yours like the field
> planted with flowers and with all sorts of fragrant plants.
> Pleasant is the canal within it,
> which your hand scooped out,
> while we cooled ourselves in the north wind.[230]

From ancient Sumer, it can be exemplified by a text with the following request from the goddess Inanna to the shepherd god Dumuzi:

> "As for me, my vulva,
> For me the piled-high hillock,
> Me—the maid, who will plow it for me?
> My vulva, the watered ground—for me,
> Me, the Queen, who will station the ox there?"
> To which the answer comes:
> "Oh Lordly Lady, the king will plow it for you,
> Dumuzi, the king, will plow it for you."
> And joyfully she responds:
> "Plow my vulva, man of my heart!"[231]

Although the erotic layer may not be the primary focus in Isaiah's use of metaphor, in light of its widespread and millennia-long history, it must have served as a backdrop for the actual message of how "the house of Israel" and "the men of Judah" remained "unfruitful" despite the "fertilization" they have been subjected to. Since it is more a backdrop than the actual focus of the text, it is difficult to derive anything normative about the erotic from it. Nevertheless, the text, at a minimum, shows that there is no distance taken from such a description of the woman and her genitals as such and that Isaiah's use of it as a backdrop implicitly reflects a positive recognition of the erotic.

Otherwise, it is in the Song of Songs that we find the most extensive and positive description of lovemaking, including the idea of the woman and her genitals being likened to a garden:

> If only he would give me a kiss of his mouth!

---

230. Quoted from Exum, *Song of Songs*, 175.
231. Quoted from Kramer, *Sacred Marriage Rite*, 59.

> Your lovemaking is sweeter than wine ... You are a locked garden, my sister, my bride; a locked garden, a sealed spring ...
> Awake, north wind, come, south wind!
> Blow on my garden, that its fragrance may spread everywhere.
> Let my beloved come to his garden
> and eat its choicest fruits.
> I have come to my garden, my sister, my bride ...
> Eat, friends, drink, and be intoxicated with love! (Song 1:2; 4:12,16; 5:1 CSB)

Tremper Longman notes in his commentary on the Song of Songs that several texts allude to the original state of creation by describing the beloved as a lush and fertile garden, and the Song of Songs' positive view of sex and eroticism should, therefore, be seen in the context of the theological framework of Gen 2.[232] Stefan Gustavsson makes a similar point when he highlights the וּנְהָרוֹת ... מַיִם רַבִּים ("mighty waters ... and rivers") in Song 8:7 as a backdrop of creation theology, describing how love possesses power comparable to God's ongoing creation, namely his control of the mighty waters, ensuring they do not exceed the boundaries set during creation (Job 26:10; 38:10; Ps 104:9; Jer 5:22).[233]

However, the most powerful expression of such a positive approach can be found in the so-called *wasf* poetry within the Song of Songs. The Arabic term *wasf* refers to a love poem that extols the lover's physique in intricate detail.[234] This is accomplished through vivid and expressive imagery derived from the natural world. Although the descriptions within the *wasf* may not explicitly depict the bodies, they instead imply, through elaborate metaphors, that the joy lovers derive from admiring their beloved can be likened to the pleasures found in nature, particularly within a garden-like setting. In the four *wasf* poems in Song of Songs (4:1–7; 5:10–16; 6:4–10; 7:1–9), every part of the beloved's body is described and praised. Even *fellatio* may be part of the described sexuality, as in 2:3 when the beloved [woman] says, "In his shadow I delight to sit, and his fruit is sweet to my taste." Marc Brettler advises caution, as there is not enough evidence to determine if פְּרִי (*pᵊrî*, "fruit") is a euphemism for sperm due to limited knowledge of sexual slang in biblical Hebrew.

232. Longman, *Songs of Songs*, 65.
233. Gustavsson, *Nøgne uden skam*, 116.
234. This genre boasts a rich history and eventually gained favor among troubadour poets and Elizabethan sonnet writers. Originating from French authors through Italian influence, this Renaissance literary form was known as *blasons anatomiques* or simply *blazon*.

"Given that much sexual slang is oral or is preserved in ephemera, it is unlikely that we will recover any additional evidence that will help us determine the extent of this slang in the Song."[235] Nonetheless, these love poems, as emphasized by Thomas Gudbergsen, show that "being created in the image of God as man and woman is closely connected to eroticism . . . If sexual intimacy between man and woman and, above all, the joy of seeing each other disappears, humanity has moved away from its image of creation."[236] In this light, the Song of Songs can be understood as a wisdom interpretation of creation, and when practiced within the bounds of the divine image, eroticism can be seen as a form of wisdom. Gudbergsen further emphasizes that these love poems highlight that "humans are fundamentally equipped with sexual drives" and that "the sexual act also aims to establish an ever deeper personal relationship and trust between the parties."[237] Therefore, he concludes, "When two people commit themselves to each other, they owe each other what is fundamentally necessary: sexual intercourse. Paul leans on this idea in his first letter to the Corinthians when he says that a wife does not have authority over her own body; her husband does. Likewise, a husband does not have authority over his own body; his wife does (1 Cor 7:4). And he says directly: 'The husband should give to his wife her conjugal rights, and likewise the wife to her husband' (v. 3)."[238] Erotic love might also be part of what Paul has in mind when he writes in Eph 5:29, "No one ever hated his own flesh, but nourishes and cherishes it," as this "nourishment" in context is about love. As Trent Rogers and John Tarwater write:

> The author of Genesis hints that God approves the purpose of pleasure in sex when he captures Adam's response at first seeing Eve: "This at last is bone of my bones and flesh of my flesh; she shall be called Woman, because she was taken out of Man" (Gen 2:23). Likewise, Paul's admonition to engage regularly in sexual relations with one's spouse suggests that sex was meant for more than just procreation (1 Cor 7:3–4). However, God did not plan for this unitive purpose to be something that was merely endured, but rather, it was to be pleasurable. Moreover, the focus of this sexual pleasure is on one's spouse and not

---

235. Brettler, "Unresolved and Unresolvable," 196.
236. Gudbergsen, "Praktiskteologiske reflektioner," 238.
237. Gudbergsen, "Praktiskteologiske reflektioner," 237, 242.
238. Gudbergsen, "Praktiskteologiske reflektioner," 243.

self. Moral sex is other-oriented and focuses on pleasing one's spouse.[239]

Such an understanding of sexuality can also be found, albeit more subdued, in the Catechism of the Catholic Church. Article 2351 of the Catechism defines "chastity" as "the successful integration of sexuality within the person and thus the inner unity of man in his bodily and spiritual being," and section 2362, quoting Pope Pius XII, describes sexuality as a source of joy and pleasure. The passage states, "The Creator ... established that in the [act of procreation], spouses should experience pleasure and happiness of body and spirit. Therefore, the spouses do nothing evil in seeking this pleasure and enjoyment. They accept what the Creator has intended for them. At the same time, spouses should know how to keep themselves within the limits of moderation."[240]

This understanding of sexuality is also significant in therapy and pastoral care in situations where it is not respected. Gudbergsen points out that "with this in mind, the pastor has ample opportunity to bring comfort to the one who has been deprived of their sexual dignity due to abuse or similar situations. The sexual body, with its desires and drives, is primarily one's own body and part of the created image of God. When the body is taken by force, it violates a person's theologically given existence."[241] Magnus Malm raises a similar point in what he calls the "Augustinian syndrome" of the church: "People with a broken and soiled sexual past are lifted out of their trauma through encounters with God. If they do not receive help later to return to a restored and healthy sexuality, they will perceive God as a substitute for sexuality, not as the source of sexuality. In this way, they only go halfway in their recovery, and polarization between God and sexuality/corporeality is established, which is then passed on to future generations in the church."[242] Malm further points out that the syndrome is reflected both in the Catholic depersonalization of Mary, who, according to Catholic tradition, never had sex and therefore had no more children than Jesus, and in the "pietistic and free church over-spirituality," where the erotic is part of the world from which one must turn away.[243] In both cases, sexuality is kept at a distance,

---

239. Rogers and Tarwater, "Biblical-Theological Framework," 565.
240. Den Katolske Kirke, "Den Katolske Kirkes Katekismus."
241. Gudbergsen, "Praktiskteologiske reflektioner," 237.
242. Malm, *Bag Billedet*, 73.
243. Malm, *Bag Billedet*, 73.

under controlled forms, and as something that destroys the pious self-image. The solution, in line with the biblical approach to sexuality and eroticism outlined above, is "to welcome sexuality as a gift from God in the name of Jesus and learn to be friends with it."[244]

Suppose Jesus's statement to the Sadducees in Mark 12:25 // Matt 22:30 // Luke 20:36 means that there will be no new marriages in the resurrection but that resurrected bodies will still be gendered. In that case, it is worth considering whether the Bible's description of eroticism for the sake of joy should also be perfected in the same way as all other aspects of the body. Christopher West goes as far as stating that "in the marriage of the Lamb, 'penetration and permeation of what is essentially human by what is essentially divine will then reach its peak.'"[245] However, this must remain a matter of speculation since the texts are few and not very explicit on this question, as mentioned above.

Furthermore, it is interesting to note that one of the elements considered distinctively human in evolutionary research is that sexual activity is relatively constant in humans, whereas for "other" mammals, sexual activity is generally periodic, corresponding to the time in their estrous cycle when the female is receptive to copulation. In contrast to *estrus* (heat) in females, human ovulation is concealed, and, as William Brown notes, "not only is human ovulation concealed, but also human copulation. Human beings engage in 'cryptic copulation,' evidenced also among chimpanzees and gorillas."[246] In light of the sexual desire that leads humans to copulate relatively constantly, it is a kind of biological testimony that sensual sexual intercourse emphasizing love, romance, and seduction is also an end and not solely for procreation.

SEPARATION AND ONENESS

Another principle behind the biblical understanding of the relationship between gender, body, and sexuality is related to the boundary-drawing or distinction that characterizes both the creation account in Gen 1 and many other texts, often referred to as priestly texts, as it was the priests' task in the tabernacle and the temple to visualize and uphold the

---

244. Malm, *Bag Billedet*, 73–74.

245. West and Metaxas, *Our Bodies Tell God's Story*, 85, quoted from John Paul II, *Man and Woman He Created Them*, 67:3.

246. Brown, *Ethos of the Cosmos*, 104.

boundaries that characterized the primordial state and presupposed the blessing within it. The creation account in Gen 1 describes the first act of creation as well organized, well structured, and well ordered. This is achieved through the quantitative use of the number seven to separate the six days of creation from the seventh day of rest and the qualitative use of the same number to symbolize the perfect result. Furthermore, the narrative repeatedly describes creation in binary terms, where an original whole is separated and given names. Both separation and naming serve to delineate and identify the new, independent parts. This applies to light and darkness (vv. 3–4), heaven and sea (vv. 6–7), sea and dry land (vv. 9–10), the creation of animals in different "kinds" (v. 21), the distinction between humans and animals, and thus also the binary creation of humans as male and female (vv. 26–27). Although Ellen van Wolde and Robert Rezetko go too far in their linguistic, exegetical, and comparative argumentation by suggesting that בָּרָא (bārā) should not be translated as "to create" but as "to spatially separate," their comprehensive argumentation shows that one of the most significant aspects of creation is to set boundaries and draw distinctions within the act of creation itself.

The functionality of the act of creation and the blessing that characterized the primordial state, in other words, depend on maintaining and adhering to the boundaries that characterized the initial act of creation. This is the rationale behind the statement in Ps 104:9 that God "set a boundary [for the deep] that it may not pass over, so as to return to cover the earth" (cf. Ps 148:6 and Jer 5:22). It is precisely this "transgression" that creates the negative cycle of sin, leading to the all-destructive flood. The boundaries of the original act of creation and the associated functionality are confirmed as still valid after the flood. The firmament will never again collapse, so the water "above" and "below" will not return to the primordial state (Gen 1:2). Thus, the associated functionality is ensured: "While the earth remains, seedtime and harvest, cold and heat, summer and winter, day and night shall not cease" (Gen 8:22).

The same principle is at play in texts that describe the new creation if one—as can be argued—sees the promised land as a symbol of the newly created world and the destination for God's people (Deut 12:8–11). Repeatedly the Israelites are warned against moving the boundaries that God set in the land before the immigration and settlement (Josh 13–22): "Cursed be the one who moves the boundary to his neighbor's field" (Deut 19:14; 27:17; cf. Prov 22:28; 23:10; Hos 5:10; Job 24:2). Furthermore, transgressions against the binary boundaries of creation are so serious that they are subject to the severest of punishments. In the apodictic laws of Lev 18, "crossovers" in sexual relationships are characterized as an "abomination" [תּוֹעֵבָה, *tôʿēvāʰ*] that pollutes the land leading to the land "vomiting out" both the Cana'anites and the Israelites (18:24–30). Similarly, in the parallel case laws of Lev 20, transgressors should be "put to death" (20:10–16), "cut off in the sight of their children of their people" (20:17–18), and die childless (20:20–21). The reason, as given in the following paragraph, is that "I am the LORD your God, who has separated you from the peoples... You shall be holy to me, for I the LORD am holy and have separated you from the peoples, that you should be mine" (20:24, 26). Only by respecting the boundaries that God has "created" can the land reflect the functionality and blessing that characterized the first creation and that will characterize the new creation. It is from the same background that we must understand the many and apparently arbitrary eating rules and impurity laws. Anthropologist Mary Douglas thus argues that we, who are characterized by rational-instrumental thinking, need to become familiar with how Leviticus in its "microcosmic thinking uses analogies as a logical basis for a total metaphysical framework."[247] Explanations and justifications are given, as I have argued elsewhere,

> not in the form of direct, logical and hierarchically constructed arguments—but in the form of analogies. In Leviticus we find, e.g., no rational explanation for the cleanliness regulations. Instead, we find for us to see a series of subtle and random connections between concrete bodies, clothes, priests and spaces— including not least God's dwelling, the tabernacle—to describe a complex and harmonious microcosm, where the concrete and the known are used to show how the unknown macrocosm is connected and works. In other words, there is no logic in which animals or things are clean and unclean. But a logically random relationship (e.g., clean—impure) is established between equally random known and concrete creatures or objects, so that this relationship, together with a large number of other relationships, can form a complex and harmonious microcosm that shows how the unknown macrocosm is connected.[248]

By adhering to the prohibitions and commands reflected in the microcosm of dietary laws and cleanliness regulations, individuals align

---

247. Douglas, *Leviticus as Literature*, 25.
248. Kofoed, "Mytebegrebet som et nødvendigt onde," 12.

with the distinctions and connections that God has established in creation as a whole. These distinctions and connections are essential for creation's functionality, "goodness," and blessing. It is the same creation theological framework that Gordon Wenham has in mind when he writes:

> It is now generally recognized that many of the most fundamental principles of Old Testament law are expressed in the opening chapters of Genesis. This applies to the laws on food, sacrifice, and the sabbath, as well as on sex. Genesis 1 repeatedly insists that God created plants, fish, birds, and other animals to breed "according to their kind." God created the different plants and animals to reproduce according to their own particular type. Hence the law forbids any mixed breeding or acts that might encourage it (Lev 19:19; Deut 22:9–11). The worst case of mixed breeding is described in Gen 6:1–4 and that prompted the flood.[249]

Perhaps most strongly, the separation is expressed in the creation's distinction between light and darkness since these states or qualities are biblically associated, on the one hand, with God and goodness and, on the other hand, with cosmic disorder, dysfunction, evil, or the Evil One. In the logic of the creation account, it is evidently not sunlight that is created first and called טוֹב (*tov*, "good") in Gen 1:3, as it only happens with the creation of "light in the expanse of the heavens" in verse 14.[250] And even if one prefers a functional interpretation of the act of creation as a condition for time, the immediate context suggests that it should also be understood as a contrast to the חֹשֶׁךְ (*ḥōshek*, "darkness") that characterizes the dysfunctional cosmos in verse 2. Based on this contrast, interpreters have proposed that light also represents an attribute or even something inherent in God's being that becomes evident or explicit with darkness as a backdrop, and not without biblical theological grounds. Regarding the attributive aspect, Ps 104:2 says of God, "You are clothed with light as with a garment." More essentially, the parallels in Job 3:20 and Ps 13:4 show that light is understood as life itself when it says, "Why does God give light to him who is in misery, and life to the bitter in soul?,"

---

249. Wenham, "Old Testament Attitude to Homosexuality," 362–63.

250. Cory Crawford has recently pointed out that a distinction between a "light" that existed prior to the creation of celestial bodies is also found in an Ur III text from the end of the third millennium BCE: "Lord Heaven illuminated heaven ... The host of heaven was not adorned ... Daylight did not yet shine, night spread, But Heaven had lit up his heavenly abode." Quoted from Crawford, "Light and Space in Genesis 1," 564–66.

and "Enlighten my eyes, lest I sleep the sleep of death." In Ezra 9:8, Ezra acknowledges how merciful it is that "our God has given us a little reviving in our slavery, to grant us a reviving to set up the house of our God, to repair its ruins" when "the people of Israel, the priests, and the Levites have not separated themselves from the peoples of the lands with their abominations" (Ezra 9:1). According to Isaiah (and later John), in the new creation, "the sun shall be no more your light by day, nor for brightness shall the moon give you light; but the Lord will be your everlasting light, and your God will be your glory" (Isa 60:19; cf. Rev 22:5). The same Isaiah also links the light with "his [the Lord's] servant," who can give life to "the one who walks in darkness and sees no light" (Isa 50:10); life is therefore neither found in Gen 1:2 nor in Isaiah's "darkness." If we make the biblical-theological leap to the New Testament, it is as indicated by John, who (despite accusations of being influenced by Greek philosophical thought) continues the approaches we find in the indisputably "non-Hellenistic" Old Testament by directly ascertaining that "God is light, and there is no darkness in him" (1 John 1:5). John also connects the light with the servant of the Lord. In John 12:38, Jesus identifies himself as this servant. In 8:12 (NET), he proclaims: "I am the light of the world. He who follows me shall never walk in darkness but shall have the light of life." In the prologue, John links the light, the life, and the servant in the same way as Isaiah: "In him was life, and the life was the light of men" (John 1:4). In the new creation, the new Jerusalem, according to John—with a slightly paraphrased quote from Isa 60.19—there will be no need for either sun or moon to shine, "for the glory of God gives it light, and its lamp is the Lamb" (Rev 21:23). The quote from Isa 60 is significant in this context because it draws upon the call or commission described in Isa 61, which serves as the foundation for the message in Isa 56–66. According to Luke 4:16–30, Jesus referenced this passage as a basis for his own mission. In the same way as it applies to Isaiah, John also links the light, the first creation, the new creation, and the Lord's Servant/Jesus/Lamb together. And if the commission is included in Isa 61, the allusion to the first creation becomes even stronger since the spirit of the Lord appears in both contexts, namely as hovering over (and clearly separated from) the still dysfunctional creation before the creation of the light in Gen 1:2 and as a starting point for the servant's work: "The spirit of the Lord God is upon me, because the Lord has anointed me" (Isa 61:1; cf. Luke 4:18).

This connection is not found in the rest of the New Testament in the same way. Instead, we find a deliberate use of "darkness" as a designation for "Satan's power" (Acts 26:18; Eph 6:12) and for existence characterized by the absence of God—whether in this life of lawlessness (2 Cor 6:14) or the eschatological consequence of such a life as "utter darkness" (2 Pet 2:17; Jude 13). Conversely, "light" is associated with God's presence, both, as we have seen, incarnationally and subsequently concerning the followers of the Incarnate One. Just as Jesus referred to himself as the "light of the world," his disciples should be that (Matt 5:14), something they—as Paul emphasizes—can only be if they have a share in or are part of the light: "For at one time you were darkness, but now you are light in the Lord. Walk as children of light" (Eph 5:8). Or, possibly concerning the initial contrast between light and darkness in creation: "For you are all children of light, children of the day. We are not of the night or of the darkness" (1 Thess 5:5).

Thus, there is a biblical-theological argument that light is not just a divine attribute or a poetic garment but an expression of something essential in God's being. The connection between light, life, creation, and renewal in Isaiah and John suggests that this is also the case in Gen 1:3. In that case, we are dealing with a kind of negative ontology where light, as an expression of life, goodness, and blessing, is explicitly articulated based on what it is not, namely, darkness as an expression of nonlife (תֹהוּ וָבֹהוּ, *tohu wabohu*, "formless and void"). And although it might be tempting to add "evil and curse" as opposed to "goodness and blessing," the text speaks against such a "reintroduction of the chaos struggle," as there is no explicit textual basis for understanding either חֹשֶׁךְ (*hōshek*), "darkness," תְהוֹם (*tᵉhôm*, "the deep") or תֹהוּ וָבֹהוּ (*tohu wabohu*, "formless and void") as evil or antagonistic to God. Rather, darkness is the backdrop without which light would not be light. The fact that darkness is not explicitly said to be created by God but that it is part of the created world could be interpreted to mean that it represents a non-world, a world as it would appear if the good, blessed act of creation described in verse 3 were deprived of "light" understood as God's life-giving and sustaining creative power, or as Augustine famously phrased it, "evil is that which is contrary to nature . . . that which falls away from essence and tends to non-existence . . . Evil was nothing but a privation of good (that, indeed, it has no being)."[251] And without formulating a proper theodicy,

---

251. Augustine, *De moribus manichaeorum* 2.2.2; *Confessiones* 3.7.

it would explain that darkness only became evil and cursed when the "serpent" and later humanity chose it, and ontologically, it is created by the one who chooses it, not by God. Such an understanding maintains that while the "serpent" and humanity could choose between "light" and "darkness," only God can define what is "light" and what is "darkness." This happens through the contrasting of light and darkness in Gen 1:2–3, just as the significant emphasis on separation in the rest of the creation account—including the distinction between man and woman—serves to underline what must be kept separate if the creation is not to become the non-world it is contrasted with in verse 2.

Such an understanding of Gen 1:2–3 would also explain the challenging statement in Isa 45:7 that "[I] form [יוֹצֵר, *yôṣēr*] light and create [בּוֹרֵא, *vôrē'*] darkness; I make [עֹשֶׂה, *ʿōśeʰ*] peace and create [בּוֹרֵא, *vôrē'*] evil; I, the Lord, do all these things." Nicolai Winther-Nielsen has shown in his article "God Does Not Act Evil!" how the creation terminology in Isa 45:6e–12 activates "a great intertextual potential in the use of the three creation verbs" in verse 7, and that in the immediate context, "there are several other linguistic allusions from Gen 1–3, so that the creation narrative can be traced behind almost every line in Isa 45:6e–12d."[252] In this context, Winther-Nielsen suggests that "when the verb about God's creative action (*ûvôrē'*) is very surprisingly combined here with rāʕ 'evil,' it may be an allusion to the serpent that seduced the woman to rebel against God," and that Isaiah is therefore implying that "God not only formed peace in Eden but also created the serpent as one of the field's animals."[253] Isaiah's purpose in activating Gen 1–3 is, therefore, that "all the evil adversaries are just created beings, subject to God's full control so that He can set the limit for evil and suffering" and that there is "a direct allusion to the serpent as a symbol of the evil enemies who are reduced to creatures rebelling against God but whom God can defeat."[254] If darkness is understood as the non-world, which only becomes evident when light is created, and if light is cast upon darkness, making it clear what is not light, it may provide an additional layer to Winther-Nielsen's interpretation. In this context, the Lord does not create darkness and evil as an expression of an evil attitude and in an ontological sense, but in the sense that they emerge as a logical contrast and a human choice when "light" and "peace" are positively created. In Isaiah's time, evil in the form

---

252. Winther-Nielsen, "Gud handler ikke ondt!," 215–16.
253. Winther-Nielsen, "Gud handler ikke ondt!," 216.
254. Winther-Nielsen, "Gud handler ikke ondt!," 216.

of "darkness" and "misfortune" was a long-realized evil that the Lord allowed to exist. Therefore—unlike the case of the first humans—it was not solely an unrealized evil potential but a visible, realized evil. By alluding to both "the serpent" in Gen 3 and the separation of light and darkness in Gen 1:2–3, Isaiah therefore suggests that the darkness and the evil/misfortune that the Lord also created in the historical context of the text were the consequence of the same rejection of "light," which had been a logical possibility since the morning of creation and which through the free choice of "the serpent" and humanity resulted in the visibly realized evil, which would also be the consequence of the people's unfaithfulness in Isaiah's time. At the same time, the possible allusion to the serpent in Gen 3 emphasizes that just as the Creator promised to crush the evil that was realized through the serpent and the first humans' fatal rejection of "light" and "goodness," so he will also crush the evil that would be the "exiled" consequence of the people's rejection in Isaiah's time—among other things by using Cyrus to crush the human agents of evil, the Babylonians. Although all of this might seem like a digression from the discussion of gender identity, there are nonetheless two points we need to take with us from the above discussion. First, only God has the right to define what is "light" and "darkness" and to describe what distinctions or separations must, therefore, be maintained in order for the goodness in "light" not to be transformed into a "dark" non-world. Second, it is evil—and results in evil—when humanity chooses "darkness" over "light." In what sense it is evil, we will return to in the discussion of what it means, for example, for same-sex intercourse to be referred to as תּוֹעֵבָה (*tôʕēvāʰ*, "abomination").

Another aspect, as far as separation is concerned, is the fundamental and explicit binary character of creation: the heavens and the earth, darkness and light, night and day, the waters above and the waters below, luminaries for day and night, male and female, working days and holy days. Although not decisive in and of itself, this binary mode of creation nevertheless speaks against an understanding of *gender* as fluid or nonbinary. It could be argued, of course, that the binary only refers to *biological* sex and, therefore, does not preclude multiple *psychological* or *social* genders. One example is Linda Herzer, who argues that "*the male or female gender binary* classification system suggested by Gen 1:27 is ... inadequate to describe the reality of those born with the innate knowledge that their *internal gender identity* does not match their external genitals."[255] Another is Austen Hartke, who states that "this verse does not discredit other sexes or genders, any more than the verse about the separation of day from night rejects the existence of dawn and dusk... In the same way we call God the Alpha and Omega, implying all things from first to last and in between, the author of Gen 1 is merely using the same dualistic poetic device to corral the infinite diversity of creation into categories we can easily understand."[256] For the same reason "intersex people are equally God's image-bearers... 'The fact that male and female are both created in the divine image is intended to convey the value, dominion, and relationality shared by both men and women, but not the idea that the complementarity of the genders is somehow necessary to fully express or embody the divine image.'"[257]

This contradicts what we saw in the discussion on the relation between body and gender. Furthermore, the text does not address a person's internal sense of who they are, that is, gender identity and masculinity/femininity, but the *biological* binary as an expression of the image. It could also be argued that just as God created all *kinds* of living creatures (Gen 2:21), he also created all kinds of humans and that the text only mentions those crucial to "fleshing out" the mandate in 2:28. This bypasses the fact, however, that לְמִינֵהֶם ("after their kinds") in 2:21 refers to species or categories, not sex. Whatever the reference is to species or broader categories, each of them is created male and female as mentioned in Gen 6:19: "And of every living thing of all flesh, you shall bring two of every sort into the ark to keep them alive with you. They shall be male [זָכָר, *zāxār*] and female [נְקֵבָה, *nᵊqēvāʰ*]." Supportive of such a rejection is also the episode in Gen 2, where Adam surveys all the male and female animals and finds no suitable partner. Only a *female* partner of his own flesh suits him as a male. The point is primarily, of course, that the partner must be "flesh of my flesh" (2:23), but the text also describes the choice as archetypically binary.

Megan K. DeFranza agrees that "in the early parts of God's story, separation equaled holiness" and that "mixing was detestable, an abomination." DeFranza continues, however, to assert that "like a great storyteller, the Master Author was writing a complicated plot with surprises in

---

255. Herzer, *Bible and the Transgender Experience*, 71. Emphasis original.
256. Hartke, *Transforming*, 57, 63.
257. Hartke, *Transforming*, 59.

store for which God's people were not prepared," and that the inclusion of eunuchs in Isa 56:3–7 adds a new plotline:

> This new trajectory is bolstered by Jesus's acknowledgment of those born with bodies that fall between male and female, and castrated men who were no longer viewed as men nor granted the privileges of masculinity in the Gospel of Matt. The narrative climaxes in the baptism of the Ethiopian eunuch in the book of Acts. The story of eunuchs parallels the narrative of clean and unclean things (food, animals, woven cloth, plants) . . . Israel had been set apart, not to remain separate forever but so that eventually "the blessing given to Abraham might come to the gentiles through Christ Jesus, so that by faith we might receive the promise of the Spirit."[258]

Whereas DeFranza is right, of course, that some of the applications of the boundary-keeping rationale behind these prohibitions "were to be left behind," it is a *non sequitur* that the *principles* also should be abandoned. In a response to DeFranza, Own Strachan notes, "Whatever their background, the repentant eunuch is not left out of the kingdom of God. This does not mean that Scripture in any way endorses personal castration; far from it. It does mean that grace is offered to all in Christ. Confession and repentance enable sinners of every kind to enter God's household as sons and daughters."[259] In his response to Justin Sabia-Tanis, Strachan writes, "Yes, every person is made in God's image, but sadly, we image-bearers hate God in our natural state. Just because we recognize that every person in some finished way reflects the likeness of God does not mean that we can affirm their lifestyle, their predilections, their self-conception. The man who cheats on his wife is an image-bearer, but the fact of his image-bearing in no way allows me to overlook or affirm his adultery."[260]

The purity regulation "A man with crushed or severed genitals may not enter the assembly of the Lord" (Deut 23:1 NET) clearly serves to maintain this boundary and would have supported prohibitions against medical or surgical interventions to facilitate a cross-gender identity.

---

258. DeFranza, "Good News for Gender Minorities," 172.
259. Strachan, "Response to Megan DeFranza," 181.
260. Strachan, "Response to Justin Sabia-Tanis," 226.

CROSS-DRESSING

It is in this context that we should understand a group of texts that address cross-dressing. When it says in Deut 22:5 that "a woman shall not wear a man's garment, nor shall a man put on a woman's cloak," it must be understood as a prohibition against obscuring the connection between the external, biological, and the internal, experienced gender. The prohibition appears immediately with prohibitions that mark boundaries between other seemingly arbitrary categories: "You shall not plow with an ox and a donkey together. You shall not wear cloth of wool and linen mixed together" (Deut 22:10–11). However, these seemingly arbitrary distinctions dissolve when viewed as symbolic acts meant to mark respect for the boundaries in creation, which, according to Gen 1–2, are embedded in it. This includes the created and thus given "boundary" between male and female. The prohibition in 22:5 is debated because it is not immediately clear what the term כְלִי־גֶבֶר ($x^{\partial}li$-gever) means. According to the *Theological Wordbook of the Old Testament*, the semantic field for כְלִי ($x^{\partial}li$), includes meanings such as "armor," "bag," "carriage," "furniture," "instrument," "jewels," "sacks," "stuff," "things," "tools," "vessels," and "weapons."[261] A classic interpretation is that it should be understood in the sense of "clothing," and therefore, it is a prohibition against transsexuality in the Canaanite fertility religion. For example, Claude Mariottini argues that "although scholars have rejected the anti-transvestitism law of Deut 22:5 to be a ban on Canaanite practices, I take the view that this Deuteronomic prohibition is a protest against the immoral practices of Canaanite fertility religion."[262] As we have seen, the challenge for these interpretations is that we have no explicit testimony that the fluctuating gender identity that characterized the Ishtar cult was also practiced in the Canaanite counterpart.[263] In a different vein, Harold Vedeler has argued in his article "Reconstructing Meaning in Deut 22:5: Gender, Society, and Transvestitism in Israel and the Ancient Near East" that כְלִי ($x^{\partial}li$), in light of the Hittite and Akkadian cognates, means "weapons," and that in Deut 22:5, it is used as a symbol of the masculine.[264] Vedeler thus writes with approval about the Hittitologist Harry Hoffner's comparison of the Hebrew lexeme and its Hittite cognate:

---

261. Harris et al., *TWOT*, 440.
262. Mariottini, "Transvestism in Ancient Israel."
263. Kimuhu, *Leviticus*, 174–75.
264. Vedeler, "Reconstructing Meaning," 459–76.

He concludes that Deut 22:5 was meant to prevent women from usurping masculine symbols and the power that went with them, but since clothing was not specifically identified with masculinity the way it was with femininity, the prevention of women taking on a male role was achieved not through a clothing ban but rather through a tool or weapon ban. Similarly, he argues that the ban on men wearing female clothing was designed not to prevent men from usurping female power, but to prevent that power from weakening them.[265]

The weakness in this interpretation is that it is normally specified that it is weapons with the construction כְּלֵי מִלְחָמָה ($k^\partial lê\ milḥāmā^h$) (Judg 18:11; 16; 17; 1 Sam 8:12; 2 Sam 1:27; Deut 1:41; Jer 21:4; 51:20).

However, there is another possibility that makes more sense both in the light of the comparative material and the biblical context, and which, despite the silence in the Canaanite texts, partially supports Mariottini's interpretation. In the review of the comparative material, we saw that fluctuating gender identity was a characteristic of the cult around the Sumerian Inanna/Akkadian Ishtar. Since Ishtar's Canaanite or Northwest Semitic counterpart ʿAshtart or ʿAthtart (cf. the Greek Ἀστάρτη, Astártē) was worshipped in Canaan from the Bronze Age to antiquity, it can be argued that such fluctuating gender identity also found expression in the Canaanite cult. This is likely the Ishtar cult mentioned in Jer 7:18 and 44:18, which refers to sacrifices to the "queen of heaven," and these references to the Canaanite counterpart to Ishtar show that there was such a cult in Jeremiah's time. As for the criticism of the Northwest Semitic texts' silence, Johnson Kimuhu points out that while there is no evidence of fluctuating gender identity in ritual texts, its attestation in the epics must be seen as a reflection of cultic practice: "While these myths are stories about gods or sacred stories, they are at the same time stories that explain the ways of the real world of Ugarit. Brunner-Traut shows that this was also the case with Egyptian mythology in which the succession in government from Osiris to his son Horus became the primordial image of royal succession."[266] However, this correspondence between the epic material and cultic practice is debated, especially because we have no texts that describe such a correspondence with the cult. Arguing that because such correspondence can be demonstrated in some

---

265. Vedeler, "Reconstructing Meaning," 471; with reference to Hoffner, "Symbols for Masculinity and Femininity," 331–34.

266. Kimuhu, *Leviticus*, 188.

parts of Egyptian context, it must also be the case in Canaanite religion. Therefore, it must stand as a thesis that can be made plausible if texts supporting it are found or falsified if texts contradict it. Correspondence or not, Canaanite religion, as far as it is reflected in the epics, included examples of transsexuality. This is also supported by the aforementioned Aqhat poem, which Cyrus Gordon believes must have been known in the society to which the prohibition in Deut 22:5 is directed: "The Israelite reaction is to forbid transvestism, another aspect of Canaanite society that they found reprehensible. Again, one needs to place this in its proper context. A close reading of the biblical prohibition reveals that the female is referred to first, then the male follows. This runs counter to most laws in the Pentateuch, which are either addressed to males solely or to males first and females second. This is not coincidental but suggests an even closer connection with Pūġatu's action detailed in the Epic of Aqhat."[267] If the transsexuality that is undeniably described in the epics had its parallel in cultic practice, the prohibition against cross-dressing in Deut 22:5 should likely be understood in this context. All interpretations may find support in ancient and medieval sources, however. Ruth Sandberg lists three instances in ancient and medieval Rabbinic sources that interpret Deut 22:5 to refer to clothing and four texts that point to armory and weapons.[268] As far as clothing is concerned, reference to sexual promiscuity and/or practice associated with the worship of other gods is mentioned by Rabbi Shlomo Yitzchaki (Rashi), Rabbi Moses ben Maimon (Rambam or Maimonides), and Thomas Aquinas.[269]

CULTIC PROSTITUTION

When it comes to the question of whether cultic prostitution was a part of the practice in Canaanite religion and whether the prohibition against cross-dressing should be seen in relation to such a practice, it is relevant to take a closer look at several biblical texts that mention the so-called קְדֵשִׁים ($q^ed\bar{e}\check{s}\hat{i}m$) and קְדֵשׁוֹת ($q^ed\bar{e}\check{s}\hat{o}t$), translated variously as a male/female "sacred prostitute" (NET), "shrine prostitute" (NIV), "cult prostitute" (NASB), and "temple prostitute" (NRSV, TEV, NLT):

267. Gordon and Rendsburg, *Bible and the Ancient Near East*, 160.
268. Sandberg, *Development and Discontinuity in Jewish Law*, 92–94; cf. Bolich, *Crossdressing in Context*, 31–36.
269. Bolich, *Crossdressing in Context*, 35–36; Aquinas, *Summa Theologica* 4.3.1.

When Judah saw her [Tamar], he thought she was a prostitute [זוֹנָה, zônā*ʰ*], for she had covered her face ... And he asked the men of the place, "Where is the cult prostitute [הַקְּדֵשָׁה, haqqᵉdēšā*ʰ*] who was at Enaim at the roadside?" And they said, "No cult prostitute [קְדֵשָׁה qᵉdēšā*ʰ*] has been here." (Gen 38:15, 20–21)

None of the daughters of Israel shall be a cult prostitute, and none of the sons of Israel shall be a cult prostitute [קְדֵשָׁה, qᵉdēšā*ʰ*, קָדֵשׁ, qādēš]. You shall not bring the fee of a prostitute [אֶתְנַן זוֹנָה, ʔetnan zônā*ʰ*] or the wages of a dog [מְחִיר כֶּלֶב, mᵉḥîr kelev] into the house of the Lord your God in payment for any vow, for both of these are an abomination to the Lord your God. (Deut 23:17–18)

For they [the Judeans] also built for themselves high places and pillars and Asherim on every high hill and under every green tree, and there were also male cult prostitutes [קָדֵשׁ, qādēš] in the land. They did according to all the abominations of the nations that the Lord drove out before the people of Israel. (1 Kgs 14:23–24)

He [Asa] put away the male cult prostitutes [הַקְּדֵשִׁים, haqqᵉdēšîm] out of the land and removed all the idols that his fathers had made. (1 Kgs 15:12)

And from the land he exterminated the remnant of the male cult prostitutes [הַקָּדֵשׁ, haqqādēš] who remained in the days of his father Asa. (1 Kgs 22:46)

He tore down the quarters of the male cultic prostitutes [הַקְּדֵשִׁים, haqqᵉdēšim] in the Lord's temple, where women were weaving shrines for Asherah. (2 Kgs 23:7 NET)

I will not punish your daughters when they commit prostitution, nor your daughters-in-law when they commit adultery. For the men consort with harlots [הַזֹּנוֹת, hazzōnot], they sacrifice with temple prostitutes [הַקְּדֵשׁוֹת, haqqᵉdēšot]. It is true: "A people that lacks understanding will come to ruin!" (Hos 4:14 NET)

The godless at heart nourish anger, they do not cry out even when he binds them. They die in their youth, and their life ends among the male cultic prostitutes [בַּקְּדֵשִׁים, baqqᵉdēšim]. (Job 36:13–14 NET)

As these texts show, the references to the so-called קְדֵשִׁים ($q^ed\bar{e}\hat{s}îm$) are consistently negative in the biblical material. At first glance, it is difficult *not* to equate זוֹנָה, ($z\hat{o}n\bar{a}^h$, "prostitute") with these קְדֵשִׁים ($q^ed\bar{e}\hat{s}îm$), and thus understand them as (cultic) prostitutes. Being collocated with זוֹנָה, ($z\hat{o}n\bar{a}^h$, "prostitute") in Genesis, Deuteronomy, and Hosea, seems compelling. However, as we shall see, such an equivalence is not generally accepted.

In interpretation literature, there has emerged a certain consensus that קְדֵשִׁים ($q^ed\bar{e}\hat{s}îm$) does *not* denote cultic prostitution but rather a type of priests or cultic workers who, though not as an integrated part of the actual cult, also offered sex within or outside the temple complex. The background for this consensus can be found in the many texts discovered from Mesopotamia and Ugarit, which have contributed to a better understanding of the cultic personnel in the temples. Patrick Michel, in summarizing the material, points out that the consonants *qdš*, which in various forms signify dedication or consecration to something that is "a holy one,"[270] often appear in administrative lists alongside *khnm*, "priests," and serve as a broad term for a group of cultic personnel.[271] In Hammurabi's law, *qadištu* is mentioned side by side with two other functionaries, *nadîtu* and *kulmašītu*. In Old Babylonian sources, *qadištu* is associated with childbirth (Atrahasis epic) and childcare,[272] while in Middle Assyrian sources,[273] this functionary is linked to magic. Other texts connect this functionary with purification rituals, and in Ugaritic texts, the male *qdš* is described as a singer.[274] Michel concludes that although a wide range of functions is associated with this type of cultic personnel, there is no evidence that cultic prostitution was included.[275] Alternatively, Gruber has argued that the biblical Hebrew קְדֵשָׁה ($q^ed\bar{e}\hat{s}\bar{a}^h$) refers to a secular prostitute, while the Akkadian cognates denote cultic functionaries whose role does not involve sexual activities.[276] In her recent study

---

270. Regarding the Hebrew terms קְדֵשָׁה ($q^ed\bar{e}\hat{s}\bar{a}^h$) and קָדֵשׁ ($q\bar{a}d\bar{e}\hat{s}$), the basic meaning of the verb קָדַשׁ ($q\bar{a}da\hat{s}$), according to *TWOT*, is "to be hallowed, holy, sanctified; to consecrate, sanctify, prepare, dedicate" (McComiskey, "1990 קדשׁ"). Thus, a קְדֵשָׁה ($q^ed\bar{e}\hat{s}\bar{a}^h$) or קָדֵשׁ ($q\bar{a}d\bar{e}\hat{s}$) must be understood, at a minimum, as someone who is (voluntarily or forcibly) consecrated to service in the sanctuary.

271. Michel, "Functions and Personalities," 441–52.

272. VAS 7 19:1–3; 37:13–17.

273. KAR 154.

274. KTU 1.112.

275. Michel, "Functions and Personalities."

276. Gruber, "Hebrew Qedešah," 133–48.

Harlot or Holy Woman, Phyllis Bird similarly argues that the Akkadian *qadištu* served as cultic officiant. Bird argues that these officiants were well known to ancient Israelite audiences and primarily associated with local outdoor sanctuaries in Israel and Judah during the eighth century BCE. Bird explains the collocation of *qᵊdēšāʰ* with *zônāʰ* "prostitute" as having arisen from a real social situation where they turned to this profession after the abolishment of local sanctuaries. The mention of *qᵊdēšîm* and *qᵊdēšôt* in the books of Deuteronomy, Kings, and Hosea should be understood, therefore, as later and possibly literarily constructed Deuteronomistic prohibitions.[277]

Kurt Noll summarizes what the comparative, non-biblical texts provide evidence for:

> Throughout the ancient Near East, a Qadesh was a male holy one, and a Qedeshah was a female holy one (see, for example, KTU 1.112). They were low-level servants who assisted in rituals and performed menial tasks associated with the upkeep of a temple. In Mesopotamia, there is evidence that these unmarried individuals became sexually promiscuous in ways that had nothing to do with religious observance (compare 1 Sam 2:22), which might be the reason for Deuteronomy's pragmatic decision to do away with the office of the "holy one" entirely.[278]

In relation to the discussion of whether the Old Testament קְדֵשָׁה (*qᵊdēšāʰ*)/קָדֵשׁ (*qādēš*) should be understood as expressions of a more general cultic prostitution, Joan Goodnick Westenholz wrote in 1989 that among the *qadištu*'s roles was a gender-specific female activity such as the task of procreation and nurture and that "'sacred prostitution' is an amalgam of misconceptions, presuppositions, and inaccuracies,"[279] while Mary Leith in 2005 formulates it as follows:

> Whereas scholars formerly saw female "sacred prostitutes" all over the Near East, they now detect a complex range of female cultic offices whose exact nature remains elusive. Terms once thought to refer to "sacred" prostitution are now understood to describe women who worked in the cult establishment. Some may have been prostitutes not because the cult required ritual sex but because of monetary vows women, even married

---

277. Bird and Glenn, *Harlot or Holy Woman?*, 359.
278. Noll, "Canaanite Religion."
279. Westenholz, "Tamar, Qĕdēšā, Qadištu," 254, 263.

women, had made to the deity in exchange for a pregnancy, cure from illness, or other favor.²⁸⁰

In the same vein, Kurt L. Noll formulates as follows:

> No ancient biblical author believed that the Canaanites or anyone else were having sex in their temple services. In the ancient world, minor temple personnel were unmarried slaves owned by the god of the temple. As such, there were numerous instances in which these "holy ones" were sexually promiscuous or engaged in the sex trade, but this had nothing to do with their status as temple personnel. It might, however, explain why Deut 23:18 desires to ban such personnel from the temple of Yahweh.²⁸¹

Noll also argues that "prostitute," זוֹנָה (zônā^h) and קְדֵשָׁה (q^{e}dēšā^h) are not synonymous in Gen 38:15 and 21–22, where Judah discreetly attempts to pay for the sexual service he unknowingly received from his daughter-in-law Tamar:

> The story claims that Judah is concerned about his reputation, so it is no surprise that when he sends payment, he tries to disguise the reason for his payment. His servant asks the local villagers for the Qedeshah, not the prostitute. If the reader equates the two words, the creative humor of the tale is lost. In ancient Canaan, a Qedeshah might receive payment connected to (nonsexual) services in the local temple. Judah's servant tries to fool the villagers into believing that he seeks to make an honorable payment.²⁸²

Edward Lipiński has recently expressed that even though "cult prostitution existed in some parts of the Near East and in Phoenician colonies of the Western Mediterranean," such cultic sex was often associated with "passage rites having a religious dimension and performed once in a lifetime," and references to sex in temples usually concerned "prostitution performed occasionally by members of the temple staff on temple grounds, thus contributing to the income of the sanctuary."²⁸³ Regarding the biblical material, Lipiński mentions that although cultic sex in this sense was part of the practice in the biblical authors' Canaanite surroundings, and although there may be a vague reference to cultic

---

280. Leith, "Gender and Religion."
281. Noll, *Canaan and Israel in Antiquity*, 21n31.
282. Noll, *Canaan and Israel in Antiquity*, 259–61, quoted from Noll, "Canaanite Religion."
283. Lipiński, "Cult Prostitution," 26–27.

prostitution in 2 Kgs 23:7, the Hebrew *qdšt*—even though it is translated as "harlot" or "prostitute"—should be understood figuratively, as other occurrences of the term serve as "metaphoric allusions to Israel's infidelity to God or as synonyms of harlotry."[284] Lipiński also mentions, in connection with 2 Kgs 23:7, that if the הַקְּדֵשִׁים (*haqqᵊdēšîm*) mentioned were involved in prostitution, they were more likely pimps than prostitutes, as "the qedeshim are thus said to have been renting houses in the temple precinct to some women, possibly for prostitution. Perhaps the men were also acting as pimps."[285] Such a figurative understanding of the Hebrew *qdšt*, according to both Leith and Lipiński, also applies to Hos 4:14, where זֹנוֹת (*zōnôt*, "prostitutes") appear parallel to קְדֵשׁוֹת (*qᵊdēšôt*). The same caution is found in more conservative literature.

Victor Matthews, Mark Chavalas, and John H. Walton distinguish between "sacred" and "cultic" prostitution in *The IVP Bible Background Commentary*, where the former covers women's sexual services as part of temple "fundraising," while the latter deals with actual ritual sex. While the existence of the former is indisputable and massively attested, "the existence of cultic prostitution on either level . . . is more difficult to prove. Cultic prostitution is not easily confirmed in Mesopotamia unless one includes the annual sacred marriage ritual." Nevertheless, it is concluded that "it is hard to imagine that prostitutes serving at the temple of Ishtar (who personified sexual force) were not viewed as playing a sacred role in the fertility cult," and that such sexual practices must have existed in the Canaanite context reflected in biblical texts and polemicized against.[286]

Based on the non-biblical comparative material, it is reasonable to understand the Hebrew קְדֵשָׁה (*qᵊdēšāʰ*)/קָדֵשׁ (*qādēš*) in a similar way, that is, as a cultic functionary who, in certain cases, also offered sex, though not as an organized part of their cultic function. The crucial point then becomes whether the biblical texts only prohibit or critically address this functionary's service in the cult, or whether the prohibition also, or even primarily, applies to their sexual "side job." The texts clearly support the latter understanding. Firstly, the reference to Tamar as קְדֵשָׁה (*qᵊdēšāʰ*) in Gen 38 shows that these functionaries were known to offer sexual services for payment. As John Day notes, the collocation of the terms make sense

---

284. Lipiński, "Cult Prostitution," 27; cf. the aforementioned argument regarding "sexual" titles as figurative language for religious devotion (or lack thereof). Anagnostou-Laoutides and Charles, "Herodotus on Sacred Marriage."

285. Lipiński, "Cult Prostitution in Ancient Israel?", 17.

286. Matthews et al., *IVP Bible Background Commentary*, Deut 23:18–20.

"only if *qᵉdēšāʰ* had broadly the same meaning as *zônāʰ*, for otherwise the men would not have understood the nature of the woman Judah was seeking! Possibly Hirah used the term *qᵉdēšāʰ* as a more elevated expression or because he was enquiring of Canaanites, but whatever the reason it makes no sense unless Tamar was perceived to be a cult prostitute."[287] Day admits that "there is no mention of a sanctuary in the narrative, although it should be noted that no other building either is mentioned in which the sexual intercourse took place," and adds that "wherever the intercourse took place, it is inexplicable that Hirah should ask about the whereabouts of a *qᵉdēšāʰ* unless Tamar was perceived on the basis of her appearance to be a cultic prostitute."[288] This applies even if Noll may be correct in pointing out the humor in Judah's attempt to disguise his visit to a זוֹנָה (*zônāʰ*, "prostitute") through his friend from Adullam. Secondly, if the female קְדֵשָׁה (*qᵉdēšāʰ*) was known to offer such services, it is reasonable to understand the prohibition in Deut 23:18 against both male and female functionaries as a prohibition that also applies to such sexual services. This is supported by Hos 4:14, where it is criticized that "the men themselves go aside with prostitutes and sacrifice with holy prostitutes." The criticism clearly focuses on the reception and offer of payment by the female cultic functionaries for the men's visits to the female prostitutes [הַזֹּנוֹת, *hazzōnôt*], which must also have been known to the female [קְדֵשָׁה, *qᵉdēšāʰ*], as indisputably indicated in Gen 38. The criticism in Hos 4:14 and in the other cases (Deut 23:18; 1 Kgs 14:24; 15:12; 22:47; 2 Kgs 23:7) must, therefore, indirectly or implicitly also refer to male functionaries engaging in prostitution. Such an understanding is also supported by the Septuagint (LXX), which translates the Hebrew קְדֵשָׁה (*qᵉdēšāʰ*)/קָדֵשׁ (*qādēš*) with πόρνη/πορνεύων ("harlot, prostitute"). In contrast, the Vulgate translates the Hebrew קְדֵשָׁה (*qᵉdēšāʰ*) with *meretrix* ("prostitute, harlot, courtesan") and קָדֵשׁ (*qādēš*) with *scortator* ("harlot, fornicator").[289] Regarding the LXX, DeYoung also mentions that the LXX uses various words to translate the Hebrew קָדֵשׁ (*qādēš*), "including 'initiates' who were dedicated to deities where homosexuality was often practiced (words from the *teleō* word group: *telesphoros, teliskomenos, teletas, tetelesmenos*), 'male cult prostitute' (*porneuōn* and *kadesim*), 'changed of sex' (*endiellagmenos*), 'bond of union' (*syndesmos*), and 'wounded' or 'crushed' (*titroskōmenē*). All of these terms allow for a

287. Day, "Does the Old Testament," 3.
288. Day, "Does the Old Testament," 3n1.
289. Lewis and Short, "Scortātor."

homosexual meaning. This finds support from the context and from the use of *bdelygma*, which relates 1 Kgs 14:24 to Lev 18 and 20."²⁹⁰

As for the "prostitute's fee" and "dog's pay" mentioned in Deut 23:19, especially the meaning of the latter is debated. Since the meaning of the former likely involves payment to the temple that included a (female) sexual service as a "commission," it is reasonable to understand "dog's pay" as the male parallel. Although *TWOT* mentions that כֶּלֶב (*kelev*) can figuratively refer to men in a derogatory sense in some instances (e.g., 1 Sam 17:43; Ps 22:17, 21; 2 Kgs 8:13), it is not used elsewhere to refer to cultic personnel or male prostitutes.

When *HALOT* suggests "male cult prostitute (pederast)" as one of the figurative meanings of the word, it is based on the word's meaning outside of the biblical material.²⁹¹ Nissinen has noted that the Sumerian ideogram UR.SAL for the cultic personnel category *assinnu* means both "female dog" and "man/woman," and Malul suggests a parallel "between this 'female dog' (a male homosexual who permits sexual intercourse per anus, in the manner of a dog?) and the 'dog' mentioned in Deut 23:19 next to the prostitute."²⁹² Relevant is also a Phoenician inscription from Kition (modern-day Larnaca in Cyprus) from the fourth century BCE, where "dogs" appear in a list of temple rations:

> For the prostitutes and the 22 musicians at the sacrifice
> For the Dogs and for the Lions 3 qr and 3 p'
> For the 3 servants 3 qp'²⁹³

Brian Peckham mentions the use of the word *klb*, "dog," in Deut 23:19. Still, he rejects the idea that it refers to male prostitutes: "There is reason to suppose that these 'Dogs' (*klbm*) and 'Lions' (*grm*, cf. Heb *gûr*) were temple servants in animal disguise, impersonating legendary figures or gods in the rituals. However, there seems to be no conclusive evidence that they were prostitutes."²⁹⁴ While some scholars argue for an interpretation of "dogs" and "lions" as literal animals or human "mask-bearers," others lean toward the figurative translation of "male prostitutes." This includes H. Donner and W. Röllig who translate it as "Temple pederasts"

---

290. DeYoung, *Homosexuality*, 135.

291. Holladay, *HALOT*, 476.

292. Nissinen, *Homoeroticism in the Biblical World*, 41; Malul, "David's curse of Joab (2 Sam 3:29)," 54; Malul, "(Leviticus 16:21)," 440.

293. Kition Inscription, B (reverse), 9–11, quoted from Peckham, "Notes," 306.

294. Peckham, "Notes," 317.

with the admitting comment that "it is questionable whether animals or humans are meant."[295] Regarding its occurrence in Deut 23:19, there are equally divided opinions on the meaning. Lawrence Stager writes about the discovery of hundreds of carefully buried dogs in ancient Ashkelon that the dogs must have been considered sacred animals, probably associated with the worship of *ršpmkl*, "Resheph-Mukol," the Canaanite god of healing. The "dog's pay" mentioned in Deut 23:19 must, according to Stager, be understood as payment to the personnel who took care of the "sacred dogs" that were likely kept outside Jerusalem.[296] In that case, the prohibition in Deut 23:19 reflects a practice that was contrary to the worship of the Lord in the temple. Elaine Adler Goodfriend is skeptical of Stager's interpretation but arrives at a similar understanding of the term "dogs" by seeing the prohibition in Deut 23:19 as

> the Bible's attempt to alienate or repulse the canine (and even that which was acquired with a dog!) from YHWH's dwelling place. The canine, the indiscriminate, blood-thirsty scavenger and antithesis of ruminating "kosher" animals should in no guise be given access to holiness! This attitude is also manifested in Matt 7, "Do not give dogs what is holy." According to 4QMMT, canines are forbidden access to the "holy camp," Jerusalem. Deuteronomy's concern is for the source of one's donation to the Temple economy. Just as a prostitute should not use her wages to pay a vow, so the barter of a detested predator is an inappropriate source of income for the sanctuary.[297]

Phyllis Bird rejects Goodfriend's interpretation but also argues that it refers to a literal dog and not a (male) prostitute. She provides three reasons for this interpretation.

Firstly, Bird points out that the grammatical second person masculine form is characteristic of addressing the collective audience in the apodictic laws. She explains that "the 2 m. sg. (alternating with pl.) is the common form for addressing the community as a whole through its adult male representatives and may be understood to include the wife of the male addressee or, collectively conceived, the women of the whole congregation. But when a woman is specifically targeted, either alone or alongside a man, the third person is always used."[298]

295. Donner and Röllig, *Kanaanäische und aramäische Inschriften: Texte*, 2.54.
296. Stager, "Why Were Hundreds," 27–42.
297. Goodfriend, "Could Keleb," 390.
298. Bird, "Of Whores and Hounds," 356.

GENDER AND BODY IN BIBLICAL CREATION THEOLOGY

Secondly, both dogs and prostitutes are presented as "ultimate symbols of dishonor" in other texts.[299] Bird references 1 Kgs 22:38, where it is mentioned that after Ahab's death, "when they washed his chariot by the pool of Samaria, the dogs licked up his blood, and the prostitutes washed themselves in it."

Thirdly, the term אֶתְנַן (?etnan), in relation to זוֹנָה (zônā*ʰ*, meaning "prostitute's fee"), is used figuratively elsewhere (Ezek 16:31, 34, 41; Hos 9:1; Mic 1:7; Isa 23:17, 18). Bird's argumentation also includes the idea that verses 18 and 19 belong to different redactional strata, and therefore the reference to קְדֵשִׁים (qᵊdēšîm) in verse 18 cannot be used as an argument for זוֹנָה (zônā*ʰ*) and כֶּלֶב (kelev) in verse 19 being cultic personnel. Even though קְדֵשִׁים (qᵊdēšîm) in verse 18 could be understood as a "literal" title for temple personnel, both זוֹנָה (zônā*ʰ*) and כֶּלֶב (kelev) in verse 19 must still be understood metaphorically. Bird concludes:

> In Deut 23:19 the prohibition appears to target "cheap" payment of vows, or possibly "dirty money," not ritual sex or foreign cults. While mention of the temple in this prohibition may suggest that the payments are ritually "unclean," "purity" language is lacking in this verse, and the secondary "abomination" clause denotes revulsion, not impurity. The emphasis appears to be on the demeaning character or negligible amount of the payments offered as fulfillment of vows, rather than the purity of the offering. "Harlot's wage" and "price of a dog" do not tell us in any specific terms what the prohibited sources of income are, but brand a class of revenue as unacceptable by identification with common symbols of dishonor and disgust. Whether they carry more specific connotations of cheap, unclean, or unethical is impossible to say.[300]

John Burns argues for the traditional understanding by pointing to using the dog as a symbol of passive submission. It was used by the Egyptian vassal kings in Canaan, who added to the conventional formula of submission, "I fall at the feet of the king, my lord, seven and seven times," sometimes the phrase "both on the stomach and on the back."[301] Vassal kings thus presented themselves as dogs, prostrating and rolling over, which Burns argues is visually documented in some cases. Burns concludes that "this is precisely the position of a dog, fawning

---

299. Bird, "Of Whores and Hounds," 360.
300. Bird, "Of Whores and Hounds," 362.
301. Burns, "Devotee or Deviate," 7; EA 63, 64, 65.

but uncertain as to its reception, the head between the front paws, the rear raised exposing the animal's anus, frequently accompanied by tail-wagging and wriggling of the hindquarters. The image of rolling from stomach to back is also telling. Thus, the line between the perception of the 'dog' as a faithful or groveling servant or as a homosexual (prostitute) submitting his rear for penetration must have been a fine one, epithet and image were easily transferred."[302]

In addition, it must be noted that while a figurative meaning of an expression such as אֶתְנַן (ʾetnan) is found in many places, a figurative meaning always presupposes a literal one. Therefore, it is not necessarily a compelling argument for understanding the expression as figurative in Deut 23:19 that it is used figuratively elsewhere.

Figure 8: Israel's King Jehu Submits to Shalmaneser III. The Black Obelisk. 825 BC.

Since it is only in Deut 23:19 that כֶּלֶב (kelev) appears in a potentially unique meaning in biblical Hebrew, it is difficult to conclude the discussion. Ultimately, the crucial question is whether the terms קְדֵשִׁים (qᵊdēšîm, "sacred prostitutes") and זוֹנָה (zônāʰ, "prostitute") should be understood figuratively or literally. On the one hand, there is an argument for a figurative understanding because "prostitute wages" are used

302. Burns, "Devotee or Deviate," 8.

in other contexts as a term for covenant violation and a lack of religious devotion. Additionally, in various places, dogs and prostitutes are representatives of the impure and dishonorable. In this case, "dog's wages" could be interpreted as an offering rejected due to covenant violations. On the other hand, there is considerable evidence for a literal interpretation. As we have seen, both economic and cultic prostitution were undeniably practiced to some extent in Mesopotamia, and it likely also occurred in the Canaanite context, where qdšm is attested as a category of cultic personnel. In this light, it would be reasonable to understand כֶּלֶב (*kelev*) as the male counterpart to זוֹנָה (*zônāʰ*, meaning "male prostitute"). The use of "dogs" as a metaphor for a specific questionable group is also illustrated not only in texts like the Armana letters but also in the New Testament, where "dogs" in Phil 3:2 is mentioned together with or as a metaphor for "evil workers" and "those who mutilate the flesh." If Burns's interpretation of the "dog position" is correct, it must also be seen as support for such a literal interpretation, where "dog's wages" would refer to payment for sex.

Regarding the concept of "harlot's wages," it is interesting that the phenomenon of using income from prostitution to finance cultic sacrifices is exemplified in the book of Proverbs. In contrast to "Lady Wisdom," "Lady Folly" in Prov 7 is described as a prostitute who, to fulfill her vows of offerings, lures the foolish man into buying sex:

> Then the woman came out to meet him,
> dressed like a prostitute and with crafty intent.
> (She is unruly and defiant;
> her feet never stay at home;
> now in the street, now in the squares,
> at every corner she lurks.)
> She took hold of him and kissed him
> and with a brazen face, she said:
> "Today I fulfilled my vows,
> and I have food from my fellowship offering at home.
> So I came out to meet you;
> I looked for you and have found you."
> (Prov 7:10–15, NIV)

This description, with its lack of explanations regarding what the fellowship offering obligation entails and its stylization of "Lady Folly" as a prostitute, indicates that such a practice must have been familiar. Even though "Lady Folly" is not referred to as a temple prostitute, it at least suggests that prostitution was taking place in connection with cultic offerings.

Cross-Dressing Revisited

Returning to cross-dressing, the formulation in 2 Kgs 23:7 is particularly relevant. It states that concerning King Josiah, "he broke down the houses of the male cult prostitutes who were in the house of the LORD, where the women wove hangings for the Asherah." Regardless of whether קְדֵשִׁים (*qᵊdēšîm*) is translated as "male cult prostitutes" or "male cult workers (who also offered sex)," and whether לָאֲשֵׁרָה (*lāʾᵃšērāʰ*) is translated as "Asherah," "Asherah pole," or "cult site" (as Lipiński argues),[303] it explicitly speaks of weaving (implied to be cloth) for a cultic questionable purpose. While there is no explicit mention of cross-dressing, considering comparative material and the prohibition in Deut 22:5, it is possible to understand these garments as expressions of such practices. Even though it might not be modern-day transgenderism, cross-dressing would still violate the binary gender identity and related sexual practices associated with the Canaanite (and Mesopotamian) gods reflected in the cult. This same underlying concept can be found in Paul's words to the Corinthian church, where he discusses head coverings (1 Cor 11:4–5) and in his admonition in 1 Cor 6:9 that "men who have sex with men" (ἀρσενοκοῖται, *arsenokoitai*) will not inherit the kingdom of God. In this context, Paul uses μαλακοί (*malakoi*) to describe the passive partner in male same-sex sexual practices, while ἀρρενοκοίτης (*arsenokoitēs*) describes the dominant partner. μαλακοί (*malakoi*) refers to the partner who should be or behaves like "the woman," thereby blurring or crossing the binary boundary between male and female.[304] As Franz Delitzsch already articulated, "The immediate design of this prohibition was not to prevent licentiousness or to oppose idolatrous practices . . . but to maintain the sanctity of that distinction of the sexes which was established by

---

303. Lipiński, "Cult Prostitution."

304. Taylor, "Bible and Homosexuality," 6; cf. n42 for bibliographic references. Lenski rejects this interpretation: "In a papyrus of ca. 245 B. C. Deissmann found the word μαλακός, which he translates 'the effeminate.' This word is used in a secondary (obscene) sense and is an allusion to the foul practices by which musicians eked out their earnings. The term is not an equivalent of *mollis*, one who submits himself to a pederast. There is no reason that this vice should be indicated twice by naming its passive and its active perpetrators. It denotes a voluptuary"; Lenski, *Interpretation*, 248.

the creation of man and woman, and with which Israel was not to sin."³⁰⁵ Cross-dressing violates the fundamental boundary set by the Creator in the act of creating humans as male and female; therefore, it is treated as a "detestable act to the Lord" [תּוֹעֲבַת יְהוָה, *tôsʿavat YHWH*]. This is what the prohibition against cross-dressing means *in principle*. What it means *in practice* is contextual, of course. Rashi remarks in his commentary, for example, that "the Torah forbids only [the wearing of] clothes that would lead to abomination [i.e., immoral and illicit behavior]," meaning that the same clothes may lead to different actions in different contexts,³⁰⁶ well-illustrated by the connotation of the two instances in the Hebrew Bible that mention the כְּתֹנֶת פַּסִּים, *kᵊtōnet passim*, "long robe with sleeves":

> Now Israel loved Joseph more than any other of his sons because he was the son of his old age. And he made him a robe of many colors [*kᵊtōnet passim*]. (Gen 37:3)

> Now she [Tamar] was wearing a long robe with sleeves [*kᵊtōnet passim*], for thus were the virgin daughters of the king dressed. So, his servant put her out and bolted the door after her. (2 Sam 13:18)

Whereas no cultural, let alone sexual connotations are attached to Joseph's wearing the robe in Genesis, in 2 Sam, it is clearly taken as a sign of Tamar's virginity and had to be torn after she was raped by David's son Amnon.

NEIGHBORING SEXES

We have very little idea of how much we have absorbed from the tradition of the neighboring Pagan cultures, except that it should be vulgar and disrespectful to speak of it. And so, when we go to the New Testament and read with fresh eyes what is written there about the neighbors who are male and female, we are very much astonished. We had forgotten that we are dealing with neighboring sexes.

—PRESTON SPRINKLE³⁰⁷

---

305. Keil and Delitzsch, *Commentary on the Old Testament*, 1:945.

306. Chavad, "Complete Jewish Bible with Rashi Commentary," Devarim 22:5.

307. Sayers, *Are Women Human?*, 103; the quote is from the essay "The Human-Not-Quite-Human," which was originally presented as a lecture at a conference on the position of women in society in 1938 and first published in Sayers, *Unpopular Opinions*.

In a work that emphasizes the "separateness" that characterizes the binary gender understanding of the biblical texts, it is appropriate to have a section on stereotypes in gender *expression*. This is especially relevant because the same texts show a wide range in describing male and female gender expression, that is, masculinity and femininity.

In the introduction, I subscribed to an essentialist and realist ontology, asserting that gender identity and sexual orientation are objective, created realities. It is now time to elaborate on another assertion: ontological essentialism and gender essentialism are not the same. While I subscribe to the former, I do not find biblical support for the notion that men and women have distinctly different natures. Instead, I will argue for a *soft* gender essentialism that distinguishes between what is universally manly and womanly according to biblical creation theology and what is culturally, socially, institutionally, or otherwise contingent.

This version aims for clarity and smooth transitions between ideas. It should be unnecessary to emphasize that the biblical texts were produced in ancient Near Eastern and Greco-Roman cultures where men held dominant positions as kings, judges, priests, and warriors and functioned within the family as patriarchs or *pater familias*. This was reflected legally, both in civil and religious law. Such stereotypes, however, were also relevant to societal status, family, and extended character traits. As Preston Sprinkle describes it:

> Men were expected to be hairy-chested, sexually charged, domineering men. And real men were military men. Joining the military and becoming a soldier "was the only way many Roman males could lay claim to being a man." Any male who cried in public, showed affection (not just lust) toward women, abstained from sex outside of marriage, or honored lower-class people—the poor, the marginalized, and children—was not considered a *real* masculine man. A real man would never have washed another man's feet.[308]

The woman's domain was within household chores, childbirth, and child-rearing. Legally, a woman did not have an independent status, but she was subject to the man as the legal head. If she was widowed or divorced, then she gained somewhat legal independence. Despite the feminist Old Testament scholar Cheryl Exum's focus on deconstructing the Old Testament texts' view of women,[309] this characterization of culture

---

308. Sprinkle, *Embodied*, 82. Emphasis original.
309. Exum, *Plotted, Shot, and Painted*.

is used to paint a much too simplified picture of the roles of men and women in the Old Testament. Exum describes the stereotypical woman as weak, passive, and identity-less, a victim suffering in silence and confined to domestic duties. Exum is correct in pointing out that the stories of the women *she* focuses on (Bathsheba, Michal, Ruth, and Delilah) reflect a male-dominated society, perspective, and value system. These stories still influence the modern reader's self-image and view of women, making it necessary to deconstruct the culture-specific elements in the text's view of women, allowing readers to "reconfigure" the text as input in constructing their own (modern) identity. In Exum's words:

> Reading is not neutral, and images are constantly competing for our allegiance. As a woman and a feminist, I have something at stake in the cultural representations of biblical women I examine in this book. Voyeurism, the positioning of the female body as object of male desire in literature, art, and film, and pornography have an urgency about them for me because they relate to contemporary issues about women's rights, and they affect my life. In view of the past and ongoing influence of the Bible and its manifold cultural representations within Western culture, it seems to me especially important to examine the roots of these social problems there. The extent to which (male) commentators reinscribe the pornographic ideology of the prophetic texts came as something of a shock to me. Their influence on Bible readers frightens me, and I hope my critique might increase critical awareness of the harmful ideology they are perpetuating.[310]

Exum's critique of the use of biblical texts to legitimize pornographic views of women is certainly timely and necessary, even nearly two decades after she conducted it. However, two objections must be raised against her approach. First, Exum does not differentiate between the text's own distinction between the culturally bound and the timeless elements. This cannot be blamed on Exum, given that she is a declared deconstructionist and social constructivist. However, it must be pointed out that, according to the hermeneutical principles mentioned above, it is possible to read the texts differently. Such a reading would recognize that alongside the culture-specific elements—whether explicitly criticized or serving as expressions of the time-bound reality the biblical ethical guidance addresses—there are also timeless ethical principles that obligate the reader to find their applications in their own, equally time-bound

310. Exum, *Plotted, Shot, and Painted*, 11–12.

reality. And this is a fundamental corrective to Exum's otherwise necessary criticism of male chauvinism.

Second, the feminist goal sometimes justifies the deconstructionist means to such an extent that it overshadows the examples that break the culturally bound stereotype and that, therefore, represent a counterculture or at least paint a more nuanced picture of men's and women's roles. For example, in Gen 4:1, Eve is conscious of the crucial role she (and Adam) plays in relation to the promise in 3:15 when she exclaims, "I have acquired a man: the LORD." Or, if the Hebrew אֵת (*?et*) is not understood as an object marker but as a preposition, it could be translated as "I have acquired a man with the help of the LORD." Similarly, Tamar and Ruth stand out in the salvation-historical thread of the promised offspring. Tamar was likely, like her first husband, Shua, a Canaanite (Gen 38:2–6), and Ruth was a Moabite (Ruth 1:4). Yet, both are described as anything but weak and passive! The same applies to the Jewish queen Esther's actions in the Persian court. In the story of Isaac, Rebekah, Esau, and Jacob, Rebekah plays a significant role in the family, often acting as the one making decisions and acting. At the same time, Isaac is portrayed as weak, passive, and silent, and Rebekah is the one who makes decisions and acts. Esau is initially presented as the "manly man" with "hairy arms" and a "real" job outside the home. At the same time, Jacob is portrayed as effeminate, excelling indoors, and clinging to his mother's skirts. Rebekah recognizes that Jacob, the one who does not fit the patriarchal stereotype, is the most competent when it comes to carrying on the family line and fulfilling the promise associated with it. The same "male" initiative can be seen in Manoah's wife in Judg 13, and towards the end of the succession narrative, Bathsheba, not the aging and impotent David, takes charge to place Solomon on the throne in the house of David (1 Kgs 1). Likewise, we see Miriam the prophetess (Exod 15:20), the prophet and judge Deborah (Judg 4:4), "warrior" Jael (Judg 4:17–24), and the prophet Huldah (2 Kgs 22:14; 2 Chr 34:22) excel in distinct "male occupations." Women appear as spies (2 Sam 17:17–21) and as "resistance fighters" who hide spies (Josh 2:1–6) or kill royal wannabes (Judg 9:53). In agriculture, outside the home, we find women (and men) who were shepherds like Rachel in Gen 29:9 and women who participated in the harvest work (Ruth 2:8–9). Zelophehad's daughters received "an inheritance among [their] father's brothers" (Num 27:4), Caleb's wife Achsah independently acquired land and water sources (Judg 1:12–15), and Job's daughters received "an inheritance along with their brothers" (Job 42:15). The Proverbs woman is not just characterized by weakness and traditional female tasks: "She considers a field and buys it; out of her earnings she plants a vineyard. She sets about her work vigorously; her arms are strong for her tasks" (Prov 31:16–17, NIV). Ephraim's daughter Sheerah is described as the one who "built Lower and Upper Beth Horon and Uzzen Sheerah" (1 Chr 7:24). Women are described as being engaged in trade (Lydia in Acts 16:14), as perfume makers, cooks, and bakers (1 Sam 18:13), and as tentmakers (Aquila and Priscilla in Acts 18:3). There were women who proclaimed military victories (Miriam in Exod 15:20–21; Deborah in Judg 5; Jephthah's daughter in Judg 11:34) and women who conducted funeral laments both publicly and within the family context (2 Sam 1:24; Jer 9:16–19; Ezek 32:16–18; Luke 8:52; 23:27–28; cf. Matt 11:17).

Also worth mentioning is Mark Brettler's article on "masculinities in the Psalms," which focuses on psalms "that explicitly contain a clearly gendered term such as *geber* and how he performs or enacts his malehood, or texts that explicitly contrast male and female."[311] Regarding *geber*, Brettler concludes that the ten occurrences of the term "are not very helpful in terms of deciding how each psalmist's idea of human masculinity, how they believed masculinity should be performed," and that the material is just as inconclusive when it comes to whether *'ish* should be translated as "man" or "person."[312] Concerning psalms that contrast man and woman, Brettler notes that such contrast primarily appears in the post-exilic part of the book of Psalms. He remarks about Ps 128 that it seems to depict clearly defined male and female roles: "Ps 128 is a man's psalm for men. Women are mentioned only to bolster the men's place. Men produce agriculture, with the result (v. 2), 'you shall be happy and you shall prosper.' Nothing is good for the vine-woman in the corner, who does not even get to eat the food she likely prepared. This psalm reinforces one well-known set of gender roles in some patriarchal societies. In this psalm, and in the one that precedes, 'gendered language serves as an ideological tool expressing, justifying, and maintaining asymmetrical relationships of power.'"[313] Both psalms, Pss 127–28, therefore suggest, Brettler argues, "that bearing children with a weak or absent wife is one role of some masculinities in the Psalms."[314]

---

311. Brettler, "Happy Is the Man," 207.
312. Brettler, "Happy Is the Man," 208.
313. Brettler, "Happy Is the Man," 210.
314. Brettler, "Happy Is the Man," 211.

Regarding Ps 144:12, which states, "Our sons are like plants grown up in their youth; our daughters are like corner pillars, cut for the structure of a palace," Brettler points out that "the dynamic nature of the sons is especially striking—they are living saplings that grow, while the daughters are a rock that is carved by others. Males have agency, females lack it—a well-known 'cross-cultural idea.' This was like part of many constructions of masculinity in ancient Israel. In addition, males are well-tended over time, and this helps them prosper, while the girls are only tended to once when they are shaped by the rock-cutter. Saplings are out in the sun; the women may be inside, as part of the house."[315] While Brettler concludes that these psalms reflect the patriarchal and male-dominated society in which they were created, he acknowledges, citing Silvia Schroer, that זָוִיֹּת (zāwiyyōt, "corner, cornerstone"), which only appears here and in Zech 9:15, can be understood as "a description of centrality and importance." In analyzing gender roles in the Psalms, one must consider that "psalms may be composed by one gender and used by another, and gendered language may have been accentuated or deemphasized as individual psalms were reworked."[316]

In the New Testament, it is also noteworthy that women, not men, play significant roles in connection with Jesus's death, and they are attributed the highly unusual role of being the first and most important witnesses to the resurrection (Matt 27:55–61; 28:1–10; Mark 15:40—16:11; Luke 23:55–56; 24:1–12; 22–24; John 19:25–27; 20:1–18). In several cases, it is women who openly declare their faith in and allegiance to Jesus (Luke 7:36–50; Mark 14:3–9), and Priscilla/Priscilla is mentioned as a significant coworker with both Paul (Rom 16:3–5) and Apollos (Acts 18:26). In Rom 16:1–2, Phoebe is described as both a διάκονος, "deacon," and a προστάτις, which, according to Louw-Nida, denotes "a woman who is active in helping—'helper, patroness' (in the sense of one engaged in supporting an individual or endeavor)," and is used in its verbal form to describe leaders in the church in 1 Thess 5:12, where Paul urges the "brothers" to "respect those who labor among you and are over you [προϊσταμένους] in the Lord and admonish you."[317] Furthermore, Jesus himself embodies a countercultural view of masculinity. He is portrayed largely in opposition to societal expectations of a messiah,

---

315. Brettler, "Happy Is the Man," 211.

316. Brettler, "Happy Is the Man," 212; cf. Schroer, "Frauenkörper Als Architektonische," 425–50.

317. Louw and Nida, *Greek-English Lexicon*, 458.

characterized as caring, low-key, peace-loving, and nonmilitant, with the spoken word as his weapon. He *did* wash other men's feet. He touched the sick, showed compassion to sinful women, loved children, wept over Jerusalem, and let people slap him in the face.

Lynn Cohick has also documented how women in the world that formed the background of the New Testament found employment in nearly every conceivable profession, far from being limited to working and fulfilling duties within the home.[318]

Although the texts undeniably reflect a patriarchal and male-dominated society, and although the roles and actions of the mentioned women are not always described positively—Bathsheba likely had personal motives for making her son the heir to the throne!—the review of the texts nonetheless shows that they are far from the stereotype if one relies solely on studies like those of Exum and Brettler. There are gentle men and assertive women; men who show care and women who go to war; passive and "monumental" men and active women with "agency"; men who excel at home and women who thrive in the field; men who stay "behind closed doors" and women who stand by their faith. While they are pieces in an "asymmetric" puzzle where the patriarchal and male-dominated is preferred, they nevertheless represent a breadth of gender roles and—as in the case of female witnesses to the resurrection—a counterculture that demonstrates the application potential in the timeless binary nature of the texts. Regarding the Hebrew Bible's countercultural potential, Katie McCoy mentions how the Prov 31 woman counters the Greek categories of male and female that had influenced Jewish culture in Rabbinic times.[319] Hellenized Jews focused on establishing households, prioritized the parent-child relationship over the husband-wife relationship, and incorporated the Greek perspective on women's roles into Hebrew marriage. Whereas the Rabbinic Jewish woman worked under her husband's instructions, and her labor's product belonged to her husband, the Prov 31 woman exemplified economic independence, creating value from raw materials, selling for profit, and investing earnings to care for her family. This marked a significant difference in the roles and agency of women in these two cultural contexts, and the emphasis on female and family identity, McCoy explains, extended to the New Testament community (John 1:12; Rom 12:4–5; Gal 3:28–29; 1 Cor 8:6; 12:12–27; Eph 2:19; Heb 2:11–12; 1 John 3:1–2):

318. Cohick, *Women*.
319. McCoy, "Recovering the Communion of Persons."

Christians were spiritually related members of one family with one Father. They collectively comprised a household. They were members of one body. This distinction is among the many reasons early Christianity attracted a disproportionate number of female converts. Amidst the debauchery and exploitation of the Greco-Roman world, the church upheld the sacredness of a woman's sexuality and defended her dignity. Further, women found a place of significant contribution in the church, despite their inferior social status and political exclusion. In other words, the early church regarded women as persons."[320]

In early Christianity, McCoy mentions with reference to Jean Bethke Elshtain that "women found that their tasks and activities were celebrated, including 'giving birth to and sustaining new life; an ethic of responsibility toward the helpless, the vulnerable, the weak, gentleness, mercy, and compassion.'"[321] And once welcomed into the Christian community, Elshtain adds, "women shared in the norms, activities, and ideals that were its living tissue," and "women, like men, might be called upon to die for a cause, not as Homeric heroes wielding great swords, but as witnesses to the strength of their inner conviction and living sacrifices to the evil that absolute political power trails in its wake."[322]

All this reflects of what Preston Sprinkle reminds us, namely that "the Bible is profoundly liberating regarding how males and females are expected to act. This is why almost every command in the Bible isn't tailored to a certain sex. Men aren't commanded to be masculine, and women aren't commanded to be feminine. They're both just commanded to be *godly*. The fruit of the Spirit (Gal 5:22–23), for instance, doesn't have male and female fruit. It's just fruit."[323] Such a perspective suggests that gender expression, including their culturally conditioned and personally chosen aspects, should be evaluated within an objective, created order framework. This means, on the one hand, that we should only speak of distinct masculinity and femininity where the biblical texts explicitly do so and where anatomy supports it. Abigail Favale mentions, for example, that the shift from "'male' and 'female' (in Gen 1) to 'man' and 'woman' (in Gen 2), an implication everywhere confirmed as the biblical narrative

---

320. McCoy, "Recovering the Communion of Persons."

321. McCoy, "Recovering the Communion of Persons"; Elshtain, *Public Man, Private Woman*, 61.

322. Elshtain, *Public Man, Private Woman*, 61.

323. Sprinkle, *Embodied*, 83. Emphasis original.

unfolds, is that *a person's biological sex reveals and determines both their objective gender* (*what* gender they, in fact, are) *and certain key gender roles* (should they be taken up). That is, human males grow into men (and potentially husbands and fathers), and human females grow into women (and potentially wives and mothers)."[324] In these *roles*, men and women are admonished to fulfill different functions. In marriage, as we have seen, husbands and wives should reflect the relationship between Christ and the church (Eph 5:22–33; 6:1–4; Col 3:18–21; 1 Pet 3:1–7; Tit 2:1–8), and fathers and mothers should represent the fatherly and motherly aspects of God's relationship with man (Isa 49:15; 66:13; Hos 11:3–4; Matt 23:37; Eph 3:14). The *expression* of these roles is, however, not prescribed in any particularly precise way but seems to depend on the individual character and personal constitution of each woman and man.

As far as the anatomical aspect is concerned, it is clearly backed by science. In a 2014 study of a very large population of 949 youths, Madhur Ingalhalikar et al., concluded that "male brains are optimized for intrahemispheric and female brains for interhemispheric communication. The developmental trajectories of males and females separate at a young age, demonstrating wide differences during adolescence and adulthood. The observations suggest that male brains are structured to facilitate connectivity between perception and coordinated action, whereas female brains are designed to facilitate communication between analytical and intuitive processing modes."[325] Fellipe do Vale, in a similar vein, adds that

> these fixed and unchangeable absolute differences in men and women (chromosomes, anatomy) are accompanied by general differences in the relative strengths of being a man or woman. The broad shoulders of men aren't accidental features, but evidence of the natural strength that males were created to innately possess. The wider hips that women possess for childbearing speak to the creational design that God wove into femaleness. The protective instinct that men are often able to harness at a moment's notice isn't an evolutionary characteristic passed down from marauding cavemen—it issues from the way that God made men. Much in the same way, women tend to enjoy what we sometimes call "motherly" instincts, such as nurturing. A woman can be protective, and a man can nurture, but we should consider whether there are natural aptitudes that men possess that make them better protectors and natural aptitudes

---

324. Smith, "Responding to the Transgender Revolution," 11. Emphasis original.
325. Ingalhalikar et al., "Sex Differences," 823.

that women possess that make them better nurturers. This does not mean to suggest that maleness or femaleness can be reduced down to aptitudes and inclinations, but that these realities are tied to the larger embodied differences of men and women. If we insist that there are no differences in aptitudes or inclinations, we are insisting upon the interchangeability of the sexes, which history and experience tells us is false.[326]

Favale writes: "Human bodies are teleologically organized according to our distinct role in reproducing the species . . . A physiology arranged to produce ova is female, and a physiology arranged to produce sperm is male. This twofold distinction between large and small gametes is stable and universal, not only throughout the human species but also among *all* plant and animal species that reproduce sexually."[327]

Subscribing to *anatomical* realism, that is, the belief that anatomical features—such as physical structures and organs—are real, objective, and tangible aspects of living organisms, does not necessarily entail a similar adherence to *gender* realism. According to gender realism, gender is an objective and inherent characteristic grounded in biological, psychological, or metaphysical realities rather than solely a social or cultural construct. Proponents of gender realism argue that fundamental, essential differences between men and women are rooted in nature or biology. In the introduction, I mentioned a feminist critique of the most recent developments within gender identity theory. One of the most heated discussions in such feminist approaches is the debate on nominalism and realism. Nominalism asserts that universals and abstract concepts do not have independent existence; they are merely names or mental constructs used to group similar objects. In contrast, realism claims that universals and abstract concepts have a real, independent existence beyond individual instances. For example, a feminist nominalist would argue that "woman" is just a social constructivist term for describing all female objects. In contrast, a realist would argue that "woman" is a real property that exists independently of any female object. Charlotte Witt, Natalie Stoljar, and Mari Mikkola in *Feminist Metaphysics* reject hard or radical nominalism and accept biological or anatomical realism and, to some extent, *gender* essentialism, not in an absolute sense but, as we saw in the introduction, as *commonsensical*. In ordinary thinking, that is, "everyday gender ascriptions," there *are* women and men, and there *are*—to use Mikkola's trait/

---

326. Walker, *God and the Transgender Debate*, 57–58.
327. Favale, *Genesis of Gender*, 124–25. Emphasis original.

norm covariance model—universal feminine and masculine traits vís-a-vís appearance, role, self-conception, etc.—that is, *nonanatomical* traits.[328] They are not absolute since the *covariance* between traits and norms changes. "Quite often, though, the [nonanatomical] trait/norm pairings are local, differing from one context to the next and depending on social and cultural factors. So, although all cultures have traits that covary with femininity and others that covary with masculinity, the configurations of these trait/norm pairings can differ depending on their location."[329] In her attempt to navigate between the Scylla of nominalism and the Charybdis of realism, Mikkola maintains the nominalist axiom that nonanatomical traits are constructed and subject to change. She argues that feminist studies serve to undermine any perceived covariance between traits and norms, thereby liberating women to change this covariance freely:

> Finally, we should work to undermine the trait/norm covariance relations that are insidious. The aim is for our judgments to change radically over time, as a result of which those future individuals picked out as women and those picked out as men won't have the same configurations of the trait/norm covariance relations that women and men currently do. But, in doing so, women and men won't be eradicated: we will have just altered how the covariance relations pan out. This is because, on my conception, no particular features must be had for one 'to be' a woman or a man.[330]

Natalie Stoljar also accepts that, *commonsensically*, there are certain unifying things about "women," but that they are not enough or of such a kind that we can speak of "sameness." Instead, Stoljar opts for "resemblance" as a descriptor of her "soft" nominalist approach. The class of women, according to Stoljar, "is heterogenous enough to raise doubts about whether 'being a woman' is a universal. But it is not an extremely gerrymandered class in which there are no substantive similarities among the members . . . *resemblance* is important for the class 'women,' but *sameness* is not."[331] Uniessentialism, developed by philosopher Charlotte Witt, posits similarly that gender is an essential aspect of social identity, serving as a unified and central role that shapes individuals' experiences and

---

328. Mikkola, "Ontological Commitments," 76–77.
329. Mikkola, "Ontological Commitments," 77.
330. Mikkola, "Ontological Commitments," 81.
331. Stoljar, "Different Women," 29. Emphasis original.

interactions within society.³³² Unlike other social roles, gender is not merely a superficial or context-dependent aspect of identity but is fundamental in organizing and integrating other aspects of an individual's self-concept. According to uniessentialism, gender provides a normative structure that guides behavior, expectations, and social interactions, influencing how individuals are perceived and treated within various social contexts. In essence, uniessentialism asserts that gender is not just one attribute among many but is a core and indispensable component of one's overall identity.

A biblical response to the rejection of gender essentialism in radical gender identity theory must be given along the same lines, that is, by refining or softening *gender* essentialism. Essentialism must be maintained because, overall, male and female roles and functions pertain to the created order. That God blesses humankind as male and female in original creation means, as we have seen, that he created them teleologically so that they were capable of fulfilling their roles as male and female. Since a male is a potential husband and father and a female a potential wife and mother, males and females are created—that is, anatomically equipped—for being a husband and father or wife and mother, respectively.

On the other hand, while there *are* such key differences between masculinity and femininity and there *are* certain natural aptitudes and inclinations tied to male and female physiology, the key binary differences are few, and character traits should be seen, not as masculine and feminine but as points in a shared spectrum. For the fun of it—but also very illustrative—I plotted my wife's and my own scores on several Hofstede's traits of masculinity and femininity into a diagram with the *traits*, not the sexes, as the main axis.³³³ The point is that as long as the key binary traits are not included, diagrams are fundamentally individual in that men and women, despite aptitudes and inclinations, share all characteristics and traits to varying degrees.

In other words, while binary gender is a good and given aspect of human nature, it is not *everything*. Looy and Bouma remind us, "Gender also does not reflect a straightforward division of humankind into two subspecies. Both within and transcending gender is much psychological, behavioral, and even physical diversity. We are called to celebrate this diversity, as reflected in Paul's repeated reminders that we are each

---

332. Witt, "What Is Gender Essentialism?," 11–25.
333. Hofstede, *Culture's Consequences*, 297–98.

uniquely gifted to contribute to the body of Christ (e.g., Rom 12:4–6; 1 Cor 12: 4–11, 27–31; Eph 4:11–12)."[334] And although anatomical differences lead to varying behavioral capacities, these differences are minor compared to the variations found within groups of women and groups of men. Yarhouse, quoting Looy and Bouma, argues that

> many differences between men and women are not categorical; rather, they are better viewed as two bell-shaped curves in which the average experiences of men and the average experiences of women are different, while having considerable overlap either in ability or with reference to a characteristic. Indeed, "all of the research on gender differences in various personality traits, cognitive abilities, and preferences consistently shows that, even when there are statistically significant differences between women and men, these differences pale in magnitude beside the variations among women and among men." It is rather artificial to focus on the differences between men and men.[335]

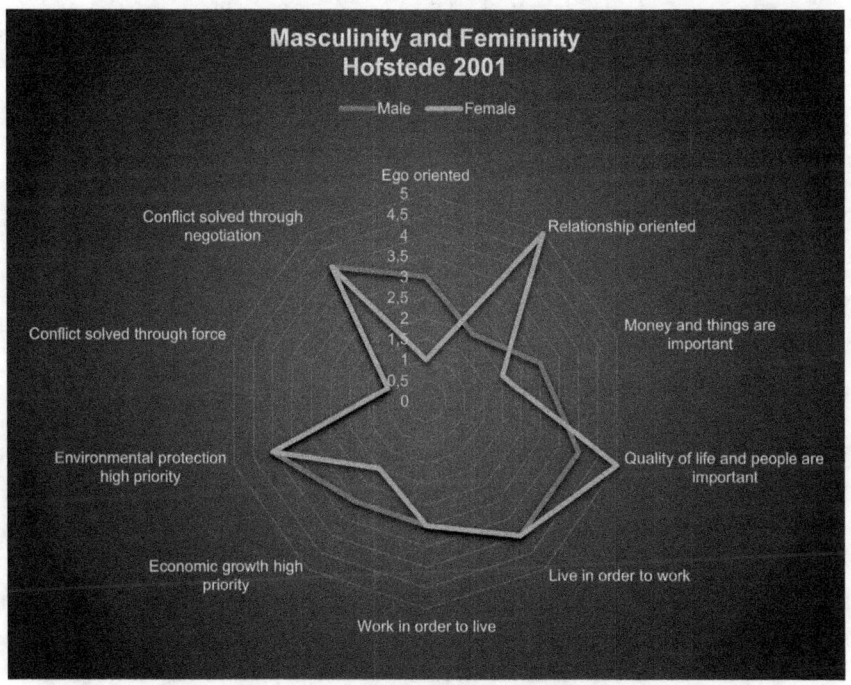

Figure 9: Hofstede Diagram

334. Looy and Bouma III, "Nature of Gender," 176.
335. Yarhouse, *Understanding Gender Dysphoria*, 37.

In conclusion, we must acknowledge that Scripture describes gender expression in binary categories to a limited extent and that the biblical texts reflect a countercultural psychological, behavioral, and physical diversity among women *and* men. Returning to Sprinkle's remark, "Men aren't commanded to be masculine, and women aren't commanded to be feminine. They're both just commanded to be *godly*."[336] The point, as far as gender expression and the corresponding gender ethics are concerned, is not, therefore, as Keller has it, "to make a single, detailed, and very specific set of 'manly' or 'womanly' characteristics that fits every temperament and culture," but rather that we "watch for and appreciate the inevitable differences that will appear between male and female in your particular generation, culture, people, and place."[337] No specific attributes (apart from reproductive capabilities) are unique to women or exclusive to men. Instead, there are shared human characteristics that, due to gendered embodiment, should naturally be expressed by women in ways that are fitting to their femininity and by men in ways that are appropriate to their masculinity. "This means," Sam Allberry notes, "that true, biblical masculinity and true, biblical femininity are, respectively, simply what naturally emerges when men and women grow in Christ. Biblically speaking, masculinity is what long-term sanctification produces in Christian men, and femininity what long-term sanctification produces in women."[338]

This is important not only on an ontological level but also for forming gender identity and sexual ethics. Firstly, such a *soft* gender essentialist approach to masculinity and femininity serves as a bulwark against cultural stereotypes. It sets men and women free to express their masculinity and femininity as *sanctification*, even when it diverges from cultural expectations and social codes. Secondly, it can be helpful for gender dysphoria. By broadening the spectrum of what it means to be masculine and feminine, some individuals may realize that they do *not* suffer from gender dysphoria but rather are pressured by cultural stereotypes and social codes. In this case, a biblical liberation from these constraints will set them free to express their masculinity and femininity in a healthy manner. For those who, despite such liberation, still suffer from gender dysphoria, the nature of the suffering will not be alleviated. However, it

---

336. Sprinkle, *Embodied*, 83. Emphasis original.
337. Keller and Keller, *Meaning of Marriage*, 200.
338. Allberry, *What God Has to Say*, 77–78.

will make it easier to cope with dysphoria if stereotypes and codes do not constantly trigger or exacerbate the dysphoria.

EUNUCHS, INTERSEX, AND TRANSGENDER

It should be clear by now that biblical creation theology operates with only two genders, not three, and does not recognize a spectrum between the two. This perspective is evident in both the creation narrative in Gen 1:1—2:3, in the narrative in Gen 2:4—3:24, and in Adam's genealogy in Gen 5:

> Then God said, "Let us make man in our image, after our likeness. And let them have dominion over the fish of the sea and over the birds of the heavens and over the livestock and over all the earth and over every creeping thing that creeps on the earth." So God created man in his own image, in the image of God he created him; male and female he created them. (Gen 1:26–27)
>
> Then the Lord God made a woman from the rib he had taken out of the man, and he brought her to the man. (Gen 2:22 NET)
>
> This is the record of the family line of Adam. When God created humankind, he made them in the likeness of God. He created them male and female; when they were created, he blessed them and named them "humankind." (Gen 5:1–2)

The reference to Gen 1 in Adam's genealogy in Gen 5 demonstrates that the same binary understanding of human gender, as expressed in Gen 1–2, applies in the postlapsarian reality. The comment that God "called their name Man when they were created" reinforces the description of man as binary.

When Jesus, as we have seen, likely refers to *both* creation texts in Matt 19, he reaffirms the theological concept of gender binary:

> Have you not read that he who created them from the beginning made them male and female, and said, "Therefore a man shall leave his father and his mother and hold fast to his wife, and the two shall become one flesh"? So, they are no longer two but one flesh. What therefore God has joined together, let not man separate. (Matt 19:4–6; cf. Mark 10:6)

Having said that, the texts also demonstrate that in the postlapsarian reality, there are individuals who do not fit within the binary understanding of gender. In Isa 56:4–5, it is stated regarding the day of the Lord or the new creation:

> For thus says the LORD:
> "To the eunuchs who keep my Sabbaths,
> who choose the things that please me
> and hold fast to my covenant,
> I will give in my house and within my walls a monument and
> a name
> better than sons and daughters;
> I will give them an everlasting name
> that shall not be cut off.

The translation "eunuchs" in most Bibles corresponds to the Hebrew סָרִיס (sārîs) and the Greek (LXX) εὐνοῦχος ("eunuch"). In this context, the new creation will eliminate the problem faced by this category of people, namely, the inability to have children and secure their lineage and legacy: "I will give them an everlasting name that shall not be cut off" (v. 5). In the New Testament, Jesus mentions the same word in Matt 19:12 to describe three categories of individuals unsuitable for marriage: "For there are eunuchs who have been so from birth, and there are eunuchs who have been made eunuchs by men, and there are eunuchs who have made themselves eunuchs for the sake of the kingdom of heaven." Jesus uses εὐνοῦχος here, in the somewhat expanded sense, to describe the category of people we might call intersex (formerly hermaphrodites), and those who have been made eunuchs by others or by themselves. Since neither Greek nor Latin had a word referring to a celibate man, Christians later used the word "eunuch" to mean celibates.

Robert Smith, referring to the distinction made in an article by F. P. Retief and J. F. G. Cilliers between "acquired and congenital eunuchism," suggests that Jesus's "first two categories were, almost certainly, informed by the common Jewish distinction between 'eunuchs of the sun' (Heb *saris hamma*)—that is, those who have been eunuchs from the moment they first saw the sun (i.e., from birth)—and 'eunuchs of man' (Heb *saris 'adam*)—that is, man-made eunuchs, either by accident or deliberately. The first of these categories would, most likely, have included the various conditions that today are included under the 'intersex' umbrella."[339] However, it is emphasized in both contexts that these conditions deviate from the prelapsarian binary norm. For this reason, it cannot be seen as an expression of fluid gender identity. It is crucial to note, as Sprinkle mentions, that eunuchs were a diverse group and always *male*:

---

339. Smith, "Responding to the Transgender Revolution"; Retief et al., "Congenital Eunuchism and Favorinus," 73.

Some eunuchs were asexual, serving as reliable guardians or military leaders without sexual distractions. Others lacked secondary male characteristics due to castration before puberty. Some were seen as sexually active but infertile, capable of serving wealthy women without the risk of pregnancy. Eunuchs were sometimes perceived as neither fully masculine nor feminine, reflecting cultural stereotypes. The literature provides no insight into the internal psychology or gender identity of eunuchs. However, a common factor among all eunuchs is their biological maleness and infertility, often stemming from a congenital condition or castration. Notably, there is no evidence in the literature of eunuchs being females; they were males culturally deemed unmasculine.[340]

When it comes to the third category, namely, "those who have made themselves eunuchs for the sake of the kingdom of heaven," there is disagreement about whether it refers to voluntary castration or a metaphorical "castration" representing celibacy, a voluntary abstention from sexual activity. Recently R. Jarrett van Tine has suggested a "Solomonic" interpretation of the third category, arguing that "Matt's eunuch metaphor is a rhetorical device exhorting would-be disciples who have illegitimately divorced their wives to 'cut off' (figuratively) what causes them to stumble (i.e., their male organ), lest they commit adultery in remarriage (cf. 5:29–30). According to this interpretation, Matt's "eunuchs" serve as literary exemplars of those who make extraordinary sacrifices in this age (i.e., a spouse and children) so that they might obtain immeasurably more in the kingdom of heaven."[341]

However, regardless of how the last category is understood, it does not alter the fact that there is no reference to a "third gender." These eunuchs are consistently referred to using masculine verbs and pronouns, which means there is no departure from the normative binary gender understanding. Instead, they refer to individuals who are not capable of functioning sexually or reproductively in the normal sense.

Relevant biblical texts for discussing the eunuch are Lev 21:16–24, Deut 23:1, Isa 56:3–5, Matt 19:12, and Acts 8:26–39, and we shall focus on the text from Matt first.

> There are some eunuchs who were born that way, and there are some who were made eunuchs by men, and there are some who

---

340. Sprinkle, *Embodied*, 99–100.
341. Van Tine, "Castration for the Kingdom," 399.

made themselves eunuchs for the sake of the kingdom of heaven. Let the one who is able to accept this accept it (Matt 19:12).

The text from Matt 19:12 is relevant because it has been argued that one or more of the categories mentioned include intersex and transgender individuals and that Jesus's words only exclude the latter from heterosexual marriage, not from being in committed same-sex relationships. Mark Olmstead states in a blog post in *The Huffington Post*, for example, that "the term *eunuchoi* was used to describe more than just a man who'd had his testicles removed," and that although Jesus clearly refers to "the biologically intersexed (previously known as hermaphrodites)," then it is by no means "a stretch to conclude that he cast a much wider net. After all, the transgendered have always been with us—treated differently according to local culture, for sure, in the same way, that boys who liked boys (and girls who liked girls) raised eyebrows in some places and caused no one to blink in others. However they get there, Jesus clearly has the same suggestion for how to treat them. *'He who is able to accept this, let him accept it'*."[342] However, it is not only in the more popular science blogosphere that such an understanding applies. Heather Looy and Hessel Bouma, in the *Journal of Psychology and Theology* and with reference to Luke 20:34–36, Gal 3:28, and Rev 14:4, argue that "it is difficult to imagine that the diversity of gender and gendered behaviors across species, and the diversity of traits within genders among humans, are all consequences of sin, that God's creational intent was monolithic females and males. Perhaps intersexed and transgendered persons are a powerful reminder that gender, while itself a good gift of God, contains within it great diversity that we tend to forget or ignore in our focus on definitions or prototypes for gender categories."[343] The influential, late (and former Evangelical) American professor of English, Virginia Mollenkott, who has not least become known for her feminist theology and LGBT activism, writes, for example, about the passage:

> Jesus' words about eunuchs in Matt 19:12 reveal an accepting, respectful attitude that ought to be the norm for the modern church: "For there are eunuchs who have been so from birth" includes at the very least all intersexual people; "and there are eunuchs who have been made eunuchs by others" includes post-operative transsexuals; "and there are eunuchs who have

---

342. Olmstead, "When Jesus Agreed with Lady Gaga." Emphasis original.
343. Looy and Bouma III, "Nature of Gender," 175.

made themselves eunuchs for the kingdom of heaven" includes not only pre-operative and non-operative transsexuals but all other transgenderists, celibates, and homosexuals who do not engage in reproductive sex. The kingdom of heaven is located within us (Luke 17:21); so perhaps what Jesus means by being eunuchs "for the sake of the kingdom of heaven" is the Jewish counsel of being true to one's deepest nature.[344]

Assistant Professor of Christian Ethics and Social Transformation Justin Sabia-Tanis states, agreeing with Mollenkott, that "we need to remember Jesus's words of acceptance for eunuchs and his way of allying himself with people outside of accepted norms of society. For way too long, Jesus has been used as a tool of exclusion and self-righteousness, when his own words counter that view and present for us a radical statement of positive inclusion in the dominion of God."[345] He then goes on to describe how the story of the Ethiopian eunuch in Acts 8:26–39 is "one of the most powerful stories in the Scriptures for gender-variant people"[346]: "Not only the eunuch's sexuality is in question, but also his gender. He did not fit into conventional categories of male and female as a castrated man who served a queen. Philip is a model for an understanding of evangelism that reaches out with Christ's message of inclusion, without the legalism that marks so many of our faith communities."[347] Sabia-Tanis then continues to argue—again in agreement with Mollenkott—that the privileging of the text in Gal 3:28 ("it does not depend on being Jew or Greek, on being slave or free, on being a man and woman") is hermeneutically disarming concerning texts such as Deut 22:5 and Lev 18:22. Sabia-Tanis summarizes in the following way what the privileged text means for the view of transgender:

> Not only will there not be divisions between Jews and Greeks, slaves and free, male and female, but the entire process of distinguishing some as superior and some as inferior is to pass away. In Christ, we are not to create categories in which some have power, influence, and privilege while others do not. If those of us who are Christian would follow this mandate, such a change would have a profound impact on how we live and are. Among other

---

344. Mollenkott, *Omnigender*, 120.
345. Sabia-Tanis, *Trans-Gender*, 75.
346. Sabia-Tanis, *Trans-Gender*, 76.
347. Sabia-Tanis, *Trans-Gender*, 77.

things, transgendered people would not be excluded from or just tolerated in communities of faith but welcomed as equals.[348]

In a similar vein, Austen Hartke argues that Gal 3:28 "seems to downgrade the importance of gender in Christian identity."[349] There are two possible interpretations, Hartke continues, of Paul's statement: "Either it means that we're all whitewashed and homogenized, and our differences are erased . . . or it means that we're called to find a way to make our different identities fit together."[350] Opting for the latter, Hartke argues—referring to the late New Testament scholar Wayne Meeks—that "Paul's vision of unity through diversity in Christ was too revolutionary" in his time and that Paul, therefore, in the rest of his letters was "telling people to keep their gender presentation as culturally traditional as possible, because the kingdom revolution that God promised hasn't happened yet. At the same time, he's telling Christians that in certain ways, they should act as if that kingdom is already here."[351] In other words, now is the time for Christians to embrace as fully as possible the gender diversity in Christian identity that Paul announced in Gal 3:28.

However, this understanding and use of Matt 19:12 and Gal 3:28 are problematic on several levels unless one explicitly states the hermeneutical principles that lead to such claims. As mentioned earlier in the section on hermeneutical principles, the criterion for considering the legislation in texts like Leviticus relevant is not whether it was originally given to ancient Israel but whether it is based on universal and timeless creation ordinances or on a particular and time-bound situation and culture in ancient Israel. A text like Gal 3:28 should indeed be given preference over texts like Deut 22:5, but the crucial question is in relation to what? When it comes to whether "the inheritance" or "righteousness" can be obtained "by the law" (v. 18) or "under the law" (v. 23), or whether it happens "by faith in Jesus Christ" (v. 22), Paul argues in the context that the law should no longer apply, and that all kinds or types of people have equal access to this inheritance and righteousness. A sinner is justified solely by faith in Jesus Christ, as Paul emphasizes in many other places, especially in Romans and Galatians. However, it is a *non sequitur* and should be evident in the context that it does not abolish the "law" in its other functions

---

348. Sabia-Tanis, *Trans-Gender*, 80.
349. Hartke, *Transforming*, 165.
350. Hartke, *Transforming*, 169.
351. Hartke, *Transforming*, 171–72.

and that the "law" must be examined to understand which parts of it still apply because they express a universal, timeless principle, and whether the particular application makes sense in a modern context or needs to be rethought. In both Romans and Galatians, Paul explicitly reintroduces the law after rejecting it as a means of salvation, not as a path to "righteousness" but as an ethical and moral compass for those justified by faith in Jesus Christ. In Galatians, Paul concludes his argument about the law as a means of salvation with the proclamation: "For freedom Christ has set us free; stand firm therefore, and do not submit again to a yoke of slavery" (Gal 5:1). But immediately afterward, he admonishes, "For you were called to freedom, brothers. Only do not use your freedom as an opportunity for the flesh, but through love serve one another" (5:13). After summarizing the law in the commandment of love (v. 14) and giving examples of what contradicts and what positively expresses such love (vv. 15–23a), he concludes that "against such things there is no law!" (v. 23b). The same applies in Romans, where Paul, in the main part of his letter, rejects "the law" as a path to "righteousness," but at the same time answers the rhetorical question he himself poses: "What shall we say then? Are we to continue in sin that grace may abound? By no means! How can we who died to sin still live in it?" (Rom 6:1–2). And from Rom 12:1, Paul shows what such "spiritual worship" consists of, namely, "to present your bodies as a living sacrifice, holy and acceptable to God." Therefore, if Gal 3:28 is used to dismantle the binding nature of "the law," it requires a hermeneutic that contradicts Paul's own hermeneutic and goes against the canonical context of the texts.

Another text that is often referenced is Isa 56:3–5:

> The foreigner who has joined himself to the Lord
> must not say,
> "The Lord will exclude me from His people";
> and the eunuch must not say,
> "I am only a dry tree."
> For the Lord says this:
> "For the eunuchs who keep My Sabbaths,
> and choose what pleases Me,
> and hold firmly to My covenant,
> I will give them, in My house and within My walls,
> a memorial and a name better than sons and daughters.
> I will give each of them an everlasting name
> that will never be cut off."

The English translation "eunuch" renders the Hebrew as סָרִיס (sārîs), which is translated as εὐνοῦχος in the Septuagint. The background of the text must be found in Deut 23:1, where it is stated about the access to become part of קְהַל יְהוָה (qᵉhal YHWH),³⁵² that "no one who has had his testicles crushed or his limb cut off has access to the assembly of the Lord," and in Lev 21:16–24, where it is stated about the priests' access to the sanctuary:

> Then the LORD spoke to Moses, saying, "Speak to Aaron, saying, 'None of your descendants throughout their generations who has an impairment shall approach to offer the food of his God. For no one who has an impairment shall approach: a man who is blind, or one who limps, or one who has a slit nose, or one with *any* conspicuous feature, or someone who has a broken foot or broken hand, or a contorted back, or one *who is* a dwarf, or *has* a spot in his eye, or a festering rash or scabs, or crushed testicles. No man among the descendants of Aaron the priest who has an impairment is to come forward to offer the LORD's offerings by fire; *since* he has an impairment, he shall not come forward to offer the food of his God. He may eat the food of his God, *both* of the most holy and of the holy, only he shall not come up to the veil or approach the altar, since he has an impairment, so that he does not profane My sanctuaries. For I am the LORD who sanctifies them.'" So Moses spoke to Aaron and to his sons and to all the sons of Israel. (NASB)

Considering both the theology of creation and the holiness legislation, there are likely several reasons for these prohibitions. These reasons include the emphasis on procreation and the function of the tabernacle/temple as a miniature of the original, perfect macrocosm.³⁵³ The emphasis in Lev 16 on "defect" [מוּם, *mûm*] can hardly be understood otherwise than a defect in comparison with the ideal, namely the biologically

---

352. Jack P. Lewis writes in *TWOT* that "a distinction between *ʿēdâ* and *qāhāl* seems to be intended in 'if the whole congregation (*ʿēdâ*) commit sin . . . and the thing is hidden from the eyes of the assembly' (*qahal* Lev 4:13). Here the *qāhāl* is the judicial representatives of the community. There is also the case where certain Israelite persons cannot enter the *qāhāl* (Deut 23:2). But elsewhere the two words are used in successive clauses in the same sense (Num 16:3) and are joined together (Prov 5:14). In general, the terms are synonymous"; Lewis, "1991 קָהָל."

353. It was also true that animals with "defects" were not to be used as sacrifices: "Any animal that has its testicles bruised or crushed or torn or cut you shall not offer to the LORD; you shall not do it within your land, neither shall you offer as the bread of your God any such animals gotten from a foreigner. Since there is a blemish in them, because of their mutilation, they will not be accepted for you" (Lev 22:24–25).

dimorphic male/female in the original creation. Therefore, it is not a moral defect but a post-fall defect that renders the individual unsuitable for visualizing pre-fall perfection. It does, however, put a strong emphasis on the biologically dimorphic *body* as a God-willed expression of his image. Additionally, eunuchs could not be circumcised and, therefore, could not become part of the covenant community. It may have also played a secondary role that eunuchs were associated with other cults where gods/goddesses or cult personnel were castrated, such as in the case of the Phrygian Agdistis, who was born as a hermaphrodite but was castrated by the gods and transformed into the goddess Cybele.

When Isa 56:3–5 states that even the eunuch should be included in the covenant and have access to the temple, it describes a fulfillment of what the Lord will do on a universal level, of which Israel was a temporary representative and demonstrative forerunner. Since the New Testament clearly describes this eschatological reality as partially realized or already breaking forth with Jesus Christ, it is surprising that Victoria Kolakowski, in her influential article "Towards a Christian Ethical Response to Transsexual Persons," notes that "this is not, unfortunately, a prophecy applicable to the present, but to some eschatological future time. Hence, it does not in and of itself change the teaching of the other scriptural passages, although it clearly indicates a favorable view by God of eunuchs."[354] Although the ultimate realization of the prophecy in Isa 56 may be placed in the eschaton, texts like Col 3:11 make it abundantly clear that the foundation has been laid with and realized through faith in Jesus Christ: "Here there is not Greek and Jew, circumcised and uncircumcised, barbarian, Scythian, slave, free; but Christ is all, and in all." Perhaps this is why the Ethiopian eunuch was reading from the prophet Isaiah when Philip met him.

The problematic aspect of privileging a text like Isa 56:3–5 is not that it does not point to a future change in the exclusion of eunuchs from the covenant community, as it clearly does. Instead, the issue lies in using the inclusion of eunuchs in both Isa 56 and Acts 8 as an *eisegetical* springboard to argue for biblical endorsement of gender transition. When Kolakowski laments that the text from Isa 56 cannot be applied as "a prophecy applicable to the present," it is because she sees it (together with the texts from Deuteronomy and Leviticus) as support for "rejection of sex reassignment as a viable treatment for transsexuals, but further, for

---

354. Kolakowski, "Toward a Christian Ethical Response," 19–20.

rejection of post-operative transsexuals from the community of faith."³⁵⁵ Kolakowski acknowledges the undeniable fact that "the development of sex reassignment surgery is undoubtedly beyond the reasonable imaginative ability of ancient Israel," but she nevertheless argues that the New Testament texts address transgenderism. She suggests that "analogy to the case of the eunuch suggests that a more compassionate response is required, and that the New Testament witness is supportive of transsexual persons. Transsexuals should be accepted into the community at face value and without condemnation. Further, a compassionate response to transsexualism, given the evidence, would be supportive of sex reassignment surgery."³⁵⁶

Similarly, Sabia-Tanis equates eunuchs with transgendered people and contends that the prophecy in Isa 56 "marks a radical change from the views of Deuteronomy" by shifting the focus "from the physical perfection and origin of worshipers to an examination of their commitment to observing the Sabbath and perpetuating justice. The emphasis is now not the external characteristics of people who worship Yahweh, but rests upon the faithfulness of the person."³⁵⁷ Sabia-Tanis concludes that "for transgendered persons who have a sense of an internal reality that is or may be in conflict with our physical bodies, the prophet speaks a word that focuses us on the faithfulness of our lives, not on the particularities of our bodies. God's emphasis is not on where our bodies came from or how they have been altered but rather on the ways in which we practice our faith. Justice, inclusion, and faithfulness become the primary indicators of people who are acceptable to God."³⁵⁸ Applying Isa 56:1–8 to the transgender experience and describing eunuchs as "one of the groups of gender-expansive people," transgender person and founder of the online community Transmission Ministry Collective Austen Hartke concurs:

> It is that . . . shared narrative that can give transgender Christians the courage to carve out a space for themselves in a global church that often ignores or actively persecutes them. To know that you belong to a God who gathers the outcasts and who commands doors to open before those sitting outside the gates: this is the kind of love that leads to liberation. God did not ask the eunuchs to pour themselves into the mold of Israel's

---

355. Kolakowski, "Toward a Christian Ethical Response," 20.
356. Kolakowski, "Toward a Christian Ethical Response," 23, 29.
357. Sabia-Tanis, *Trans-Gender*, 69–70.
358. Sabia-Tanis, *Trans-Gender*, 70.

previous societal norms, nor to bend themselves to fit by taking on specifically gendered roles in the current system. Instead, God called for a transformed community that looked like nothing the people had ever seen.[359]

In the same way that the privileging of the New Testament texts involved reading them *eisegetically*, there is also an element of *eisegesis* when it is claimed that the Hebrew סָרִיס (*sārîs*), the Septuagint's εὐνοῦχος, and the Vulgate's *spado* and *eunuch* validate gender transition. Retief, Cilliers, and Riekert include Isa 56:3–5 among the texts that, according to their analysis of cognate terms, refer to "someone (usually a man) whose testes (and sometimes also penis and scrotum) have been destroyed or removed." Therefore, there is no inherent notion of gender transition in the terminology itself.[360] This does not mean that we can etymologically determine why a person—whether by force or voluntarily—was castrated. This must be determined through sociocultural studies that uncover the norms and deviations from those norms that existed in the area of gender identity. Although Retief, Cilliers, and Riekert refer to Joshua Levinson, who has demonstrated that "cultural androgyny" was a theme in Rabbinic Judaism with Joseph's imprisonment interpreted as a punishment for his "effeminacy" or "gender-slippage" in relation to Potiphar's "sexually voracious" wife, such cases do not involve eunuchs.[361] Additionally, Joseph's alleged gender-bending is criticized because his imprisonment is seen as deserved. While none of the fifty texts identified by Retief, Cilliers, and Riekert as referring to eunuchs in the sense mentioned above describe castration as a desire to change gender, it cannot be denied that such cases existed. However, if such a case existed and was even behind the castration in some of the Old Testament texts mentioning eunuchs, then the castration must be evaluated in relation to the normative context of the Old Testament, namely, the binary gender understanding reflected in the texts.

Such an understanding of "the neighboring sexes" and the texts concerning eunuchs has significant implications in several areas. Firstly, and fundamentally, it must be emphasized that although "all have sinned and fall short of the glory of God," without exception or any form of differentiation, all "are justified freely by his grace through the redemption

---

359. Hartke, *Transforming*, 110, 107–8.
360. Retief et al., "Eunuchs in the Bible," 248.
361. Levinson, "Cultural Androgyny in Rabbinic Literature," 119–40.

that is in Christ Jesus" (Rom 3:23-24). *This* is the primary point that the various "eunuch texts" address.

Secondly, and because of this, it must be emphasized that biological anomalies such as intersex conditions are not in themselves considered a moral issue. When eunuchs are excluded from temple service, it is not because they are morally unfit for it, but because they (like many others with bodily defects) are unable to symbolize and visualize prelapsarian perfection. The same applies to marriage, where the issue is not a moral problem related to their status as eunuchs but rather their "unsuitability" within the prelapsarian symbolism attached to marriage, as they cannot procreate. The text from Isa 56 is exceedingly important in this context, not because it speaks of a third gender but because it emphasizes that anyone who does not fall within the binary spectrum is included in the new creation that will restore the devastations wrought by the fall upon body and soul.

Even though the texts do not mention conditions we today call intersex and gender dysphoria, it is a natural extension of their interpretation to include these conditions in the proclamation of the hope of restoration. This is crucial for trans* persons, particularly because gender dysphoria is a painful condition that statistically leads to a challenging life. Although the broad parameters of Scripture for gender expression can be helpful for many, they do not apply to all. For some, dysphoria is a given condition. Yarhouse and Sadusky write, "We do see evidence that gender dysphoria in childhood tends to resolve on its own in the vast majority of cases. However, once a person reaches late adolescence or adulthood, if their gender dysphoria has not resolved, it does not tend to. The person is living with more of an enduring condition."[362]

In this situation, it is crucial to state the most important point first, namely that gender dysphoria is not a sin but a consequence of the fall. As Yarhouse and Sadusky formulate it: "We can expect that gender identity and the potential for incongruence and distress associated with that incongruence demonstrate the fallen reality in which we live. It seems likely that the sense of maleness or femaleness, in varying degrees with different people, would be fallen like every other aspect of human experience."[363]

---

362. Beilby, *Understanding Transgender Identities*, 88.
363. Yarhouse and Sadusky, "Complexities of Gender Identity," 112.

Here, Jesus's words to his disciples concerning the healing of the man born blind must be brought into consideration, as the blindness that Jesus healed was also not due to the man's own fault: "Neither this man nor his parents sinned, but he was born blind so that the acts of God may be revealed through what happens to him" (John 9:3 NET). The blindness was due to the consequences of the fall. However, it also allowed Jesus to demonstrate the power of restoration and new creation. In other words, Jesus shows that the man—despite his blindness—was still an image-bearer of God after the fall and that he was included in the restoration promised from the beginning (Gen 3:15). This underscores that every person born blind—and, by extension, anyone who experiences the consequences of the fall on body and soul without personal fault—is an "image-bearer" so valuable that they are included in the same free decision of new creation as was God's decision to create humanity in the beginning. As Owen Strachan formulates it in relation to gender dysphoria: "The first thing—the very first thing—that must be said about individuals who experience gender dysphoria at any level is that they are fully, substantially, immovably human . . . They are inexorably image-bearers made by God."[364] If we assert—according to the Bible's view—that these conditions are results of the fall, we must ensure to convey this in a non-dehumanizing way. We are all fallen and marred by the fall in some way or another. Intersex persons are not more fallen than non-intersex persons. However, that distinction is sometimes lost in translation. We need, therefore, as Preston Sprinkle reminds us, "to exercise much caution in how we speak about 'conditions' and 'issues' and 'concepts' that are embodied in the lives of real people who already have many social cards stacked against them in ways non-intersex persons will never truly understand."[365]

Finally, we need to return to the difficult issue of brain gender. If, as mentioned in the first part of the book, it were possible to identify and describe a female or male brain, the term "intersex," for example, could be expanded to include conditions where a person experiences a mismatch between the biological brain and the biological (physiological) sex, thereby supporting the argument that physiological sex is subordinate to the biological brain sex. While neuroscientists are divided, and studies that seem to support such a conclusion are disputed, both

---

364. Beilby, *Understanding Transgender Identities*, 92.
365. Sprinkle, "Sex, Gender, and Transgender Experiences: Part 6."

because studies are contradictory and due to the factor of neuroplasticity, one question remains: Could gender dysphoria be described as a form of brain intersex? Yarhouse and Sadusky write that "we understand Gen 1 and 2 as indicating that God's creational intent was a male/female binary for sex and alignment between one's gender identity and one's biological sex. The reality today is that, for a small percentage of persons, gender identity does not align with biological sex. In other words, some people don't live at either side of the binary (they live in between or outside the binary) when it comes to gender identity or gender expression."[366] Yarhouse and Sadusky suggest that Milton Diamond's view of gender dysphoria as "a form of brain intersex" may be accurate. They address the question "Is gender transitioning a solution?" with cautious responses. They say it should only be considered "with great caution," not as "the first and best option." Instead, transitioning should be reserved for "life-threatening gender dysphoria." They compare it to other medical or psychiatric conditions where invasive treatments are used only when all other approaches have failed and the situation is severe.[367] Furthermore, "If one's gender is tainted by the fall, it remains a difficult decision whether to bring one's anatomy into accordance with one's gender identity. After all, a person's chromosomes, gonads, and genitalia are intact and are typically understood as instructive of creational intent. However, a person's gender identity—again, as a result of the fall—may be due to something akin to an intersex condition of the brain, which may present a different decision tree for Christians."[368]

Given that, as we have seen, it is interpretatively defensible to include any form of involuntary physical or psychological defect after the fall in the point of Isa 56 (and, by extension, also in Matt 19), there is good reason to describe gender dysphoria as a form of intersex, that is, a condition that is congenital, involuntary, and a consequence of the fall. In this case, it is characterized by a lack of congruence between biological and psychological gender, but equally a condition that implies being "unsuitable for marriage" because one cannot symbolize what marriage was originally created to visualize. The critical point is not so much the designation of intersex but the question of how to address the psychological and physical challenges the condition brings.

---

366. Yarhouse and Sadusky, "Complexities of Gender Identity," 108.
367. Yarhouse and Sadusky, "Complexities of Gender Identity," 108, 112–13.
368. Yarhouse and Sadusky, "Complexities of Gender Identity," 112.

As cited above, Yarhouse and Sadusky suggest that in "cases of life-threatening gender dysphoria," aligning anatomy with experienced gender might be a solution. In light of the comorbidity and suicide rate statistically associated with gender dysphoria, Yarhouse and Sadusky's cautious openness seems to be a biblically defensible solution to a dilemma where the lesser of two evils must be chosen because the optimal solution appears unattainable. This may be compared to other bioethical dilemmas. Is it right to perform an abortion if a pregnancy would otherwise cost the mother's life? Where is the line for attempting to save a premature baby? What are the limits for palliative (and potentially life-ending) treatment of terminally ill patients? Without definitively answering these questions, the primary biblical ethical task must be to point to the "rule" rather than the "exception that confirms the rule," naturally considering more fundamental creation theology.

As we have seen, there are several reasons why anatomical gender is indicative of psychological gender. First, we saw that the biblical texts necessitate the correlation between זָכָר (zāxār, "[biological] male" (Gen 1:27; 5:2) and אִישׁ (ʔîš, "[complementary] man" on the one hand, and נְקֵבָה (nᵉqēvāʰ, "[biological] female" and אִשָּׁה (ʔiššāʰ, "[complementary] woman" on the other. Secondly, we saw in the discussion of "soul stuff" that body and soul form a unity in biblical anthropology and that there is, therefore, no "I" behind or before the body. If a substance ontology is maintained as a biblically coherent foundation for scriptural anthropology, it follows that since "the body is the matter that a soul informs," there cannot be a mismatch between the "soul's" and the body's gender. The soul and the matter would simply be two constituents that constitute the person, and the gender manifests in the body. Gender dysphoria must consequently be regarded as a delusion stemming from original sin. Biological gender reflects psychological gender accurately.

Without excluding the rare solution to the bioethical dilemma mentioned above, a biblical ethic vis-à-vis gender dysphoria must, therefore, uphold that anatomical gender determines psychological gender and that a creation-theological boundary is crossed when the body is manipulated to align with experienced gender. This is written with great understanding and empathy for the bodily and psychological challenges that gender dysphoria entails, emphasizing that pastoral counseling must start from the forgiveness available to all who make choices that do not reflect the ideal, accessible through faith in Jesus Christ. It must allow for the sanctification process, which for many means that until the new creation, they must be on the journey, living with and receiving the repeated nudging of forgiveness towards the ideal and the new creation.

It also needs to be emphasized that the notion of being "unsuitable" for temple service and marriage (Isa 56; Matt 19) does not prevent an intersex (or otherwise infertile or bodily defect) person from serving Christ or marrying, nor does it render such a ministry or marriage second-rate. It *does* mean that there are certain things the intersex (or otherwise infertile or bodily defective) person cannot do, namely represent bodily perfection as a visualization of prelapsarian creation and perform sexual intercourse and/or procreate as a symbol of Christ's "procreative" union with the church. However, since such conditions, as we have seen, are not a moral issue, we need to look at it in terms of function and role. Both in the Old and New Testament, *all* members of the congregation/church were unsuitable for *something*. Esau was unsuited as a patriarch because he lacked the character for it. Saul was unsuited for kingship for the same reason. Judahites, Zebulunites, and Naphtalites were unsuited for service in the temple for the (nonmoral) reason only that they were not Levites! David was unsuited as a temple builder because he was *not* a man of peace. These "lacks" were not moral failings but rather pointed to other traits and attributes that made them suitable for different roles and functions. The tribe of Judah was made "king material" (Gen 49). The Zebulunites and Naphtalites were loyal, willing, and courageous "team players" suited for backing Deborah and Barak against the Canaanites (Judg 4–5). Esau's character was suited for securing the subsistence and security of the patriarchal family (Gen 25), and Jacob was chosen over him because he, as a type (at least later in his life), represented repentance, remorse, and dependency on God. Saul, though lacking these traits, was entrepreneurial and good at acting. And it would have been—and in some of these cases, it really *was*—disastrous for these people to do what they were not suited for. On the other hand, they were just as valuable if they had chosen to do—and in some of these cases, they *did*—what they were suited or equipped for. And this is precisely the logic in Paul's use of the body metaphor in 1 Cor 12, where the members are not interchangeable but, nonetheless, equally valuable:

> So now there are many members, but one body. The eye cannot say to the hand, "I do not need you," nor in turn can the head say to the foot, "I do not need you." On the contrary, those members that seem to be weaker are essential, and those members we consider less honorable we clothe with greater honor, and our

> unpresentable members are clothed with dignity, but our presentable members do not need this. Instead, God has blended together the body, giving greater honor to the lesser member, so that there may be no division in the body, but the members may have mutual concern for one another. If one member suffers, everyone suffers with it. If a member is honored, all rejoice with it. Now you are Christ's body, and each of you is a member of it. (1 Cor 12:20–27 NET)

There is a difference, of course, between *not* being equipped with a certain character trait or ability and being deprived of a bodily function that belongs to the normal human body but is defective due to the fall. And it should not be minimized that humans are created with a longing for the complementarity, union, and reproduction inherent in marriage. However, there is still a matter of degree. Just as one can be born with other physical or psychological disabilities or be genetically predisposed to develop alcoholism, depression, breast cancer, or other conditions and thus be naturally prevented from doing certain things, there will always be other qualities that are equally valuable in "the body of Christ." Therefore, both Jesus and Paul highlight those who are "unsuitable for marriage"—whether by choice or not—as individuals who should accept with great blessing the service they are suitable for. When Jesus says, "Not everyone can accept this statement, except those to whom it has been given . . . The one who can accept this should accept it" (Matt 19:11–12), it means precisely that it can be "given" to accept a different role and function than being married. This is the "gift" Paul refers to when he says, "I wish that everyone was as I am. But each has his own gift from God, one this way, another that" (1 Cor 7:7).

SAME-SEX RELATIONS

It is high time that we turn our attention to the relatively few biblical texts that address same-sex sexual relations. However, precisely because there are few texts that explicitly deal with this issue, it has been necessary to construct a creation-theological foundation that supports these statements. This foundation implies that even if one or more of the so-called "seven gay texts" were not to concern "a sexual relationship between

Genesis 9:20-27

> Noah, the farmer, was the first to plant a vineyard. When he drank from the wine, he became drunk and uncovered himself [וַיִּתְגַּל, *wayyitgal*] inside his tent. Ham, the father of Canaan, saw his father's nakedness [אֶת עֶרְוַת אָבִיו, *ʔēt ʕerwat ʔāvîw*] and told his two brothers outside. Shem and Japheth took a garment and placed it across their shoulders; then they walked backward and covered their father's nakedness [אֶת עֶרְוֹת אֲבִיהֶם, *ʔēt ʕerwat ʔᵃvîhem*]. They turned their faces away so as not to see their father's nakedness [וְעֶרְוַת אֲבִיהֶם לֹא רָאוּ, *ʕerwat ʔᵃvîhem lōʔ rāʔû*]. When Noah awoke from his wine and learned what his youngest son had done to him, he said, 'Cursed be Canaan! The lowest of slaves will he be to his brothers.'

The reason for including this text is that it has been interpreted as a narrative of incestuous, homosexual rape. With extensive reference to interpretation literature, Robert Gagnon explains how such an interpretation addresses the questions that other interpretations fall short of, namely, what Ham did that led to such a severe punishment, and why it was his son Canaan who was cursed.[370] The "simple" interpretation, Gagnon mentions, is that the Canaanites were cursed because their ancestor saw his father, Noah, lying naked in his tent, thereby arousing his father's anger. The argument for this being solely "voyeurism" is supported by the fact that Shem and Japheth "turned their faces away and did not see their father's nakedness" (v. 23). However, this interpretation may be too simplistic. If Ham's offense was solely accidentally seeing his father naked inside the tent, there must have been a custom prohibiting his son from seeing or entering their parents' tents—a custom about which we know nothing from other texts or sources. And how could Ham know that his father was naked if he merely looked into the tent? And when the punishment was so severe, it must have meant that Ham, who, in the interpretation, solely saw his father naked, had a sexual desire to exploit the situation but did not act upon it. Thus, it would be one of the earliest

---

369. Gnuse, "Seven Gay Texts," 68–87.
370. Gagnon, *Bible and Homosexual Practice*, 63–71.

GENDER AND BODY IN BIBLICAL CREATION THEOLOGY

examples of a person being punished for sinful lust. This still does not explain why it was Canaan and not Ham who was cursed. Therefore, a significant portion of the interpretation literature points to another explanation, namely that Ham committed incestuous homosexual rape. Gagnon presents four main arguments for this interpretation:

First, the narrative places Ham inside the tent, which suggests more than just "voyeurism." In verse 22, where it is mentioned that Ham told "it" to his two brothers, Ham was also outside the tent. When we hear that his brothers took "the garment, the robe," in definite form, it is most natural to understand it as Noah's robe. It is, therefore, obvious to understand the event in the way that Ham commits an offense against his father, taking his robe outside to boast about it to his brothers.

Secondly, Noah becomes aware of what Ham had done to him when he wakes up from his drunkenness. Gagnon also argues that the hitpael form וַיִּתְגַּל (*wayyitgal*) in verse 21 should be translated as "he [Noah] was uncovered [by Ham]" instead of the normal reflexive "he uncovered himself." The actions in verses 21 and 22 are connected; both verses are about what Ham did inside his father's tent.

Thirdly, the language itself is suggestive. The expressions "uncover nakedness" and "see nakedness" are often used in the context of sexual intercourse. In Leviticus, the term is used several times, especially concerning incest (Lev 18:6–19; 20:11, 17–21), although it should be noted that in these cases, it is constructed with a piel form of גלה (*GLH*). The same applies to various other instances where it describes prostitution, adultery, and rape (Deut 23:1; 27:20; Isa 47:3; Ezek 16:36–37; 23:10, 29). Similarly, the term "see nakedness" is used in Lev 20:17 to describe incest with siblings, while in several other places, it denotes occasions of rape (Isa 47:3; Ezek 16:37; Hab 2:15; Nah 3:5; Lam 1:8–10).

Fourthly, Gagnon points out that if one understands Ham's offense as incestuous, homosexual rape, it closely resembles the situations described in the Mesopotamian omen text and the Egyptian myth of Horus and Seth, where the assault serves to emasculate, that is, deprive the victim of his masculinity by placing him sexually in the receptive, feminine role. In this case, it demonstrates power, where Ham tries to take on the leading role as the family patriarch.

Fifthly, the brothers' reaction shows that while Ham committed the worst possible offense against his father, the brothers did the opposite. They not only "covered their naked father" but also entered "backward" so they did not even see their father's nakedness in the literal sense. Their reaction clearly contrasts Ham's actions and shows that Ham did in the worst possible way what the brothers would never even think of doing.

Sixth, such an interpretation explains better than other interpretations why the curse hit Ham's son Canaan. In relation to the Canaanites, the Lord later explains to Moses that "you must not behave as they do in Canaan" (Lev 18:3), and that the reason why "the land became unclean, and I punished it for its sin, and the land spat out its inhabitants" was that the actions of the Canaanites—including incest and homosexual sex—were זִמָּה (*zimmāʰ*, "shamelessness") (v. 17), תּוֹעֵבָה (*tôʿēvāʰ*, "abomination)" (v. 22), and תֶּבֶל (*tevel*, "uncleanness, disgrace") (v. 23). This applies to both Lev 18:24–30 and 20:22–26. Gagnon also mentions that the Yahwist's both direct and indirect allusions to the moral abominations of the Canaanites—including the remark in the following text that "the territory of the Canaanites extended 'to Sodom and Gomorrah'"—show that "the etiological thrust of Gen 9:20–27 lies at the forefront: The Canaanites deserve to be dispossessed of the land and made slaves because they are, and always have been, avid practitioners of immoral activity. In the new post-diluvian world, it was their ancestor that committed the most heinous act imaginable—not just rape, but incest; not just incestuous rape, but homosexual intercourse; not just incestuous, homosexual rape, but the rape of one's own father, to whom supreme honor and obedience are owed."[371] The punishment, therefore, corresponds to the crime: "Just as Ham committed a heinous act with his ʿseed' (sperm), so too the curse fell on his 'seed' (son, descendants)."[372]

The most significant and obvious weakness of Gagnon's interpretation is unquestionably the argument that the hitpael form וַיִּתְגַּל (*wayyitgal*) in verse 21 is translated reflexively as "he [Noah] was uncovered [by Ham]." According to BDB, it is usually the piel form of גלה (*GLH*) that is used in the sense of "uncover nakedness." However, in Gagnon's defense, BDB translates the hitpael form in Gen 9:21 as "was uncovered." Nevertheless, even with this translation, interpreters are generally more inclined to suggest that Noah himself was responsible for the uncovering.

There is another reading, however, that is more likely, since it avoids the unusual and probably incorrect reflexive translation of the hitpael form in verse 21 and, to a higher degree, aligns with the description of "seeing" and "uncovering" in Lev 20:17 (NET):

---

371. Gagnon, *Bible and Homosexual Practice*, 67.
372. Gagnon, *Bible and Homosexual Practice*, 67.

> If a man has sexual intercourse with his sister, whether the daughter of his father or his mother, so that he sees [רָאָה, rāʔāʰ] her nakedness and she sees his nakedness, it is a disgrace. They must be cut off in the sight of the children of their people. He has exposed [גִּלָּה, gillāʰ] his sister's nakedness; he will bear his punishment for iniquity.

What is important here is the comparison between "seeing" and "exposing" or "uncovering" since uncovering is clearly a euphemism for sexual intercourse. Ham, in other words, engage not only in voyeurism but in actual sexual intercourse. The question is, however, with *whom* this sexual intercourse takes place. Now, in Lev 18:7–8 (NET; cf. 18:14, 16; 20:11, 30), it is clear that the father's nakedness actually refers to the *mother*:

> You must not expose your father's nakedness by having sexual intercourse with your mother. She is your mother; you must not have intercourse with her. You must not have sexual intercourse with your father's wife; she is your father's nakedness.

What Ham does, therefore, is to have sexual intercourse with his *mother*, thereby usurping his father's role as leader of the clan. It makes good sense, therefore, that Canaan, not Ham, is punished since it is a cutting off of Ham's line. John Sietze Bergsma and Scott Walker Hahn conclude their review of the various interpretations as follows:

> In the review of the various interpretive options for Gen 9:20–27 above, it has been seen that the voyeurist position, which understands Ham's deed as nothing more than looking, fails to explain the gravity of Ham's sin or the cursing of Canaan. The castration view suffers from a lack of textual support. The currently popular paternal-incest interpretation has much to commend it, but in almost every case the evidence marshalled for this view actually better suits the maternal-incest theory. The heuristic strengths of the maternal-incest interpretation are manifold: it explains (1) the gravity of Ham's sin, (2) the rationale for the cursing of Canaan rather than Ham, (3) Ham's motivation for committing his offense, (4) the repetition of "Ham, the father of Canaan," and (5) the sexually charged language of the passage. In addition, biblical and ancient Near Eastern analogues for Ham's crime are easy to find, and the related passages of the Pentateuch fit together more elegantly on this interpretation.[373]

---

373. Bergsma and Hahn, "Noah's Nakedness," 39–40.

If the narrative is to be understood in this way, it only contributes to the biblical assessment of same-sex intercourse in a very indirect way. Ham's offense is not about same-sex intercourse but maternal incest. Though it involves grave offenses such as rape, incest, and the dishonoring of the patriarch, in light of the broader context, same-sex intercourse is only referred to in connection to the later practices of Ham's line, i.e., the Canaanites (which were clearly not terminated), where male homosexual intercourse is explicitly included (Lev 20:13). When Nissinen argues that the narrative "does not speak of Ham's homosexual orientation but his hunger for power,"[374] he is right in the sense that the assault (which Nissinen believes was homosexual) was a means to gain status as a patriarch or at least dominance over his brothers. And since the assault probably was *maternal* incest, the text does not address homosexuality directly.

Genesis 19 and Judges 19

> They called out to Lot: "Where are the men who came to you tonight? Bring them out to us! We want to have sex with them [וְנֵדְעָה אֹתָם, *nēdəʿāh ʾōtām*]!" But Lot went out to the entrance to them, and after he had shut the door behind him, he said, "No, my brothers! Don't do this wicked thing!" (Gen 19:5–7 CSB)

> While they were enjoying themselves, the men of the city, some wicked men, surrounded the house. They pounded on the door and shouted to the old man who owned the house, "Bring out the man who came to your house. We want to have sex with him [נֵדְעֶנּוּ, *nēdāʿennû*]!" (Judg 19:22 NIV)

In discussions of these texts, it is often claimed that they explicitly refer to gang rape, making them irrelevant to our discussion. The "sin" in these texts is thus primarily about the unprecedented attack on the helpless guests who, according to the unwritten rules of hospitality at the time, should have been protected and welcomed. This is also evident from the earliest reception history, as expressed in Ezek 16:49 (NIV): "Now this was the sin of your sister Sodom: She and her daughters were arrogant, overfed and unconcerned; they did not help the poor and needy." However, it is worth noting that the episode in Gen 19, in the broader context, serves as a parallel to Gen 6:1–4, which also deals with "boundary-crossing" sexual behavior between angels (assuming בְּנֵי־הָאֱלֹהִים, *vᵊnê-hāʾᵉlōhîm*, is

---

374. Nissinen, *Homoeroticism*, 53.

to be interpreted as such) and humans, and that the boundary-crossing not only consists of rape but also of unnatural and creation-conflicting intercourse. Gordon Wenham notes in support of such an understanding that just as the first episode is followed by a judgment consisting of destruction (the flood), the episode in Gen 19 is also followed by such a judgment, namely, the destruction of Sodom and Gomorrah.[375] The rapes are obviously not the sole cause of the judgments, but they undoubtedly contribute to them, as indicated in Ezek 16:49–50. When Ezekiel uses the term תּוֹעֲבוֹתֵיהֶ ($tô^{a}vôtêhen$, "their abominations") to describe Sodom's sin, it is the same word used in Lev 18:22 and 20:13 to describe homosexual practices. Furthermore, Lot's daughters' subsequent incestuous acts with their father demonstrate that sexual excesses were not foreign to the Sodomites. Kevin DeYoung further points out that three texts from the Second Temple period, namely, the Testaments of Naphtali and Benjamin and the book of Jubilees, testify to the same understanding of the sin of the Sodomites:

> But you, my children, shall not be like that: In the firmament, in the earth, and in the sea, in all the products of his workmanship discern the Lord who made all things, so that you do not become like Sodom, which departed from the order of nature.[376]
>
> From the words of Enoch the Righteous I tell you that you will be sexually promiscuous like the promiscuity of the Sodomites and will perish, with few exceptions.[377]
>
> And in that month the LORD executed the judgment of Sodom and Gomorrah and Zeboim and all of the district of the Jordan. And he burned them with fire and sulphur and he annihilated them till this day just as (he said), "Behold, I have made known to you all of their deeds that (they were) cruel and great sinners and they were polluting themselves and they were fornicating in their flesh and they were causing pollution upon the earth." And thus the LORD will execute judgment like the judgment of Sodom on places where they act according to the pollution of Sodom.[378]

The references to Gen 19, DeYoung argues, demonstrate that the dating of the texts to the second–first centuries BCE underscores that

---

375. Wenham, "Old Testament Attitude to Homosexuality"; cf. Gagnon, *Bible and Homosexual Practice*, 75.

376. T. Naph. 3:4; Charlesworth, *Old Testament Pseudepigrapha*, 1:812.

377. T. Benj. 9:1 Charlesworth, *Old Testament Pseudepigrapha*, 827.

378. Jub. 16:5–6; Charlesworth, *Old Testament Pseudepigrapha*, 2:88.

their understanding of the sin of the Sodomites cannot be explained by suggesting that Philo and/or Josephus introduced a new interpretation contrary to the original interpretive tradition.[379] This argument probably holds true but must be cautiously presented since only fragments of the Testaments of Levi and Naphtali (and not those of the other ten) have been found at Qumran. The likely explanation is that there is such a great similarity between the text in the fragments of Levi's Testament and the later standard text that the text from Qumran may well be a copy of the original text.[380] The same understanding is also supported by the New Testament, where in Jude 7 (NLT), it is stated about the angels, "And don't forget Sodom and Gomorrah and their neighboring towns, which were filled with immorality and every kind of sexual perversion." Likewise, in 2 Pet 2:7 (NLT), it is said of Lot, "But God also rescued Lot out of Sodom because he was a righteous man who was sick of the shameful immorality of the wicked people around him." Here, it is asserted that the crime is not same-sex intercourse as such but rather the purpose that the sexual assault served, namely, to dishonor or shame Lot. Leland White argues, therefore, that there is no evidence that the Sodomites wanted to engage in same-sex intercourse "unless we want to believe that all the men of Sodom are homosexual."[381] This statement requires some qualification. The claim is not that all Sodomites were homosexuals but that some were. And while the text does not give us a basis for determining whether the Sodomites only intended to violate hospitality and thus Lot's honor or whether they (also) desired same-sex intercourse and considered it within the moral realm, the context—as described above—shows that the narrator's critical assessment of the assault is not just about whether they committed an assault but also about how they did it, by forcibly obtaining morally objectionable same-sex intercourse. Whether the objectionable behavior is solely forced or consensual same-sex intercourse can likewise be determined by the context, where the conclusion, as formulated by Gagnon, must be that "as with the author(s) of the Levitical prohibitions, the Yahwist is less concerned with motives than with the act of penetrating a male as if he were a female, and that by its very nature is demeaning regardless of how well it is done."[382]

379. DeYoung, *What Does the Bible Really Teach*, 36.
380. Bible Gateway, "Testaments of the Twelve Patriarchs."
381. White, "Does the Bible Speak about Gays," 20, quoted from Gagnon, *Bible and Homosexual Practice*, 77.
382. Gagnon, *Bible and Homosexual Practice*, 78.

Leviticus 18:22 and 20:13

וְאֶת־זָכָר לֹא תִשְׁכַּב מִשְׁכְּבֵי אִשָּׁה תּוֹעֵבָה הִוא

You shall not lie with a male as with a woman; it is an abomination. (Lev 18:22)

וְאִישׁ אֲשֶׁר יִשְׁכַּב אֶת־זָכָר מִשְׁכְּבֵי אִשָּׁה תּוֹעֵבָה עָשׂוּ שְׁנֵיהֶם מוֹת יוּמָתוּ דְּמֵיהֶם בָּם

If a man lies with a male as with a woman, both of them have committed an abomination; they shall surely be put to death; their blood is upon them. (Lev 20:13)

There is not much in these prohibitions that is not debated! The challenge in understanding that the prohibition lies in both how to translate תִשְׁכַּב (*tiškav*) and the subsequent description of the kind of "lying" that is forbidden. This further specification is given in the form of two nouns in construct state, מִשְׁכְּבֵי אִשָּׁה (*miškᵃvê ʔiššāʰ*), with מִשְׁכָּב (*miškāv*, "bed, lying") as the governing noun (the governing noun), and אִשָּׁה (*ʔiššāʰ*, "woman") as the governed noun (the governed noun). In 2 Sam 4:5, we have a similar expression in a subordinate clause, where, in the complementary construct connection (about Ishbosheth), it says: וְהוּא שֹׁכֵב אֵת מִשְׁכַּב הַצָּהֳרַיִם (*wᵉhûʔ šōxēv ʔēt miškav haṣṣāhᵒrāyim*, "and he lay in the bed at noon"), where מִשְׁכַּב (*miškav*, "bed, lying") is the governing noun, and צָהֳרַיִם (*ṣāhᵒrayim*, "noon") is the governed noun. In other words, Ishbosheth is lying down as people typically do at noon, namely, "taking a nap." Concerning Lev 18:22, where the bed or lying is not specified by using צָהֳרַיִם (*ṣāhᵒrayim*, "noon") but by using אִשָּׁה (*ʔiššāʰ*, "woman") the traditional translation has been "as with womankind" (KJV) or "as with a woman" (NKJV, ESV). The meaning of these traditional translations is that a man is not allowed to "go to bed with" or "have sexual intercourse with" another man. The argument for this translation is drawn from, among other things, Num 31:17–18, 35 (cf. Judg 21:11–12), where the phrase (with and without negation) יָדְעוּ מִשְׁכַּב זָכָר, *yādᵉʕû miškav* (*zāxār*), refers to any woman who "has known [a man] by lying with a man" or "has had an experience [with a man] by lying with a man." Since the phrase מִשְׁכַּב זָכָר, *miškav* (*zāxār*), here elaborates or specifies the frequently used euphemism for "having sexual intercourse with," in casu יָדְעוּ, *yādᵉʕû*, the argument is that מִשְׁכַּב זָכָר, *miškav* (*zāxār*), or מִשְׁכְּבֵי אִשָּׁה, *miškᵃvê ʔiššāʰ*, must also elsewhere refer to having sexual intercourse with a man/woman. However, Jerome T. Walsh has pointed out that while Num 31:17–18, 35, and Judg 21:11–12 use the verb יָדַע to say that women "have known" or "experienced" מִשְׁכַּב זָכָר (*miškav zāxār*, "having sexual intercourse with a man") Lev 18:22 and 20:13 use the verb שָׁכַב in their statement that a man shall not "lie" (ה אִשָּׁה מִשְׁכְּבֵי, *miškᵃvê ʔiššāʰ*). Furthermore, since מִשְׁכְּבֵי, *miškᵃvê*, has the same root as תִשְׁכַּב (*tiškav*), it is more interesting to understand it in the light of other similar occurrences of the Hebrew idiom, such as "dream a dream" (Judg 7:13). "This construction," argues Walsh, "regularly describes an action performed by the subject, not the subject's experience of someone else's action." Therefore, the prohibitions in Lev 18:22 are addressed to "the one who performs the 'lying down of a woman'—that is, the one who acts as the receptive partner . . . The זכר with whom a man is forbidden to lie is the penetrator; the person addressed by the laws is the receptive partner. Thus the phrase אשה משכבי את־זכר ישכב is best translated as 'to lie with a male as a woman would.'"³⁸³ Walsh also argues that while in Lev 18:22 it is only the passive, receptive role that is forbidden, Lev 20:13 extends the prohibition to make the active, penetrating party responsible for making a man take on the passive, receptive, or "female" role.³⁸⁴ Furthermore, it is Walsh's point that the legislation applies to free Israelite men. Therefore it does not—or at least not explicitly—address same-sex sexual practices where a free Israelite man penetrates a passive, receptive partner who is not yet a man (but still a boy or young man) or is not a free man. Walsh concludes:

> The two legislative texts in Lev 18:22 and 20:13 have very narrow and very precise purview. They envisage one situation only: anal intercourse between two men, one of whom is a free adult Israelite and takes the passive sexual role of being penetrated by the other. The underlying system of social values within which such laws should be understood is the gender construction of maleness in a society where honor and shame are foundational social values. The male sexual role is to be the active penetrator; the passive role of being penetrated brings shame to a man (at least to a free adult male citizen) who engages in it and, in the later redactional stratum, also to the one who penetrates him. Apart from this situation, the Hebrew Bible is silent.³⁸⁵

Walsh also appeals to the unusual juxtaposition of זָכָר (*zāxār*, "[biological] male)" with אִשָּׁה (*ʔiššāʰ*, "woman") instead of the corresponding

---

383. Walsh, "Leviticus 18:22 and 20:13," 205.
384. Walsh, "Leviticus 18:22 and 20:13," 206.
385. Walsh, "Leviticus 18:22 and 20:13," 208.

term נְקֵבָה (nᵊqēvāʰ, "[biological] female"). Gordon Wenham is representative of the traditional explanation for the choice of זָכָר (zāxār, "[biological] male") when he writes that "clearly this very general term prohibits every kind of male-male intercourse not just pederasty."[386] Against this, Walsh argues that since the text reads זָכָר (zāxār, "[biological] male") and not אִישׁ (ʔîš, "man"), it should be translated as "a penetrator." However, the reason אִישׁ (ʔîš) is not used is probably different, namely that it is used generically about humans without reference to gender. At the same time, זָכָר (zāxār) unambiguously refers to "males," and therefore here to the biological male. The choice of זָכָר (zāxār) does not necessarily imply that it specifically refers to "a penetrating [male]." At the same time, the argument is a bit of a boomerang. If the construct connection מִשְׁכְּבֵי אִשָּׁה (miškᵊvê ʔiššāʰ) should define a man who plays the passive, receptive role in the same-sex sexual relationship, why then is נְקֵבָה (nᵊqēvāʰ) not used, which indeed means—at least etymologically—"one who is penetrated?" Against Walsh, it must be argued that his interpretation of the Hebrew idiom is a *non sequitur*. It is true, of course, that the idiom describes "an action performed by the subject." However, even though the man in Lev 18:22 actively performs a "lying down," it does not necessarily follow that he also plays the passive, receptive role in this "lying down." Such a meaning is not inherent in the idiom itself but depends on how we understand the construct connection. If it is translated as a subjective genitive in the sense of "[as] the lying [of a woman with a man]," then it is most obvious to understand it as a general prohibition against sexual intercourse between men, since the narrower meaning would be "[as] the [receptive] lying [of a woman with a man]." Suppose it is translated as an objective genitive. In that case, the translation becomes "[in the same way as] lying with a woman." Here, the woman becomes the object of the man's "lying," and what is forbidden to a man is, therefore, to take on the active, penetrating role in the sexual contact. Ian Paul mentions—including with reference to the parallel formulation in 2 Sam 4:5 about Ishbosheth's lying "at noon"—that he prefers the traditional translation of the governed noun "with a woman," as it is in line with all other uses of the expression:

> This is based on the observation that the verbal sentence to which the construct chain is a shortcut in all attested cases has a complement. (As pointed out above, "x lies down" only refers

---

386. Wenham, "Old Testament Attitude to Homosexuality," 362.

to sex when it has a complement "with y.") The subject of the verbal sentence implied (the x who performs the lying down) is implied in the verbal idea expressed in the construct noun. This makes it more likely, in my view, that the postconstructus provides the complement ("with a woman") rather than a specification of the subject ("[as] a woman").[387]

Although there are significant objections to the necessity of understanding and translating as Walsh does, it is not decided that the traditional translation is correct. To determine which understanding is the most likely out of the possible translations, we need to consider both the immediate and remote context. Before we move on to this, however, we need to take a closer look at the extended prohibition in Lev 20:13, as it is the most likely source for the prohibitions against same-sex activity in 1 Cor 6:9 and 1 Tim 1:10. The Septuagint translates זָכָר (zāxār) in Lev 18:22 and 20:13 with the rarely occurring word ἄρσενος (arsenos) instead of using the more commonly occurring words ἄνθρωπος (anthrōpos) or ἀνήρ (anér),[388] and since the term ἀρσενοκοίτης (arsenokoites) in 1 Cor 6:9 and 1 Tim 1:10 does not occur in texts outside the New Testament, it is highly likely that the phrase ἄρσενος κοίτην (arsenos koitēn, "male-lie") in Lev 20:13 is Paul's source text. David Instone-Brewer mentions in this regard that "even if this form was not inspired by Lev 20:13, and its absence in surviving literature was merely an accident of history, its use in the NT would still be significant because no Greek Jew or Christian would fail to make the link between this word and the text of Lev 20:13."[389] Therefore, the understanding of the texts in Lev 18:22 and 20:13 becomes crucial for the understanding of 1 Cor 6:9 and 1 Tim 1:10. But more on this later. Before discussing the related but extended prohibition in Lev 20:13, a variant of Walsh's interpretation should be mentioned. It concerns Jacob Milgrom, who argues that the illegal sexual practice denoted by the expression מִשְׁכְּבֵי אִשָּׁה (miškᵃvê ʔiššāʰ) may indeed be directed at the penetrating part, but that it must also be understood in light of the other prohibitions in the context so that it only applies to "the equivalent degree of forbidden heterosexual relations," and that "sexual liaisons

---

387. Paul, "Grammar of Leviticus 18.22."

388. The normal words ἄνθρωπος (anthropos) and ἀνήρ (anêr) appear approximately 1,400 and 1,500 times respectively in the Septuagint. In contrast, ἄρσην (arsēn) is used only 59 times and always emphasizes the masculine aspect.

389. Instone-Brewer, "Are There Two Types of Men," 33.

occurring with males outside these relations would not be forbidden."³⁹⁰ Because the list of prohibitions in Lev 18:6–23 is organized in relation to family relations, Milgrom argues that same-sex activity between men outside the domain controlled by the paterfamilias is not covered by the prohibition. The expression מִשְׁכְּבֵי אִשָּׁה (*miškᵃvê ʔiššāʰ*) which normally refers to illegal heterosexual relations, is according to Milgrom transferred to illegal homosexual sex, so the rationale for the prohibition becomes: "Do not have sex with a male with whose widow sex is forbidden. In effect, this means that the homosexual prohibition applies to Ego, with father, son, and brother (subsumed in v. 6) and to grandfather-grandson, uncle-nephew, and stepfather-stepson, but not to any other male."³⁹¹ Against Milgrom, it must be said that it is an interpretive reading of the text, which may be possible but which is in no way explicit in the prohibition itself and must, therefore, be assessed in light of the wider biblical-theological context. Milgrom begins his interpretation by saying, "It may be plausibly suggested."³⁹²

The challenge in Lev 20:13 lies in the asymmetry between אִישׁ (*ʔîš*) and זָכָר (*zāxār*). As mentioned earlier, Walsh argues that the prohibition in 20:13 extends the prohibition in 18:22 to hold the active, penetrating partner responsible for causing a man to assume the passive, receptive, or "female" role. However, it is not explicitly evident that same-sex intercourse per se is prohibited here. Such an interpretation implies that the "asymmetrical" word pair אִישׁ (*ʔîš*) and זָכָר (*zāxār*) refers to two different "types" of men, namely the penetrating role and the penetrated role. Nevertheless, it is not immediately clear that זָכָר (*zāxār*) should be understood this way. In addition to Walsh's solution, commentary literature suggests two other solutions: One posits that the asymmetry may result from combining two more or less identical but originally independent sources. In contrast, the other suggests that the words are used synonymously.

Regarding the "source-critical" solution, Instone-Brewer argues that the two sources in Lev 18:17–22 and Lev 20:10–21 each have an "appendix" (18:20–23 and 20:17–21) that incorporates elements from the other source. However, he notes that while such a redactional blending of sources may shed light on the textual history, it doesn't explain why two

---

390. Milgrom, *Leviticus 17–22*, 1569.
391. Milgrom, *Leviticus 17–22*, 1569.
392. Milgrom, *Leviticus 17–22*, 1569.

separate words are used in a legal text. In legal contexts, using the same words for the same entity is typical.³⁹³

As for the "synonymous" solution, early translations did not understand אִישׁ (*ʾîš*) and זָכָר (*zāxār*) as synonyms. Instone-Brewer mentions that in the case of the Targums, they all use the normal Aramaic equivalent *gevar* for the Hebrew אִישׁ (*ʾîš*), "but for '*zakar*,' they employ the phonetically similar '*dekar*,' which carries the sense of 'maleness.'"

> The Syriac translation Peshitta "follows the pattern set by the Targums. The Septuagint translates the opening '*ish asher*... as '*hos an*' (ὃς ἂν ...,"anyone who...") throughout this list... However, when it comes to translating '*zakar*,' the Septuagint uses the relatively rare term '*arsēn*' (ἄρσην), which has a sense of "male" as opposed to "man." The Vulgate followed this pattern by translating it as '*masculo*.' It appears that all ancient translations wanted to reflect the meaning of '*zakar*' as distinctively referring to maleness.³⁹⁴

In relation to the third interpretation, namely that with אִישׁ (*ʾîš*) and זָכָר (*zāxār*), there are references to two different "male roles," Instone-Brewer makes the point that while we may not be able to verify this interpretation, we can attempt to falsify it. He argues, "If it can be shown that ancient society had no concept of non-masculine or homoerotic men, then this interpretation should be regarded as false."³⁹⁵ However, such an attempt at falsification does not make much sense in the context of Old Hebrew since the Hebrew Bible is essentially the only source we have. It is a different situation with Akkadian, though. After analyzing Mesopotamian texts, Instone-Brewer concludes that such an interpretation in Akkadian cannot be definitively falsified. Therefore, an alternative version of the third interpretation can be argued for.

As we saw in the examination of Mesopotamian material, Instone-Brewer argues that the Akkadian phrase *la zikaru* should be understood to mean "not a he-man." Regarding the understanding of Lev 18:22 and 20:13, Instone-Brewer further asserts that the Akkadian phrase *zikarim u sinništim* corresponds to the Hebrew זָכָר וּנְקֵבָה (*zāxār ûnqēvāʰ*), and therefore, both the Akkadian *zikaru* and the Hebrew זָכָר (*zāxār*) must be understood to mean "heteroerotic" as opposed to "homoerotic."³⁹⁶

393. Instone-Brewer, "Are There Two Types of Men," 34–38.
394. Instone-Brewer, "Are There Two Types of Men," 39.
395. Instone-Brewer, "Are There Two Types of Men," 40.
396. Instone-Brewer, "Are There Two Types of Men," 48.

Consequently, what is prohibited in Leviticus is same-sex intercourse between a man with a "heteroerotic" orientation, and it is not a prohibition against same-sex intercourse between men with a "homoerotic" orientation. The latter, Instone-Brewer adds, would likely be considered shameful but not prohibited, similar to the case of the cultic prostitute, קְדֵשָׁה ($q^ǝdēšā^h$) in Gen 38:21–22. Such an understanding of the prohibitions does not explain why the text uses two different words for "man," but because the words are different, Instone-Brewer argues that it is difficult "to interpret this legislation as meaning: 'a man may not sleep with [an identical type of] man.'"[397]

Instone-Brewer's conclusion is, therefore, as follows:

> Because of the paucity of data, we cannot be sure if this distinction between 'ish and zakar relates to sexuality. It may, for example, relate to marriage status, so that the law would mean that no man may sleep with an unmarried man. Or the distinction may refer to age (as Alan Millard argued), so that the law would mean that no man may sleep with another man-or-boy. These alternatives are interesting possibilities, but they have no support in the usage of zakar in Hebrew nor in cognate languages. However, there is evidence (though not enough to be certain), [sic] that Lev 20:13 forbids any man from sleeping with a heteroerotically inclined man.[398]

As a comment on his conclusion, Instone-Brewer adds the somewhat unusual remarks that "in the end, personal or doctrinal agendas are likely to determine the conclusion," and "where dogmatic interpretations of these passages may have ruinous consequences for many individuals, this uncertainty is important, and should not be ignored."[399] This can be understood as an appeal not to use Lev 18:22 and 20:13 as arguments against same-sex relations. While the desire to approach the topic with leniency is commendable, it does not alter the fact that criticism must be directed towards Instone-Brewer's argumentation.

The conclusion that both the Akkadian term zikaru and the cognate Hebrew term זָכָר (zāxār) fundamentally emphasize masculinity in their semantic fields is unassailable. However, it is a *non sequitur* to argue that these terms, therefore, denote a sexual orientation that can be understood independently of biological gender, exclusively applying to

397. Instone-Brewer, "Are There Two Types of Men," 48.
398. Instone-Brewer, "Are There Two Types of Men," 48–49.
399. Instone-Brewer, "Are There Two Types of Men," 49.

biological males with a heterosexual orientation. If these terms signify a biologically masculine gender that, within the context of creation theology, is normatively associated with a lived heterosexual gender, then the use of זָכָר (zāxār) in the prohibitions would apply to all biological males, not just those with a heterosexual orientation. Based on the above argumentation about the creation-theological, normative connection between biological gender and heterosexual orientation, Instone-Brewer's conclusion must be rejected. While it may be defensible in isolation, it is untenable within the creation-theological framework in which the prohibitions are embedded.

Jacob Milgrom has an interesting interpretation that, because the list of prohibitions in Lev 20:9–21, unlike the list in Lev 18:6–23, is arranged with the severity of the offenses and their corresponding penalties as the organizing principle, the prohibition in Lev 20:13 must be understood as an "absolute ban on homosexuality." This broader prohibition "contrasts strikingly with the Hellenistic and Roman world, where homosexuality was sanctioned with those of inferior status, such as slaves, foreigners, and youths."[400]

Regarding the immediate context, the prohibitions in Lev 18:22 and 20:13 are part of the so-called Holiness Code in Lev 17–26. Regardless of its redactional history in relation to the rest of Leviticus, it's considered a priestly text concerned with the holiness that should be a prerequisite for access to the sanctuary and the boundaries that should be observed in respect to the order of creation. Concerning holiness, both the commandments and prohibitions in the Holiness Code should be understood ritually and within the dichotomy of טָהֵר (ṭāhēr, "to be clean") and טָמֵא (ṭāmēʾ, "to be unclean"). As ritual categories, they reflect, according to a representative definition, "a symbolic system according to which a pure person or object is qualified for contact with the Temple and related sancta (holy objects and spaces) while an impure person or object is disqualified from such contact. Ritual impurity arises from physical substances and states associated with procreation and death, not in themselves sinful. Ritual impurities are in general permitted (if not unavoidable or obligatory) and in this they can be distinguished from moral impurities, which arise from prohibited acts."[401]

---

400. Milgrom, *Leviticus 17–22*, 1749.
401. Hayes, "Purity and Impurity, Ritual."

However, there is disagreement regarding how holiness and ritual purity should be understood. One strong trend in recent decades is the anthropological approach, particularly influenced by Mary Douglas, an anthropologist, and her seminal work *Purity and Danger: An Analysis of Concepts of Pollution and Taboo* (1966). The main idea is that rituals restore the world's order and protect against threats that could disrupt this order.[402] These rituals encompass taboos, defined as rules of correct behavior that serve to define, separate, and "discard" existential and moral "dirt"—that is, "waste" that has no place and threatens the stability of the group or society. According to Douglas, such taboos are necessary for a society to function as they both reflect and, through their enforcement, guarantee the understanding of reality that defines the group or society:

> Without the taboos, which turn basic classifications into automatic psychological reflexes, no thinking could be effective, because if every system of classification was up for revision at every moment, there would be no stability of thought. Hence there would be no scope for experience to accumulate into knowledge. Taboos bar the way for the mind to visualize reality differently. But the barriers they set up are not arbitrary, for taboos flow from social boundaries and support the social structure. This accounts for their seeming irrational to the outsider and beyond challenge to the person living in the society.[403]

In her work *Natural Symbols*, Douglas introduced her "group-grid" theory, which distinguishes "group," referring to an individual's social position within or outside a given group, and "grid," indicating the clarity with which an individual's social role is defined within networks of social privileges, demands, and obligations. Douglas argues that ritual, as a behavior-regulating code, "enables a given pattern of values to be enforced and allows members to internalize the structure of the group and its norms."[404]

Another aspect associated with taboos is that the bipolar distinction between purity and impurity helps individuals distinguish the sacred from the profane. This notion is explicitly formulated in Leviticus, where it states that the regulations should serve to "distinguish between the holy and the common, and between the unclean and the clean" (Lev 10:10 NLT) with the rationale that "you shall be holy to me, for I, the Lord, am

---

402. Douglas, *Purity and Danger*.
403. Douglas, "Taboo," 71.
404. Douglas, *Natural Symbols*, 54.

holy and I have separated you from the peoples, that you should be mine" (Lev 20:26 NLT).

Mary Douglas's influence on biblical scholarship is due, in no small part, to her extensive application of her theories to priestly texts in the Old Testament.[405] This influence is evident, for instance, in the work of David Janzen, who writes about texts from the book of Leviticus, stating that "rituals function as a kind of rhetoric to convince their participants to lend their allegiance to the worldview and moral system of one social group in particular."[406] It's also seen in the work of Margaret Barker, who understands the term חַטָּאת הַכִּפֻּרִים (*ḥaṭṭaʾt hakkippurîm*, the "sin offering of atonement") as a cosmic healing and restoration of the world's order.[407]

In this context, mention must also be made of Jacob Milgrom, who, over a long scholarly career, has focused on describing the rationality in the priestly texts of the book of Leviticus. He has argued that חַטָּאת הַכִּפֻּרִים (*ḥaṭṭaʾt hakkippurîm*) is not a "sin offering for atonement"—that is, a substitutionary offering for forgiveness—but rather serves to cleanse the altar in the sanctuary when it has become contaminated due to the sins of the people. According to Milgrom, "Humans can drive God out of the sanctuary by polluting it with their moral and ritual sins. All that the priests can do is periodically purge the sanctuary of its impurities and influence the people to atone for their wrongs."[408]

Milgrom argues, therefore, that the verb כִּפֶּר (*kipper*) should be translated as "purge" or "cleanse," rather than as suggested in BDB as "pacify" or "make propitiation." In his commentary on the book of Leviticus, Milgrom also notes that the central issue is not so much the sins of individuals or the community but rather the fact that the altar has become impure due to these sins. Consequently, the verb סָלַח (*sālaḥ*), often translated as "to forgive," should be understood more as "to reconcile" or "to make amends." Thus, the sin offering primarily focuses on the purification of the sanctuary and the continuation of God's presence within the sanctuary: "The offender who brings the *ḥaṭṭāʾt* does so because he knows that his wrong, though committed inadvertently, has polluted the altar and, hence, has alienated him from God. By his sacrifice he hopes to repair the broken relationship. He therefore seeks more than forgiveness. If God will accept his sacrifice he will be once again restored to grace, at

---

405. Cf. Douglas, *Leviticus as Literature*.
406. Janzen, *Social Meanings of Sacrifice*, 5.
407. Barker, "Atonement," 1–20; Barker, *Great High Priest*.
408. Milgrom, *Leviticus 1–16*, 43.

one with his deity."⁴⁰⁹ This "more than forgiveness" shows that Milgrom does not reject forgiveness as an aspect of the cleansing sacrifice but that forgiveness must first and foremost be understood as the assurance of God's continued presence that the cleansing of the sanctuary facilitates. This emphasis on purification rather than forgiveness is made clear in a slightly longer quote where Milgrom characterizes the people's sin as a physical substance or aerial miasma, "air pollution," which has a magnetic attraction in relation to the sanctuary:

> The dynamic, aerial quality of biblical impurity is best attested by its graded power. Impurity pollutes the sanctuary in three stages: (1) The individual's inadvertent misdemeanor or severe physical impurity pollutes the courtyard altar, which is purged by daubing its horns with the [חטאת] blood ([Lev] 4:25, 30; 9:9). (2) The inadvertent misdemeanor of the high priest or the entire community pollutes the shrine, which is purged by the high priest by placing the [חטאת] blood on the inner altar and before the [כפרת] ([Lev] 4:5–7, 16–18). (3) The wanton unrepented sin not only pollutes the outer altar and penetrates into the shrine but it pierces the veil and enters the adytum, housing the Ark and [כפרת], the very throne of God (cf. Isa 37:16). Because the wanton sinner is barred from bringing his [חטאת] (Num 15:27–31), the pollution wrought by his offense must await the annual purgation of the sanctuary on the Day of Purgation, and it consists of two steps: the purging of the adytum of the wanton sins and the purging of the shrine and outer altar of the inadvertent sins ([Lev] 16:16–19). Thus the entire sacred area or, more precisely, all that is most sacred ... is purged on Purgation Day ([הכפרים יום]) with the [חטאת] blood.⁴¹⁰

The insights from anthropology and Milgrom's understanding of חַטָּאת (*ḥaṭṭaʾt*) have convincingly demonstrated that the preservation of the world order and the purification of the sanctuary are rational motives behind the laws of purity in Leviticus. This becomes evident, for example, in Lev 15:31, where it states, "Thus you shall keep the people of Israel separate from their uncleanness, lest they die in their uncleanness by defiling my tabernacle that is in their midst." However, there are two significant problems with the *exclusive* use of this anthropological theory.

---

409. Milgrom, *Leviticus 1–16*, 245; see Zohar, "Repentance and Purification," 609–18; cf. n2 for further references to Milgrom.
410. Milgrom, *Leviticus 1–16*, 257.

Firstly, in its purest form, this theory leads to a narrow understanding of the sin offering and the verb סָלַח (sālaḥ). Olivier Randrianjaka has documented that "several occurrences of the niph'al וְנִסְלַח 'and it will be forgiven' describes the state of the offerer after the completion of the כִּפֶּר rites. The use of the passivum divinum וְנִסְלַח לוֹ 'and it will be forgiven for him' in these cases clearly shows that only God can forgive sins. The officiating priest is only there to perform the ritual. He has nothing to do with the outcome of the sacrifice."[411] Similarly, Stephen Finlan argues that if "sin-sacrifice" is too narrow a term for the *ḥaṭṭā 't* ritual, it's also overly limited to call it a "purification sacrifice" if it is meant to exclude the possibility of sin-purgation or expiation. Milgrom's insistence on "purification" alone minimizes the fact that it's the impurity caused by sin that is being cleansed.[412] Joshua Vis points to the broader meaning of חַטָּאת (*ḥaṭṭā't*) when he concludes, based on his analysis of Lev 4:1—5:13 and Lev 16, that the Israelite and the sanctuary are in a reciprocal relationship. It's the presence of YHWH in the tabernacle that underlies all of these ritual relationships and procedures: "As Lev 16 indicated, the Israelite and the sanctuary, especially the altars of the sanctuary, are in a reciprocal relationship. The sin of the Israelite can stain the sanctuary, and the sanctuary, through sacrifice offered within it and on parts of it, can purge the Israelite of his/her sin. Underlying all of this is the continued and necessary presence of YHWH in the Tabernacle. These ritual relationships and procedures rely on and must be realized in the presence of YHWH."[413]

Secondly, this theory tends to understand impurity solely as ritual and not morally culpable. Jonathan Klawans has argued for the presence of both ritual and moral impurity in biblical texts. Klawans writes:

> What we will call "moral impurity" results from committing certain acts to heinous that they are explicitly referred to in biblical sources as defiling. Thus describing these acts as impurities is not our choice to make: the biblical authors have explicitly described these sin as impurities. These defiling acts include sexual sins (e.g., Lev. 18:24–30), idolatry (e.g., Lev. 19:31; 20:1–3), and bloodshed (e.g., Num. 35:33–34). These three sinful behaviors are also frequently referred to as "abominations" (תוֹעֵבוֹת). They bring about an impurity that *morally*—but

---

411. Randrianjaka, "Sin, Purification and Sacrifice," 71.
412. Finlan, *Background and Contents*, 33.
413. Vis, "Purification Offering of Leviticus," 204.

not *ritually*—defiles the sinner (Lev. 18:24), the land of Israel (Lev. 18:25; Ezek 36:17), and the sanctuary of God (Lev. 20:3; Ezek 5:11). This defilement, in turn leads to the expulsion of the people from the land of Israel (Lev. 18:28; Ezek 36:19).[414]

Characteristic of ritual impurity, Klawans continues, is that it's "natural," meaning it arises in connection with situations, conditions, or actions that are part of life and therefore can also be "contagious" through physical contact (e.g., with bodily fluids). However, these impurities are not inherently prohibited and thus not associated with guilt. Actions that lead to moral impurity, on the other hand, render the individual guilty of sin and require purification through a substitutionary offering for the individual to be forgiven. Since this impurity is personal, it does not transmit through physical contact; nevertheless, it "pollutes" its surroundings by bringing a curse upon both the land and the temple, understood as an idealized miniature model of the land.[415]

This detour has been necessary because the more purist anthropological approach and Milgrom's emphasis on the ritual purification aspect significantly influence the interpretation of prohibitions against same-sex sexual intercourse in Lev 18:20 and 20:13. A common interpretation of these prohibitions suggests that they are taboos, and a violation of these prohibitions is understood as a breach of the code prevailing in the honor/shame culture to which the Israelites belonged. In this context, Walsh's interpretation of the prohibition of same-sex sexual intercourse revolves around situations where a free Israelite man is "feminized" as the passive, receptive partner, thereby bringing shame upon the community in relation to the ethical framework promoted by the priestly authors.

> The language of the laws, therefore, is fully consonant with what we know of other contemporary Mediterranean societies in which an honor/shame dynamic was central to social and sexual behavior. Thomas M. Thurston applied Douglas's categories specifically to Lev 18:22: in an act of male-male anal intercourse the boundary between "male" and "female" is being transgressed, since a man is acting in the sexually receptive role proper to a woman. Similar reasoning can be extended as well to the other two instances of sexual category confusion in the immediate context: adultery, which confuses the categories of

---

414. Klawans, *Impurity and Sin in Ancient Judaism*, 26 (emphasis original); cf. Klawans, *Purity, Sacrifice, and the Temple*.

415. Klawans, *Impurity and Sin in Ancient Judaism*, 22–31.

one's own sexual property and one's neighbors, and bestiality, which transgresses the boundary between human and animal.[416]

The Israelites were to abstain from the type of same-sex sexual practices that were associated with shame in the general cultural code. As Walsh put it, this was "fully consonant with what we know of other contemporary Mediterranean societies" and not unique to the Israelites. Another interpretation, also influenced by anthropological insights, suggests that the prohibition should be understood as a specific and narrow prohibition against temple sex, which was an integral part of the West Semitic expression of the Ishtar cult or which occurred in temples without being explicitly ritualized. In this case, the prohibition must be seen as part of what anthropologists call ethnic negotiation, specifically the priestly authors' efforts to construct an Israelite identity vis-à-vis the Canaanites.[417] Therefore, Israelites were supposed to refrain from engaging in the same-sex sexual practices associated with the worship of Canaanite gods to set themselves apart from the Canaanites (and Egyptians). However, there was no general prohibition against same-sex sexual practices. Even proponents of the narrow or cultic interpretation of the prohibition, while not explicitly or only incidentally using anthropological arguments, have increasingly relied on these arguments implicitly. This is evident in the fact that these interpretations often do not distinguish between the ritual impurity resulting from violations of the rules in Lev 17 and the moral impurity due to violations of the prohibitions in Lev 18. As we have seen, research has convincingly demonstrated that within the "symbolic system" reflected in many purity regulations, there are actions that only trigger ritual impurity. However, this cannot be used to conclude that there are no cases where these actions also result in moral impurity and, therefore, require atonement to cleanse the impurity. This is why Hayes, in the abovementioned text, emphasizes the need to distinguish between ritual impurity caused by actions that are inherently permitted and moral impurity resulting from violations of prohibited

416. Walsh, "Leviticus 18," 207.

417. In the above quote, Walsh also indirectly subscribes to the concept of *ethnic negotiation* when he points to adherence to prohibitions as a transgression of boundaries between categories. While the Israelites shared with the Canaanites a view on the boundary between "male" and "female" behavior, this does not apply to the prohibition against bestiality, which was part of the Canaanite pantheon's sexual repertoire and is not condemned in Canaanite texts. Here, the priestly authors highlight a distinctive aspect of the Israelite ethos, which cannot be justified by any other rationale than that it reflects the order of creation as expressed in Gen 1.

actions. The first category includes discharges (Lev 15:2), emissions of semen (Lev 15:16), and menstruation (Lev 15:19), which are "natural" situations or conditions that are not inherently prohibited or morally sinful and are often associated with ritual cleansing. The second category stands out in several ways. Firstly, impurities resulting from violations in this category cannot be cleansed through ritual washing. Secondly, moral categorization and responsibility are emphasized, as actions in this category are usually described as a תּוֹעֵבָה (tôʕēvā^h, "abomination").

> But you shall keep my statutes and my rules and do none of these abominations [הַתּוֹעֵבוֹת, hattôʕēvôt], both the native and the stranger who sojourns among you (for the people of the land, who were before you, did all of these abominations [הַתּוֹעֵבֹת, hattôʕēvôt], so that the land became unclean), lest the land vomit you out when you make it unclean, as it vomited out the nation that was before you. For everyone who does any of these abominations [הַתּוֹעֵבוֹת, hattôʕēvôt], the persons who do them shall be cut off from among their people. So keep my charge never to practice any of these abominable customs [מֵחֻקּוֹת הַתּוֹעֵבֹת mēḥuqqôt hattôʕēvōt], that were practiced before you, and never to make yourselves unclean by them: I am the Lord your God! (Lev 18:26–30 NET)

Ronald Youngblood argues in *TWOT* that the term תּוֹעֵבָה (tôʕēvā^h) is not limited to cultic impurity: "Whereas *tôʕēbâ* includes that which is aesthetically and morally repulsive, its synonym *šeqeṣ* denotes that which is cultically unclean, especially idolatry."[418] According to Jacob, who quotes Picket, "it should not be forgotten that the term *tôʕēbâ* is used to characterize all the illicit cohabitation (vv. 26, 27, 29. 30). [This term] carries 'moral (rather than legal) weight and serves primarily to characterize the undesirability and unacceptability of the (referred) offenses.'"[419] This understanding would undermine the argument, especially as put forward by John Boswell in his influential work *Christianity, Social Tolerance, and Homosexuality*, where the prohibition is understood solely as a prohibition against cultic impurity and not moral impurity. Boswell argues that the prohibition "does not usually signify something intrinsically evil, like rape or theft (discussed elsewhere in Leviticus), but something which is ritually unclean for Jews, like eating pork or engaging in

---

418. Youngblood, "2530a תּוֹעֵבָה."
419. Milgrom, *Leviticus 17–22*, 1569–70.

intercourse during menstruation, both of which are prohibited in these same chapters."[420] However, this perspective is not as clear-cut as Youngblood's quote might indicate. As Jay Sklar points out, the term, in most cases, "refers to things that are detestable because they are intrinsically immoral, that is, they go directly against God's universal intent for the world."[421] In contrast, in some cases, it "refers to things that are *not* intrinsically wrong, including at least one reference to ritually impure animals (Deut 14:3)."[422] The exception to the rule suggests that Boswell's view that there is no explicit account of which meaning of the term is employed in Lev 18 and 20 is a possibility and that it falls under the category of "exceptions." One argument for this understanding is that Lev 18 explicitly mentions that the land becomes unclean through these violations. On the other hand, an alternative perspective is that the abomination stands in contrast to the holiness of the Lord and that the violation, if one understands "holiness" as an expression of something essential to the Lord's being, breaks something inherently in conflict with the "godlikeness" in the Lord's nature. Furthermore, contrary to what Boswell claims about the use of the term תּוֹעֵבָה (*tôʕēvāʰ*), a closer examination reveals that out of the 118 occurrences of the term, it is used only once for cultic impurity. Moreover, Boswell fails to distinguish between ritual and moral impurity, whereas Lev 18 and 20 deal with the latter, i.e., inherently prohibited actions.

Another aspect of the prohibition in Lev 18:22 is why it is grouped with child sacrifice (v. 21) and bestiality (v. 23). Milgrom, in his commentary on Leviticus, argues that the common denominator for all prohibitions is procreation. Specifically, they all involve the emission of semen for copulation resulting either in incest or illicit progeny (vv. 6–20), the destruction of progeny (v. 21), or no progeny (vv. 22–23). The consequence of child sacrifice, homosexual intercourse, and bestiality, respectively, is profanation of God's name (תְּחַלֵּל אֶת־שֵׁם אֱלֹהֶיךָ, *tᵉhallēl ʔet-šēm ʔᵉlōheʸxā*), abomination (תּוֹעֵבָה, *tôʕēvāʰ*), and perversion (תֶּבֶל, *tevel*). These acts are singled out from the other offenses as transgressions directly against God because these acts are contrary to creation order. In essence, they involve copulating with somebody who could not procreate or copulating to destroy the procreated result. Such an understanding

---

420. Boswell, *Christianity, Social Tolerance, and Homosexuality*, 100.

421. E.g., idolatry (Deut 7:25), human sacrifice (Deut 12:31), conducting one's business dishonestly (Deut 25:13–16). Cf. also the list of moral offenses in Prov 6:16–19.

422. Sklar, "Prohibitions," 167. Emphasis original.

only adds to the conclusion above, namely that the rationale is not only cultic prostitution, a distinction between penetrator and penetrated, or pederasty, but a total ban against homosexuality. The reason why lesbianism is not mentioned (here or elsewhere in the Old Testament) is probably due to the prevailing prescientific idea that the child was in the male seed, and copulation "planted" the child in the woman's womb where it "took root" and grew. Consequently, lesbian sex, as it did not involve the emission of semen, did not belong to a list of prohibitions with procreation as a common denominator. This omission does not mean, however, that lesbian sex is exonerated since the most fundamental reason against homosexual practice is creation order.

Moving on to the broader context, the prohibitions appear as a specific application of the Decalogue in Exod 20 and the creation narrative in Gen 1. Notably, Lev 19 can be viewed as a condensed version of the Torah, echoing aspects of the Ten Commandments and encompassing various laws and commandments representative of the entire Torah. In contrast, chapter 20 revisits the apodictic laws on specific sexual behaviors outlined in Lev 18, providing a more detailed explanation of the prohibition of "mixtures," encompassing diverse areas such as sexual relationships, fabrics, animal breeding, and planting. Within this context, these prohibitions are explored in the worldview context presented in the Old Testament. Regarding sexual relationships, same-sex sexual practices are rejected along with a range of other violations of the sixth commandment in Lev 18:6–23 and 20:10–21. Especially noteworthy is that in Lev 20:10–21, the prohibition of same-sex sexual practices is part of a broader interpretation of the various apodictic commandments in the Decalogue. Furthermore, there are several reasons to see the Holiness Code considering the priestly creation theology in Gen 1 and 2. Firstly, there are numerous allusions to creation in Exod 19–24. The rationale for the Sabbath commandment in Exod 20:8–11 is God's rest on the seventh day (Gen 2:1–3). While a different term, namely פֶּסֶל (*fesel*, "idol, graven image") is used in the prohibition of images in Exod 20:4, it should be interpreted in the light of the "image"—צֶלֶם, *ṣelem*,—in Gen 1:26: the divine image that God had already created could not be recreated by those who themselves were divine images. Additionally, there are several subtle links between the creation narrative in Gen 1 and the creation of Israel in Exod 19–24. In the rabbinic tradition, it is noted in Pirqe Avot that the world was created with ten words (5:1), that Israel's ancestor Abraham was the tenth generation after Noah (5:2), and that God performed ten wonders in connection with the exodus from Egypt (5:4). Similarly, both Jewish and Christian interpreters have drawn attention to the parallel between God's ten words in creation and God's ten words at Sinai. Notably, Martin Buber, for instance, states that "since the power of the Ten Words of Creation is hidden in the land and the fathers have lived in the strength of the Ten Words, Israel, to whom God 'proclaimed the power of His work,' as 'to His own people,' was able to come into the land with the Ten Words revealed to them. Thus Israel's appropriation of the land is the encounter and association of Creation and Revelation."[423] Similarly, Jonathan Burnside notes that "this relationship between the Decalogue and creation suggests that there is a relationship between the particular and the universal, viz., between that which is given specifically to Israel and that which is common to the world."[424] Israel, as God's new, particular creation, should be understood in the light of God's original, universal creation. To put it succinctly, Joseph Ratzinger notes: "The creation narrative anticipates the Ten Commandments. This makes us realize that these Ten Commandments are, as it were, an echo of the creation; for they are not arbitrary inventions for the purpose of erecting barriers to human freedom but signs pointing to the spirit, the language, and the meaning of creation; they are a translation of the language of the universe, a translation of God's logic, which constructed the universe."[425] As an interpretation and specification of the sixth commandment, the prohibitions in Lev 18:22 and 20:13 are thus rooted in the created order of the world. Specifically, this is particularly true to Gen 1 but also concerns the subsequent description in Gen 2 of the relationship between man and woman as "one flesh." Furthermore, in this context, it is worth considering whether the somewhat unusual juxtaposition of זָכָר (zāxār, "male") and אִשָּׁה (ʔiššāʰ, "female") in Lev 18:22 could be a subtle yet conscious reference to both the binary, biological gender identity in the form of זָכָר (zāxār, "male") and נְקֵבָה (nᵉqēvāʰ, "female") in Gen 1 and the heterosexual "joining" of אִישׁ (ʔîš, "man") and אִשָּׁה (ʔiššāʰ, "woman") in Gen 2.

However, there is another and perhaps even more significant reason to understand the prohibition considering the creation order in Gen 1–2. Namely, if the temple is accepted as an idealized miniature model of the created world, then, by nature, it must be the prelapsarian created world—as described in Gen 1–2—that forms the framework for

---

423. Buber, *On Zion*, 102.

424. Burnside, *God, Justice, and Society*, 51.

425. Ratzinger, "In the Beginning," 26.

interpreting the prohibitions. As noted by Frank Gorman in the introduction to "The Ideology of Ritual," "the present study takes these works as its starting point and seeks to develop more fully the precise nature of the conceptual, ideological, and theological framework that informs specific priestly rituals and which is, in turn, constructed, in part, by those rituals. It is argued that the priestly ritual system is best understood as the meaningful enactment of world [sic] in the context of priestly creation theology."[426] Samuel Balentine similarly points out that the understanding of reality that underlies the priestly rituals in Leviticus reflects two principles: "The first is the conviction that God has created the world and purposefully designed the rhythmic orders that keep it tuned to its capacity to be 'very good.' . . . [In essence, t]he second priestly conviction is that God's creational order is generative of and sustained by human observance of an imaging ritual order."[427] Klawans also notes that "if the temple symbolizes the cosmos, then maintaining the temple can easily symbolize maintaining the world, and the sacrificial activity that takes place there can be seen on some level as part of that effort."[428] Sklar also argues that the parallels between Gen 1–2 and Leviticus show that "the Israelites are not only to be a signpost back to Eden, they are to become a manifestation of it and a people who extend Eden's borders to every corner of the earth,"[429] and that this leads to two conclusions: "First, because these chapters are a backdrop to Leviticus, it's natural to understand that the moral logic behind the Levitical prohibitions against homosexual sex is rooted in the fact that there is a pattern laid down in creation that helps us to understand what sex and marriage are to look like . . . Second, because the pattern is creational, it has ongoing relevance for today. Such an understanding is rooted in Jesus's own approach to these chapters."[430]

Israel Knohl has argued against Gorman, Balentine, and Klawans by pointing out the significant shift in the priestly material's understanding and characterization of God after the revelation of the divine name Yahweh in Exod 6. In "the Genesis period," Knohl claims, God speaks and acts directly, while in "the period of Moses," God appears much more impersonal, distant, and indirect.[431] Joshua Vis avers that "Knohl's analysis

426. Gorman, *Ideology of Ritual*, 9.
427. Balentine, *Leviticus*, 4.
428. Klawans, *Purity, Sacrifice, and the Temple*, 112.
429. Sklar, *Leviticus*, 28.
430. Sklar, "Prohibitions," 189–90.
431. Knohl, *Sanctuary of Silence*, 125.

is extremely helpful and insightful, but it fails to uncover the simplest explanation for this clear contrast between the P material after Exod 6 and the material that has been traditionally assigned to P before Exod 6 (a text that Knohl somewhat ironically, but correctly, attributes to H32). Instead of assuming a drastic change in the conception of God in P, the texts of Genesis that have been identified as belonging to P should be understood as belonging to H."[432] This is a solution that Milgrom, according to Vis, almost anticipates when he writes in his commentary on Leviticus:

> Knohl also observes that in P, God's contact with man is direct and unmediated prior to the revelation of the Tetragrammaton (Exod 6:2). Afterward, however (Exod 7ff.), his address to man is no longer in the first person (not even to Moses) but is distant, indirect, and mediated (e.g., "and the Glory of the Lord appeared to all of the people. Fire came forth from before the Lord," Lev 9:23b–24a). H, by contrast, continues the Genesis pattern: God's revelation is direct and anthropomorphic (e.g., "I shall set My face against that man and his family and I shall excise him..." 20:5).[433]

The point made by both Milgrom and Vis is that there are numerous similarities between the creation account in Gen 1:1—2:4a (P) and the Holiness Code (H), suggesting that both must be attributed to H. When considering this source-critical discussion in the context of the texts' canonical relationship, it becomes clear that the resemblance between these texts is so substantial that, even under the source-critical framework, a solution is needed that incorporates both texts in the same source.

It's also worth mentioning G. Geoffrey Harper's study, "The Rhetorical Function of Allusion to Gen 1–3 in the Book of Leviticus." Harper employs eight diagnostic criteria to determine when allusions are highly probable and four criteria to establish whether these allusions are intentional on the part of the author. Based on this methodological framework, Harper demonstrates that there are numerous lexical, syntactical, and conceptual similarities between Lev 11, 16, and 26 and Gen 1–3. These elements are integral to recontextualizing patterns in these chapters of Leviticus. This suggests a deliberate use and recontextualization of Gen 1–3. Although chapters 18 and 20 are not part of Harper's main analysis or proposals for other chapters that seem to use allusions

---

432. Vis, "Purification Offering of Leviticus," 27.
433. Milgrom, *Leviticus 1–16*, 15.

with the same level of intentionality, such as chapters 13–15 and 23–25,[434] Harper mentions that "the presence of allusion in each of the representative chapters of Leviticus I investigate is suggestive of a wider strategy to utilize intertextual connection for rhetorical aims," and that

> the allusions discussed in this study are mutually reinforcing. For example, the banishment motif investigated in relation to Lev 16 finds support in the conceptualization of Canaan as a new Eden in Lev 26. Similarly, the paralleling of Adam with Israel in Lev 26 is mutually reinforced by the use of allusion in Lev 11 to portray Israel as facing the same diet-based test of obedience that Adam faced in the garden of Eden. Thus, the interplay between lexical, syntactical, and conceptual parallels observed at the pericope level is supported by a wider strategy evident across the book. Allusion is meant to be noticed; indeed, it must be to be effective. Therefore, repeated connections to the same set of texts (i.e., Gen 1 and Gen 2–3), across multiple pericopes (i.e., Lev 11, 16, and 26), lessen the chance of allusion being missed.[435]

And since terms and central concepts such as זֶרַע (*zeraʕ*) meaning "seed, offspring," אֶרֶץ (*ʔāreṣ*) meaning "earth, land," and מוֹת (*môt*) meaning "death" appear both in Gen 1–3 and in chapters 18 and 20, this strengthens Harper's argument that the connection between Gen 1–3 and Leviticus should be considered as "a wider strategy." Therefore, the statements about homosexual practices in Lev 18:22 and 20:13 must be viewed within the framework of the creation theology in Gen 1–2.

To this should be added that the story of the fall clearly functions as a pretext for the exodus-conquest. Paraphrasing P. Wayne Townsend,[436] parallels to Eve's words can be identified in Lev 11 and Deut 14. Leviticus 11 outlines the dietary laws for the Israelites, specifying which foods are permissible. Concerning unclean land animals, verse 8 states, "You must not eat their meat or touch their carcasses; they are unclean for you." The language and structure of this verse are strikingly similar to Eve's words in Gen 3:3: "You must not eat fruit . . . and you must not touch it." This parallel is particularly significant as it highlights a special prohibition against touching unclean (forbidden) food, extending beyond the prohibition against touching dead clean animals mentioned

---

434. Harper, "I Will Walk Among You," 231–32.
435. Harper, "I Will Walk Among You," 229.
436. Townsend, "Eve's Answer to the Serpent," 406.

in Lev 11:39–40. Additionally, this combined prohibition against eating and touching is reiterated throughout the chapter in reference to various forbidden foods. The emphasis on not touching becomes increasingly pronounced: for unclean water creatures, "since you are to detest them, you must not eat their meat and you must detest their carcasses" (v. 11); for flying creatures, "these are the birds you are to detest and not eat because they are detestable [to you] ... whoever touches their carcasses will be unclean till evening" (v. 13, 24b); and again for land animals, "whoever touches the carcasses of any of them will be unclean ... whoever touches their carcasses will be unclean until evening. Anyone who picks up their carcasses must wash his clothes, and he will be unclean until evening" (v. 26b, 27b–28a). Deut 14:8b reiterates this pattern, using language identical to Lev 11:8a, which closely parallels Gen 3:3. Even if Deut 14 is derived from Lev 11, this does not diminish the strength of the parallel to Gen 3:3. The choice of this phrase, whether by derivation or common source, underscores its importance in teaching prohibitions against unclean food. In this context, the original readers of Gen 3 would have perceived Eve's words as a natural extension of God's command in Gen 2:17.

David and Jonathan

In his *Jonathan Loved David* from 1978, Tom Horner explores the close relationship between Jonathan and David, suggesting that their bond goes beyond mere friendship.[437] He examines biblical passages that describe their love for each other, such as Jonathan's covenant with David and their emotional parting. Horner argues that the language used to describe their relationship includes elements that can be interpreted as homoerotic, highlighting a form of love and commitment that transcends conventional platonic friendships. Horner contests traditional interpretations that frequently overlook or disregard the potential homoerotic aspects of these relationships. He advocates for a reexamination of biblical texts with an open mind toward the diverse expressions of love and affection they encompass. In essence, Horner's book seeks to illuminate the presence and importance of same-sex love in the Bible, promoting a more inclusive understanding of biblical narratives that recognize the complexity of human relationships.

437. Horner, *Jonathan Loved David*.

Given the current cultural environment, it is no surprise that the relationship between David and Jonathan continues to be interpreted as a homosexual relationship.[438] In isolation, several passages in the narrative can indeed be understood that way:

> When David had finished talking with Saul, Jonathan and David became bound together in close friendship. Jonathan loved David as much as he did his own life. (1 Sam 18:1 NET)

> David said to Jonathan, "Tomorrow is the new moon, and I am certainly expected to join the king for a meal. You must send me away so I can hide in the field until the third evening from now. If your father happens to miss me, you should say, 'David urgently requested me to let him go to his city Bethlehem, for there is an annual sacrifice there for his entire family.' If he should then say, 'That's fine,' then your servant is safe. But if he becomes very angry, be assured that he has decided to harm me. You must be loyal to your servant, for you have made a covenant with your servant in the Lord's name. If I am guilty, you yourself kill me! Why bother taking me to your father?" (1 Sam 20:5–8 NET)

> Saul and Jonathan were greatly loved during their lives, and not even in their deaths were they separated. They were swifter than eagles, stronger than lions. O daughters of Israel, weep over Saul, who clothed you in scarlet as well as jewelry, who put gold jewelry on your clothes. How the warriors have fallen in the midst of battle! Jonathan lies slain on your high places! I grieve over you, my brother Jonathan! You were very dear to me. Your love was more special to me than the love of women. (2 Sam 1:23–26 NET)

However, there are good reasons to reject this interpretation. First and foremost, considering the context, it's clearly a political friendship. Despite God's rejection of Saul and Samuel anointing David as king, many must have viewed him as a usurper, and there were likely strong forces working to ensure that Saul's house continued to represent royal power. In the ancient Near East, such a struggle for the throne often meant the losing party and their household were put to death. In this context, the relationship between David and Jonathan is a countercultural expression of an attempt to avoid such bloodshed. If Saul seeks to kill David, Jonathan tries to shield him from his father's wrath, and after David is crowned, he shows mercy to Saul's house for Jonathan's sake.

---

438. Thatcher, *God, Sex, and Gender*; Guest, *Beyond Feminist Biblical Studies*; Carr, *Holy Resilience*.

> Then David asked, "Is anyone still left from the family of Saul, so that I may extend kindness to him for the sake of Jonathan?" Now there was a servant from Saul's house named Ziba, so he was summoned to David. The king asked him, "Are you Ziba?" He replied, "At your service." The king asked, "Is there not someone left from Saul's family, that I may extend God's kindness to him?" Ziba said to the king, "One of Jonathan's sons is left; both of his feet are crippled." The king asked him, "Where is he?" Ziba told the king, "He is at the house of Makir son of Ammiel in Lo Debar." So King David had him brought from the house of Makir son of Ammiel in Lo Debar. When Mephibosheth, son of Jonathan, the son of Saul, came to David, he bowed low with his face toward the ground. David said, "Mephibosheth?" He replied, "Yes, at your service." David said to him, "Don't be afraid, because I will certainly extend kindness to you for the sake of Jonathan your father. You will be a regular guest at my table." Then Mephibosheth bowed and said, "Of what importance am I, your servant, that you show regard for a dead dog like me?" Then the king summoned Ziba, Saul's attendant, and said to him, "Everything that belonged to Saul and to his entire house I hereby give to your master's grandson." (2 Sam 9:1–9 NET)

The fact that it concerns a *political* friendship is underscored by the repeated descriptions of David and Jonathan making a covenant with each other (1 Sam 18:3; 20:8, 16; 23:18), which employs covenant language. Deuteronomy explains that God's love for the fathers was the reason for the deliverance from Egypt.

> It is not because you were more numerous than all the other peoples that the Lord favored and chose you—for in fact you were the least numerous of all peoples. Rather it is because of his love for you and his faithfulness to the promise he solemnly vowed to your ancestors that the Lord brought you out with great power, redeeming you from the place of slavery, from the power of Pharaoh king of Egypt. (Deut 7:7–8 NET)

A characteristic of the covenant is that Israel reciprocates God's love.

> Listen, Israel: The Lord is our God, the Lord is one! You must love the Lord your God with your whole mind, your whole being, and all your strength. (Deut 6:4–5 NET)

> So realize that the Lord your God is the true God, the faithful God who keeps covenant faithfully with those who love him

and keep his commandments, to a thousand generations. (Deut 7:9 NET)

Understanding the nineteen occurrences of the term "love" in Deuteronomy as a political metaphor for covenant fidelity or loyalty is supported considering similar covenant language in comparative material. In 1963, William Moran noted that, in the Amarna period, "'love' unquestionably belongs to the terminology of international relations." An example given is the correspondence between Tusratta of Mitanni and the Egyptian court in which the friendship between the rulers, who are independent and equals ("brothers"), is described.[439]

> Say [to Nim]mureya, the king of [Egypt], my brother, my son-in-law, [whom I l]ove and who love[s me: Thus T]ušratta the king of Mitt[ani], your father-in-law, [who l]oves, your brother. [Fo]r me all goes well. For you [may a]ll go well. For your household, for [your] wives, for your [s]ons, for your magnates, [for] your [ch]ariots, for your horses, for your warriors, [f]or your country and whatever else belongs to you, may all go very, very well. In view of friendly relations, Mane, my brother's messenger, came to take my brother's wife to become the mistress of Egypt. I read and reread the tablet that he brought to me, and I listened to its words. Very pleasing indeed were the words of my brother. I rejoiced on that day as if I had seen my brother in person. I made that day and night a [fes]tive occasion.[440]

From the Neo-Assyrian period, Moran mentions a reminder by Esarhaddon to a vassal that he must still love Esarhaddon's successor Assurbanipal: "You will love as yourselves Assurbanipal." And in another text we find similar language in a declaration under oath: ". . . the king of Assyria, our lord, we will love."[441] It is in full correspondence with such covenantal language that we learn in 1 Kgs 5:15 that the Tyrian king Hiram "had always loved David" (אֹהֵב הָיָה חִירָם לְדָוִד כָּל־הַיָּמִים, *ʾōhēv hāyāʰ ḥîrām lᵉdāwid kol-hayyāmîm*), or, as the NET Bible translation has it, "Hiram had always been an ally of David."

When we hear in the story of David and Jonathan that they "loved" each other, it makes much more sense in context to understand it as a political metaphor and conventional covenant language. This is also underscored by the fact that David laments the deaths of *both* Saul and

---

439. Moran, "Ancient Near Eastern Background," 79.
440. EA 20.1–13, in Moran, *Amarna Letters*, 47.
441. Quoted from Moran, "Ancient Near Eastern Background," 80.

Jonathan in 2 Sam 1. Jonathan's treatment of David and David's subsequent mercy upon the house of Saul is highly unusual, and therefore, it suggests that the political relationship must be understood against the background of a personal relationship in the form of a close friendship. While it's initially largely due to Jonathan that the covenant is made (1 Sam 18:2-4; cf. 20:8, 16; 23:18), there is no doubt that it was rooted in a mutual friendship, as David bitterly mourns Jonathan's death and shows mercy to his house for Jonathan's sake (2 Sam 1:11, 25-26; 9). Thus, David's love for Jonathan being "more special ... than the love of women" (2 Sam 1:26) is much better understood as an expression of a particularly special personal friendship that had highly unusual political consequences. This interpretation is supported by Martti Nissinen, who, in his book *Homoeroticism in the Biblical World: A Historical Perspective*, contextualizes the relationship within the broader spectrum of male-male relationships in the ancient Near East, suggesting that the intensity of the bond between David and Jonathan fits within a recognized cultural pattern of close, affectionate male friendships, which may or may not have included physical and emotional intimacy.[442] He highlights that such relationships were not necessarily categorized in the same way as contemporary understandings of sexual orientation. As mentioned above, Nissinen suggests that some of these relationships "exemplify less a homoerotic than a homosocial type of bonding, which is often seen in societies in which men's and women's worlds are segregated."[443]

An interesting analogy can be found in the letters of John Henry Newman, one of the most significant Anglican converts to Catholicism. In a letter to Lord Blachford in 1875, he described his friendship with Ambrose St. John, with whom he shared communitarian life for thirty-two years: "From the first he loved me with an intensity of love, which was unaccountable. At Rome 28 years ago he was always so working for and relieving me of all trouble, that being young and Saxon-looking, the Romans called him my Angel Guardian."[444] When St. John died, Newman clung to the body all night and expressed his grief in the following manner: "I have ever thought no bereavement was equal to that of a husband's or a wife's, but I feel it difficult to believe that any can be

---

442. Nissinen, *Homoeroticism in the Biblical World*.

443. Nissinen, *Homoeroticism in the Biblical World*, 24.

444. Newman, *John Henry Newman*, 20, quoted from Roderick Strange; cf. Newman, *Letters and Diaries* 27.

greater, or anyone's sorrow greater, than mine."[445] Perhaps most notably, the two requested to be buried together in the same grave. They selected the epitaph for their tombstone to read *Exod umbris et imaginibus in veritatem*, "Out of shadows and phantasms into Truth," a phrase that, according to Francis DeBernardo, could serve as a fitting motto for any contemporary Catholic LGBTQ equality organization.[446] And when, on April 23, 2008, the Vatican approved the beatification of John Henry Newman and decided that Newman's body was to be reinterred in a sarcophagus, leaving the remains of his friend Ambrose St. John behind, it led "some people to question whether the Church is embarrassed about their relationship and doesn't want to raise attention to it at the time of Newman's beatification."[447] DeBernardo, in a talk for University College Dublin's LGBTI History Month Event on February 26, 2021, argues that Newman was not "gay" since the word in its modern use implies that the person "is sexually active—and oftentimes thought of as promiscuously so. . . . And most likely, since he was probably very dedicated to celibacy, he would not have thought of himself as gay or as St. John as a gay loved one." He was, nevertheless, *homosexual*, since "not having the language to describe the relationship doesn't mean that such a relationship didn't exist." It was a homoerotic relationship that was "being emotionally sensitive, tender, and affectionate with one another."[448]

The allegation that Newman had homosexual inclinations was made as early as 1933 by Geoffrey Faber who claimed that the Oxford Movement contained a significant stream of homoeroticism and that Newman's friendship with Hurrell Froude and Ambrose St. John was at least subconsciously homosexual. Biographers have interpreted Newman similarly over time.

Ian Ker, a prominent biographer of John Henry Newman, especially in his "Afterword," has addressed allegations regarding Newman's sexuality by firmly rejecting the notion that Newman was gay.[449] Ker argues that such allegations are anachronistic and misunderstand the nature of

---

445. Newman, *Letters and Diaries* 9.

446. DeBernardo, "Question Is Not." DeBernardo is executive director of New Ways Ministry, a Catholic outreach that educates and advocates for equity, inclusion, and justice for LGBTQ+ persons.

447. Censor Librorum, "Church Defies."

448. DeBernardo, "Was Cardinal John Henry Newman Gay?"; cf. the critique of this interpretation in Ker, "Cardinal John Henry Newman's Exhumation Objectors."

449. Ker, *John Henry Newman*, 746–50.

Newman's close friendships. He emphasizes that Newman's deep emotional relationships with men, such as his friendship with Ambrose St. John, were expressions of intense spiritual and platonic love, not sexual relationships. Ker maintains that Newman was a celibate priest whose relationships were marked by a profound spiritual connection rather than physical or romantic involvement.

Regarding his sexual inclinations, Ker highlights that at the age of fifteen, he became convinced it was God's will for him to live a single life. When praying for protection from temptations awaiting him during his return home from boarding school for Christmas, he specifically mentioned dances and parties. This, Ker suggests, carries a clear implication: "There he will meet girls, from whom he is shielded at a boys' boarding school."[450] Regarding same-sex burials, Ker notes:

> Certainly, the assumption that the desire to be buried in the same grave as someone else may, if not must, indicate some sort of sexual attraction would have greatly astonished previous generations. G. K. Chesterton's devoted secretary, Dorothy Collins, whom he and his wife regarded as a daughter, while thinking it presumptuous to ask to be buried in the same grave as the Chesterton's, nevertheless directed that she be cremated and her ashes buried in the same grave. C. S. Lewis and his brother Warnie are buried in the same grave in accordance with both brothers' wishes. For Newman, Ambrose St John, a fellow priest of the Birmingham Oratory, was the equivalent of a brother.[451]

Frederick S. Roden, a scholar and author known for his work in the fields of Victorian literature, gender studies, and queer theory, also does not argue that Newman was homosexual but characterizes him as "cultural dissident" or "queer" in its very general meaning "to include any dissonant behaviors, discourses or claimed identities" in relation to Victorian norms.[452] In Newman's case, Roden argues, *homoaffectivity* "is contained in friendships, in relationships that are not overtly sexual."[453] Roden also uses the term *homosociality*.[454]

Read in isolation, the expressions of love in the Jonathan and David narrative and in Newman's letters are open to interpretation. And if

---

450. Ker, *John Henry Newman*, 748.
451. Ker, *John Henry Newman*, 747.
452. Roden, *Same-Sex Desire*, 1.
453. Roden, *Same-Sex Desire*, 7.
454. Roden, *Same-Sex Desire*, 1, 4, 7.

interpretation is made in the context of queer ideology and recent gender identity theory, they *could* be understood as evidence of homoerotic relationships. If the context is changed, however, to the contemporary cultures of the ancient Near East and Victorian England, homoeroticism becomes an unlikely interpretation. What we find, instead, is homoaffectivity or homosociality that may be expressed by both heterosexuals and homosexuals but, in these cases, arguably occurs in relationships between heterosexual men.

Romans 1:26-27

> For this reason, God gave them up to dishonorable passions. For their women exchanged natural relations for those that are contrary to nature; and the men likewise gave up natural relations with women and were consumed with passion for one another, men committing shameless acts with men and receiving in themselves the due penalty for their error.

The text from the book of Romans is undoubtedly the most significant text in the New Testament concerning the issue of same-sex relationships. Rom 1:26–27 is part of a longer section in Rom 1:18—3:20, where Paul writes about God's wrath against Jews and gentiles. Just as the introduction in 1:18–32 describes the situation for all of humanity, the first main section also concludes in 3:20 with a universal perspective: "For by works of the law no human being will be justified in his sight, since through the law comes knowledge of sin."

Torben Kjær argues that Rom 1:18–32 forms a unified whole, and Paul presents a category of people with four characteristics: God has revealed his wrath in the lives of these people, their ungodliness, unrighteousness, and suppression of the truth. This revelation is universal and begins with creation. Paul does not use ethnic labels, and this natural revelation, starting from creation, describes not only Jews but all of humanity. In verse 18, the thesis is presented, namely, that "the wrath of God is revealed from heaven against all ungodliness and unrighteousness of men, who by their unrighteousness suppress the truth," and verses 19–32 elaborate on this thesis.

In verses 24–31, there are three sections (verses 24–25, 26–27, and 28–31), each of which elaborates on the revelation of God's wrath. In the first section (verses 24–25), Paul describes how this wrath is expressed as giving up to impurity. In the following section, verses 26–27, Paul shows how this wrath is manifested in people who practice same-sex sexual activity.[455] The crucial points are many:

1. What is the cause of the manifestation of wrath? Kjær convincingly argues that there are two causes, one religious and one ethical: "There is a religious cause. Διὸ τοῦτο explicitly tells us that the cause of God's wrath is found in verse 25, and this cause is religious. The justification in verses 26–27abc also tells us explicitly that there is an ethical cause. In the justification, Paul describes homosexual practice, which describes the condition these people were in when God's wrath struck them."[456] Same-sex sexual acts are, therefore, the direct cause of God's wrath, not just a consequence of it.

2. How should "gave them up" be understood? Kjær rejects the permissive and judicial interpretation in favor of the privative one, where the dishonorable passions "already exist in these people, but 'gave them up' means that the dishonorable passions intensify and break forth with renewed strength.[457] "Giving up" should be understood considering God's sustaining work on the ethical level. Through natural law, as part of natural *revelation*, God has given humanity an ethical foundation that protects it. With the act of "giving up," God withdraws from this area, the ethical foundation breaks down, and sin bursts forth with irresistible force.[458]

3. What does the "exchange of natural relations for those that are contrary to nature" mean? Regarding the expression παρὰ φύσιν ("contrary to nature"), Kjær provides a useful overview of the eleven instances where Paul uses the noun φύσις ("nature") and the two instances where he uses the adjective φυσικός ("natural").[459] Based on this examination, Kjær concludes that "'nature' is a comprehensive term for 'the law written in human nature' or 'the work of the law

---

455. Kjær, *Naturlig åbenbaring*, 11–12, 79–80, 99–100.

456. Kjær, *Naturlig åbenbaring*, 104; for a detailed argumentation, cf. 80–84 and 102–4.

457. Since the permissive and judicial interpretations are not relevant to the understanding of what kind of same-sex desire/sex Paul is referring to, they will not be reviewed here.

458. Kjær, *Naturlig åbenbaring*, 105.

459. Kjær, *Naturlig åbenbaring*, 135–39.

written on their hearts.'"[460] Concerning Paul's use of φύσις/φῠσικός in Rom 1:26-27, Kjær rejects interpretations that define these words as expressions of cultural convention or human constitution.[461] Such rejection also applies to the dominant and influential interpretation that Paul uses φύσις/φῠσικός in the same sense as in the Hellenistic Jewish tradition of his time, where (male) same-sex sexual activity is considered against nature because it hinders reproduction, violates the dominant nature of the man (in the case of the penetrated man), and because passion is uncontrollable. Kjær demonstrates with his analysis of Paul's use of φύσις/φῠσικός that "we find none of this in Paul... Therefore, it is not reasonable to claim that Paul simply follows the contemporary ideas and associates with them,"[462] especially when these contemporary understandings of φύσις/φῠσικός are not explicitly mentioned in the text and when the text explicitly specifies a different normative frame of reference for these terms.

Overall, there can be no doubt that Paul alludes to the creation account in his argumentation. The replacement of "the immortal God's glory... with images resembling mortal man and birds and animals and creeping things" in verse 23 clearly refers to the divine image in Gen 1:26-27,[463] and the worship of "the creature rather than the Creator" in verse 25 expresses the *raison d'être* of Gen 1, namely that God is the Creator, and humanity is his creation. Furthermore, the "creation of the world" is explicitly mentioned in verse 20, just as there is an unmistakable allusion to Gen 2:17 in verse 32 when it says about the "men who by their unrighteousness suppress the truth" (verse 18) that "they know God's decree, that those who practice such things deserve to die."

---

460. Kjær, *Naturlig åbenbaring*, 135.

461. Thus, Nissinen argues that, "In antiquity, *physis* expresses a fundamental cultural rule or a conventional, proper, or inborn character or appearance, or the true being of a person or a thing rather than 'nature' in a genetic-biological sense, as a modern reader would perceive it." Nissinen, *Homoeroticism in the Biblical World*, 105.

462. Kjær, *Naturlig åbenbaring*, 143.

463. Torben Kjær (in my translation) writes regarding this, "I also do not believe that a 'likeness of an image' (verse 23) alludes to Genesis 1:26, where 'image' and 'likeness' are used concerning the divine likeness of humanity; in verse 23, a likeness of an image refers to idols." Kjær, *Naturlig åbenbaring*, 144. It is correct to a certain extent, but if by the "replacement" of "God's glory" one thinks of that "glory of God" which was expressed in the divine likeness of humanity, then the "replacement" in verse 23 nonetheless entails that instead of understanding oneself in a theocentric manner, humans now define themselves anthropocentrically.

The Greco-Roman World

It would go beyond the scope of this study to include all the extensive material from ancient Greece and Rome, but since arguments in the interpretation of Rom 1 involve the Greco-Roman material, a brief introduction is in order.

Having said that, gender roles were important to the Romans. Generally, the Romans were particularly concerned with the issue of who penetrated whom. Joseph Fantin, in his "Sexualities in the First-Century World," explains:

> Citizen adult males could only properly be *penetrators*, and females could only be *penetrated*. The status of male slaves and male noncitizens was more ambiguous. As males, they could be *penetrators*; their social status (or lack of status), however, made it acceptable to be *penetrated*. To be clear, a male being penetrated was not seen positively. However, the social stain was either minimal or nonexistent, because of slaves' lesser status. It seems likely that in the Roman context, penetrated males were prostitutes, slaves, and/or adolescent males (children)... [A]n adult male Roman citizen must be a penetrator. He should never be penetrated. This standard has social connotations as well as sexual. However, whom he penetrated (within the law), male or female, was unimportant. The male penetrator experienced no specific shame or negative stigma for penetrating another man. He was viewed as doing what he was supposed to do: penetrate. Of course, the penetrated male in this sex act could be viewed negatively. Women could only be penetrated. This is why same-sex relations between women were unacceptable. In such situations, at least one of the women needed to function as a penetrator, that is, like a male.[464]

John Collins mentions that, in Plato's *Symposium*, there seem to be precedents for the modern idea of a homosexual orientation and way of life: "In Plato's Symposium, Aristophanes offers a playful explanation of three different sexual orientations. The primeval human being was round, his back and sides forming a circle; he had four hands and four feet, one head with two faces, looking opposite ways. These primeval beings were fearsome and mounted an attack on the gods. To subdue them, Zeus cut them in two and made them walk upright on two legs. This

---

464. Fantin, "Sexualities in the First-Century World," 57–58. Emphasis original.

division of the original human being is the origin of desire."⁴⁶⁵ Aristophanes, in Plato's *Symposium*, argues:

> Each of us, then, is but a tally of a man, since every one shows like a flat-fish the traces of having been sliced in two; and each is ever searching for the tally that will fit him. All the men who are sections of that composite sex that at first was called man-woman are woman-courters; our adulterers are mostly descended from that sex, whence likewise are derived our man-courting women and adulteresses. All the women who are sections of the woman have no great fancy for men: they are inclined rather to women, and of this stock are the she-minions. Men who are sections of the male pursue the masculine, and so long as their boyhood lasts they show themselves to be slices of the male by making friends with men and delighting to lie with them and to be clasped in men's embraces; these are the finest boys and striplings, for they have the most manly nature. Some say they are shameless creatures, but falsely: for their behavior is due not to shamelessness but to daring, manliness, and virility, since they are quick to welcome their like.⁴⁶⁶

Aristophanes, Collins remarks, "defends such people against the charge of shamelessness, and waxes rhapsodic about their love," and though "Plato's categories do not correspond to the modern distinction between heterosexuals and homosexuals," they nonetheless "suggest that sexual orientation is inborn and determined by a person's make-up. Such theorizing about sexuality was exceptional in antiquity, however, and is not attested at all in the Bible."⁴⁶⁷

The texts not only mention pederasty, however. Greenberg concludes his analysis of the Greco-Roman material by arguing that

> by the time the Greeks emerged from the Dark Age and produced the writings that tell us of life in the classical age, they considered these cult practices [the homosexual component of tribal initiation] to be alien... The desexualization of Greek initiations did not, however, lead to the disappearance of homosexuality: vase painting, drama, poetry, oratory, and philosophical treatises show that from the sixth century on, secularized male homosexuality flourished in many of the Greek city-states.

---

465. Collins, *What Are Biblical Values?*, 64.

466. Plato, *Symposium*, 191d–192a, quoted from Loeb Classical Library 166, 136.137.

467. Collins, *What Are Biblical Values?*, 64–65.

Nowhere was is prohibited by law. Public opinion was complex and undoubtedly not uniform, but did not generally stigmatize sexual contacts between males. Relations between women were also known. Few written records of it survive, but vase paintings show lesbian activities among female prostitutes.[468]

Greenberg suggests that it wasn't just the widespread idealized pederasty between the adult *erastes* ("lover") and the young, receptive *eromenos* ("beloved") that was socially acceptable but that there are sources, such as texts about the relationship between Achilles and Patroclus, which also reflect other types of same-sex relationships.[469] Indeed, Plato's *Symposium*, Lucian's (or Pseudo-Lucian's) *Amores*, and Xenophon's novel, *An Ephesian Tale*, testify to compassionate same-sex love in Greco-Roman literature. Mark Smith even argues that by the time of the first century, pederasty had significantly declined, and "there was a significant increase in homosexual behavior among consenting adults."[470] These examples indicate that the authors of the New Testament (and intertestamental Jewish literature) not only addressed pederasts but also other types of same-sex sex—in other words, same-sex sex in general.

This is contrary, of course, to mainstream voices like John J. Collins, who argues that Paul's argumentation was "not very satisfactory."

Collins highlights that the distinction between "in accordance with nature" and "contrary to nature" is a key theme in Greco-Roman popular philosophy. He points out, for instance, a character in Plutarch's *Dialogue on Love* who condemns same-sex relationships as contrary to nature, contrasting them with heterosexual relationships, which are described as natural. It should also be noted that while Plato had expressed positive views on homosexual relations in the *Symposium*, in his final work, the *Laws*, he wrote, "And whether one makes the observation in earnest or in jest, one certainly should not fail to observe that when male unites with female for procreation the pleasure experienced is held to be due to nature, but contrary to nature when male mates with male or female with female, and that those first guilty of such enormities were impelled by their slavery to pleasure."[471]

Hellenistic Jewish literature generally took a strict stance against homosexual relations, particularly those between males. One of the

468. Greenberg, *Construction of Homosexuality*, 141–42.
469. Cf. Holmen, "Examining Greek Pederastic Relationships."
470. Smith, "Ancient Bisexuality," 233.
471. *Laws* 1.636c, quoted from Perseus Digital Library.

most explicit passages on this topic, Collins notes, is found in Pseudo-Phocylides, a collection of moralizing sayings likely dating to the first century CE:

> Do not outrage your wife for shameful ways of intercourse.
> Do not transgress the natural limits of sexuality for unlawful sex,
> For even animals are not pleased by intercourse of male with male,
> And let not women imitate the sexual role of men.
> Do not deliver yourself wholly unto unbridled sensuality towards your wife.
> For eros is not a god, but a passion destructive of all.[472]

As for Philo of Alexandria, he describes relations between a man and a woman in her menstrual period, relations between a man and a boy, and relations between different species of animals as "contrary to nature."[473] Philo saw nature as an expression of the divine Logos ("Word" or "Reason"). For Philo, the Logos was a mediating principle between God and the world, and nature was a manifestation of God's rational order. Living according to nature meant living according to virtue and reason. Human beings, endowed with reason, should align their lives with the rational order of nature, which reflects God's will. This ethical dimension of nature suggests that moral laws are embedded in the fabric of the universe, and humans are meant to discover and follow these laws. It's fully in line with this line of thought that Philo, in his assessment of these sexual relations as contrary to nature, specifically refers back to creation and points to procreation as the rationale behind his judgment. This rationale is entirely consistent with that of Lev 18 and 20 as well, and it's indeed the punishment in these texts that Josephus refers to when he writes, "The Law recognizes no sexual connections, except the natural union of man and wife, and that only for the procreation of children. But it abhors the intercourse of males with males and punishes any who undertake such a thing with death."[474]

The "not very satisfactory" argument by Paul, Collins explains, is due to Paul's reliance on *both* Hellenistic Judaism and Greco-Roman culture. On the one hand, Paul, "like Leviticus, holds both active and passive parties equally responsible, and liable for the death penalty. Unlike Philo,

---

472. Pseudo-Phocylides 189–94; van der Horst, *Sayings of Pseudo-Phocylides*, 237–41.
473. Philo, *On the Special Laws* 3.7–82.
474. Josephus, *Against Apion*, 199, quoted from Perseus Digital Library.

Paul was not concerned about procreation. Neither was he concerned about purity laws, such as those involving menstruating women."[475] On the other hand, "he was surely influenced by Greco-Roman and Hellenistic Jewish conceptions of what was natural and unnatural," and used the expression "contrary to nature" accordingly in the meaning "seriously unconventional." This becomes clear, according to Collins, in light of 1 Cor 11, where Paul strains to make an argument that any woman who prays or prophesies should veil her head. Assessing Paul's argumentation, Collins writes: "But nature only teaches this in specific cultural contexts ... Paul himself seems to have sensed the weakness of his argument, for he concludes: 'But if anyone is disposed to be contentious, we have no such custom, nor do the churches of God.' Custom, not nature, is what was at stake, and this was no less true in Rom 1, on the subject of same-sex relations."[476]

Such an understanding of Paul is untenable, however, if the interpretation given above is correct. Paul may very well have been familiar with the Greco-Roman concept of nature, but it's a *non sequitur* that he, for that reason, relied more on Greco-Roman culture than he was informed by Old Testament creation theology. And if Collin's prooftext from 1 Cor 11 is interpreted along the lines given above, it cannot be used to argue for a Greco-Roman versus Hellenistic Jewish *tension* in Paul's epistles. It's correct, in my view, that the "natural" or "seriously unconventional" character of long hair is dependent on the culturally specific contexts. The question is, however, what φύσις "nature" in 1 Cor 11:14 *refers to*. If it refers to the long hair; Collins is right, of course. But if it refers to the observance of the boundary given in creation between man and woman and the long hair is a culturally contingent way to demonstrate or signal adherence to this boundary, then Collins is mistaken.

Arvid Tångberg argues in the article "The Concept of Nature and Homosexuality in the Old Testament" that even though there is no Hebrew equivalent lemma for the Greek φύσις that Paul uses in Rom 1:26 in his critique of homosexual practices, in light of the terminological parallels in Jewish literature, it's "quite plausible that Paul refers to the canonical texts about the Creator and creation in the Torah (the Books of Moses) as normative. Paul's use of the specific word pair for 'male/female' (*arsen/thelys*) plays on the creation account of Gen 1:27 and the Holiness

---

475. Collins, *What Are Biblical Values?*, 78.
476. Collins, *What Are Biblical Values?*, 78–79.

Code (Lev 18:22).... In this way, Paul confirms the normative content of the pre-Mosaic and Mosaic Torah—strikingly similar to Philo's exegetical interpretation of physis as a normative concept. At the same time, it becomes clear that Paul's ethics is based to a very large extent on the Old Testament."[477] The same-sex sexual acts forbidden in Lev 18:22 are, therefore, not just תּוֹעֵבָה (tôʕēvāʰ, "an abomination") because the Canaanites practiced them (18:3) or because they caused impurity (18:24-27) but because they conflict with the created order. Tångberg further argues that the justification has a broader basis in protecting the family. This is achieved by limiting sexual intercourse exclusively to legal marriage, as also presupposed in the sixth commandment. This is reflected in Josephus's interpretation of the law in *Against Apion* 2.199: "What are our marriage laws? The law does not recognize any sexual relations except the natural union of man and woman and that only for procreation's sake. It abhors sodomy."[478]

Gordon Wenham writes about the Old Testament background (with reference to C. E. B. Cranfield) that "St Paul's comment that homosexual acts are 'contrary to nature' (Rom 1:26) is thus probably very close to the thinking of the Old Testament writers . . . By 'contrary to nature,' Paul clearly means 'contrary to the intention of the Creator.'"[479] Thomas Schreiner similarly argues that "Paul's use of the relatively unusual words *thelys* for female and *arsen* for males suggests that he draws on the creation account of Gen (Gen. 1:27, LXX) where the same two words are used," and the phrase "contrary to nature" reflects "Stoic and Hellenistic Jewish traditions, which saw homosexual relations as a violation of the created order."[480] Robert Gagnon also refers to the texts in Gen 1-2 and Lev 18 and 20 as the rationale for Paul's argument: "Minimally, Paul is referring to the anatomical and procreative complementarity of male and female. Put in more crude terms, Paul in effect argues that same-sex eroticism is 'contrary to nature' because the primary sex organs fit male to female, not female to female or male to male. Again, by fittedness, I mean not only the glove-like physical fit of the penis and vagina but also clues

---

477. Tångberg, "Naturbegrepet og homifili," 245-46.

478. Tångberg, "Naturbegrepet og homifili," 248. For a review of a series of texts from ancient Judaism which demonstrates how Philo, in particular, is influenced by Hellenistic thought in his use of the terms φύσις ("nature"), κατὰ φύσιν ("according to nature"), and παρὰ φύσιν ("against nature"), cf. Kjær, *Naturlig åbenbaring*, 132-35.

479. Wenham, "Old Testament Attitude to Homosexuality," 363; Cranfield, *Epistle to the Romans I*, 125.

480. Schreiner, "New Testament Perspective on Homosexuality," 65.

to complementarity provided by procreative capacity and the capacity for mutual and pleasurable stimulation."[481] According to Gagnon, Paul uses the term παρὰ φύσιν about "the material shape of the created order."[482]

Kevin DeYoung goes a step further in interpreting the phrase τὴν φυσικὴν χρῆσιν ("natural relations") in Rom 1:26 when he writes:

> Natural revelation itself suggests that our physiology corresponds to a divine moral injunction. When two men are together sexually, the member that is supposed to give life is often placed in a part of the body where death and decay are expelled. Even apart from supernatural revelation, the very body God has given us suggests that our bodies are designed for a certain purpose, and using our members for any alternative purpose is unnatural and rebellion against the creator. Why is it that the sexual act is so powerful? Why is it that God determined sex as the moment of one flesh union? Why not holding hands or locking arms? Because God endowed the unique male/female sexual union with the procreative ability—the ability to fulfill the creation mandate in Gen 1, to replenish the earth, to multiply, to fill the earth and subdue it.[483]

Both Oliver O'Donovan and Nancey Pearcey make the same physiological argument, i.e., that it's not only God's special revelation that designates same-sex sex as being contrary to the created order. Even if we set aside texts like Lev 18 and 20, the "material shape" of the body (penis and vagina) and human "physiology" (reproductive capability) would testify to the unnaturalness of same-sex sex:

> To have a male body is to have a body structurally ordered to loving union with a female body, and *vice versa*.[484]

> To engage in same-sex behaviors, then, is implicitly to say, Why should my body inform my psychological identity? Why should the structural order of my body have anything to say about what I do sexually? Why should my moral choices be directed by its *telos*?[485]

A point could be made, of course, that we cannot determine whether "nature" is based on the visible anatomical difference between man

481. Gagnon, *Bible and Homosexual Practice*, 254.
482. Gagnon, *Bible and Homosexual Practice*, 256.
483. DeYoung, "How Are Men and Women Different?"
484. O'Donovan, *Transsexualism and Christian Marriage*, 19.
485. Pearcey, *Love Thy Body*, 30.

and woman, and Gagnon and others may, therefore, overemphasize the anatomical difference when talking about male-female complementarity. However, it must be acknowledged that human physiology—the biological, binary gender function in relation to reproduction—is evident even from a purely visual perspective.

So, if we stick to what is explicit in the text, there is no doubt that it's the theology and anthropology as expressed in Gen 1–2 that forms the normative backdrop for Paul's understanding of same-sex sex as being παρὰ φύσιν, "contrary to nature, unnatural." Or as Kjær concludes, "In the immediate context, 'natural intercourse' and 'against nature' have normative significance. Natural intercourse is the 'right' intercourse; it's without dishonor, and it's according to God's will. Intercourse against nature is the 'wrong' intercourse; it's associated with dishonor, and it's against God's will, that is, it's a sin. 'Nature,' therefore, is a normative concept for human behavior . . . It's reasonable, based on this, to understand 'natural' as a divine order and 'unnatural' as a violation of this order."[486] When you add what Paul expresses elsewhere based on Gen 2:24, namely that sex belongs exclusively within heterosexual, monogamous, and lifelong marriage (1 Cor 7; Eph 5:22–33; 1 Thess 4:3–8), it becomes clear that Paul also regards Gen 2:24 as defining what is "natural" and "contrary to nature." Therefore, human binary gender identity and the associated monogamous, heterosexual practice are grounded in creation even before the fall and confirmed afterward as the ideal for humanity's understanding of the relationship between gender, body, and sexuality, regardless of how it's experienced and practiced in the fallen world.

Such an understanding naturally disqualifies interpretations that attempt in various ways to narrow down what type of same-sex sex Paul designates as "unnatural, contrary to nature" in Rom 1:26–27 by rejecting the creation-theological framework in favor of the cultural conventions prevalent in Hellenistic Judaism. Paul is not only thinking about prostitutional or feminizing relationships but any form of same-sex sex. In other words, Paul does not just go along with the cultural currents of his time but stands critically against them, and such ethics, as Eva Cantarella points out in the chapter "The Metamorphoses of Sexual Ethics," must have attracted attention:

> It immediately shows the Christian attempt to introduce a different sexual ethic, which replaced the old contrast between

---

486. Kjær, *Naturlig åbenbaring*, 141, 144.

activity and passivity with a new, fundamental dichotomy between heterosexuality and homosexuality. The novelty of this principle is underlined, if it needs underlining, by a consideration which is by no means of negligible or secondary importance: in his letter to the Romans... Paul condemns not only male but also female homosexuality. For him, clearly, the problem is not the typical one experienced by Roman laws and ethics in the era before Justinian, of how to proclaim the principle that a man must be manly. His concern is to impose respect for a rule which is for the first time defined as natural, which demands that men should always and only couple with women, and vice versa. In Paul, the expressions *kata physin* and *para physin*, unlike the situation in previous times, signalled the imperative and inescapable rule of heterosexuality, and the abnormality of any practice which moves away from it.[487]

The discussion regarding Paul's use of φύσις/φυσικός in Rom 1 is a classic example of parallelomania, as the majority interpretation uses Hellenistic-Jewish texts to create similarities even when they are not explicit. But even if the force of parallels were conceded, it would speak *against* the cultural conventions prevalent in Hellenistic Judaism since there is no evidence whatsoever of older women sexually involved with girls. A more balanced comparative method, on the other hand, would reveal the contrasts that stand out when reading the text at hand and would stick to what the text explicitly expresses. Or, as J. Glen Taylor formulates it in his summary: "Significantly then, only when the reference to God as creator and the clear allusions to the creation story in Gen 1–3 are ignored or significantly downplayed (as in the works of William Countryman, Scroggs and Furnish for example) can Paul's clear teaching that homosexual union is 'unnatural' plausibly be regarded as culturally conditioned and thus of very limited (or no) relevance for the modern issue of homosexual relations and the church."[488]

That Paul's teaching is culturally conditioned has been demonstrated to be exegetically wrong, but there is also reason to believe that it's wrong on the basis of "culturally conditioned" relevance. It's a myth (in the New Testament sense of the word) that the ancient world knew nothing about committed same-sex relationships between adults. Several Roman emperors are known to have had same-sex relationships. Julius

---

487. Cantarella, *Bisexuality in the Ancient World*, 193.

488. Taylor, "Bible and Homosexuality," 6; cf. Countryman, *Dirt, Greed and Sex*; Scroggs, *New Testament and Homosexuality*; Furnish, *Moral Teaching of Paul*.

Caesar was rumored to have had a relationship with King Nicomedes IV of Bithynia. Tiberius was alleged to have engaged in sexual activities with young boys on Capri. Nero famously married a freeman named Pythagoras in a public ceremony. Hadrian had a well-documented relationship with Antinous, whom he deified after his death. Elagabalus was noted for numerous same-sex relationships and alleged desires for sex reassignment surgery. These examples illustrate the complex and varied attitudes toward same-sex behavior in Roman society, particularly among the elite. In his *Apology*, father of the church and Ante-Nicene Christian apologist Athenagoras of Athens (ca. 133—ca. 190 CE) urges Christians not to be like their pagan neighbors:

> For those who have set up a market for fornication and established infamous resorts for the young for every kind of vile pleasure—who do not abstain even from males, males with males committing shocking abominations, outraging all the noblest and comeliest bodies in all sorts of ways, so dishonouring the fair workmanship of God... These adulterers and pederasts defame the eunuchs and the once-married (while they themselves live like fishes; for these gulp down whatever falls in their way, and the stronger chases the weaker: and, in fact, this is to feed upon human flesh, to do violence in contravention of the very laws which you and your ancestors, with due care for all that is fair and right, have enacted).[489]

It's evident that Athenagoras not only targeted "pederasts," but also practitioners of other male-male sexual relations in Athens, including homosexual relationships between free citizens. So both in Rome and Athens, Paul's negative view on all types of homosexual practice was indeed "culturally conditioned" relevant.

1 Corinthians 6:9 and 1 Timothy 1:10 (8-11)

> Do you not know that the unrighteous will not inherit the kingdom of God? Do not be deceived! Neither fornicators, nor idolaters, nor adulterers, nor homosexuals [μαλακοί], nor sodomites [ἀρσενοκοῖται], nor thieves, nor covetous, nor drunkards, nor revilers, nor extortioners will inherit the kingdom of God.

---

489. Athenagoras, *Plea for the Christians*, 34.

> But we know that the law is good if one uses it lawfully, knowing this: that the law is not made for a righteous person, but for the lawless and insubordinate, for the ungodly and for sinners, for the unholy and profane, for murderers of fathers and murderers of mothers, for manslayers, for fornicators, for sodomites [ἀρσενοκοίταις], for kidnappers, for liars, for perjurers, and if there is any other thing that is contrary to sound doctrine, according to the glorious gospel of the blessed God which was committed to my trust.

Just as in the discussion about the meaning of φύσις/φυσικός in Rom 1:26–27, it has also been suggested in relation to 1 Cor 6:9 and 1 Tim 1:10 that ἀρσενοκοίτης (*arsenokoites*) refers to male prostitutes, and that "sexual immorality" does not refer to every form of male same-sex sex.[490] John Boswell, in his influential *Christianity, Social Tolerance, and Homosexuality*, suggested that the meaning of ἀρσενοκοίτης is not entirely clear and that it might not specifically refer to homosexuality as we understand it today.[491] He explores various possibilities, including the idea that it could refer to exploitative or abusive sexual practices, rather than consensual same-sex relationships. However, David Wright rejected such an understanding as a reaction to Boswell's assertion, arguing that the expression indeed means "a man who lies with a man." After reviewing Boswell's argumentation and the sources he refers to, Wright concludes:

> ἀρσενοκοιτία came into use, under the influence of the LXX of Leviticus, to denote that homoerotic vice which Jewish writers like Philo, Josephus, Paul and Ps-Phocylides regarded as a signal token of pagan Greek depravity. It is not apparent that investigation of the sources of the New Testament's Lasterkataloge serves to establish further than this the meaning of the term. But it is probably significant that the word itself and comparable phrases used by Philo, Josephus and Ps-Phocylides81 spoke generically of male activity with males rather than specifically categorized male sexual engagement with παῖδες. It is difficult to believe that ἀρσενοκοιτία was intended to indict only the commonest Greek relationship involving an adult and a teenager. The interchangeability demonstrated above between ἀρσενοκοιτία and παιδοφθορία argues that the latter was encompassed within the

---

490. Scroggs, *New Testament and Homosexuality*, 106–7; Boswell, *Christianity, Social Tolerance, and Homosexuality*, 342.

491. Boswell, *Christianity, Social Tolerance, and Homosexuality*.

former. A broader study of early Christian attitudes to homosexuality would confirm this.[492]

In this context, it's interesting that in the earliest Christian literature outside the New Testament, a distinction is made between pederasty and general same-sex sex. For example, in Polycarp's (69–155 CE) letter to the Philippians 5:3, states, "In like manner, let the young men also be blameless in all things, being especially careful to preserve purity, and keeping themselves in, as with a bridle, from every kind of evil. For it's well that they should be cut off from the lusts that are in the world, since every lust wars against the spirit; 1 Pet 2:11 and neither fornicators, nor effeminate, nor abusers of themselves with mankind, shall inherit the kingdom of God, 1 Cor 6:9–10 nor those who do things inconsistent and unbecoming."[493] Here, the same expression used in 1 Cor 6:9, namely "males who lie with males," is used. Since it then mentions those "who let themselves be used for such purposes," it's obvious to understand this second group as boys who, as the receptive party, allow themselves to be exploited for same-sex sex. Thus, we have an exhortation that encourages "abstaining from desires in the world," that is, refraining from the practice that must have been prevalent in the readers' context, which first mentions same-sex sex (between males) in general and pederasty/receptive same-sex sex in particular.

Regarding 1 Tim 1:10, it has also been argued by, among others, Scroggs, that the nouns πόρνοις, ἀρσενοκοίταις, and ἀνδραποδισταῖς, which in the Septuagint and the New Testament according to the *Greek-English Lexicon* mean "fornicator," "sodomite," and "slave dealer," respectively, are related and should be understood to mean "male prostitutes, males who lie [with them], and slave dealers [who procure them]."[494] Scroggs argues that "lawbreakers and rebels" refer to civil law; "ungodly," "sinners," "mockers," and "the unholy" to religious law; and "patricide," "matricide," "manslayers" to the part of the law dealing with murder, while πόρνοις, ἀρσενοκοίταις, and ἀνδραποδισταῖς are allegedly referring to prostitution.[495] Taylor concedes that several of the terms in verses 9–10 seem to be related, but the key point is what the various groups refer to. In light of verse 8, it's more appropriate to see the catalog of vices and its possible

---

492. Wright, "Homosexual or Prostitutes?," 145–46.
493. Quoted from *New Advent* at https://www.newadvent.org.
494. Scroggs, *New Testament and Homosexuality*, 120.
495. Scroggs, *New Testament and Homosexuality*, 120.

groupings of sins as referring to the Mosaic law: "On this understanding, the list beginning with 'patricide' and 'matricide' refers to extreme violations against the fifth commandment (to honour one's parents); 'murder' applies to the sixth commandment; 'fornicators' and 'sodomites' refers to the seventh commandment concerning adultery; 'kidnappers' refers to the eighth commandment concerning stealing, and 'liars' and 'perjurers' refers to the ninth commandment concerning bearing false witness."[496] Therefore, instead of interpreting the terms as referring to prostitution or pederasty, it's better to understand πόρνοις in its general meaning of "sexual immorality" and as referring to a violation of the commandment "you shall not commit adultery" (Exod 20:14). Similarly, ἀρσενοκοίταις, as argued below, is best understood as referring to a general prohibition of same-sex sex. If ἀνδραποδισταῖς should be understood as part of this "group," there is nothing preventing it from denoting persons who deal in sex slaves, but the term does not provide a boundary in relation to the previous two, so these only refer to prostitution.

In the discussion of the prohibition in Lev 20:13, we saw that this text is likely the background for Paul's mention of same-sex sex in 1 Cor 6:9 and 1 Tim 1:10 since the same rare Greek word ἄρσενος (*arsenos*) underlies both the Septuagint's translation of the Hebrew זָכָר (*zāxār*) in Lev 18:22 and 20:13 and Paul's use of the term ἀρσενοκοίτης (*arsenokoites*) in 1 Cor 6:9 and 1 Tim 1:10. Wright points out the same in his analysis. In contrast, P. D. M. Turner, in the same vein, writes that "probably, then, the compound, whether chosen or coined in 1 Cor, is intended to evoke the Holiness Code with its emphasis on male penetration of the male. Actually, as a biblical Hellenist and Hebraist, I should put it more strongly; in the absence of earlier attestation, a deliberate, conscious back-reference by the Apostle is as certain as philology can make it. (He may or may not have known that he was dropping into 'translationese'.) Fascinatingly, by avoiding the available *paiderastēs*, he [Paul] sees to it that 'loving, consensual, adult relations' are fully covered."[497] Once again, it must be noted that the backdrop for Paul's understanding of same-sex sex can be found in the Old Testament, this time in Lev 18:22 and 20:13, and that according to the analysis of these prohibitions, the term ἀρσενοκοίτης (*arsenokoites*) refers to any form of same-sex (male) sex.

---

496. Taylor, "Bible and Homosexuality," 7.

497. Quoted from Taylor, "Bible and Homosexuality," 6; cf. Turner, "Biblical Texts Relevant," 435–45.

Furthermore, it is noteworthy that in 1 Cor 6:9, Paul uses two different terms for "males." The term μἄλᾰκός ("soft") is likely used to describe the passive partner in the specific male same-sex sexual practice, while ἀρσενοκοίτης denotes the dominant partner; μἄλᾰκός is thus the partner who is to be or behaves like "the woman" and thus blurs or crosses the binary boundary between male and female.[498] Regardless of the role the man plays in same-sex sex, it is included in the category of "unrighteous" in 1 Cor 6:9. In this regard, it is also worth noting that "unrighteousness" is one of the four characteristics that Paul mentions among the category of people he refers to in Rom 1:18-32. Thus, all three Pauline texts are tied together into a consistent view of same-sex sex.

It should also be noted that, according to John J. Collins, the use of ἀρσενοκοίτης in the Judeo-Hellenistic Sibylline Oracles support such an understanding. In Sib. Or. 2.70-77, probably written in the first century BCE,[499] the verb ἀρσενοκοίτεῖν is used in conjunction with terms associated more with injustice than with sexual transgressions. Collins mentions, however, that the Sibylline Oracles consistently include male homosexual relations in lists of moral wrongs. For instance, in Sib. Or. 3.185, it is expressed as "male will approach male." Additionally, in Sib. Or. 3:595-96, the Jews are commended for their mindfulness of holy wedlock and refraining from impious intercourse with male children. Furthermore, in Sib. Or. 3:764, the Sibyl encourages people to "avoid adultery and indiscriminate intercourse with males." Collins writes, "Since warnings against male homosexual intercourse is a *topos* in Sibylline literature, there can be little doubt about the meaning of *arsenokoitai* in Sib. Or. 2, or indeed in Paul. The word suggests an allusion to Leviticus, but Paul's position on the subject absolutely conforms with the prevalent position in Hellenistic Judaism."[500] The last statement betrays Collins' interpretation of the texts from Leviticus and the Pauline corpus as *not* addressing the modern concept of homosexual relationships. Given that

---

498. DeYoung, *What Does the Bible Really Teach*, 59-67; Taylor, "Bible and Homosexuality," 6; cf. n42 for bibliographical references. It should be noted that Lenski rejects this interpretation: "In a papyrus of ca. 245 B. C. Deissmann found the word μαλακός, which he translates 'the effeminate.' This word is used in a secondary (obscene) sense and is an allusion to the foul practices by which musicians eked out their earnings. The term is not an equivalent of *mollis*, one who submits himself to a pederast. There is no reason that this vice should be indicated twice by naming its passive and its active perpetrators. It denotes a voluptuary." Lenski, *Interpretation*, 248.

499. Buitenwerf, *Book III*.

500. Collins, *What Are Biblical Values?*, 80.

Collins' interpretation is wrong, the warning in the Sibylline Oracles against male homosexual intercourse supports the interpretation of the biblical texts advocated by the present study, namely, they articulate a *general* warning against male homosexual intercourse.

SUMMARY AND CONCLUSION

The present study has examined various theological perspectives on gender identity and sexual orientation in relation to biblical texts with a particular focus on the views of social constructivism and queer ideology. A "Lord-of-the-Rings-theology," where individual biblical passages are isolated from their broader canonical context, is rejected since it overlooks the Bible's comprehensive structure and theological context, which could offer a more nuanced understanding of sexuality and gender issues.

In developing a gender hermeneutics based on biblical texts, I have laid out my foundational assumptions as ontological realism and essentialism. These assumptions align with what Pope John Paul II called prescientific hermeneutics, which posits that ontology precedes biology, sociology, and anthropology. This perspective emphasizes that the ontology of man and woman is a given rather than a social construct.

My approach also uses the principles outlined by Ryan Peterson's notion of human identity and John Webster's definition of Christian theology with the triune God as the central object and key to understanding the biblical narrative within the divine economy. Webster's theological thought centers on the nature and character of God, focusing profoundly on divine self-revelation. For Webster, theology is not merely an academic pursuit but a deeply theological endeavor that seeks to understand God's being and attributes, an endeavor that seeks to understand God's being, attributes, and works through the lens of Christian tradition and doctrine. His emphasis on the doctrine of the Trinity highlights how God's triunity impacts our understanding of salvation, creation, and the Christian life. Webster suggests that the Trinity introduces a "disturbance of order" in traditional philosophical categories, challenging our natural understanding by showing that God's historical actions are inextricably linked to his eternal being. This perspective implies that the relationship between God's inner life and his external works cannot be compartmentalized, reflecting a profound unity in God's essence and actions. The creation of gendered man thus reflects God's essence and the relations within the Trinity.

Ryan Peterson, on the other hand, approaches the concept of the *imago Dei*, or the image of God, with a focus on human identity. Influenced by Richard Bauckham's distinctions between identity, function, and ontology, Peterson argues that the *imago Dei* is foundational to understanding human identity. This identity, he suggests, is dynamic and relational, reflecting God's character and imbuing human life with intrinsic dignity and purpose. For Peterson, the *imago Dei* informs our understanding of human relationality, connecting it with the relational nature of God as revealed in the Trinity. This view posits that human identity is not static but is continually shaped by our relationship with God, challenging conventional notions of identity formation. What it means to be a man or a woman is, therefore, defined by the relational nature of God's triune being.

Applying these theological insights to biblical sexual ethics reveals that any understanding of gender and sexuality must be consistent with God's essence. If biblical sexual ethics are grounded in who God is, they must align with divine revelation and cannot be viewed as merely situational or subject to change. This understanding also implies that any evolution in the understanding of these ethics must be consistent with God's immutable nature and the foundational truths revealed in Scripture.

In conclusion, integrating Webster's and Peterson's theological perspectives with the hermeneutics of the gift provides a comprehensive framework for understanding biblical teaching on gender and sexuality. This approach emphasizes that our personal ethics and identity must align with divine revelation and the fundamental truths about human existence and purpose as reflected in God's nature and relational design.

Humanity as the Apex of Creation

Man is portrayed as the apex of creation. In Gen 1, man is made in the image of God and given dominion over the earth. Genesis 2 further highlights humanity's central role by showing that creation is incomplete without humans to till the earth and care for the garden of Eden. Human solitude and self-consciousness, as discussed by Pope John Paul II, also set humans apart from animals, emphasizing humanity's unique personal and rational nature.

Biblical texts, including Jer 1:5, Ps 139:16, and Job 35:10–11, reinforce the qualitative difference between humans and animals. Ps 8 describes humans as being made "a little lower than God," reflecting a special status and divine intention. The New Testament continues this distinction, emphasizing humans' value and unique role compared to other creatures. This biblical anthropology, therefore, integrates both physical and metaphysical aspects with the image of God providing the framework for understanding human identity.

The hermeneutics of the gift, as articulated by John Paul II, offers a complementary perspective. This framework emphasizes that life should be viewed as a gift rather than a construct. According to this view, reality is received from God rather than created by us. This perspective contrasts with theories that suggest reality, including gender and sexual identity, is a social or psychological construct. A hermeneutics of the gift asserts that the biblical texts on creation should be understood as reflecting this gift-giving nature of God, which is expressed relationally through male and female identities.

Man as Body and Soul

The relationship between body and soul is fundamental to discussing gender identity. The Bible presents body and soul as distinct yet interconnected components of human nature. Ecclesiastes 12:7 describes how "the dust returns to the earth as it was, and the life's breath returns to God who gave it." Similarly, Job 34:14–15 notes that if God were to gather in his spirit and breath, all flesh would perish and return to dust. These texts suggest a separation between body and soul.

In the New Testament, Jesus distinguishes between body and soul in Matt 10:28, where he says to "fear the one who is able to destroy both soul and body in hell." This separation appears temporary, as other New Testament passages, like Acts 7:59 and Luke 9:28–36, suggest that the soul exists after the body's death. The distinction implies that body and soul are separate entities that interact but are not the same.

The challenge is determining the nature of the relationship between body and soul and how this impacts gender identity. The issue becomes whether one's biological sex or psychological gender should determine their "true" gender, especially in cases of gender dysphoria. Nancy Pearcey highlights the debate surrounding the body and soul. She criticizes perspectives seeing the body as a mere vessel to be manipulated and others emphasizing the unity of body and soul.

The debate on the origin of the soul remains unresolved, and the relationship between body and soul and their role in defining gender identity is complex and multifaceted. We need, therefore, a nuanced understanding of how biological and psychological aspects of gender intersect with theological views on the nature of human beings.

The idea that the body is merely a vessel for the soul, often termed a "tomb" or a "prison," has ancient philosophical roots. Socrates, referencing orphic thought, suggests that the body is perceived as a tomb (σῶμα σῆμα) where the soul is confined and undergoes punishment until it is liberated. In contrast, biblical anthropology presents a more integrated view of the body and soul. According to the Bible, the body is not a mere hindrance but an essential component of human identity, created by God as "very good" (Gen 1:31). The body is seen as integral to the divine image. It continues to reflect God's glory, even after the fall. Passages from the Old Testament and New Testament indicate an expectation of bodily resurrection and redemption. For example, Job speaks of seeing God in his flesh after death, and Isaiah and Daniel foretell the resurrection of the dead.

Genesis describes humanity as created in the image of God, suggesting that both physical form and spiritual essence are vital to human nature. The concept of the body as a visible representation of divine presence is supported by comparisons with ancient royal ideologies, where kings were seen as earthly embodiments of deities. This idea extends to Christian theology, where Christ's incarnation demonstrates the body's value and significance. Christ's flesh is portrayed as a means of revealing divine glory, and his bodily resurrection affirms the redemption of both body and soul.

Paul's writings reinforce this view, emphasizing the inseparability of body and soul. He urges believers to offer their bodies as living sacrifices and to recognize their bodies as temples of the Holy Spirit. Paul's teachings reflect a holistic understanding of human identity, where the physical body and spiritual life are intertwined.

The biblical perspective contrasts with dualistic gnostic views that devalue the body. Biblical thought sees the body as a trustworthy vessel designed to host the divine presence, opposing the notion that spiritual truth can be divorced from physical reality. Early Christian theologians such as Irenaeus and Ignatius of Antioch were crucial in defending the reality of Christ's physical existence against such dualistic views. They insisted on the truth of Christ's bodily suffering and resurrection, emphasizing that salvation involves the full reality of human existence, including the body.

Genesis describes humanity's creation as male and female, affirming that gender is a fundamental aspect of human identity and a good part of God's creation. The concept of male and female being made in the image of God implies that gender is integral to human nature and not merely a superficial or temporary state. The union of male and female in marriage, as described in Gen 2:24, reflects the intended complementarity and relational nature of gender.

The New Testament further explores these issues in the context of resurrection. Passages like Gal 3:28 and Jesus's words in Mark 12:25 discuss the nature of human relationships and gender in the resurrected state. While Jesus indicates that marriage will not continue in the resurrection, this does not necessarily imply that gender itself will be abolished, suggesting that gender, as part of the created order, retains significance even in the eschatological vision. The resurrection affirms the goodness of the body and its role in the divine plan, including aspects of gender. This continuity suggests that while certain social constructs and roles related to gender may shift, the essential goodness and significance of gender as part of human identity remain. The biblical view upholds the dignity of the body and the significance of gender, offering a theological perspective that integrates these elements into a coherent understanding of human identity and salvation.

The Bible describes God in various gendered terms, though God is spirit and not bound by human gender. Descriptions of God include maternal imagery (e.g., Isa 66:13; Deut 32:11) alongside traditional masculine imagery. These portrayals reflect the "genderfulness" of God, expressing attributes and relational qualities rather than literal gender. The biblical understanding of human gender is rooted in a binary framework, allowing for complex theological interpretations of divine attributes and human identity. In biblical texts, the terms for humans and their biological and functional distinctions reveal much about the nature of gender and relationships. The term הָאָדָם (hāʔādām) generically denotes humanity, while זָכָר (zāxār) and נְקֵבָה (nᵊqēvāʰ) specify biological sex as male and female, respectively. On the other hand, אִישׁ (ʔîš) and אִשָּׁה (ʔiššāʰ) refer to the complementary aspects of gender, indicating functional and existential roles in human relationships. These terms illustrate how gender roles are both complementary and reflective of the divine image, emphasizing that male and female were created to counteract the "aloneness" experienced before their creation.

Gender and Marriage

Heterosexual marriage is portrayed in the Bible as part of the divine creation order, particularly in Gen 2. Here, the unity of man and woman in marriage is described as a fundamental aspect of God's design. Genesis 2:24 underscores this by stating that a man and woman become "one flesh," signifying a deep, enduring bond intended by God.

Procreation is also central to the biblical understanding of gender and marriage. Genesis 1:28 commands humanity to "be fruitful and multiply," linking the creation of male and female to the purpose of procreation. This view, supported by scholars like Gordon Wenham and Jacob Milgrom, argues that the prohibition of homosexual acts in the Bible is rooted in the belief that procreation is a fundamental purpose of the male-female relationship.

Pope John Paul II's theology emphasizes that human solitude—described as the initial state where man recognizes himself as a unique, embodied person—is foundational. This solitude reveals the human person as a subject with inherent subjectivity linked to their physical body. The experience of being a subject is not merely a matter of intellectual realization ("I think, therefore I am") but a recognition of oneself as an embodied being ("I am embodied, therefore I am"). This understanding is crucial for grasping the "second delineation" of solitude, where man is seen as incomplete without a helper. God's creation of woman addresses this lack and establishes their union as an original unity.

John Paul II suggests a significant interpretative approach by linking the narratives of the trees and the creation of woman in Gen 2. Adam's awareness of death, which he had never experienced, is understood through an internal consciousness rather than external knowledge. This internal awareness, a form of spiritual self-awareness, is crucial for understanding the meaning of solitude and the subsequent creation of woman.

In Gen 1, humanity is created male and female from the beginning. However, Gen 2 focuses on a man in his embodied form before the distinction between male and female is made. The narrative highlights that man's initial solitude precedes the realization of sexual differentiation, emphasizing that the human body's "spousal" or "nuptial" meaning is integral to understanding personal subjectivity and unity.

John Paul II argues that while the human body carries signs of sex (male or female), the deeper significance is its embodiment, which precedes and underpins the sexual distinction. The terms used in Gen 2—אִישׁ (ʾîš) for "man" and אִשָּׁה (ʾiššāʰ) for "woman"—underscore a fundamental kinship and unity that transcends mere physical differences. These terms are more accurately translated as "man" and "woman" rather than just "male" and "female," reflecting a unique human dimension of kinship and unity. The "one-flesh" union described in Gen 2 is a matter of physical or anatomical complementarity and a profound expression of shared humanity and kinship. This union symbolizes a deeper spiritual and relational connection, affirming that male and female unite in a way that reflects divine creation and unity. The concept of "one flesh" highlights the mutual recognition and fulfillment that arises from this union.

The discussion on nakedness in Gen 2:25—whether it refers to physical or spiritual nakedness—reveals the original state of harmony and transparency between man and woman. The term עָרוֹם (ʿārôm) used here, typically signifies a state of being without protection or barrier, symbolizing the purity and openness of the original human relationship. This nakedness reflects internal completeness and mutual recognition that exists prior to any sense of shame or disunity.

Pope John Paul II's theology asserts that the human body's spousal meaning reflects its role in expressing love and communion. This "nuptial" significance of the body aligns with God's design for human relationships, emphasizing that the body is not just a physical entity but a means of expressing profound spiritual and relational truths. Marriage, therefore, is viewed as a reflection of divine love and participation in God's plan for creation and redemption.

In summary, as Pope John Paul II interpreted it, the theological exploration of solitude, unity, and nakedness in Genesis underscores a vision of human existence deeply intertwined with divine intention. The biblical narratives reveal that the human body and its sexual differentiation are integral to understanding personal identity, relational unity, and the ultimate purpose of human existence as a reflection of divine love and communion.

The theological reflection on marriage in the Bible often explores how it serves as a profound symbol of the divine relationship between God and his people. This divine-marital imagery extends throughout the Bible. From Gen 2's first marriage to Rev 19's "wedding of the Lamb," the Bible presents a coherent narrative of divine commitment and union. The union of heaven and earth is akin to the complementary nature of male and female relationships, symbolizing a larger cosmic harmony and purpose.

The Old Testament prophets like Isaiah, Ezekiel, and Hosea use marital imagery to express God's deep commitment to Israel. They portray God as a bridegroom rejoicing over his bride, which symbolizes the intimate and enduring nature of his covenant with his people. This imagery continues into the New Testament, where Paul extends it to describe Christ's relationship with the church. For instance, Eph 5:31-32 underscores this metaphor, stating that marriage is a profound mystery, reflecting Christ and the church.

Heterosexual marriage thus reflects the divine union of Christ and the church, making deviations from this model—such as homosexual practices—contrary to this symbol.

Marriage and Singleness

The New Testament's portrayal of singleness, especially in the teachings of Jesus and Paul, provides a counterbalance to the often marriage-centric views found in some traditions. Singleness and celibacy, far from being a state of deficiency, can be a means of devoted service and an expression of the ultimate union with Christ. Singleness, like marriage, points towards the greater reality of union with Christ. Singles can embody the "covenantal love of self-giving" that marriage symbolizes, offering a unique witness to the world.

Both married and single individuals can experience and express this divine love in their respective states. The biblical vision of marriage and singleness both reflect a broader theological truth about human relationships and divine communion.

Marriage, as a reflection of Christ's union with the church, thus holds deep theological significance. At the same time, singleness is not a lesser state but a different expression of faith and devotion. Both are integral to understanding the fullness of God's design for human relationships and the divine communion they signify.

Eroticism

Human sexuality has long been a subject of theological and philosophical debate, with contrasting views on its nature and purpose. In early Christian thought, a significant strand of tradition viewed eroticism and sexual pleasure with suspicion, often considering them as manifestations of sinful desire. This perspective can be traced back to Greek Platonism, which sharply distinguished between the body and the soul, influencing early Christian attitudes toward sexuality. Figures like Ambrose and Origen, for instance, advocated for celibacy and saw sexual desire as a hindrance to spiritual growth. Augustine's adoption of Manichaean views on sexuality further reinforced this negative view, with sexual intercourse being considered a necessary evil within marriage but still tainted by sin.

In contrast, some Christian thinkers, influenced by Neoplatonism and other philosophical traditions, offered more nuanced interpretations of desire and eroticism. Dionysius the Areopagite, for example, envisioned desire as a reflection of divine abundance rather than a sign of lack. This understanding suggests that human desire, including eroticism, could be viewed as a positive force that mirrors divine generosity and creativity. Such an interpretation aligns with biblical texts that celebrate eroticism in the context of love and creation.

For instance, the Song of Songs provides an extensive and positive portrayal of erotic love, depicting it as a joyous and integral part of human existence. The imagery in this book likens erotic love to a fertile garden, emphasizing the beauty and delight found in romantic and sexual intimacy. This perspective contrasts with the more restrained views of early church fathers and highlights a different aspect of biblical teaching on sexuality.

Theological interpretations of Genesis also play a crucial role in understanding sexuality. Genesis 1 emphasizes procreation as part of the divine mandate, but Gen 2 offers a more holistic view of marriage and sexuality, focusing on the relational and existential aspects of human unions. This suggests that while procreation is significant, the relational and erotic dimensions of sexuality are equally important.

Moreover, in therapeutic and pastoral contexts, acknowledging and affirming the positive aspects of sexuality can aid in healing and understanding. Recognizing sexuality as a gift from God rather than a source of sin or shame aligns with a more holistic and affirming view of human sexuality.

Gender and Creation Order

In biblical understanding, the relationship between gender, body, and sexuality is deeply tied to the concept of separation and oneness, which is evident in the creation account of Gen 1. This account emphasizes a structured and ordered creation, achieved through the separation and naming of elements. In Gen 1, we see a binary division: light from darkness, heaven from sea, land from water, and male from female. This binary creation, characterized by distinct boundaries, reflects a divine order that is integral to the created world's functionality and blessing.

In the biblical framework, maintaining these separations is crucial in the initial creation and the context of the new creation, symbolized by the promised land and the laws governing it. The Israelites are repeatedly warned against altering the boundaries set by God, as doing so is seen as a serious offense. The laws in Leviticus about sexual relationships and impurity further reflect the seriousness with which these boundaries are regarded. Violations are considered abominations that disrupt the land's sanctity and are met with severe penalties.

The binary nature of creation extends to the understanding of gender, evidenced by the creation of male and female in Gen 1 and 2. The Bible acknowledges the existence of individuals who do not fit neatly into this binary framework. Isaiah 56:4–5 mentions eunuchs, promising them a place in God's covenant and an everlasting name, suggesting an inclusion beyond the traditional gender norms. In Matt 19:12, Jesus refers to eunuchs, including those born as such, made eunuchs by others, or who have chosen celibacy for the sake of the kingdom of heaven. This term covers a range of conditions, from congenital intersex variations to voluntary celibacy, though it does not explicitly address transgender identities.

Some modern interpretations seek to expand the understanding of eunuchs to include transgender individuals, suggesting that Jesus's inclusive attitude towards eunuchs could extend to those with diverse gender identities. For instance, scholars like Heather Looy and Hessel Bouma argue that biblical texts on eunuchs and gender diversity reflect God's acceptance of a broader range of gender experiences. Similarly, Virginia Mollenkott and Justin Sabia-Tanis interpret these texts as supportive of transgender and gender-variant individuals, arguing that the focus should be on faithfulness rather than strictly adhering to binary norms.

Despite these interpretations, the biblical texts do not explicitly mention gender transition as understood today. The discussions about eunuchs and intersex conditions do not directly equate to contemporary concepts of transgender identity. The emphasis in texts like Isa 56:3–5 and Matt 19:12 is more on inclusion and acceptance within the covenant community rather than an endorsement of gender transition.

The discussion on gender dysphoria and its theological implications explores whether this condition could be conceptualized as a form of brain intersex and how it aligns with Christian teachings and creation theology. The central idea is that gender dysphoria might be understood as a mismatch between an individual's biological sex and their gender identity due to a neurobiological factor, a condition potentially seen as congenital and involuntary. Milton Diamond's suggestion that gender dysphoria could be regarded as a form of brain intersex provides a framework for integrating contemporary understandings of gender with traditional Christian perspectives.

The biblical texts often emphasize the alignment between biological sex and gender identity, suggesting that the original creation was intended for a clear male/female binary. This interpretation posits that any deviation from this alignment results from the fall, introducing disorders and imperfections into human existence. Thus, the concept of being "unsuitable" for marriage or temple service, as found in texts like Isa 56 and Matt 19, can be understood as reflecting functional differences rather than moral failings. This notion extends to gender dysphoria, where individuals might be seen as unsuited for certain roles due to their condition. Yet, they remain valuable members of the community with unique contributions.

The pastoral response to gender dysphoria should involve understanding, empathy, and support. It must recognize the real psychological and physical challenges individuals face while maintaining a creation-theological perspective on gender. This approach suggests that individuals with gender dysphoria should be encouraged to find meaning and purpose within their unique circumstances and roles in the faith community despite not aligning with the biblical ideal of anatomical and psychological unity. The goal is to honor the inherent value of each person while navigating the challenges posed by gender dysphoria in a manner consistent with Christian teachings and pastoral care.

The biblical framework emphasizes that since all individuals are made in God's image, adherence to the boundaries and distinctions set by God is crucial for maintaining the order and blessing of creation. Such a framework does not, therefore, endorse all variations of gender or sexuality but rather underscores the importance of respecting divine boundaries and the created order.

The passage on cross-dressing from Deut 22:5 should also be understood within this framework as an attempt to maintain divinely established boundaries. The command is part of a broader set of laws that preserve distinctions in creation as outlined in Gen 1–2, which delineate male and female roles and identities. The prohibition is placed alongside other seemingly arbitrary distinctions, such as not mixing different types of animals or fabrics. This broader context suggests that the laws were designed to uphold the natural order and boundaries that the biblical text associates with divine intent.

The term כְּלִי־גֶבֶר (*xᵊlī-gever*), often translated as "men's clothing" or "masculine article," has a wide range of meanings. It can refer to "armor," "tools," or "weapons," among other things. Traditional interpretations often understand it as referring to clothing, with the prohibition seen as a measure against cross-dressing, which was perceived as a disruption of gender norms. This prohibition might be a reaction against Canaanite fertility cult practices, which might have included gender transgressions or rituals involving gender fluidity. According to this interpretation, the prohibition against cross-dressing served to distance the Israelites from these practices associated with Canaanite religious rites.

The idea of fluctuating gender identities in Canaanite religion, particularly in worshiping deities like Ishtar, adds another layer to the interpretation. Although direct evidence of such practices in Canaanite texts is limited, parallels with other ancient Near Eastern cultures suggest that gender fluidity might have been part of their religious practices. Thus, the prohibition in Deuteronomy could be seen as a response to these practices aimed at maintaining clear gender boundaries as part of the religious and social order.

Understanding Deut 22:5 thus requires considering a range of factors, including cultural and historical contexts, linguistic analysis, and interpretations from various religious traditions. The prohibition against cross-dressing can be seen as part of a broader effort to maintain distinct gender roles and uphold religious norms within the ancient Near Eastern framework.

When examining whether cultic prostitution was practiced in Canaanite religion and how this relates to the biblical prohibition against cross-dressing, several biblical texts mentioning "sacred prostitutes" or "cult prostitutes" (Hebrew קְדֵשִׁים, *qᵊdēšîm*; קְדֵשׁוֹת, *qᵊdēšôt*) should be analyzed. For example, Gen 38:15 and 21–22 describe Judah mistaking Tamar for a prostitute, using the term קְדֵשָׁה ($q^ed\bar{e}š\bar{a}^h$), which some interpret as a cultic prostitute. Deuteronomy 23:18–19 prohibits both male and female cult prostitutes from entering the house of the Lord, suggesting a negative view towards such practices. Other texts, like 1 Kgs 14:23–24 and 2 Kgs 23:7, describe the presence and removal of male cult prostitutes, indicating their role in the religious landscape.

Scholars generally agree that the terms קְדֵשִׁים and קְדֵשׁוֹת likely refer to a category of temple personnel rather than to cultic prostitution per se. Victor Matthews, Mark Chavalas, and John H. Walton differentiate between "sacred" prostitution (a form of temple fundraising) and actual ritual sex, suggesting the latter is harder to confirm in Mesopotamian texts. They argue that cultic prostitution may have existed but was likely not a formal part of worship in the Canaanite context.

In discussing Deut 23:19, interpretations of the term "dog's pay" vary. Some scholars, like Brian Peckham, suggest that "dogs" might refer to temple servants in disguise, while others argue that the term symbolizes dishonor or unethical income. Elaine Adler Goodfriend views the prohibition as targeting undesirable forms of payment, not ritual sex. Phyllis Bird concurs with this interpretation, suggesting that terms like "prostitute's fee" and "dog's pay" represent symbols of dishonor rather than literal practices.

Ultimately, while figurative interpretations are supported by the symbolic use of terms for dishonor and impurity, substantial evidence from comparative ancient Near Eastern contexts suggests that literal cultic prostitution did occur. Thus, the biblical prohibitions likely reflect both the actual practice and a broader condemnation of dishonorable or unethical income related to temple practices.

In 2 Kgs 23:7, King Josiah's actions are described, including the destruction of male cult prostitutes' houses and the women who wove hangings for Asherah. Although this verse does not explicitly mention cross-dressing, it is part of a broader narrative about rejecting idolatrous and sexual practices. The weaving of garments for cultic purposes might imply a connection to gender practices in these rituals, though direct evidence of cross-dressing is not present in the text itself.

In the Pauline epistles, 1 Cor 11:4–5 addresses head coverings, which indicate gender roles within the Corinthian church. This passage reflects the broader cultural and religious significance of gender-specific attire in the context of early Christian practices. Meanwhile, in 1 Cor 6:9,

Paul uses the terms *malakoi* ("soft") and *arsenokoitai* ("men who have sex with men") to describe certain immoral behaviors. While *malakoi* has been interpreted to describe the passive partner in same-sex relations, its application to cross-dressing or gender identity is subject to debate.

Overall, the biblical prohibition against cross-dressing is deeply rooted in maintaining gender distinctions and avoiding behaviors associated with idolatrous practices. Understanding these texts requires careful consideration of their cultural, historical, and theological contexts and an awareness of how the meanings of similar garments can shift depending on the narrative in which they appear.

Gender and Concepts of Gender

In exploring gender roles and stereotypes in biblical texts, it is important to approach the discussion with an understanding of the historical and cultural context in which these texts were written. Ancient Near Eastern and Greco-Roman societies had rigid gender roles, with men predominantly occupying positions of power and authority while women were largely confined to domestic roles. These cultural norms influenced the biblical depiction of gender roles, reflecting a male-dominated society.

However, the biblical narrative also presents a more nuanced view of gender roles that challenges simplistic stereotypes. For instance, women in the Bible are depicted in various roles that transcend traditional expectations. Figures like Tamar, Ruth, and Esther display strength and agency, while characters like Rebekah and Bathsheba take significant actions in their respective stories. This suggests that the biblical texts contain elements affirming and challenging the stereotypical gender roles of their time.

Feminist scholars such as Cheryl Exum critique biblical texts, highlighting their patriarchal nature and how they have been used to justify gender inequalities. Exum's work is crucial for understanding how ancient gender roles have been perpetuated and how they impact contemporary views of women. Yet, her approach sometimes overlooks the texts' distinction between culturally specific elements and timeless ethical principles. Her focus on deconstructing gender roles might overshadow instances where women break stereotypes and exhibit agency.

In the New Testament, women play significant roles that counter traditional gender expectations. They are the first witnesses to Jesus's resurrection and contribute actively to the early Christian community. Notable figures like Phoebe, Priscilla, and Junia challenge the notion that women were passive or secondary to men in the early church.

Furthermore, discussions about masculinity and femininity in biblical texts often intersect with broader debates about gender essentialism. While anatomical differences between men and women are real and significant, gender essentialism—asserting that there are fixed, inherent differences between the sexes—requires careful consideration. While the Bible acknowledges certain gender-specific roles, it does not prescribe rigid behavior or character traits for men and women.

Modern studies in neuroscience and psychology also contribute to the conversation by examining differences in male and female brain function and aptitude. However, these differences should not be interpreted as rigid or absolute but rather as tendencies that exist within a broader spectrum of human behavior.

Ultimately, while binary gender distinctions are important to human nature, they do not encompass the full range of individual traits and abilities. Gender diversity and individual variation within and across sexes reflect a more complex reality than traditional stereotypes suggest. When read with an understanding of their cultural and historical context, the biblical texts reveal a rich and diverse portrayal of gender that goes beyond simplistic binary notions.

Homosexual Practice

The biblical texts from Genesis and Judges are considered irrelevant to the discussion of homosexual practice. While Gen 9:20–27 indirectly touches upon severe offenses, it does not explicitly address same-sex relations. Instead, it has been linked to the later practices of the Canaanites, who engaged in homosexual acts as condemned in Lev 20:13. Thus, at the same time, the story may inform broader discussions on sexual morality, but it does not provide a direct assessment of same-sex relationships. As for Gen 19 and Judg 19, their primary emphasis appears to be on the violent and immoral acts committed rather than on a blanket condemnation of same-sex intercourse. The broader context of these texts suggests that their critical assessment is not solely about the nature of the sexual acts but also about how they were carried out and the underlying moral failures they represent.

On the other hand, the prohibitions in Lev 18:22 and 20:13 are deeply rooted in the creation narrative of Genesis. They reflect an effort to maintain divine order and purity as understood by ancient Israelites. The laws against homosexual practices, along with other prohibitions, are seen as expressions of this broader theological framework, aiming to preserve the divine design of creation. This interpretation provides a comprehensive understanding of the prohibitions in Leviticus, linking them to a larger vision of maintaining the order and sanctity established by God.

The interpretation of the story of David and Jonathan's relationship as homoerotic is influenced by contemporary understandings of sexuality. When viewed through the lens of ancient Near Eastern political alliances or Victorian attitudes towards friendship, the relationship appears more as an example of intense homosocial bonding rather than a modern conception of homosexuality.

Paul's teaching in Rom 1:26–27, similar to the texts from Leviticus, is deeply rooted in the Old Testament creation theology and reflects a divine perspective on human sexuality. While Greco-Roman and Hellenistic Jewish views influenced the cultural context, Paul's argument is grounded in a normative understanding of nature and creation. This perspective challenges interpretations that see Paul's views as culturally conditioned and highlights the theological significance of his teachings on same-sex relations.

1 Corinthians 6:9 and 1 Tim 1:10, alongside their Old Testament background, contribute to a view of same-sex relationships that is generally negative within the New Testament context. The term ἀρσενοκοῖτης appears to indicate a broad condemnation of male same-sex acts, consistent with the prohibitions found in Leviticus and reflected in other Jewish and early Christian writings.

It is of utmost importance to notice that the texts address homosexual *practice*, not homosexual orientation or homoeroticism in itself. We shall return to this in the final chapter on the pastoral implications.

In Sum

Just as human life is a gift, so too is humanity's creation as man and woman a given. What it means for humans to be male and female must, therefore, be defined by the Giver, and several aspects crystallize in biblical texts. First, man and woman reflect God's "genderfulness," and the distinction between male and female distinguishes different attributes of God's nature. Second, the relationship between man and woman mirrors the relationship among the persons of the Trinity. Finally, and derived from the foregoing, the relationship between man and woman represents and visualizes God's relationship to humanity. Lifelong heterosexual marriage and the sexual union between man and woman are fundamentally ordained to demonstrate the relationship between Christ and the church. Each of these "reflections" excludes the possibility that homosexual marriage and divorce can represent and visualize what God has created human gender and sexuality to embody.

As God's physical creation, the body is also a good and reliable testimony to God's intention for humanity and is, therefore, endowed with inherent moral boundaries. Consequently, our bodies reflect moral agency. The physical body serves as a symbol to the world of God's presence and redemptive plans. Our bodies act as "living temples" with a mission-oriented presence in the world, culminating in our bodily resurrection at the end of the ages.

Celibacy and singleness signify the onset of the future new creation and the marriage supper of the Lamb, which will be fully realized at the consummation of the ages.

That this ideal is challenged and, in many respects, not the norm "east of Eden" does not mean that the ideal must be abandoned. Because the ideal is rooted in God's essence and actions, it must still be sought and strived for. It remains normative in the church and is an ethical guideline in political and social engagement. More on this will be discussed in the pastoral afterword.

Part Four

Pastoral Implications

WHY DON'T WE PUT adulterers to death anymore as prescribed in, for example, Lev 20:10–16? And since we do not, why insist on the enduring importance of the prohibitions on adultery in the same passage? What are the criteria for discarding some of the Mosaic laws and upholding others? The purpose of the following is not to review the centuries-long discussion on which Old Testament laws are binding for Christians as such but to present a new perspective on Old Testament law with two examples of how to transfer its ethical guidance to a New Testament context.[1]

Since the Mosaic law has often been read in light of or compared to modern legal statuary norms, the relevance of comparative studies is obvious. As far as the laws' cultural rootedness is concerned, Nicolai Winther-Nielsen summarizes current research:

> Comparative studies of the use of legal collections from the Near East have created a new synthesis, as it is now clear that the laws were never used in the courts but instead served as exercise texts for training judges. Near Eastern legal collections functioned as descriptive treatises and compilations of legal rules and customary law derived from traditional practice. In difficult cases, judges could consult them to guide existing practices that embodied the law. It is highly likely that the oral tradition

---

1. The following section is a summary of the more detailed presentation in Kofoed, "Old Testament Law."

culture, which dominated ancient Israel, treated the laws in Exod 21–22 as "self-executing laws," that is, a self-regulating system characterized by the oral culture.[2]

Referring to the research of Michael Lefevre, Winther-Nielsen argues that

> only in Hellenistic Judaism and under the influence of Ptolemy II's court reforms do the collections of the book of Moses assume a completely new function as a binding constitutional law, a code of law. Therefore, it is not during the time of Ezra and Nehemiah, but under later Hellenistic influence, that the law acquires its new legalistic status because it is no longer sufficient to regard "the law book as an ideal, but not itself as 'the law.'" According to this new research synthesis, it is, therefore, Hellenistic legalism and not the original Mosaic guidance that is challenged in the New Testament.[3]

Such a contextually and culturally rooted understanding of the law book as guidance in the light of an ideal makes all the difference in the world. If, for example, the exhortation in Lev 18:5 ("You shall therefore keep my statutes and my rules; if a person does them, he shall live by them: I am the LORD") is understood in legalistic terms, it would be only natural to understand Paul's rejection of legalism in the New Testament as a rejection of the Mosaic law *as such*. However, understood as an expression of an ideal with respect for the *context*, it becomes clear, as Winther-Nielsen argues, that

> when it is said about Israel that they must *ḥay bāhem* "live by them," this living according to God's ordinances and laws should be understood as a contrast to Canaanite religion, not as a reward for good deeds. Up until now, the Books of Moses have used the verb *ḥāyāh* "live" in contexts of preserving life in contrast to death: Girls are to survive (Exod 1:19;22), Israel will not survive contact with the mountain (19:13), you must not let a sorceress live (22:17), Moses cannot survive seeing God (33:20), and subsequently it is stated that the impoverished shall survive among you (Lev 25:35–36). Both contextually and linguistically, living by God's guidance means avoiding losing life by breaking away from God's guidance. In other words, it's a guidance that

---

2. Winther-Nielsen, "Mosebøgernes brug som vejledning," 20–21; all Winther-Nielsen translations are mine.

3. Winther-Nielsen, "Mosebøgernes brug som vejledning," 21.

warns against Canaanite ways of living and sexual transgressions, which could lead to God's punishment with the threat of being wiped out in the same manner as the Canaanites.[4]

In addition, Thomas Schreiner agrees with Lefevre and Winther-Nielsen by pointing to Jewish traditions that understood the exhortation in Lev 18:5 as promising *eternal* life to those who kept the law, not, as was the case in its original context, life in the *land* to those who had already been "saved" and given "eternal life." Targum Onkelos and Pseudo-Jonathan,[5] respectively, thus render Lev 18:5 as

> And you shall keep my statutes and my judgments, which if a man do he shall live by them an everlasting life.
>
> And you shall keep my statutes, and the order of my judgments, which if a man do he shall live in them, in the life of eternity, and his position shall be with the just.

Schreiner backs up his point by referring to the same "eternal" understanding of Lev 18:5 in later Jewish tradition:

> In a thorough study of Lev 18:5 in the Old Testament and Second Temple Judaism, Preston Sprinkle shows that in some texts the verse is interpreted as requiring obedience for eternal life (cf. CD III, 15–16; 4Q266 11, I–II, 12; *Pss. Sol.* 14:1–5; cf. also 4Q504; Philo, *Prelim. Studies* 86–87). Simon Gathercole also argues that an eschatological reading of Leviticus 18:5 is evident both in the New Testament and in Second Temple Judaism. He rightly remarks, "There is an 'eternalization' of the life that, in its original context in Leviticus, would have been understood in terms of lengthened life and prosperity of one's descendants and the nation as a whole."[6]

Similarly, Averbeck writes that ancient Near Eastern law collections did not serve statutory purposes: "They are *descriptive* of legal practice as it occurred in the courts, not *prescriptive* for that practice. Therefore, the law collections reflect 'common' or 'customary' law. The practice of 'statutory' law in which lawyers and judges consult written codes for making decisions in court does not seem to have existed in the ancient

---

4. Winther-Nielsen, "Mosebøgernes brug som vejledning," 59.

5. Quoted from Longenecker, *Galatians*, 120.

6. Schreiner, *40 Questions*, 61; cf. Sprinkle, *Law and Life*, 1–130; Gathercole, "Torah, Life, and Salvation," 126–45.

Near East."[7] Introducing various models for explaining the relationship between the cuneiform and biblical law collections, Averbeck points to the diffusion model as the most likely: "The *diffusion* model proposes that the biblical law codes draw partly from the oral legal tradition and partly from the written cuneiform tradition that had spread throughout the ancient Near East. This created a common legal tradition reflected also in the Israelite law collections since the ancient Israelites were ancient Near Eastern people too."[8] As for the law in the Pentateuch, Averbeck argues that the Ten Commandments are the primary principles of law for ancient Israel and that all other law collections in the Pentateuch are examples of how these principles should be unpacked in *real* life:

> The Mosaic law displays its core ideals in the Ten Commandments, but it was not idealistic. It was realistic for application to the life of ancient Israel in its real-world cultural context. In fact, in many instances, to read it well depends on a wider understanding of the political-sociological, familial, psychological, and economic realities of the world in which they lived, most of which are evident within the Bible itself... The Lord intended that the Mosaic law serve as the foundation for such judicial wisdom in ancient Israel. The written law could not and did not intend to deal with every possible situation people faced, but it could provide ideals and precedents to guide the decisions of the judicial officers, whether they were local city elders (Deut 16:18–20), Levitical priestly judges (Deut 17:8–13), or kings (Deut 17:18–10).[9]

Kenneth Bergland, referring to his monograph *Reading as a Disclosure of the Thoughts of the Heart*, also argues that the laws of the Pentateuch should be applied in practical, real-life situations: "A scribe's task therefore consisted of inscribing a text not only on clay tablets, skin, papyrus, or other material, but also on one's own lips and heart. At the same time memorization was only a means for embodying the texts in lived life. Orality and writing functioned together so the scribe could embody and perform the treasured tradition."[10]

---

7. Averbeck, *Old Testament Law*, 87. Emphasis original.
8. Averbeck, *Old Testament Law*, 87–88 (emphasis original); cf. Barmash, "Biblical and Ancient Near Eastern Law," e12262.
9. Averbeck, *Old Testament Law*, 89–90.
10. Bergland, "Memorized Covenantal Instruction," 108.

This understanding is also the rationale behind another aspect of Mosaic law that has often been overlooked, namely that there is a progressive growth of the Mosaic law not only in the addition of new laws but also in the revision of *existing* laws. Berman, in the eighth chapter of his *Inconsistencies in the Torah*, shows how legislations from different law collections in the Pentateuch are combined in later biblical texts and that this combination means that the author or editor may not have understood them as mutually exclusive.[11] Averbeck notes that "the placing of Exod 18 before this [the giving of the Ten Commandments], even though the event took place later, is strategic in a literary and judicial way. It suggests that the law began to grow case by case almost immediately after they arrived at Sinai, as the people brought cases to Moses for him to gain resolution directly from the Lord."[12] Averbeck furthermore notes that the three parallel law collections in Exodus through Deuteronomy—i.e., the book of the covenant (Exod 21–23), the holiness regulations (Lev 17–27), and the Deuteronomic regulations (Deut 12–26)—demonstrate that changing circumstances, namely the construction of the tabernacle, required revision of the altar regulations in Exod 20:24–26 as evident in Lev 17:1–12.[13] The best way to characterize these laws, therefore, is to use the term frequently used in the biblical text itself, namely תּוֹרָה (*tôrā*ʰ) in its essential meaning of "teaching, guidance." Bergland, in a similar manner, proposes "a model for how to best account for the dual phenomena of pointillistic exact correspondence of lexemes, phrases, and concepts coupled with a certain fluidity and creativity in legal reuse in Torah" by suggesting

> that seeing Torah as normative covenantal instruction and being reused from memory might better account for this dual phenomenon than source-critical solutions or traditional harmonizations. That we find legal dissimilarity and variation between the different legal corpora of Torah seems to be where we need to take our departure when reflecting on this dual phenomenon. While both critical and traditional scholarship tend to insist on a concept of literary coherence, either in the Pentateuch as a whole or subdocuments or fragments such as J, E, P, and D, the proposed model here rather suggests that we should

---

11. Berman, *Inconsistency in the Torah*; cf. Barmash, *Laws of Hammurabi*, 231–50.
12. Averbeck, *Old Testament Law*, 99.
13. Averbeck, *Old Testament Law*, 100–101.

expect a certain legal dissimilitude and variation, even revision, given Torah as covenantal instruction and memorized reuse.[14]

Backing this modified perspective on Mosaic law is another evolution within jurisprudence.[15] In his influential essay "Nomos and Narrative" from 1983, the late legal scholar Robert Cover of Yale University contended that instead of regarding law solely as a system of rules imposed by a sovereign, it is more apt to conceptualize law as a normative universe, a "nomos," wherein "we constantly create and maintain a world of right and wrong, of lawful and unlawful, of valid and void."[16] According to Julen Etxabe, Cover's initial proposition represents a significant departure from traditional perspectives on law—not as a collection of institutional rules and principles, not as a series of policies and mechanisms for social control, but rather as a narrative prism through which we perceive and filter the realms of right and wrong, valid and void, good and bad. From this standpoint, law is most accurately characterized not as a rigid system but rather as an exceptionally rich and adaptable set of resources for all aspects of the normative life of individuals and communities.[17] Cover contends that neither law nor legal institutions can be comprehended in isolation from the narrative in which they are immersed:

> For every constitution there is an epic, for each decalogue a scripture. Once understood in the context of the narratives that give it meaning, law becomes not merely a system of rules to be observed, but a world in which we live. In this normative world, law and narrative are inseparably related. Every prescription is insistent in its demand to be located in discourse—to be supplied with history and destiny, beginning and end, explanation and purpose. And every narrative is insistent in its demand for its prescriptive point, its moral. History and literature cannot escape their location in a normative universe, nor can prescription, even when embodied in a legal text, escape its origin and its end in experience, in the narratives that are the trajectories plotted upon material reality by our imaginations.[18]

---

14. Bergland, "Memorized Covenantal Instruction," 111.

15. The following is a to a large extent a paraphrase of different sections from Kofoed, "Encoding and Decoding Culture," 243–44.

16. Cover, "Supreme Court, 1982 Term—Foreword," 4.

17. Etxabe, "Legal Universe After Robert Cover," 116.

18. Cover, "Supreme Court, 1982 Term—Foreword," 4–5.

Cover's essay was of landmark importance as it pioneered a new field of research, offering a fresh perspective on the interplay between law and narrative. In Old Testament research, it is evident in, for example, Mary Douglas' *Leviticus as Literature* and Assnat Bartor's *Reading Law as Narrative*.[19] Bartor explains:

> It seems that the fundamental approach which guided the authors of the narrative laws is the very same approach that is common and agreed upon until today. Narrative is a mode of thought, a cognitive tool that allows us to attribute significance to actions and events, and therefore serves as a foremost means for the recognition of the world, humankind, and human reality. The authors made use of the medium of narrative, understanding that the story is efficacious for the understanding of moral rules and principles, and that narrativity serves as a means of argumentation and persuasion. The context for understanding the narrative legal texts is therefore suasion.[20]

Similarly, Averbeck has demonstrated that regarding Pentateuchal slave law, the law, given at Sinai, begins and ends with the native Hebrew indentured servant and the release law considering the Lord's liberation from slavery in Egypt. The liberation from slavery in Egypt is mentioned as the entire premise for the law in the first of the Ten Commandments (Exod 20:2), and the non-cultic regulations in the book of the covenant commence with provisions on indentured servitude and release (Exod 21:2–11). Similarly, the law given at Sinai concludes with the same subject (Lev 25:39–43 and 47–55), again emphasizing the liberation from slavery in Egypt as the entire premise for the law (Lev 25:38, 42–43, 55). This is the fundamental historical fact and theological rationale underlying the covenant and the law. God had set his people free, so he is their God, and they are his people (Lev 25:55—26:1).[21]

God's free and unforced creation of Israel through liberation from slavery is itself embedded in the larger narrative of God's universal creation and redemption of humanity. In Deut 4, God leading Israel "out of the iron furnace, out of Egypt" (4:20) is described as God's greatest act "since the day God created [בָּרָא] man on the earth" (4:32). There are numerous references to the creation account in the introduction to the narrative of covenant formation in Exod 19–24. The rationale for observing

19. Bartor, *Reading Law as Narrative*.
20. Bartor, "Reading Biblical Law as Narrative," 298.
21. Averbeck, "Egyptian Sojourn," 169–70.

the Sabbath in Exod 20:8–11 is provided with a reference to God's rest on the seventh day in the creation account (Gen 2:1–3), and the parallel between the rest after the creation of heaven and earth and the creation of Israel is evident from the rationale for observing the Sabbath day in Deut 5:15.

As far as the *emic* approach is concerned, Richard Averbeck has recently proposed that the law is not limited or irrelevant but rather a unified whole written on the heart of the new covenant believer.

Averbeck's proposal is based on three principles:

1. The law is good: The Old Testament law is not only good but also useful for Christians, applying it to their lives in a new covenant sense.
2. The law is weak: The law cannot change a human heart; only the Holy Spirit can. The law is good, holy, and spiritual, but it is weak because it cannot control our flesh.
3. The law is one unified whole: The law should not be divided into different types (moral, civil, ceremonial) or applied selectively. Rather, every law element supports or works out the implications of the two greatest commandments.[22]

Averbeck's approach has implications for understanding the application of the law in the Christian life. He argues that the law should be applied in a way that is consistent with its redemptive context rather than as a set of abstract principles. Jesus's teachings in Matt 5:17–19 suggest that the laws remain valid until heaven and earth pass away. According to Averbeck, Jesus's fulfillment of the law is not about abolishing it but about teaching and living it fully. This means that the law, as understood and lived by Jesus, remains valid today.

The laws were originally given to separate Israel from Gentile peoples and to make them a "light to the nations." However, Jesus clarified their original intent and subjected observance to their redemptive-historical purpose. The key to understanding the laws is the "deliberation" behind them. The connection between the "deliberation" and the prohibited foods was disconnected, as the food regulations were no longer necessary to separate Israel from gentiles.[23]

The New Testament does not abandon the "deliberation" to make God's people distinct but rather applies it in a new way. The repetition of

---

22. Averbeck, *Old Testament Law*, 17.
23. Averbeck, *Old Testament Law*, 246, 221.

the call to be a "chosen race, a royal priesthood, a holy nation" in 1 Pet 2:9 is no longer connected to specific food taboos. Still, it is given under the general principle that "all things are lawful, but not all things are helpful."

The Old Testament laws were not intended to create divisions between God's people but rather to illustrate God's character and interaction with them. The physical requirements of the purity laws corresponded to the physical presence of the Lord in the tabernacle, and since God is present with his people in a different way in the church, the content or rationale behind these laws has to be applied differently.

The New Testament teaches us to transpose the laws in the light of Christ's presence through the Holy Spirit. This is not about abandoning the laws but about understanding them in a new way. The entire Old Testament law is valid in the New Testament, and the question is not which laws to apply but how to transpose them in the light of Christ's presence.

Before we proceed to the implications for contemporary guidance in sexual ethics, it is pertinent to introduce and interact with the model suggested by Winther-Nielsen to understand how Mosaic law itself differentiates between the different tiers of spheres in the ethical vision of Mosaic guidance: essential (creation, salvation, faith), ethical (love of neighbor, compassion), and existential (legal, social-economical). Based on the inspiration from Peter W. Gosnell especially, Winther-Nielsen has developed a model based on the current research of how ancient Near Eastern laws functioned in their contemporary context and how the laws are embedded in the foundation stories of the books of Moses: "In this model, the community between God and His people and the individual is created through the grand narrative of creation, judgment, and salvation. This relationship is established by grace, expressed in holiness, and affirmed in love. The divine grace, holiness, and love of the grand narrative then function in the laws of the Books of Moses as motivation for obedience that concretely motivates care for the weak in love for the neighbor, but the ethics are also inspired by the Creator's desire to maintain the good order in the world of creation."[24] Winther-Nielsen's own contribution is to develop this model of "divine guidance on three different tiers," where the first tier is the essential relationship with God, which he establishes in creation, judgment, and salvation, often solemnly affirmed in various forms of covenant ceremonies, and which is intended to lead to obedience in faith. The first tier, the foundational

---

24. Winther-Nielsen, "Mosebøgernes brug som vejledning," 23; cf. Gosnell, *Ethical Vision of the Bible*.

narrative, is represented by the main narrative thread in the Pentateuch and characterized by its emphasis on God's salvation-historical dealings with Israel and their celebration thereof in the cult. As ethical guidance, it emphasizes Israel's obedience as a *response* to God's grace (Gen 15:6), and holiness, on this tier, is primarily understood as theological and ritual, that is, holiness *coram Deo*. The second tier focuses on personal morality regarding love for the neighbor and individual ethics intending to produce righteousness *coram Mundo*. The second tier focuses on the family's concrete, practical, and spiritual formation and on the patriarchs and Israel as a royal priesthood serving God in purity and holiness. The third tier focuses on the existential conditions in contemporary society by "regulating legislation in society in a way that protects fellow human beings so that they can live a righteous life."[25] Winther-Nielsen further demonstrates how "justice is fundamentally grounded in an ethics that derives socio-economic guidance from the grand narrative" and how new historical contexts entail that while "the grand narrative's demands for obedience are maintained," law and ethics are updated and reformulated to address a new situation.[26] Transposing the three-tier model to the New Testament, Winther-Nielsen argues that "Paul does away with salvation by the law, without excluding that it may well be a guide for the saved as in Gal 5:13–15," and that "Paul is not engaged in an antinomian rejection of the books of Moses, but instead offers a prophetic foundation in the Old Testament, which includes both a prediction of Christ and a proclamation of God's will for the liberated people. Therefore, if Eph 2:15 is read in the light of its context, it does not exclude that the books of Moses can be used as a guide for believers who, to keep Paul's terminology, are under construction as a temple of God by the Spirit (2:21–22)."[27] "In my own three-tiered model," Winther-Nielsen continues, "I maintain judgment, salvation, and obedience as the basic righteousness. However, it also makes room for derived ethical guidance in the justice of life in relation to fellow human beings, and it is related to the admonitions in the epistolary literature on this point. Its strength is that it makes room for the books of Moses to 'provide an essential foundation to developing a basic moral sense of direction.' Gosnell calls it a moral compass, but we could also call it landmarks or milestones for the good life."[28] The guid-

25. Winther-Nielsen, "Mosebøgernes brug som vejledning," 25.
26. Winther-Nielsen, "Mosebøgernes brug som vejledning," 43, 47; my translation.
27. Winther-Nielsen, "Mosebøgernes brug som vejledning," 62.
28. Winther-Nielsen, "Mosebøgernes brug som vejledning," 62–63.

ance of the books of Moses, according to Winther-Nielsen, is fully upheld as consistent with the guidance found in the New Testament, since "the books of Moses can also today guide how the foundational narrative can be maintained in obedience. At the same time, the ethics and law of the books of Moses are applied in new contexts."[29]

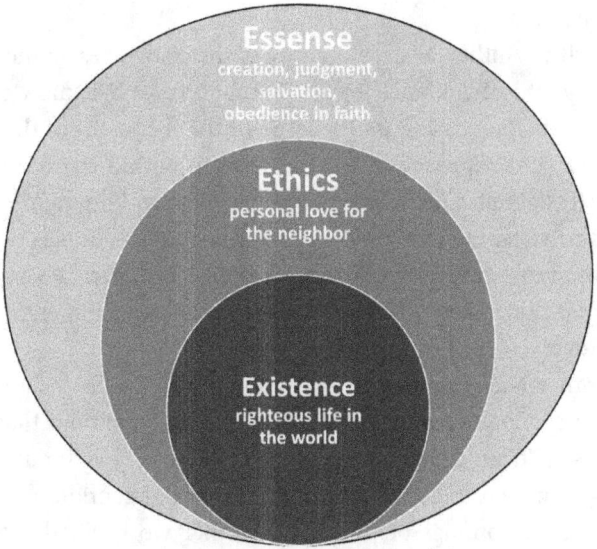

Figure 10: Nicolai Winther-Nielsen's Model

Winther-Nielsen's model addresses several questions that arise when life is to be lived between ideal and reality and has several strengths. First and foremost, it "follows the books of Moses' own distinction between Yahweh's Torah being revealed to the desert generation from Abraham and up to the end of Numbers, and Moses' Torah being formulated for the next generation in Deuteronomy." This approach, Winther-Nielsen continues, "provides the contemporary reader with a historically rooted interpretation key, where Moses can also today provide guidance on how the foundational narrative can be maintained in obedience, while at the same time applying the ethics and law of the books of Moses in new contexts.[30]

Secondly, by distinguishing between the three tiers of Mosaic guidance as they appear in the Pentateuch, it enables the reader to determine which Mosaic laws and principles should also be maintained in their

29. Winther-Nielsen, "Mosebøgernes brug som vejledning," 63.
30. Winther-Nielsen, "Mosebøgernes brug som vejledning," 63.

application because they are reasoned or justified by the foundational narrative and which laws and principles should be maintained only in principle and applied to new contexts. Here is the hermeneutical rationale, for example, for rejecting the claim that if we do not maintain the death penalty (which belongs to the third tier), we should also not enforce other commandments (which belong to the second tier) in the same context.

Thirdly, Winther-Nielsen is aware of the challenges on the third tier in applying ethical guidance to modern contexts and acknowledges that there is an obvious discontinuity between the theocracy of the books of Moses and contemporary societal legislation within the framework of the New Testament's distinction between the two kingdoms' realms of church and state. He nevertheless provides some examples of how the patriarchs' and Israel's very different responses to their changing existential conditions may inspire the believer to choose different models for societal involvement.

Winther-Nielsen notes the limitations of his article as far as Mosaic guidance in a Christian context is concerned and mentions that he must limit himself "from the full extent of the problem."[31] Without removing anything from an otherwise very helpful model, attention must be paid to several shortcomings or points for further work. Firstly, the model provides little help in distinguishing between absolute and guiding applications of core principles. This is illustrated well by the example given by Winther-Nielsen on the admonition in Lev 25:37–38 that "you shall not lend him your money at interest, nor give him your food for profit. I am the LORD your God, who brought you out of the land of Egypt to give you the land of Canaan, and to be your God." Applying his three-tier model, Winther-Nielsen fleshes out how the guidance looks like on each tier:

> Interest rates belong to judicial ethics which depends on the social structure in different social models and eras (tier 3), and the ban could usefully inspire god-fearing legislators and economists today. The very requirement to pay special attention to a fallen countryman defines a social ethic that the godly must live by as a concretization of charity (tier 2), and it can always guide godly people in similar situations. The most comprehensive guidance lies in the fact that the claim is made absolute by being grounded in the fundamental revelation of God's historical work in the deliverance of Israel from Egypt (tier 1), and this

---

31. Winther-Nielsen, "Mosebøgernes brug som vejledning," 58.

understanding of the mission of God's people can inspire the church today.[32]

I have no quibble with how Winther-Nielsen extracts guidance for "god-fearing legislators and economists today" on the third tier and "godly people at all times" on the second tier. But what exactly is made "absolute" by referring to "the fundamental revelation of God's historical work" on the first tier? The implications on the third and second tiers or the obligation to reflect the ethos displayed by God in his "historical work" on the first tier? It must, of course, be admitted that Winther-Nielsen, in the same sentence, notes that "this understanding ... can inspire the church today" and that Winther-Nielsen hardly understands the application on the third tier to be absolute. But again, where is the boundary between absolute and inspiring? Or put differently, how do we determine whether only the core principle derived from God's historical work on the first tier or also the concrete implications on the second and third tiers are timeless and absolute? The problem can be illustrated well by turning to sexual ethics. Winther-Nielsen discusses the patriarchs' "violations" of the prohibitions against marrying one's father's sister (Amram in Exod 6:20 contra Lev 18:12–14), sexual relationship with a half-sister (Abram's marriage with Saraj contra Lev 18:9;11; 20;17; Deut 27:22), and taking the wife's sister as a second wife (Jacob marrying Leah and Rachel in Gen 29:16–30 contra Lev 18:18). Winther-Nielsen comments on this discrepancy that "in the three-tier model, it would not be a problem to draw inspiration for an ethical reflection on caring for women's sexual integrity based on these texts and address the breakdown of sexual morality through preaching and teaching." I have no objections against how the model explains the different applications of "sexual morality" on the second and third tiers, but again, what exactly is "sexual morality?" And if the application of it is time-bound and flexible, does it also apply to the prohibition of practiced homosexuality? And if not, why? One could point to the fact that there is no flexibility attested in this prohibition, but the argument is weak since the examples on applications are not exhaustive, and it could, therefore, be argued that it is coincidental that there are no examples of flexibility concerning sexual orientation. On this point Winther-Nielsen's model could be improved by emphasizing, as Averbeck does, the foundational character of God's creational order, especially for issues related to gender identity and sexuality, but also regarding,

---

32. Winther-Nielsen, "Mosebøgernes brug som vejledning," 25.

for example, slavery. Winther-Nielsen probably includes God's creation in the "foundational narrative on God's works," but it needs to be made much more explicit if concepts like "sexual morality" and references to "absolute" principles are not to become empty of content and subject to subjective interpretation.

A second suggestion for improvement has to do with the discontinuity of the theocracy in the New Testament. While all three tiers operated within the same theocratic framework in ancient Israel, the church—understood as God's people of all tribes and languages—in the New Testament is the place where the foundational narrative serves as a basis for teaching and instruction on "how personal morality unfolds in righteous living and genuine love for one's neighbor," and where, based on such principles, church discipline is exercised concerning individuals who live inconsistently with the principles that can be derived from the foundational narrative. In this task, the church's leadership in its "spiritual realm" has only the power of the word and wields solely "the sword of the Spirit." When it comes to the third tier, which is the civil or "secular realm" of law and governance, the church—understood both collectively and as individuals—contributes on an equal footing with everyone else to influence legislation in a way that serves to protect fellow human beings and promote a righteous life. The question of how the church makes such a contribution is naturally inseparable from the derivation of guidance from the foundational narrative, which takes place in the church on the first and second tiers, but it will typically appear differently on the second and third tiers, as it is generally easier to derive and enforce guidance that is closer to the ideal in the church than in society. When it comes to discussing engagement on the third tier, that is, societal involvement and efforts to influence legislation, it is beyond the scope of the purpose of the perspective in this work, and therefore we will focus on ethical guidance in the second tier in the following. The potential for improvement in Winther-Nielsen's model lies in clarifying on which tier the church's role as instructor and guardian of the "absolutes" should be placed. One possibility would be to place it on tier 2, but this means that tier 2 is no longer confined to personal morality in terms of love for the neighbor and individual ethics intending to produce righteousness *coram mundo* with the family as the primary setting for concrete, practical, and spiritual formation (unless, of course, "family" is redefined to also encompass the spiritual family). But the focus is clearly on instruction and guidance on this tier, not sanction. Alternatively, it could be placed on the first tier, since one of the characteristics of this tier, according to Winther-Nielsen, is the communal emphasis on Israel as God's children who obey him in response to the imputed righteousness through his grace.[33] A natural correlation would be that the community, Israel in the Old Testament and the church in the New, also had the obligation to draw the consequences when such an obedience was *not* practiced, but that the consequences and the means of affecting them in a New Testament non-theocratic setting would be different on tier 1 and 3. The best solution is probably to place the defensive guarding and sanctioning obligations of the church on tier 1 and the more positive instruction on tier 2.

EPILOGUE

The fact that no "Leviticus" is in the New Testament is both obvious and challenging! It is obvious because ethical guidance in the church and society exist in their respective domains, but it is also challenging—or perhaps even frustrating—because there is no direct reuse of the guidance given to ancient Israel. When it comes to deriving ethical guidance from these ideals in the New Testament and the modern contexts, the complexity of the task is not only due to the distinction between the spiritual and secular domains but also the complexity found in the examples of guidance found in both the Old and New Testaments.

Firstly, some texts show that while the ideal or "absolute" is maintained, there are variations in the specific guidance regarding what an ideal means in each context. For instance, when it comes to the prohibition in Deut 22:5 against cross-dressing, as we have seen, it is most likely directed at the fluid gender identity that characterized the worship of Ishtar and its Canaanite counterpart in ancient Israel during the monarchy. The absence of explicit references to cross-dressing in the New Testament does not mean that the binary understanding of gender, which cross-dressing violates, has been abandoned. Instead, it suggests that the specific form of cross-dressing addressed in Deut 22:5 was apparently not a concern in the contexts discussed in the New Testament. However, we do find the ideal applied to other types of "boundary-crossing behavior." When Paul speaks in 1 Tim 2:9–10 about women adorning themselves modestly and not with elaborate hairstyles, gold, pearls, or expensive clothing, but rather with good deeds that befit women professing

---

33. Winther-Nielsen, "Mosebøgernes brug som vejledning," 24.

godliness, the implicit argument is that if something is befitting for women, there is also something befitting for men. Women who engage in the behaviors that Paul advises them against are crossing boundaries within the context of the binary gender understanding depicted in the foundational narrative. The same applies to 1 Cor 11:13–15, where Paul, in response to his own rhetorical question about whether it is proper for a woman to pray with her head uncovered, gives the following answer: "Judge for yourselves: is it proper for a wife to pray to God with her head uncovered? Does not nature itself teach you that if a man wears long hair it is a disgrace for him, but if a woman has long hair, it is her glory? For her hair is given to her for a covering." Here, too, the rationale behind Paul's exhortation is that the boundary between the two genders should be respected, and in the Corinthian context, it meant that men did not let their hair grow long while women did. Although there are interpreters who understand φύσις ("nature") as an expression of divine order, it is more plausible to understand it here as an expression of a cultural convention, that is, what is "naturally" appropriate due to custom and usage. After all, women's hair does not grow faster than men's! Alternatively, "nature," in the same manner as in Rom 1, refers to the binary gender as part of the created order without understanding men's short and women's long hair as *timeless* and *necessary* implications. In any case, however, the ideal from the foundational narrative is upheld while the guidance is applied to new culturally conditioned contexts. In this type of guidance for the church (on the second tier), the derivation should be understood as a direct but flexible application of the ideal (on the first tier).

Furthermore, there are examples of casuistic guidance that confront reality with the aim of directing towards the ideal, but where the guidance reflects the ideal to a lesser or weakened extent. This is evident in texts that narratively or juridically address or mention polygamy without idealizing it, such as stories about Abraham's, Jacob's, David's, and Solomon's polygamy and the levirate law in Deut 25:5–6. Similarly, New Testament texts that regulate slavery without idealizing it (e.g., 1 Cor 7:20–24; Col 3:22–25; 4:1; Eph 6:5–9; and Titus 2:9–10) do not outright reject polygamy or slavery. However, when viewed in the light of the foundational narrative, it becomes clear that texts are guidance that, based on a culture where polygamy and slavery were common, seeks to move the culture towards the ideal. The polygamy of Abraham, Jacob, David, and Solomon is described in a way that leaves no doubt that it is not ideal. For instance, Sarah sends Hagar away (Gen 16), Jacob must endure the jealousy between Rachel and Leah (e.g., Gen 29:34), David experiences his greatest crisis because of Bathsheba (2 Sam 11–12), and Solomon is criticized for his harem because "his wives had turned his heart away to other gods" (1 Kgs 11:4). In all these cases, the reader is invited to limit or abolish polygamy. The same applies to slavery in the New Testament. Although Paul regulates slavery in his letter to the Christians in Colossae without prohibiting it (Col 3:22–25), he concludes with a countercultural exhortation to slaveholders: "Masters, treat your slaves justly and fairly, knowing that you also have a Master in heaven." Similarly, in Eph 6:5–9, the ideal is emphasized, namely that slaveholders do not have a privileged relationship with God because all people are created equal. Additionally, when Paul writes to the Christian slaveholder Philemon, he encourages him to receive his slave Onesimus "no longer as a slave, but more than a slave, as a beloved brother. Especially to me, but how much more to you, both in the flesh and in the Lord!" (Phlm 16 NRSV). When these instructions on the second tier are viewed in light of the foundational narrative on the first tier, it becomes clear that man was not created to have multiple wives, that no human being was created to be owned by another human being, and that these instructions encourage small steps towards the ideal. As Lenski notes in his commentary on Eph 6:5, "Christ and the apostles did not denounce slavery and call for its immediate abolition. Christianity followed a deeper, more thorough method, [sic] it undermined slavery with the spirit of Christianity by destroying it from within."[34] Or, as Douglas Moo notes in a more recent commentary on Phlm 16, although Onesimus will technically remain and continue to be Philemon's slave, Paul's point is that "your [i.e., Philemon's] relationship with Onesimus will no longer be dictated by your legal relationship (master-slave) but by your spiritual relationship (brothers)."[35] This implies such a thorough transformation of power dynamics that, as Miroslav Volf puts it, "slavery has been abolished even if its outer institutional shell remains as an oppressive reality."[36]

The discussion about the Bible's relationship to slavery is, of course, more complicated than that, as "slavery" in the ancient Middle East and in antiquity encompasses a range of practices, from the "transatlantic" type that we associate with the exploitation of slaves from Africa by colonial powers to labor conditions that resemble what we would today label

---

34. Lenski, *Interpretation*, 652.
35. Moo, *Letters*, 422.
36. Volf, *Public Faith*, 92.

as "debt slavery" or even the looser concept of "wage slavery." Therefore, it is not given that the ideal necessitates the abolition of all forms of "slavery," but rather that the relevance of the foundational narrative for deriving a work ethic primarily concerns the fundamental theological equality inherent in creation, which should characterize both parties in the employment relationship and undoubtedly disqualifies several forms of slavery, but not necessarily all forms at all times and places.

Gender Issues

The same tension between the ideal and reality is what Jesus refers to when he addresses the divorce regulation in Deut 24:1–4, telling the Pharisees, "Because of your hardness of heart Moses allowed you to divorce your wives, but from the beginning it was not so. And I say to you: whoever divorces his wife, except for sexual immorality, and marries another, commits adultery." (Matt 19:8–9). Jesus upholds the ideal by referring to the creation order in the preceding verses 4–6: "Have you not read that he who created them from the beginning made them male and female, and said, 'Therefore a man shall leave his father and his mother and hold fast to his wife, and the two shall become one flesh?' So, they are no longer two but one flesh. What therefore God has joined together, let not man separate." Jesus upholds the ideal in creation as primary while acknowledging that, in the fallen world, divorce due to "hardness of heart" may be a condition that needs regulation to minimize harm. Legal and casuistic approaches may be necessary in this case, but Jesus's indirect response to their legal-casuistic question highlights the need for a different starting point. First, the ideal must be described. When Jesus then adds his "I tell you"—"Anyone who divorces his wife, except for sexual immorality, and marries another woman commits adultery"—and earlier in the Gospel of Matthew says, "But I say to you that everyone who divorces his wife, except on the ground of sexual immorality, makes her commit adultery, and whoever marries a divorced woman commits adultery" (Matt 5:32), it is reasonable to understand the permission of divorce in the Mosaic law as something that, in a New Testament and Christian context, belongs to the third plane, namely civil law. Similarly, Paul's guidance to the Corinthian Christians that if "the unbelieving spouse separates, let it be so. In such cases, the brother or sister is not bound. God has called you to peace" (1 Cor 7:14) pertains to someone who is not part of the church. In contrast, Jesus's statement, "I tell you," stands out. Here, the foundational narrative on the first tier is made directly or "absolutely" applicable as the basis for guidance, aligning the ethical standard of God's people with the ideal. Sexual immorality inherently breaks the union that marriage represents, effectively ending the marriage when one of the parties commits it. However, only sexual immorality, by definition, breaks the union. In cases of other conflicts, the marriage stays intact, allowing Paul to guide the Corinthian Christians that "to the married, I give this charge (not I, but the Lord): the wife should not separate from her husband (but if she does, she should remain unmarried or else be reconciled to her husband)—and the husband should not divorce his wife" (1 Cor 7:10–11).

The crucial point regarding the derivation of ethical guidance concerning gender identity and sexuality from the foundational narrative is whether the casuistic approach should be applied not only in the third tier but in the second tier—within the church community. Should the same casuistic approach be applied to the church community, as in the examples where the ideal of the foundational narrative is upheld, and the guidance considers the postlapsarian, nonideal reality to point towards the ideal? When Paul applies casuistic-oriented guidance regarding slavery to the communities in Colossae and Ephesus, should something similar not also be possible in regulating the diverse reality where people practice their homosexuality in lifelong, committed relationships so that these groups can feel just as at home in the church as the slaves did in Paul's time?

It is striking that very similar guidance is formulated in contexts that span both temporally and culturally from ancient Near Eastern and theocratic Israel in the late second millennium BCE to the early church in a Greco-Roman context in the early first millennium CE. While the New Testament provides casuistic guidance regarding slavery, it exclusively emphasizes the ideal and does not provide similar casuistic guidance regarding gender identity and homosexual practice. Despite navigating different contexts in the early churches, Paul's guidance regarding homosexual practice to the Christian communities in Rome and Corinth is identical to the instructions of the Old Testament for ancient Israel. However, the question is whether Paul's guidance regarding homosexual practice should be considered exhaustive from the second tier in Winther-Nielsen's model based on the ideal in the foundational narrative on the first tier. Alternatively, might Paul's casuistic guidance on slavery permit a similar casuistry on homosexual practice? In other words, just because the New Testament authors do not engage in casuistic discussions about homosexual practices in the church does not necessarily mean that they could not have done so if needed. It appears there are two possible trajectories (and hybrids) to consider.

The first one would argue that the New Testament guidance is not exhaustive and that the church community, therefore, can address homosexual practices in the same casuistic way as the communities in Colossae and Corinth were encouraged to address slavery. In practice, this would mean that the church follows the ideal wherever possible, for example, by not offering marriage or blessings to same-sex couples and by highlighting the ideal in preaching and teaching, while at the same time acknowledging practicing homosexuals who, for example, have been civilly married and who live in such committed, registered partnerships without subjecting them to church discipline but still reminding them of the ideal, binary understanding of gender with the aim that they may eventually choose a sexually abstinent life—together or individually. The same applies to practicing homosexuals who were married before their conversion—somewhat similar to the ethical practice in, for example, an African context, where a man who has received forgiveness for marrying multiple wives is not asked to separate from the "surplus" wives because it would be a greater evil to ask him to separate from them than to discuss how the extended family can best handle the situation together. Only in the next generation is the monogamous marriage enforced. In many ways, this is the approach advocated by Mikael Wandt Laursen in his book *Tro, kirke og homoseksualitet* [*Faith, Church, and Homosexuality*] where he writes, for example, about the Baptist Church in Denmark: "Today it is possible, as a divorced person, to be active in service in all areas of the church, even though the church clearly confesses that marriage lasts 'until death do us part.' Churches live with solutions that reflect our fallen world. It is a journey from which we can draw inspiration regarding the service of LGBT+ individuals in the church."[37]

The second trajectory would maintain that even though the church in other matters—including the question of slavery—does not consistently or idealistically confront practices and systems that are contrary to the ideal in the foundational narrative, this does not apply to issues related to the binary understanding of gender, including the question of gender identity and homosexual practice. The reason for this difference

---

37. Wandt, *Tro, Kirke Og Homoseksualitet*, 140.

in ethical guidance could be that when it comes to ethical questions related to the binary understanding of gender, we are so close to the heart of what it means to be created in God's image that we are dealing with a boundary that must not be crossed in the church. Members should be subjected to church discipline if they do so. Human sexuality is so intimately connected to who we are created to be that it cannot be held at arm's length and separated from a person's innermost and *created* identity. Applying the three-tier model—with the suggested improvements—to this issue, this trajectory seems to offer the best reading of the biblical texts, since it considers the importance of the creational embeddedness of the various guidance in guarding a timeless, absolute, and *blessed* practice of gender identity and sexuality. And though Pless focuses on homosexual practice, the same conclusion must be drawn from the embeddedness of guidance in the creational order on other issues related to gender identity:

> Homosexuality is a disordering of God's design expressed in Gen 1–2. Whatever else may be said about the causes of homosexuality, it cannot be attributed to God. From the standpoint of theological ethics, it is irrelevant whether homosexuality is a result of a genetic disorder, environment or personal choice as the Scriptures teach us that all of creation after the fall is subject to bondage, disorder, and death. Robert Jenson is on target here: "We need not here resolve the question of whether there are such things as 'sensual orientations' and if so how they are acquired. What must anyway be clear is that 'homosexuality,' if it exists and whatever it is, cannot be attributed to creation; those who practice forms of homoerotic sensuality and attribute this to 'homosexuality' cannot refer to the characteristic as 'the way God created me,' if 'create' has anything like its biblical sense. No more in this context than in any other do we discover God's creative intent by examining the empirical situation; as we have seen, I may indeed have to *blame* God for the empirically present in me that contradicts his known intent, but this is an occasion for unbelief, not a believer's justification of the evil."[38]

Precisely because gender identity and sexual orientation are related to a person's innermost being, the call to resist the desire and inclination that runs contrary to "foundational idealism" must be extended with an understanding of how deeply the knife cuts into personal identity and with an awareness that much forgiveness may be needed in the process.

38. Pless, "Use and Misuse," 54.

At the same time, the ideal of the foundational narrative must also serve as a bulwark against problematic culturally or socially conditioned gender stereotypes. This applies to stereotypes that can never be accepted as an expression of human *imago Dei* and to stereotypes that may be fruitful expressions of the biblical ideal in certain cultures and social contexts but not in others. What it meant for Solomon to "be strong and show yourself a man" (1 Kgs 2:2) may not necessarily mean the same in our cultural or social contexts as in others. It is, therefore, up to us to unfold what the broader framework in the Bible's description of the gender differentiation of the *imago Dei* entails.

Seventy-Seven Times

We must be careful not to rank sins and stigmatize certain individuals or groups due to specific sins that we consider particularly serious. We must remind ourselves of what Jesus says: "Therefore whoever relaxes one of the least of these commandments and teaches others to do the same will be called least in the kingdom of heaven, but whoever does them and teaches them will be called great in the kingdom of heaven" (Matt 5:19). At the same time, we still need to distinguish how we do not live according to how God created us, particularly in terms of gender identity and sexual orientation. Living in a heterosexual relationship aligns with God's creation order. In a homosexual relationship, this is not the case. Here, God allows us to discern and call one situation good and another sinful. This does not change the fact that even we who live in a heterosexual relationship fall short in many other areas and, therefore, cannot claim to be free from sin. However, when it comes to the fundamental creation order, we are allowed to uphold the heterosexual relationship as being in accordance with God's creation order.

Regardless of whether a practicing homosexual transgresses a more fundamental boundary in God's creation, there is no difference in forgiveness. While I do not cross that boundary but live in a heterosexual relationship, I still sin in other areas and need the same forgiveness as the practicing homosexual. I know there is a difference in how we *experience* sin. There is a difference between refraining from stealing or gossiping and refraining from practicing one's homosexual orientation. We should not downplay this! And I believe it is such deeply rooted tendencies that Jesus has in mind when he says, "So watch yourselves! If your brother or sister sins against you, rebuke them; and if they repent, forgive them. Even if they sin against you seven times in a day and seven times come back to you saying, 'I repent,' you must forgive them" (Luke 17:3–4 NIV). And, replying to Peter, who attempted to hold Jesus to a literal interpretation of forgiving "seven times," Jesus emphasized the boundless nature of forgiveness. He said, "I tell you, not seven times, but seventy-seven times" (Matt 18:22 NIV). Jesus's point was not to limit forgiveness to a specific number but to illustrate that forgiveness should be limitless, reflecting the boundless grace and mercy that God extends to us. In essence, Jesus was teaching that human limitations do not confine our call to forgive but should mirror the infinite forgiveness that God offers. This perspective challenges us to move beyond rigid interpretations and embrace a more profound understanding of grace and reconciliation. So, as we navigate the complexities of human fallibility and moral discernment, let us remember that our focus should be on embodying the same mercy and forgiveness that God shows us without succumbing to a judgmental or exclusionary mindset. As Matt Lee Anderson reminds us: "This is the paradox of the body: The body is a temple, but the temple is in ruins. The incarnation of Jesus affirms the body's original goodness. The death of Jesus reminds us of the need for redemption. And the resurrection of Jesus gives us hope for its restoration."[39]

---

39. Anderson, *Earthen Vessels*, 31.

Bibliography

Allberry, Sam. *What God Has to Say about Our Bodies: How the Gospel Is Good News for Our Physical Selves*. Wheaton, IL: Crossway, 2021.

Allison, Gregg R. "Four Theses Concerning Human Embodiment." *The Southern Baptist Journal of Theology* 23.2 (2019) 157–80.

Anagnostou-Laoutides, Eva, and Michael B. Charles. "Herodotus on Sacred Marriage and Sacred Prostitution at Babylon." *Kernos. Revue Internationale et Pluridisciplinaire de Religion Grecque Antique* 31 (2018) 9–37.

Anderson, Matthew Lee. *Earthen Vessels: Why Our Bodies Matter to Our Faith*. Minneapolis: Bethany House, 2011.

Andresen, Steffen Ringgaard, and Ulla Salicath. "Forfejlet kætteranklage. Velsignelse er delagtiggørelse i kristusvirkelighed." *Kristeligt Dagblad*, June 23, 2010.

———. "Når Det Gamle Testamente skygger for Det Nye." *Kristeligt Dagblad*, June 17, 2010.

———. "Nej til splittelsens retorik. Vi må forstå os selv i lyset af kristusvirkeligheden." *Kristeligt Dagblad*, 17 June 2010.

Anselm. *The Prayers and Meditations of St. Anselm with the Proslogion*. Translated by Benedicta Ward. Rev. ed. Harmondsworth: Penguin Classics, 1973.

Aquinas, Thomas. *Summa Theologica*. Vols. 1, 4. New York: Cosimo, 2013.

———. *Summa Theologica. Volume IV. Part III. First Section*. New York: Cosimo, 2013.

———. *Light of Faith: The Compendium of Theology*. Translated by Cyril Vollert. Manchester, NH: Sophia Institute, 1993.

Assante, Julia A. "Bad Girls and Kinky Boys?: The Modern Prostituting of Ishtar, Her Clergy and Her Cults." In *Tempelprostitution Im Altertum: Fakten Und Fiktion*, edited by Tanja Scheer and Martin Lindner, 23–54. Berlin: Verlag Antike, 2009.

———. "From Whores to Hierodules: The Historiographic Invention of Mesopotamian Female Sex Professionals." In *Ancient Art and Its Historiography*, edited by Alice A. Donohue and Mark D. Fullerton, 13–47. Cambridge: Cambridge University Press, 2003.

———. "The Erotic Reliefs of Ancient Mesopotamia." PhD diss., Columbia University, 2000.

———. "The Kar.Kid/Harimtu, Prostitute or Single Woman: A Reconsideration of the Evidence." *Ugarit-Forschungen* 30 (1998) 5–96.

———. *The Last Frontier: Exploring the Afterlife and Transforming Our Fear of Death*. Novato, CA: New World Library, 2012.

BIBLIOGRAPHY

Athenagoras. *A Plea for the Christians*. Translated by B. P. Pratten. In *Ante-Nicene Fathers* 2, edited by Alexander Roberts et al. Buffalo, NY: Christian Literature, 1885. Revised and edited for New Advent by Kevin Knight. http://www.newadvent.org/fathers/0205.htm.

Augustine. *Augustins Bekendelser*. Translated by Torben Damsholt. København: Sankt Ansgars Forlag, 1998.

———. *The Literal Meaning of Genesis*. Translated by John Hammond Taylor. Ancient Christian Writers 2. Mahwah, NJ: Paulist, 1982.

Averbeck, Richard E. "The Egyptian Sojourn and Deliverance from Slavery in the Framing and Shaping of the Mosaic Law." In *"Did I Not Bring Israel Out of Egypt?": Biblical, Archaeological, and Egyptological Perspectives on the Exodus Narratives*, edited by James K. Hoffmeier et al., 143–75. Winona Lake, IN: Eisenbrauns, 2016.

———. *The Old Testament Law for the Life of the Church: Reading the Torah in the Light of Christ*. Downers Grove, IL: IVP Academic, 2022.

Bahrani, Zainab. *Women of Babylon: Gender and Representation in Mesopotamia*. London: Routledge, 2013.

Balentine, Samuel. *Leviticus*. Interpretation. Louisville: Westminster John Knox, 2002.

Barker, Margaret. "Atonement: The Rite of Healing." *Scottish Journal of Theology* 49.1 (1996) 1–20.

———. *Great High Priest: The Temple Roots of Christian Liturgy*. London: T & T Clark, 2003.

Barmash, Pamela. "Biblical and Ancient Near Eastern Law." *Religion Compass* 12 (2018) e12262.

———. *The Laws of Hammurabi: At the Confluence of Royal and Scribal Traditions*. Oxford: Oxford University Press, 2020.

Barnes, Cory Ryan. "The Curious Setting of Eden: The Ethical Implications of the Narrative Setting of Genesis 2–3." *Christus Cultura: The Journal of Christianity in the Social Sciences* 2.1 (2020) 5–14.

Barth, Karl. *Church Dogmatics* 3.1. Translated by T. F. Torrance. Edinburgh: T & T Clark, 1958.

Bartor, Assnat. "Reading Biblical Law as Narrative." *Prooftexts* 32.3 (2012) 292–311.

———. *Reading Law as Narrative: A Study in the Casuistic Laws of the Pentateuch*. Atlanta: Society of Biblical Literature, 2010.

Bavinck, Herman. *God and Creation*. Vol. 2 of *Reformed Dogmatics*. Translated by John Vriend. Edited by John Bolt. Grand Rapids: Baker Academic, 2004.

Bavinck, Herman, and James Eglinton. *The Christian Family*. Translated by Nelson D. Kloosterman. Grand Rapids: Christian's Library, 2012.

Beauvoir, Simone de. *L'expérience Vécue*. Vol. 2 of *Le Deuxième Sexe*. Paris: Gallimard, 1949.

———. *The Second Sex*. Translated by Constance Borde and Sheila Malovany-Chevallier. New York: Vintage, 2011.

Beckman, Gary. "Ištar of Nineveh Reconsidered." *Journal of Cuneiform Studies* 50 (1998) 1–10.

Beilby, James K. *Understanding Transgender Identities: Four Views*. Grand Rapids: Baker Academic, 2019.

Bergland, Kenneth. "Memorized Covenantal Instruction and Legal Reuse in Torah." In *Exploring the Composition of the Pentateuch*, edited by L. S. Baker Jr. et al., 95–112. Bulletin for Biblical Research Supplement 27. University Park, PA: Eisenbrauns, 2020.

BIBLIOGRAPHY

Bergsma, John Sietze, and Scott Walker Hahn. "Noah's Nakedness and the Curse on Canaan." *Journal of Biblical Literature* 124.1 (2005) 25–40.

Berman, Joshua A. *Inconsistency in the Torah: Ancient Literary Convention and the Limits of Source Criticism*. 1st ed. New York: Oxford University Press, 2017.

Bible Gateway. "Testaments of the Twelve Patriarchs." Encyclopedia of the Bible, October 10, 2022. https://www.biblegateway.com/resources/encyclopedia-of-the-bible/Testaments-Twelve-Patriarchs.

Bigwood, Carol. "Renaturalizing the Body (With the Help of Merleau-Ponty)." *Hypatia* 6.3 (1991) 54–73.

Bird, Phyllis A. *Faith, Feminism, and the Forum of Scripture: Essays on Biblical Theology and Hermeneutics*. Eugene, OR: Cascade, 2015.

———. "Of Whores and Hounds: A New Interpretation of the Subject of Deuteronomy 23:19." *Vetus Testamentum* 65.3 (2015) 352–64. https://doi.org/10.1163/15685330-2301200.

Bird, Phyllis A., and Anna Glenn. *Harlot or Holy Woman?: A Study of Hebrew Qedešah*. University Park, PA: Eisenbrauns, 2019.

Bolich, G. G. *Crossdressing in Context*. Transgender & Religion 4. Raleigh, NC: Psyche's, 2008.

Bonhoeffer, Dietrich. *Letters and Papers from Prison*. Translated by Reginald H. Fuller. Edited by Eberhard Bethge. New York: Touchstone, 1997.

Boswell, John. *Christianity, Social Tolerance, and Homosexuality: Gay People in Western Europe from the Beginning of the Christian Era to the Fourteenth Century*. 1st ed. Chicago: University of Chicago Press, 1981.

Boyce, Natalie M., et al. "Estimates of the Prevalence of Klinefelter Syndrome." *Journal of the American Medical Association* 19 (2020) 1941–42.

Brannan, Rick, ed. *Lexham Research Lexicon of the Greek New Testament*. Bellingham, WA: Lexham, 2020.

Brettler, Marc. "Happy Is the Man Who Fills His Quiver with Them (Ps 127:5) Constructions of Masculinities in the Psalms." In *Being a Man: Negotiating Ancient Constructs of Masculinity*, edited by Ilona Zsolnay, 198–220. London: Routledge, 2016.

———. "Unresolved and Unresolvable Problems in Interpreting the Song." In *Scrolls of Love: Reading Ruth and the Song of Songs*, edited by Peter S. Hawkins and Lesleigh Cushing Stahlberg, 185–98. New York: Fordham University Press, 2006.

Brown, Francis, et al. *Enhanced Brown-Driver-Briggs Hebrew and English Lexicon*. Logos Research ed. Oxford: Clarendon, 1977.

Brown, William P. *The Ethos of the Cosmos: The Genesis of Moral Imagination in the Bible*. Grand Rapids: Eerdmans, 1999.

Brownson, James V. *Bible, Gender, Sexuality: Reframing the Church's Debate on Same-Sex Relationships*. Grand Rapids: Eerdmans, 2013.

Buber, Martin. *Between Man and Man*. London: Routledge, 2003.

———. *On Zion: The History of an Idea*. Syracuse, NY: Syracuse University Press, 1997.

Budin, Stephanie Lynn. *Freewomen, Patriarchal Authority, and the Accusation of Prostitution*. London: Routledge, 2021.

———. *Gender in the Ancient Near East*. London: Routledge, 2023.

———. *The Myth of Sacred Prostitution in Antiquity*. Cambridge: Cambridge University Press, 2009.

Budziszewski, J. *On the Meaning of Sex*. New York: Simon and Schuster, 2023.

BIBLIOGRAPHY

Buitenwerf, Rieuwerd. *Book III of the Sibylline Oracles and Its Social Setting: With an Introduction, Translation, and Commentary*. Leiden: Brill, 2021.

Burns, John Barclay. "Devotee or Deviate: The 'Dog' (Keleb) in Ancient Israel as a Symbol of Male Passivity and Perversion." *Journal of Religion & Society* 2 (2000) 1–10.

Burnside, Jonathan. *God, Justice, and Society: Aspects of Law and Legality in the Bible*. 1st ed. Oxford: Oxford University Press, 2010.

Butler, Judith. *Gender Trouble: Feminism and the Subversion of Identity*. London: Routledge, 1990.

———. "Performative Acts and Gender Constitution: An Essay in Phenomenology and Feminist Theory." *Theatre Journal* 40.4 (1988) 519–31.

———. *Undoing Gender*. London: Routledge, 2004.

Byrd, Aimee. *The Sexual Reformation: Restoring the Dignity and Personhood of Man and Woman*. Grand Rapids: Zondervan, 2022.

Cagni, Luigi. *The Poem of Erra*. Malibu, CA: Undena, 1977.

Callender, Dexter E. *Adam in Myth and History: Ancient Israelite Perspectives on the Primal Human*. Harvard Semitic Studies 48. Winona Lake, IN: Eisenbrauns, 2000.

Cameron, Ron, ed. *The Other Gospels: Non-Canonical Gospel Texts*. 1st ed. Philadelphia: Westminster John Knox, 1982.

Cantarella, Eva. *Bisexuality in the Ancient World*. Translated by Cormac O. Cuilleanain. 2nd ed. New Haven, CT: Yale University Press, 2002.

Carr, David M. *Holy Resilience: The Bible's Traumatic Origins*. New Haven, CT: Yale University Press, 2014.

Censor Librorum. "Church Defies Cardinal Newman's Dying Wish." *Nihil Obstat* (blog), July 24, 2008. https://nihilobstat.info/2008/07/24/church-defies-cardinal-newmans-dying-wish/.

Charlesworth, James H., ed. *The Old Testament Pseudepigrapha*. 1st ed. The Old Testament Pseudepigrapha 1. Garden City, NY: Doubleday, 1983.

———, ed. *The Old Testament Pseudepigrapha: Expansions of the "Old Testament" and Legends, Wisdom and Philosophical Literature, Prayers, Psalms and Odes, Fragments of Lost Judeo-Hellenistic Works*. The Old Testament Pseudepigrapha 2. Garden City, NY: Doubleday, 1985.

Chavad. "The Complete Jewish Bible with Rashi Commentary." *Chavad.org*, 2024. https://www.chabad.org/library/bible_cdo/aid/9986/jewish/Chapter-22.htm.

Chesterton, G. K. *Poems*. 1st ed. London: Burns and Oates, 1915.

Chisholm, Robert B. "Male and Female in the Genesis Creation Accounts: A Mission, an Ideal, and a Tragic Loss." In *Sanctified Sexuality: Valuing Sex in an Oversexed World*, edited by Sandra L. Glahn and C. Gary Barnes, 65–75. Grand Rapids: Kregel, 2020.

Cohick, Lynn. *Women in the World of the Earliest Christians: Illuminating Ancient Ways of Life*. Grand Rapids: Baker Academic, 2009.

Collins, Francis. *The Language of God: A Scientist Presents Evidence for Belief*. New York: Simon and Schuster, 2006.

Collins, John J. *What Are Biblical Values?: What the Bible Says on Key Ethical Issues*. New Haven, CT: Yale University Press, 2019.

Cooper, Alan M. "Canaanite Religion: An Overview." *Encyclopedia.com*, 1987. https://www.encyclopedia.com/environment/encyclopedias-almanacs-transcripts-and-maps/canaanite-religion-overview.

BIBLIOGRAPHY

Cornwall, Susannah. *Sex and Uncertainty in the Body of Christ: Intersex Conditions and Christian Theology.* London: Routledge, 2016.

Cortez, Marc. *ReSourcing Theological Anthropology: A Constructive Account of Humanity in the Light of Christ.* Grand Rapids: Zondervan Academic, 2018.

Countryman, William. *Dirt, Greed, and Sex: Sexual Ethics in the New Testament and Their Implications for Today.* London: SCM, 2013.

Cover, Robert. "The Supreme Court, 1982 Term—Foreword: Nomos and Narrative." *Harvard Law Review* 97.4 (1983) 4–68.

Cranfield, C. E. B. *The Epistle to the Romans I.* Edinburgh: T & T Clark, 1975.

Crawford, Cory D. "Light and Space in Genesis 1." *Vetus Testamentum* 68.4 (2018) 556–80.

Crisp, Oliver D. "Pulling Traducianism out of the Shedd." *Ars Disputandi* 6.1 (2006) 265–87. https://doi.org/10.1080/15665399.2006.10819933.

Cuneiform Digital Library Initiative. "CDLI Literary 000771, Ex. 039 Artifact Entry." CDLI, 2003. https://cdli.mpiwg-berlin.mpg.de/artifacts/223416.

Dalley, Stephanie. *Myths from Mesopotamia: Creation, the Flood, Gilgamesh, and Others.* Oxford: Oxford University Press, 1989.

Dansk Regnbueråd. "12 opgør med wokeness & kønsaktivisme i Danmark." *Dansk Regnbueråd*, June 7, 2022. http://danskregnbueraad.dk/12-opgoer-med-wokeness-koensaktivisme-i-danmark/.

———. "Pressemeddelelse." *Dansk Regnbueråd*, June 9, 2022. https://danskregnbueraad.dk/presse-meddelelse/.

Dashu, Max. "Goddess Temples in Western Asia I—Veleda." *Veleda* (blog). http://www.sourcememory.net/veleda/?p=229. Accessed on September 1, 2023.

Day, John. "Does the Old Testament Refer to Sacred Prostitution and Did It Actually Exist in Ancient Israel?" In *Biblical and Near Eastern Essays: Studies in Honour of Kevin J. Cathcart*, edited by David J. A. Clines and Philip R. Davies, 2–21. Journal for the Study of the Old Testament Supplement Series 375. London: T & T Clark, 2004.

DeBernardo, Francis. "The Question Is Not 'Was Cardinal John Henry Newman Gay?' But 'Was He Straight?'" *New Ways Ministry* (blog), October 9, 2021. https://www.newwaysministry.org/2021/10/09/the-question-is-not-was-cardinal-john-henry-newman-gay-but-was-he-straight/.

———. "Was Cardinal John Henry Newman Gay?: A Talk for University College Dublin's LGBTI History Month Event: 'Cardinal John Henry Newman: Saint; Cardinal; Egalitarian; Gay?'" *New Ways Ministry* (blog), February 26, 2021. https://www.newwaysministry.org/newman/.

DeFranza, Megan K. "Good News for Gender Minorities." In *Understanding Transgender Identities: Four Views*, edited by James K. Beilby and Paul Rhodes Eddy, 147–78. Grand Rapids: Baker Academic, 2019.

Den Katolske Kirke. "Den Katolske Kirkes Katekismus." *Den Katolske Kirke i Danmark*, 2006. http://exist-db.katolsk.dk:18080/exist/apps/cathdb/cathdb.xql?func=lookupid&lookupid=CCC.PART0003.SEC0002.CHAP0002.ART0003&work=CCC.

DeYoung, James B. *Homosexuality.* Grand Rapids: Kregel Academic, 2000.

DeYoung, Kevin. "How Are Men and Women Different?" 9Marks, November 12, 2019. https://www.9marks.org/article/how-are-men-and-women-different/.

———. *What Does the Bible Really Teach about Homosexuality?* Wheaton, IL: Crossway, 2015.

BIBLIOGRAPHY

Diggory, Terrence. "Reading the Bible in the Same-Sex Marriage Debate." *Covenant Network of Presbyterians*, January 20, 2014. https://covnetpres.org/2014/01/20/reading-bible-sex-marriage-debate/.

do Vale, Fellipe M. *Gender as Love: A Theological Account of Human Identity, Embodied Desire, and Our Social Worlds*. Grand Rapids: Baker Academic, 2023.

Donner, H., and W. Röllig. *Kanaanäische und aramäische Inschriften: Texte, Band 2*. Wiesbaden: Harrassowitz, 1973.

Douglas, Mary. *Leviticus as Literature*. Oxford: Oxford University Press, 1999.

———. *Natural Symbols: Explorations in Cosmology*. New York: Pantheon, 1982.

———. *Purity and Danger: An Analysis of Concepts of Pollution and Taboo*. London: Routledge and Kegan Paul, 1966.

———. "Taboo." In *Magic, Witchcraft, and Religion: An Anthropological Study of the Supernatural*, edited by Arthur C Lehmann and James E. Myers, 68–72. New York: McGraw Hill, 2001.

Dreifus, Claudia. "A Conversation with Anne Fausto-Sterling; Exploring What Makes Us Male or Female." *New York Times*, January 2, 2001.

Eddy, Paul Rhodes, and James K. Beilby. "Understanding Transgender Experiences and Identities: An Introduction." In *Understanding Transgender Identities: Four Views*, edited by James K. Beilby and Paul Rhodes Eddy, 1–54. Grand Rapids: Baker Academic, 2019.

Ehalt, Kelsie. "Assumptions About the Assinnu: Gender, Sex, and Sexuality in Ancient Texts and Modern Scholarship." MA thesis, Brandeis University, 2021.

Elmelund, Rasmus. "Er kirkebryllup virkelig værd at kæmpe for?" *Information*, October 9, 2011. https://www.information.dk/indland/2011/10/kirkebryllup-virkelig-vaerd-kaempe.

Elshtain, Jean Bethke. *Public Man, Private Woman: Women in Social and Political Thought*. 2nd ed. Princeton: Princeton University Press, 1993.

Epictetus. *Discourses*. In *The Works of Epictetus: His Discourses, in Four Books, the Enchiridion, and Fragments*, translated by Thomas Wentworth Higginson. New York: Thomas Nelson and Sons, 1890.

Etxabe, Julen. "The Legal Universe After Robert Cover." *Law and Humanities* 4.1 (2010) 115–47.

Exum, J. Cheryl. *Plotted, Shot, and Painted: Cultural Representations of Biblical Women*. New York: Bloomsbury, 1996.

———. *Song of Songs: A Commentary*. Louisville: Westminster John Knox Press, 2005.

Fantin, Joseph D. "Sexualities in the First-Century World: A Survey of Relevant Topics." In *Sanctified Sexuality: Valuing Sex in an Oversexed World*, edited by Sandra L. Glahn and C. Gary Barnes, 41–62. Grand Rapids: Kregel, 2020.

Farris, Joshua R. *The Creation of Self: A Case for the Soul*. Lanham, MD: Iff Books, 2023.

———. "Maybe the Idea of the Soul Isn't Crazy After All." *American Mind*, 2023. https://americanmind.org/salvo/maybe-the-idea-of-the-soul-isnt-crazy-after-all/.

———. "The Soul and Science: Challenging the 'Consensus.'" The City. Houston Christian University, March 22, 2019. https://hc.edu/news-and-events/2019/03/22/the-soul-and-science-challenging-the-consensus.

———. *The Soul of Theological Anthropology: A Cartesian Exploration*. London: Routledge, 2017.

Farris, Joshua R., and Marc Cortez. *An Introduction to Theological Anthropology: Humans, Both Creaturely and Divine*. Grand Rapids: Baker Academic, 2020.

Farris, Joshua R., and Charles Taliaferro, eds. *The Ashgate Research Companion to Theological Anthropology*. London: Routledge, 2015.
Favale, Abigail. *The Genesis of Gender: A Christian Theory*. San Francisco: Ignatius, 2022.
Favale, Abigail Rine. *Into the Deep: An Unlikely Catholic Conversion*. Eugene, OR: Cascade, 2018.
Finlan, Stephen. *The Background and Contents of Paul's Cultic Atonement Metaphors*. Leiden: Brill, 2004.
Fischer, Loren R. "Creation at Ugarit and in the Old Testament." *Vetus Testamentum* 15 (1965) 313–24.
Foster, Benjamin R. *Before the Muses: An Anthology of Akkadian Literature*. 3rd ed. Bethesda, MD: CDL, 2005.
———. *The Age of Agade: Inventing Empire in Ancient Mesopotamia*. 1st ed. London: Routledge, 2015.
Foucault, Michel. *The History of Sexuality*. Translated by Robert Hurley. 3 vols. New York: Random House, 1978.
Freud, Sigmund. *Jenseits des Lustprinzips*. Ditzingen: Reclam, 2013.
Frisch, Morten, et al. "Sex in Denmark: Key Findings from Project SEXUS 2017–2018." Statens Serum Institute and Aalborg University, 2019. https://files.projektsexus.dk/2019-10-26_SEXUS-rapport_2017-2018.pdf.
Furnish, Victor Paul. *The Moral Teaching of Paul: Selected Issues*. 3rd ed. Nashville: Abingdon, 2010.
Gagnon, Robert A. J. *The Bible and Homosexual Practice: Texts and Hermeneutics*. Nashville: Abingdon, 2001.
Garr, Randall. *In His Own Image and Likeness: Humanity, Divinity, and Monotheism*. Leiden: Brill, 2003.
Gathercole, Simon J. "Torah, Life, and Salvation: Leviticus 18:5 in Early Judaism and the New Testament." In *From Prophecy to Testament: The Function of the Old Testament in the New*, edited by Craig A. Evans. Peabody, MA: Hendrickson, 2004.
Gentry, Peter J., and Stephen J. Wellum. *Kingdom through Covenant: A Biblical-Theological Understanding of the Covenants*. 2nd ed. Wheaton, IL: Crossway, 2018.
George, A. R. *The Babylonian Gilgamesh Epic: Introduction, Critical Edition and Cuneiform Texts*. Vol. 1. Oxford: Oxford University Press, 2003.
Gerle, Elisabeth. *Passionate Embrace: Luther on Love, Body, and Sensual Presence*. Eugene, OR: Cascade, 2017.
Giffney, Noreen. "Introduction: The 'q' Word." In *The Ashgate Research Companion to Queer Theory*, edited by Noreen Giffney and Michael O'Rourke. Burlington, VT: Ashgate, 2009.
Giversen, Søren. *Thomasevangeliet*. København: Gyldendal, 1990.
Glahn, Sandra L. "Reproduction, Contraception, and Infertility." In *Sanctified Sexuality: Valuing Sex in an Oversexed World*, edited by Sandra L. Glahn and C. Gary Barnes, 198–209. Grand Rapids: Kregel, 2020.
Glinister, Fay. "The Rapino Bronze, the Touta Marouca, and Sacred Prostitution in Early Central Italy." *Bulletin of the Institute of Classical Studies. Supplement* (2000) 18–38.
Glintborg, Dorte, et al. "Socioeconomic Status in Danish Transgender Persons: A Nationwide Register-Based Cohort Study." *Endocrine Connections* 10.9 (2021) 1155–66.

Gnuse, Robert K. "Seven Gay Texts: Biblical Passages Used to Condemn Homosexuality." *Biblical Theology Bulletin* 45.2 (2015) 68–87.
Goodfriend, Elaine Adler. "Could Keleb in Deuteronomy 23:19 Actually Refer to a Canine?" In *Pomegranates and Golden Bells: Studies in Biblical, Jewish, and Near Eastern Ritual, Law, and Literature in Honor of Jacob Milgrom*, edited by Jacob Milgrom, 381–97. Winona Lake, IN: Eisenbrauns, 1995.
Gordon, Cyrus H. *Ugaritic Textbook*. Rome: Pontifical Biblical Institute, 1965.
Gordon, Cyrus H., and Gary Rendsburg. *The Bible and the Ancient Near East*. New York: Norton, 1997.
Gorman, H. Frank. *The Ideology of Ritual: Space, Time, and Status in the Priestly Theology*. Journal for the Study of the Old Testament Supplement 91. Sheffield: Sheffield Academic, 1990.
Gosnell, Peter W. *The Ethical Vision of the Bible: Learning Good from Knowing God*. Downers Grove, IL: IVP Academic, 2014.
Goss, Robert. *Jesus Acted Up: A Gay and Lesbian Manifesto*. San Fransisco: HarperSanFrancisco, 1993.
Greenberg, David F. *The Construction of Homosexuality*. Chicago: University of Chicago Press, 2008.
Greggs, Tom. "The Call to Focus on God: A Review of Webster's *God Without Measure*." *Modern Theology*, January 1, 2018, 657–63.
Gruber, Mayer I. "Hebrew Qedešah and Her Canaanite and Akkadian Cognates." *Ugarit-Forschungen* 18 (1986) 133–48.
Gudbergsen, Thomas. "Praktiskteologiske reflektioner med henblik på det erotiske og på parforholdet i lyset af udvalgte gammeltestamentlige tekster om seksualitet." *Teologisk Tidsskrift* 3 (2016) 228–47.
Guest, Deryn. *Beyond Feminist Biblical Studies*. Bible in the Modern World 47. Sheffield: Sheffield Phoenix, 2012.
Gustavsson, Stefan. *Nøgne uden Skam: Om den seksuelle revoluton og et revolutionært syn på sex*. Fredericia: Credo, 2022.
Hailes, Sam. "N. T. Wright Attacks 'Fashionable Fantasy' of Allowing Children to Choose Their Own Gender." *Premier Christianity*, April 8, 2017. https://www.premierchristianity.com/home/nt-wright-attacks-fashionable-fantasy-of-allowing-children-to-choose-their-own-gender/543.article.
Harper, G. Geoffrey. *"I Will Walk Among You": The Rhetorical Function of Allusion to Genesis 1–3 in the Book of Leviticus*. 1st ed. University Park, PA: Eisenbrauns, 2018.
Harris, R. L., et al., eds. *Theological Wordbook of the Old Testament*. Electronic ed. Chicago: Moody, 1999.
Hartke, Austen. *Transforming: The Bible and the Lives of Transgender Christians*. Updated ed. Louisville: Westminster John Knox Press, 2023.
Hasker, William. "The Dialect of Soul and Body." In *Contemporary Dualism: A Defense*, edited by Andrea Lavazza and Howard Robinson, 215–29. New York: Routledge, 2014.
———. *The Emergent Self*. Ithaca, NY: Cornell University Press, 1999.
Hayes, Christine. "Purity and Impurity, Ritual." In *Encyclopedia Judaica*, 746–56, 2006. https://ia903008.us.archive.org/12/items/EncyclopediaJudaica_201905/Encyclopedia%20Judaica.pdf.

BIBLIOGRAPHY

Hays, Christopher B. and Richard B. Hays. *The Widening of God's Mercy: Sexuality Within the Biblical Story.* 1st ed. New Haven, CT: Yale University Press, 2024.

Heacock, Anthony. "Wrongly Framed?: The 'David and Jonathan Narrative' and the Writing of Biblical Homosexuality [Sic]." *The Bible and Critical Theory* 3.2 (2011). https://novaojs.newcastle.edu.au/ojsbct/index.php/bct/article/view/141.

Heggheim, Arne, et al. "Kjønn—en betenkning. Tverrfaglig blikk på kjønnsidentitet og kjønnsinkongruens." Oslo: Norges Kristelige Lege-og Tannlegeforening, 2023.

Helle, Sophus. "'Only in Dress?': Methodological Concerns Regarding Non-Binary Gender." In *Gender and Methodology in the Ancient Near East: Approaches from Assyriology and Beyond*, edited by Stephanie Lynn Budin et al., 41–53. Barcino Monographica Orientalia 10. Barcelona: Edicions Universitat Barcelona, 2018.

———. "Weapons and Weaving Instruments as Symbols of Gender in the Ancient Near East." In *Fashioned Selves: Dress and Identity in Antiquity*, edited by Megan Cifarelli, 105–16. Oxford: Oxbow, 2019.

Heller, Lee Francis. "Is God Against Us?: Grace and Lace Letters: 1990–1997." Institute for Welcoming Resources, 1996. http://www.welcomingresources.org/graceofgod3.pdf.

Herman, Jody L., et al. "How Many Adults and Youth Identify as Transgender in the United States?" *Williams Institute*, 2022. https://williamsinstitute.law.ucla.edu/publications/trans-adults-united-states.

Herodotus. *Herodotus I.* Translated by A. D. Godley. Loeb Classical Library. Cambridge, MA: Harvard University Press, 1920.

Herzer, Linda. *Bible and the Transgender Experience: How Scripture Supports Gender Variance.* Cleveland: Pilgrim, 2016.

Hoffner, Harry A. "Symbols for Masculinity and Femininity: Their Use in Ancient Near Eastern Sympathetic Magic Rituals." *Journal of Biblical Literature* 85.3 (1966) 326–34.

Hofstede, Geert. *Culture's Consequences: Comparing Values, Behaviors, Institutions and Organizations Across Nations.* Thousand Oaks, CA: Sage, 2001.

Høgenhaven, Jesper. "Adam in Qumran Wisdom Literature." In *Adam and Eve Story in the Hebrew Bible and in Ancient Jewish Writings Including the New Testament*, edited by Antii Laato and Lotta Valve, 177–209. Studies in the Reception History of the Bible 7. Åbo: Åbo Akademi University; Winona Lake, IN: Eisenbrauns, 2016.

Holladay, William L. *A Concise Hebrew and Aramaic Lexicon of the Old Testament.* Electronic ed. Leiden: Brill, 2000.

Holmen, Nicole. "Examining Greek Pederastic Relationships." *Inquiries Journal* 2.2 (2010). http://www.inquiriesjournal.com/articles/175/examining-greek-pederastic-relationships.

Horner, Tom. *Jonathan Loved David: Homosexuality in Biblical Times.* Philadelphia: Westminster, 1978.

Horst, P. W. van der. *The Sayings of Pseudo-Phocylides.* Leiden: Brill, 1978.

Houtman, Alberdina. "The Development of the Adamic Myth in Genesis Rabbah." In *Religious Stories in Transformation: Conflict, Revision and Reception*, 36–51. Leiden: Brill, 2016.

Ingalhalikar, Madhura, et al. "Sex Differences in the Structural Connectome of the Human Brain." *Proceedings of the National Academy of Sciences* 111.2 (2014) 823–28. https://doi.org/10.1073/pnas.1316909110.

BIBLIOGRAPHY

Instone-Brewer, David. "Are There Two Types of Men in Leviticus 20:13?" *HIPHIL Novum* 6.1 (2020) 33–49.

Isherwood, Lisa. "Impoverished Desire." In *The Poverty of Radical Orthodoxy*, edited by Marko Zlomislic, 1–12. Eugene, OR: Pickwick, 2012.

Jacobsen, Mia Rahr, and Viggo Julsgaard Jensen. "Køn og bibellæsning." *Kritisk Forum for Praktisk Teologi*, December 18, 2023.

James, Montague Rhode. *The Apocryphal New Testament*. Oxford: Clarendon, 1924.

Janzen, David. *The Social Meanings of Sacrifice in the Hebrew Bible: A Study of Four Writings*. New York: de Gruyter, 2012.

Johnson, Luke Timothy. "Homosexuality and the Church: Scripture and Experience." *Commonweal*, June 11, 2007. https://www.commonwealmagazine.org/homosexuality-church-0.

Jones, Clay. "We Don't Hate Sin So We Don't Understand What Happened to the Canaanites." *Philosophia Christi* 11.1 (2009) 53–72.

Jørgensen, Theodor. "Er bøsser og lesbiske skabt i Guds billede?" *Kristeligt Dagblad*, January 28, 2012. https://www.kristeligt-dagblad.dk/kronik/er-b%C3%B8sser-og-lesbiske-skabt-i-guds-billede.

Keel, Othmar. *700 Skarabäen und Verwandtes aus Palästina/Israel. Die Sammlung Keel*. Orbis Biblicus et Orientalis. Series Archaeologica 39. Leuven: Peeters, 2020.

Keil, Carl Friedrich, and Franz Delitzsch. *Commentary on the Old Testament* 1. Peabody, MA: Hendrickson, 2002.

Keller, Timothy. "The Gospel and Sex." *Gospel in Life* (2010) 1–14.

Keller, Timothy, and Kathy Keller. *The Meaning of Marriage: Facing the Complexities of Commitment with the Wisdom of God*. New York: Dutton, 2011.

Ker, Ian. "Cardinal John Henry Newman's Exhumation Objectors." *EWTN Global Catholic Television Network*, September 3, 2008. https://www.ewtn.com/catholicism/library/cardinal-john-henry-newmans-exhumation-objectors-5696.

———. *John Henry Newman: A Biography*. Oxford: Oxford University Press, 2010.

Kimuhu, Johnson M. *Leviticus: The Priestly Laws and Prohibitions from the Perspective of Ancient Near East and Africa*. New York: Peter Lang, 2008.

Kiraxes. "Amazing NDE and Conversion Testimony by Dr. Donald Whitaker (RIP)." Reddit Post. *Reddit*, March 21, 2022. www.reddit.com/r/Christianity/comments/tjetmu/amazing_nde_and_conversion_testimony_by_dr_donald.

Kirby, Peter. "Gospel of the Egyptians." *Early Christian Writings*, 2021. http://www.earlychristianwritings.com/gospelegyptians.html.

Kjær, Torben. *Naturlig Åbenbaring. Romerbrevet 1, 18–12, 16*. Frederiksberg: Bache og Kjær, 2021.

Klawans, Jonathan. *Impurity and Sin in Ancient Judaism*. Oxford: Oxford University Press, 2004.

———. *Purity, Sacrifice, and the Temple: Symbolism and Supersessionism in the Study of Ancient Judaism*. Oxford: Oxford University Press, 2005.

Knohl, Israel. *The Sanctuary of Silence: The Priestly Torah and the Holiness School*. 1st ed. Winona Lake, IN: Eisenbrauns, 2007.

Kofoed, Jens Bruun. "Encoding and Decoding Culture." In *Write That They May Read: Studies in Literacy and Textualization in the Ancient Near East and in the Hebrew Scriptures: Essays in Honour of Professor Alan R. Millard*, edited by Daniel I. Block et al., 240–62. Eugene, OR: Wipf & Stock, 2020.

———. *Fra begyndelsen—Køn og seksualitet i skabelsesteologisk perspektiv*. Fredericia: Kolon, 2023.

———. "Mytebegrebet som et nødvendigt onde." *Dansk Tidsskrift for Teologi Og Kirke* 1 (2016) 5–27.

———. "Old Testament Law, Pastoral Counseling, and Community Engagement." *Hiphil Novum* 9.2 (2024) 115–64.

Kolakowski, Victoria S. "Toward a Christian Ethical Response to Transsexual Persons." *Theology & Sexuality* 6 (1997) 10–31.

Korpel, Marjo. "The Adamic Myth from Canaan." In *Religious Stories in Transformation: Conflict, Revision and Reception*, 21–35. Leiden: Brill, 2016.

Korpel, Marjo C. A., and Johannes C. de Moor. "Adam, Eve, and the Devil." *The Bible and Interpretation* 1–12. https://bibleinterp.arizona.edu/sites/bibleinterp.arizona.edu/files/docs/Paper_Korpel_De_Moor_0.pdf.

———. *Adam, Eve, and the Devil: A New Beginning*. 2nd enlarged ed. Sheffield: Sheffield Phoenix, 2015.

Krafft-Ebing, R. von. *Neue Forschungen Auf Dem Gebiet Der Psychopathia Sexualis: Eine Medicinisch-Psychologische Studie*. Stuttgart: Verlag Von Ferdinand Enke, 1891.

Kramer, Samuel Noah. *The Sacred Marriage Rite; Aspects of Faith, Myth, and Ritual in Ancient Sumer*. Bloomington: Indiana University Press, 1969.

Kvanvig, Helge. *Primeval History: Babylonian, Biblical, and Enochic: An Intertextual Reading*. Leiden: Brill, 2011.

Lambert, Wilfred G. *Babylonian Wisdom Literature*. Winona Lake, IN: Eisenbrauns, 1996.

Lambert, Wilfred G. and Alan R. Millard. *Atra-ḫasīs: The Babylonian Story of the Flood*. Oxford: Oxford University Press, 1969.

Lapinkivi, Pirjo. "The Sumerian Sacred Marriage and Its Aftermath in Later Sources." In *Sacred Marriages: The Divine-Human Sexual Metaphor from Sumer to Early Christianity*, edited by Martti Nissinen and Risto Uro, 7–41. Winona Lake, IN: Eisenbrauns, 2008.

Larsen, Irene. "Homoseksualitet og kristendom." *Irene Larsen*, August 2022. http://irenelarsen.dk/Religion/homoseksualitet_kristendom.pdf.

Larsen, Irene, and Anne-Birgitte Zoëga. "Præst og teolog: Ja, der står sætninger i Bibelen, som man kan læse som et forbud mod homoseksualitet." *Politiken*, August 19, 2021. https://politiken.dk/debat/kroniken/art8325469/Ja-der-st%C3%A5r-s%C3%A6tninger-i-Bibelen-som-man-kan-l%C3%A6se-som-et-forbud-mod-homoseksualitet.

Layton, Bentley, et al. *The Gnostic Scriptures: A New Translation with Annotations and Introductions*. 2nd ed. New Haven, CT: Yale University Press, 2021.

Leichty, Erle Verdun. *The Omen Series Šumma Izbu*. Texts from Cuneiform Sources 4. Locust Valley, NY: J. J. Augustin, 1970.

Leith, Mary Joan Winn. "Gender and Religion: Gender and Ancient Near Eastern Religions." *Encyclopedia.com*, 2005. https://www.encyclopedia.com/environment/encyclopedias-almanacs-transcripts-and-maps/gender-and-religion-gender-and-ancient-near-eastern-religions.

Lenski, R. C. H. *The Interpretation of St. Paul's First and Second Epistle to the Corinthians*. Minneapolis: Augsburg, 1963.

Levinson, Joshua. "Cultural Androgyny in Rabbinic Literature." In *From Athens to Jerusalem*, edited by Samuel Kottek and Manfred Horstmanshoff, 119–40. Rotterdam: Erasmus, 2000.

Lewis, C. S. *The Four Loves*. London: HarperCollins UK, 2002.
Lewis, Charlton T., and Charles Short. "Mĕrētrix." In *A Latin Dictionary*. Oxford: Clarendon, 1879. http://www.perseus.tufts.edu/hopper/text?doc=Perseus:text:1999.04.0059:entry=scortator.
———. "Scortātor." In *A Latin Dictionary*. Oxford: Clarendon, 1879. http://www.perseus.tufts.edu/hopper/text?doc=Perseus:text:1999.04.0059:entry=scortator.
Lewis, Jack P. "1991 קָהָל." In *Theological Wordbook of the Old Testament*, edited by R. L. Harris et al. Chicago: Moody, 1999. https://ref.ly/logosref/TWOT.TWOT_No._1991d.
Lichtheim, Miriam. *The New Kingdom*. Vol. 2 of *Ancient Egyptian Literature*. Berkeley: University of California Press, 1976.
Liddell, H. G. *A Lexicon: Abridged from Liddell and Scott's Greek-English Lexicon*. Logos Research Systems, 1996.
Lind, Laura Elisabeth. "Folkekirken ønsker tænkepause i strid om homoseksuelle vielser." *Kristeligt Dagblad*, March 25, 2010. https://www.kristeligt-dagblad.dk/kirke-tro/folkekirken-%C3%B8nsker-t%C3%A6nkepause-i-strid-om-homoseksuelle-vielser.
Lipiński, Edward. "Cult Prostitution and Passage Rites in the Biblical World." *The Biblical Annals* 3.1 (2013) 9–27.
———. "Cult Prostitution in Ancient Israel?" *Biblical Archaeology Review* 40.1 (2014) 49–56, 70.
Løgstrup, K. E. *Skabelse og tilintetgørelse: Religionsfilosofiske betragtninger. Metafysik IV*. Gyldendals, 1995.
Longenecker, Richard N. *Galatians*. Word Biblical Commentary 41. 61 vols. Waco, TX: Thomas Nelson, 1990.
Longman, Tremper. *Songs of Songs*. Grand Rapids: Eerdmans, 2001.
Looy, Heather. "Male and Female God Created Them: The Challenge of Intersexuality." *Journal of Psychology and Christianity* 21.1 (2002) 10–20.
Looy, Heather, and Hessel Bouma III. "The Nature of Gender: Gender Identity in Persons Who Are Intersexed or Transgendered." *Journal of Psychology and Theology* 33.3 (2005) 166–78.
Louw, Johannes P., and Eugene Albert Nida. *A Greek-English Lexicon of the New Testament: Based on Semantic Domains*. 2nd ed. Electronic ed. New York: United Bible Societies, 1996.
Lundbom, Jack R. *Deuteronomy: A Commentary*. Grand Rapids: Eerdmans, 2013.
Luther, Martin. *Christian in Society II*. Vol. 45 of *Luther's Works*. Edited by Walther I. Brandt. Philadelphia: Fortress, 1962.
Malm, Magnus. *Bag Billedet*. Frederiksværk: Boedal, 2004.
Malul, Meir. "David's Curse of Joab (2 Sam 3:29) and the Social Significance of Mhzyq Bplk." *Aula Orientalis* 10.1 (1992) 49–67.
———. "איש עתי (Leviticus 16:21): A Marginal Person." *Journal of Biblical Literature* 128.3 (2009) 437–42.
Mansfield, Harvey C. *Manliness*. New Haven, CT: Yale University Press, 2006.
Marasco, Robyn. "On Womanly Nihilism: Beauvoir and Us." *boundary 2* 47.1 (2020) 43–64.
Marcus, Joel. *Mark 8–16*. Anchor Bible 27A. New Haven & London: Yale University Press, 2009.

BIBLIOGRAPHY

Mariottini, Claude. "Transvestism in Ancient Israel." *Dr. Claude Mariottini—Professor of Old Testament* (blog), January 26, 2009. https://claudemariottini.com/2009/01/26/transvestism-in-ancient-israel/.

Marsh, Michael N. *Out-of-Body and Near-Death Experiences: Brain-State Phenomena or Glimpses of Immortality?* Oxford Theological Monographs. Oxford: Oxford University Press, 2010.

Marsman, Hennie J. *Women in Ugarit and Israel: Their Social and Religious Position in the Context of the Ancient Near East.* Leiden: Brill, 2003.

Martyr, Justin. *On the Resurrection.* In vol. 1 of *Ante-Nicene Fathers*, edited by Alexander Roberts et al. Buffalo, NY: Christian Literature, 1885. Revised by Kevin Knight. http://www.newadvent.org/fathers/0131.htm.

Mathis, David. "Brother Ass: Stewarding the Body as Christian Hedonists." *Desiring God*, March 2, 2022. https://www.desiringgod.org/messages/brother-ass.

Matthews, Victor Harold, et al. *The IVP Bible Background Commentary: Old Testament.* Electronic ed. InterVarsity Press, 2000.

Matuszak, Jana. "Don't Insult Inana!: Divine Retribution for Offense against Common Decency in the Light of New Textual Sources." In *Fortune and Misfortune in the Ancient Near East: Proceedings of the 60th Rencontre Assyriologique Internationale at Warsaw 21–25 July 2014*, edited by Olga Drewnowska and Malgorzata Sandowicz, 359–70. Winona Lake, IN: Eisenbrauns, 2017.

Mayer, Lawrence, and Paul McHugh. "Special Report on Sexuality and Gender: Findings from the Biological, Psychological, and Social Sciences." *The New Atlantis* 50 (2016).

McCaulley, Esau. "Esau McCaulley Talks about 'Reading While Black.'" Interview by Anna Gissing. Facebook, August 31, 2020. https://www.facebook.com/ivpacademic/videos/597870104422145.

McComiskey, Thomas E. "1990 קָדַשׁ." In *Theological Wordbook of the Old Testament*, edited by R. L. Harris et al., 786. Chicago: Moody, 1999.

McCoy, Katie J. "Recovering the Communion of Persons: How Hebrew Anthropology Counters Aristotelian Thought Concerning Male and Female Roles." *Council on Biblical Manhood and Womanhood*, November 20, 2019. http://cbmw.org/2019/11/20/recovering-the-communion-of-persons-how-hebrew-anthropology-counters-aristotelian-thought-concerning-male-and-female-roles/.

———. "What It Means to Be Male and Female." In *Created in the Image of God: Applications and Implications for Our Cultural Understanding*, edited by David S. Dockery and Lauren McAfee, 141–57. Nashville, TN: Forefront, 2023.

Meadowcroft, Tim. "Vive La Différence!: Reflections on Human Sexuality from the Old Testament Creation Tradition." *ANVIL* 14.3 (1997) 196–206.

Menzel, Brigitte. *Assyrische Tempel* 2. Rome: Biblical Institute, 1981.

Merillat, Herbert Christian. "The Gnostic Apostle Thomas: 'Twin' of Jesus?" *Gnostic Society Library*, 1997. http://gnosis.org/thomasbook/ch24.html.

Metodistkirken i Danmark. "Kirken Og Homoseksualitet." Metodistkirken, 2011. https://www.metodistkirken.dk/wp-content/uploads/2018/06/Studiedokument-om-homoseksualitet.pdf.

Michel, Patrick M. "Functions and Personalities of 'Syrian' Priestesses in the Bronze Age: Priestesses at Mari, Emar, and Ugarit." In *Women in Antiquity: Real Women Across the Ancient World*, edited by Stephanie Lynn Budin and Jean MacIntosh Turfa, 441–52. London: Routledge, 2016.

Middleton, J. Richard. "Image of God." In *Encyclopedia of the Bible and Ethics*, edited by Samuel E. Ballentine, 516–23. 2. Oxford: Oxford University Press, 2015.

———. *Liberating Image: The Imago Dei in Genesis 1*. Grand Rapids: Brazos, 2005.

Mikael Wandt. *Tro, kirke og homoseksualitet*. Christiansfeld: ProRex, 2022.

Mikkola, Mari. "Ontological Commitments, Sex and Gender." In *Feminist Metaphysics: Explorations in the Ontology of Sex and the Self*, edited by Charlotte Witt, 67–83. New York: Springer, 2011.

Milgrom, Jacob. *Leviticus 1–16: A New Translation with Introduction and Commentary*. New York: Doubleday, 1991.

———. *Leviticus 17–22: A New Translation with Introduction and Commentary*. New York: Doubleday, 2000.

Milton, John. *Paradise Lost*. John Milton Reading Room. https://milton.host.dartmouth.edu.

Mollenkott, Virginia R. *Omnigender: A Trans-Religious Approach*. Cleveland: Pilgrim, 2001.

Monson, John. "The New 'Ain Dara Temple: Closest Solomonic Parallel." *Biblical Archaeology Review* 26.3 (2000) 20–35, 67.

Moo, Douglas J. *The Letters to the Colossians and to Philemon*. The Pillar New Testament Commentary. Grand Rapids: Eerdmans, 2008.

Moran, William L. *The Amarna Letters*. Baltimore, MD: Johns Hopkins University Press, 1992.

———. "The Ancient Near Eastern Background of the Love of God in Deuteronomy." *The Catholic Biblical Quarterly* 25.1 (1963) 77–87.

Morgan, Cheryl. "Evidence for Trans Lives in Sumer." *NOTCHES* (blog), May 2, 2017. https://notchesblog.com/2017/05/02/evidence-for-trans-lives-in-sumer/.

Muchnik, Malka. *The Gender Challenge of Hebrew*. Leiden: Brill, 2014.

Nataf, Francis, trans. "Sefer HaChinukh." *Sefaria*, 2018. https://www.sefaria.org/topics/tumtum.

Naus, Eric. "God's Feminine Attributes." *Moody Church* (blog), July 5, 2011. https://www.moodychurch.org/gods-feminine-attributes/.

Nelson, James B. *Body Theology*. Philadelphia: Westminster John Knox, 1992.

———. "Embracing the Erotic: The Church's Unfinished Sexual Revolution." *Reflections*, 2006. https://reflections.yale.edu/article/sex-and-church/embracing-erotic-church-s-unfinished-sexual-revolution.

———. "On Doing Body Theology." *Theology & Sexuality* 1.2 (1995) 38–60.

Newman, John Henry. *The Controversy with Gladstone: January 1874–December 1875*. The Letters and Diaries of John Henry Newman 27. Edited by Charles Stephen Dessain and Thomas Gornall. Oxford: Clarendon, 1975.

———. *John Henry Newman: A Portrait in Letters*. Edited by Roderick Strange. Oxford: Oxford University Press, 2015.

———. *Littlemore and the Parting of Friends, May 1842–October 1843*. The Letters and Diaries of John Henry Newman 9. Edited by Francis McGrath. Oxford: Oxford University Press, 2006.

Nielsen, Kirsten Busch, et al. *Forkynd evangeliet for al skabningen. Om kirkelig velsignelse af registrerede par*. 2nd ed. Frederiksberg: Anis, 1996.

Nietzsche, Friedrich. *Die Fröhliche Wissenschaft*. Leipzig: E. W. Fritzsch, 1882.

Nietzsche, Friedrich. *Beyond Good and Evil*. Translated by R. J. Hollingdale. New York: Penguin Classics, 2003.

Nissinen, Martti. *Homoeroticism in the Biblical World: A Historical Perspective.* Minneapolis: Fortress, 1998.

———. "Homosexuality." In *Encyclopedia of the Bible and Its Reception*, edited by Constance M. Furey et al., 289–97. Vol. 12. Berlin; New York: De Gruyter, 2009.

———. "Homosexuality." In *Encyclopedia of the Bible and Its Reception Online*, edited by Constance M. Furey et al., 289–94. Berlin: De Gruyter, 2016.

Noll, K. L. *Canaan and Israel in Antiquity: A Textbook on History and Religion.* London: T & T Clark, 2013.

———. *Canaan and Israel in Antiquity: An Introduction.* Sheffield: Sheffield Academic, 2001.

Noll, Kurt L. "Canaanite Religion." *Religion Compass* 1.1 (2007) 61–92. https://people.brandonu.ca/nollk/canaanite-religion.

Nonbinary Hebrew. "Nonbinary Hebrew Project." 2022. https://www.nonbinaryhebrew.com.

O'Donovan, Oliver. *Transsexualism and Christian Marriage.* Cambridge: Grove, 1982.

Olmstead, Mark. "When Jesus Agreed with Lady Gaga: What the Bible Says About the Transgendered." *Huffington Post*, August 31, 2017. https://www.huffpost.com/entry/when-jesus-agreed-with-lady-gaga-what-the-bible-says_b_59a813cce4b096fd8876c0d1.

Olson, Kristina R. "When Sex and Gender Collide." *Scientific American*, September 1, 2017. https://www.scientificamerican.com/article/when-sex-and-gender-collide/.

Oppenheim, A. Leo, ed. "Ḫarīmtu." In *Chicago Assyrian Dictionary*, 101. Vol. 6. Chicago: Oriental Institute, 1956. https://isac.uchicago.edu/sites/default/files/uploads/shared/docs/cad_h.pdf.

Origen. *Prologue to the Commentary on the Songs of Songs.* Classics of Western Spirituality. Mulwah, NJ: Paulist, 1979.

Ortlund, Ray, et al. *Marriage and the Mystery of the Gospel.* Wheaton, IL: Crossway, 2016.

Panoussi, Vassiliki. *Brides, Mourners, Bacchae: Women's Rituals in Roman Literature.* Baltimore: Johns Hopkins University Press, 2019.

Parpola, Simo. *Letters from Assyrian Scholars to the Kings Esarhaddon and Ashurbanipal. Part I: Texts.* Winona Lake, IN: Eisenbrauns, 2007.

Paul, Ian. "The Grammar of Leviticus 18.22." *Psephizo* (blog), January 21, 2015. https://www.psephizo.com/biblical-studies/the-grammar-of-leviticus-18-22/.

———. "Will We Be Male and Female in the Resurrection?" *Psephizo* (blog), August 27, 2019. https://www.psephizo.com/biblical-studies/will-we-be-male-and-female-in-the-resurrection/.

Paul, John II. *Man and Woman He Created Them: A Theology of the Body.* Boston: Pauline, 2006.

———. *Mulieris Dignitatem.* The Vatican: Dicastero per la Comunicazione—Libreria Editrice Vaticana, 1988. https://www.vatican.va/content/john-paul-ii/en/apost_letters/1988/documents/hf_jp-ii_apl_19880815_mulieris-dignitatem.html.

———. *The Redemption of the Body and Sacramentality of Marriage (Theology of the Body).* Vatican: Libreria Editrice Vaticana, 2006. https://d2y1pz2y630308.cloudfront.net/2232/documents/2016/9/theology_of_the_body.pdf.

Paz, Yitzhak, Ianir Milevski, and Nimrod Getzov. "Sound-Track of the 'Sacred Marriage?': A Newly Discovered Cultic Scene Depicted on a 3rd Millennium BC Cylinder Seal Impression from Bet Ha-Emeq, Israel." *Ugarit-Forschungen* 44 (2013) 243–59.

BIBLIOGRAPHY

Pearcey, Nancy R. *Love Thy Body: Answering Hard Questions about Life and Sexuality.* Grand Rapids: Baker, 2018.

Peckham, Brian. "Notes on a Fifth-Century Phoenician Inscription from Kition, Cyprus (CIS 86)." *Orientalia* 37.3 (1968) 304–24.

Pedersen, Else Marie Wiberg. "Radical Incarnation and Creative Ambiguity." *Studia Theologica—Nordic Journal of Theology*, January 2, 2019, 4–22.

Pedersen, Håkon Sunde. "The Retributive and Suffering God of the Book of Jeremiah: A Study of YHWH's 'Āzab-Complaints." PhD diss., MF Norwegian School of Theology, Religion, and Society in Oslo, 2018.

Peled, Ilan. "Kula'ūtam Epēšum: Gender Ambiguity and Contempt in Mesopotamia." *Journal of the American Oriental Society* 135.4 (2015) 751–64. https://doi.org/10.7817/jameroriesoci.135.4.751.

———. *Masculinities and Third Gender: The Origins and Nature of an Institutionalized Gender Otherness in the Ancient Near East.* Alter Orient und Altes Testament 435. Münster: Ugarit Verlag, 2016.

Petersen, Carsten Elmelund. "Samkønnet sex i et historisk lys." *Nordisk Teologi* (2010) 1–38.

Peterson, Ryan S. *The Imago Dei as Human Identity: A Theological Interpretation.* Journal of Theological Interpretation Supplement 14. Winona Lake, IN: Eisenbrauns, 2016.

Plato. *Plato in Twelve Volumes.* Vol. 9. Translated by W. R. M. Lamb. Cambridge, MA: Harvard University Press, 1925.

———. *Plato in Twelve Volumes*, Vol. 12. Translated by Harold N. Fowler. Cambridge, MA: Harvard University Press, 1921.

———. *Lysis, Symposium, Gorgias.* Translated by W. R. M. Lamb. Loeb Classical Library 166. Cambridge, MA: Harvard University Press, 1925.

Pless, John T. "The Use and Misuse of Luther in Contemporary Debates on Homosexuality: A Look at Two Theologians." *LOGIA*, February 21, 2009.

Pritchard, James B. *Ancient Near Eastern Texts Relating to the Old Testament with Supplement.* 3rd ed. Princeton, NJ: Princeton University Press, 1969.

Randrianjaka, Olivier. "Sin, Purification and Sacrifice: Analysis and Comparison of Texts from the Book of Leviticus and Malagasy Traditional Rituals." 295. VID vitenskapelige høgskole, Stavanger, 2020. https://vid.brage.unit.no/vid-xmlui/handle/11250/2738157.

Ratzinger, Joseph. *"In the Beginning . . .": A Catholic Understanding of the Story of Creation and the Fall.* Grand Rapids: Eerdmans, 1995.

Reimer-Barry, Emily. "A Queer Reading of Genesis 1–2 for Pride Month." *Catholic Moral Theology* (blog), June 7, 2022. https://catholicmoraltheology.com/a-queer-reading-of-genesis-1-3-for-pride-month/.

Retief, F. P., et al. "Congenital Eunuchism and Favorinus." *South African Medical Journal (Suid-Afrikaanse Tydskrif Vir Geneeskunde)* 93.1 (2003) 73–76.

———. "Eunuchs in the Bible." *Acta Theologica* 26.2 (2006) 247–58.

Rochberg, Francesca. *Before Nature: Cuneiform Knowledge and the History of Science.* Chicago: University of Chicago Press, 2016.

Roden, Frederick S. *Same-Sex Desire in Victorian Religious Culture.* New York: Palgrave Macmillan, 2002.

Rogers, Eugene F. "Doctrine and Sexuality." In *The Oxford Handbook of Theology, Sexuality, and Gender*, edited by Adrian Thatcher. Oxford: Oxford University Press, 2015.

BIBLIOGRAPHY

Rogers, Trent A., and John K. Tarwater. "A Biblical-Theological Framework for Human Sexuality: Applications to Private Sexuality." *Themelios* 47.3 (2022) 559–72.

Roselli, C. E. "Neurobiology of Gender Identity and Sexual Orientation." *Journal of Neuroendocrinology* 30.7 (2018) 1–14. https://doi.org/10.1111/jne.12562.

Rothenberg, Naftali. *The Wisdom of Love: Man, Woman and God in Jewish Canonical Literature*. Translated by Shmuel Sermoneta-Gertel. 1st ed. Boston: Academic Studies, 2009.

Sabia-Tanis, Justin. *Trans-Gender: Theology, Ministry, and Communities of Faith*. Eugene, OR: Wipf & Stock, 2018.

Sandberg, Ruth N. *Development and Discontinuity in Jewish Law*. Lanham, MD: University Press of America, 2001.

Sartre, Jean-Paul. *Existentialism Is a Humanism*. New Haven, CT: Yale University Press, 2007.

Savage, Helen. "Changing Sex?: Transsexuality and Christian Theology." PhD diss., Durham University, 2005. http://etheses.dur.ac.uk/3364/1/185.PDF?DDD32+.

Sawyer, Deborah F. "Gender-Play and Sacred Text: A Scene from Jeremiah." *Journal for the Study of the Old Testament* 24.83 (1999) 99–111.

Sayers, Dorothy L. *Are Women Human?: Penetrating, Sensible, and Witty Essays on the Role of Women in Society*. Grand Rapids: Eerdmans, 2005.

———. *Unpopular Opinions: Twenty-One Essays*. Victor Gollancz, 1946.

Schmitz, Matthew. "N. T. Wright on Gay Marriage." *First Things*, June 11, 2014. https://www.firstthings.com/blogs/firstthoughts/2014/06/n-t-wrights-argument-against-same-sex-marriage.

Schreiner, Thomas R. *40 Questions about Christians and Biblical Law*. 40 Questions Series. Edited by Benjamin L. Merkle. Grand Rapids: Kregel Academic & Professional, 2010.

———. "A New Testament Perspective on Homosexuality." *Themelios* 31.3 (2006) 62–75.

Schroer, Silvia. "Frauenkörper Als Architektonische Elemente. Zum Hintergrund von Ps 144, 12." In *Bilder Als Quellen/Images as Sources: Studies on Ancient Near Eastern Artefacts and the Bible Inspired by the Work of Othmar Keel*, edited by Susanne Bickel, 425–50. Orbis Biblicus et Orientalis, Sonderband. Fribourg: Vandenhoeck & Ruprecht, 2007.

Schroer, Silvia, and Othmar Keel. *Die Ikonographie Palästinas/Israels und der Alte Orient: eine Religionsgeschichte in Bildern: Die Mittelbronzezeit*. Fribourg: Academic Press Fribourg/Paulusverlag Freiburg, 2008.

Scroggs, Robin. *The New Testament and Homosexuality: Contextual Background for Contemporary Debate*. Minneapolis: Fortress, 1983.

Selmys, Melinda. "John Paul II, Intimate Friendship, and the Fluidity of Philia and Eros." *Catholic Authenticity* (blog), February 16, 2016. https://www.patheos.com/blogs/catholicauthenticity/2016/02/john-paul-ii-intimate-friendship-and-the-fluidity-of-philia-and-eros/.

Seneca. *Epistles*. In *Seneca IV. Ad Lucilium Epistulae Morales I*. Translated by Richard M. Gummere. Cambridge, MA: Harvard University Press, 1979.

Silver, Morris. *Sacred Prostitution in the Ancient Greek World: From Aphrodite to Baubo to Cassandra and Beyond*. Ugarit-Verlag, 2020.

———. "Temple/Sacred Prostitution in Ancient Mesopotamia Revisited." *Ugarit-Forschungen* 38 (2006) 631–63.

Sklar, Jay. *Leviticus: An Introduction and Commentary*. Edited by David G. Firth. Tyndale Old Testament Commentaries 3. Downers Grove, IL: InterVarsity, 2013.

———. "The Prohibitions against Homosexual Sex in Leviticus 18:22 and 20:13: Are They Relevant Today?" *Bulletin for Biblical Research* 28.2 (2018) 165–98.

Smith, Mark D. "Ancient Bisexuality and the Interpretation of Romans 1:26–27." *Journal of the America Academy of Religion* 64.2 (1996) 223–56.

Smith, Robert S. "Responding to the Transgender Revolution." *The Gospel Coalition*, October 17, 2017. https://www.thegospelcoalition.org/article/responding-to-the-transgender-revolution/.

Søndergaard, Morten, and Sophus Helle. *Gilgamesh*. København: Gyldendal, 2019.

Song, Robert. *Covenant and Calling: Towards a Theology of Same-Sex Relationships*. London: SCM, 2014.

Sprinkle, Preston M. *Embodied: Transgender Identities, the Church, and What the Bible Has to Say*. Colorado Springs: David C. Cook, 2021.

———. *Law and Life: The Interpretation of Leviticus 18:5 in Early Judaism and in Paul*. Tübingen: Mohr Siebeck, 2008.

———. "Sex, Gender, and Transgender Experiences: Part 6—What about Intersex?" *Center for Faith, Sexuality & Gender*, August 26, 2019. https://www.centerforfaith.com/blog/sex-gender-and-transgender-experiences-part-6-what-about-intersex.

———. "Sex, Gender, and Transgender Experiences: Part 7—Male and Female in the Image of God." *Center for Faith, Sexuality & Gender*, October 14, 2019. https://centerforfaith.com/blog/sex-gender-and-transgender-experiences-part-7-male-and-female-in-the-image-of-god.

Stager, Lawrence. "Why Were Hundreds of Dogs Buried at Ashkelon?" *Biblical Archaeology Review* 17.3 (1991) 27–42.

Steenhoff, Eirik A., 2021. "Om det nye synet på kjønn og seksualitet og en adekvat kristen respons [On the New Approach to Gender and Sexuality and a Proper Christian Response]," paper presented at the research seminar on the theology of the body, Fjellhaug Internasjonale Høgskole, Oslo, November 29.

———. "The Body That Reveals the Person(s): On Phenomenology and Metaphysics in the Catechesis on Human Love." Pontifical John Paul II Institute, 2019. https://www.academia.edu/43547113/The_Body_That_Reveals_the_Person_s_On_Phenomenology_and_Metaphysics_in_the_Catechesis_on_Human_Love.

Steinsaltz, Rabbi Adin Even-Israel, trans. *The William Davidson Talmud*. Koren Publishers. https://www.sefaria.org/Niddah.

Stol, Marten. *Women in the Ancient Near East*. Translated by Helen Richardson and Mervyn Richardson. Berlin: de Gruyter, 2016.

Stoljar, Natalie. "Different Women: Gender and the Realism-Nominalism Debate." In *Feminist Metaphysics. Explorations in the Ontology of Sex and the Self*, edited by Charlotte Witt, 27–46. New York: Springer, 2011.

Stone, Ken. "Homosexuality and the Bible or Queer Reading?: A Response to Martti Nissinen." *Theology & Sexuality* 14 (2001) 107–18.

Strachan, Owen. "Response to Justin Sabia-Tanis." In *Understanding Transgender Identities. Four Views*, edited by James K. Beilby and Paul Rhodes Eddy, 223–27. Grand Rapids: Baker Academic, 2019.

———. "Response to Megan DeFranza." In *Understanding Transgender Identities: Four Views*, edited by James K. Beilby and Paul Rhodes Eddy, 179–83. Grand Rapids: Baker Academic, 2019.

BIBLIOGRAPHY

Stuckey, Johanna H. "Shaushka and 'Ain Dara: A Goddess and Her Temple." *MatriFocus* 7.2 (2008) 1–8.

Sunde Pedersen, Håkon. *The Retributive and Suffering God of the Book of Jeremiah: A Study of YHWH's 'Azab-Complaints.* Forschungen Zum Alten Testament. 2. Reihe 140. Tübingen: Mohr Siebeck, 2023.

Tångberg, Arvid. "Naturbegrepet og homifili i Det Gamle Testamente." *Tidsskrift for Teologi Og Kirke* 4 (1998) 243–52.

Taylor, J. Glen. "The Bible and Homosexuality." *Themelios* 21.1 (1995) 4–9.

Tennent, Timothy C., and Ajith Fernando. *For the Body: Recovering a Theology of Gender, Sexuality, and the Human Body.* Grand Rapids: Zondervan, 2020.

Teologisk Forum. "Om homoseksuelles plads i menigheden." *Baptistkirken*, 2012. https://baptistkirken.dk/wp-content/uploads/pdf/120215_homofili_teologisk_forum_2012.pdf.

Thatcher, Adrian. *God, Sex, and Gender: An Introduction.* West Sussex: Wiley-Blackwell, 2011.

The General Presbytery, Assemblies of God. "Transgenderism, Transsexuality, and Gender Identity." *Assemblies of God*, 2017. https://ag.org/Beliefs/Position-Papers/Transgenderism-Transsexuality-and-Gender-Identity.

Townsend, P Wayne. "Eve's Answer to the Serpent: An Alternative Paradigm for Sin and Some Implications in Theology." *Calvin Theological Journal* 33 (1998) 399–420.

Trible, Phyllis. *Texts of Terror: Literary-Feminist Readings of Biblical Narratives.* Philadelphia: Fortress, 1984.

Trueman, Carl R. "The Triumph of the Social Scientific Method." *First Things*, June 15, 2020. https://www.firstthings.com/web-exclusives/2020/06/the-triumph-of-the-social-scientific-method.

Turner, P. D. M. "Biblical Texts Relevant to Homosexual Orientation and Practice: Notes on Philology and Interpretation." *Christian Scholar's Review* 26.4 (1997) 435–45.

Van Tine, R Jarrett. "Castration for the Kingdom and Avoiding the Αἰτία of Adultery (Matthew 19:10–12)." *Journal of Biblical Literature* 137.2 (2018) 399–418.

Vanstiphout, Herman L. J. *Epics of Sumerian Kings: The Matter of Aratta.* Atlanta: Society of Biblical Literature, 2003.

Vedeler, Harold Torger. "Reconstructing Meaning in Deuteronomy 22:5: Gender, Society, and Transvestitism in Israel and the Ancient near East." *Journal of Biblical Literature* 127. 3 (2008) 459–76.

Vis, Joshua M. "The Purification Offering of Leviticus and the Sacrificial Offering of Jesus." PhD diss., Duke University, 2012. https://dukespace.lib.duke.edu/dspace/bitstream/handle/10161/6144/Vis_duke_0066D_11667.pdf.

Volf, Miroslav. *A Public Faith: How Followers of Christ Should Serve the Common Good.* Grand Rapids: Brazos, 2011.

Walker, Andrew T. *God and the Transgender Debate: What Does the Bible Actually Say About Gender Identity?* Epsom: The Good Book Company, 2022.

Walsh, Jerome T. "Leviticus 18:22 and 20:13: Who Is Doing What to Whom?" *Journal of Biblical Literature* 120.2 (2001) 201–9.

Webster, John. *God Without Measure: Working Papers in Christian Theology: Volume 1: God and the Works of God.* London: Bloomsbury, 2015.

Wengert, Timothy J. *The Roots of Reform.* Vol. 1 of *The Annotated Luther.* Minneapolis: Fortress, 2015.

Wenham, Gordon J. "The Old Testament Attitude to Homosexuality." *Expository Times* 102.9 (1991) 359–63.

West, Christopher. "Our Bodies Tell God's Story." In *Sanctified Sexuality: Valuing Sex in an Oversexed World*, edited by Sandra L. Glahn and C. Gary Barnes, 15–24. Grand Rapids: Kregel, 2020.

West, Christopher, and Eric Metaxas. *Our Bodies Tell God's Story: Discovering the Divine Plan for Love, Sex, and Gender*. Grand Rapids: Brazos, 2020.

Westenholz, Joan Goodnick. "Heilige Hochzeit und kultische Prostitution im Alten Mesopotamien, Sexuelle Vereinigung im sakralen Raum?" In *Geschlechterforschung in der Theologie: Studien aus feministisch-theologischer Perspektive*, edited by Luise Schottroff and Marie-Theres Wacker, 43–62. Wort und Dienst 23. Bielefeld: Kirchliche Hochschule Bethel, 1995.

———. "Tamar, Qědēšā, Qadištu, and Sacred Prostitution in Mesopotamia." *The Harvard Theological Review* 82.3 (1989) 245–65.

Westenholz, Joan Goodnick, and Ilona Zsolnay. "Categorizing Men and Masculinity in Sumer." In *Being a Man: Negotiating Ancient Constructs of Masculinity*, edited by Ilona Zsolnay, 12–41. London: Routledge, 2017.

Weyde, Karl William. "Does Mal 2:15a Refer to Adam and Eve in the Creation Account in Gen 2:4–25?" In *Adam and Eve Story in the Hebrew Bible and in Ancient Jewish Writings Including the New Testament*, edited by Antti Laato and Lotta Valve, 73–90. Studies in the Reception History of the Bible 7. Åbo: Åbo Akademi University; Winona Lake, IN: Eisenbrauns, 2016.

White, Leland J. "Does the Bible Speak about Gays or Same-Sex Orientation?: A Test Case in Biblical Ethics: Part I." *Biblical Theology Bulletin* 25.1 (1995) 14–23.

Wilson, Douglas. *Future Men*. Moscow, ID: Canon, 2001.

Wimber, K. Michelle. "Four Greco-Roman Era Temples of Near Eastern Fertility Goddesses: An Analysis of Architectural Tradition." MA thesis, Brigham Young University, 2007. https://scholarsarchive.byu.edu/etd/1277/.

Winther-Nielsen, Nicolai. "Gud handler ikke ondt!: Et opgør med Guds alvirksomhed i Gammel Testamente." *Theofilos Supplement* 6.2 (2014) 206–26.

———. "Mosebøgernes brug som vejledning." In *Den kristne forkyndelse—Teori og praksis fra Bibelen, i historien, til verden*, edited by Jakob Olsen, 14–67. Fredericia: Kolon, 2018.

Witt, Charlotte. "What Is Gender Essentialism?" In *Feminist Metaphysics: Explorations in the Ontology of Sex and the Self*, edited by Charlotte Witt, 11–25. New York: Springer, 2011.

Wright, David F. "Homosexual or Prostitutes?: The Meaning of Arsenokoitai (1 Cor. 6:9, 1 Tim. 1:10)." *Vigilia Christianae* 38.2 (1984) 125–53.

Wright, N. T. *Surprised by Hope: Rethinking Heaven, the Resurrection, and the Mission of the Church*. New York: HarperOne, 2008.

Yarhouse, Mark A. *Understanding Gender Dysphoria: Navigating Transgender Issues in a Changing Culture*. Downers Grove, IL: InterVarsity, 2015.

Yarhouse, Mark A., and Julia Sadusky. "The Complexities of Gender Identity. Towards a More Nuanced Response to the Transgender Experience." In *Understanding Transgender Identities: Four Views*, edited by James K. Beilby and Paul Rhodes Eddy, 101–35. Grand Rapids: Baker Academic, 2019.

Yates, John. "A New Vision of the Father." *CrossConnect*, January 26, 2007. https://crossconnect.net.au/a-new-vision-of-the-father/.

BIBLIOGRAPHY

Youngblood, Ronald F. "2530a תּוֹעֵבָה." In *Theological Wordbook of the Old Testament*, edited by R. L. Harris et al., 344. Chicago: Moody, 1999.

Zehnder, Markus. "A Fresh Look at Malachi II 13–16." *Vetus Testamentum* 53.2 (2003) 224.

Zohar, Noam. "Repentance and Purification: The Significance and Semantics of חטאת in the Pentateuch." *Journal of Biblical Literature* 107.4 (1988) 609–18.